# Managing Financial Risks

# Managing Financial Risks: From Global to Local

*Edited by*
Gordon L. Clark, Adam D. Dixon, and
Ashby H. B. Monk

OXFORD
UNIVERSITY PRESS

# OXFORD
**UNIVERSITY PRESS**

Great Clarendon Street, Oxford OX2 6DP

Oxford University Press is a department of the University of Oxford.
It furthers the University's objective of excellence in research, scholarship,
and education by publishing worldwide in

Oxford New York

Auckland Cape Town Dar es Salaam Hong Kong Karachi
Kuala Lumpur Madrid Melbourne Mexico City Nairobi
New Delhi Shanghai Taipei Toronto

With offices in

Argentina Austria Brazil Chile Czech Republic France Greece
Guatemala Hungary Italy Japan Poland Portugal Singapore
South Korea Switzerland Thailand Turkey Ukraine Vietnam

Oxford is a registered trade mark of Oxford University Press
in the UK and in certain other countries

Published in the United States
by Oxford University Press Inc., New York

British Library Cataloguing in Publication Data

Data available

Library of Congress Cataloging in Publication Data

Data available

Typeset by SPI Publisher Services, Pondicherry, India
Printed in Great Britain
on acid-free paper by the
MPG Books Group, Bodmin and King's Lynn

ISBN 978-0-19-955743-1 (hbk.)

1 3 5 7 9 10 8 6 4 2

For Shirley, Olga, and Courtney

# Contents

## Contents

# Notes on Contributors

**Gordon L. Clark** is the Halford Mackinder Professor of Geography, holds a Professorial Fellowship at St Peter's College and is currently a Faculty Associate in the Smith School of Enterprise and the Environment at Oxford University. His current research is on pension fund governance focusing upon the competence and consistency of decision-makers and the design of rules and regulations to enhance the investment performance of these crucial institutions (supported by the National Association of Pension Funds and Watson Wyatt). Related work centers on individual financial decision-making in defined contribution plans emphasizing the intersection between cognition and context (supported, in part, by the ESRC, Mercers, and Watson Wyatt). Recent books include *The Geography of Finance* (OUP, 2007) (with Dariusz Wójcik), *Pension Fund Capitalism* (OUP, 2000), *European Pensions and Global Finance* (OUP, 2003), and the coedited *Pension Security in the Twenty-First Century* (OUP, 2003) and the *Oxford Handbook of Pensions and Retirement Income* (OUP, 2006).

**Adam D. Dixon** is a D.Phil. candidate in economic geography at the OUCE, University of Oxford. His doctoral research focuses on developing conceptualizations of European and global financial geography in the context of globalization and institutional diversity. He holds a graduate degree from the Institute d'Etudes Politiques de Paris and an undergraduate degree from The George Washington University Elliott School of International Affairs. He has published in *New Political Economy and Soziale Welt*, and has a forthcoming article in the *Journal of Economic Geography*. He is also the International Economy Editor for Oxford Analytica.

**Gary A. Dymski** is founding Director of the University of California Center, Sacramento (UCCS), and professor of economics at the University of California, Riverside. He received his B.A. in urban studies from the University of Pennsylvania in 1975, an MPA from Syracuse University in 1977, and a Ph.D. in economics from the University of Massachusetts, Amherst in 1987. He was a research fellow in economic studies at the

Brookings Institution in 1985–6. He has taught at the University of Southern California and has been a visiting scholar at Tokyo University, the Bangladesh Institute for Development Studies, the Federal University of Rio de Janeiro, and the University of São Paulo. Gary's research spans economics and geography, focusing on banking, financial instability and crises, urban development and inequality, and on credit-market discrimination and financial exclusion. Gary's books include *The Bank Merger Wave* (M. E. Sharpe, 1999), and *Reimagining Growth: Toward a Renewal of the Idea of Development*, coedited with Silvana DePaula (Zed, 2005).

**Ewald Engelen** is associate professor at the Amsterdam Metropolitan institute for Development Studies of the University of Amsterdam. He was trained as a political philosopher and wrote a Ph.D. thesis about corporate democracy. After a number of postdoctoral positions, he moved to the field of economic geography, focusing in particular on the intricate interactions between welfare state restructuring and financial markets. After a spell of three years at the Scientific Council for Government Policy, a prestigious public Dutch think-tank, Engelen was awarded a five-year grant by the Dutch Council for Scientific Research to investigate the effects of financial internationalization on the historical financial center of Amsterdam.

**Lisa A. Hagerman** is the Director of the Mission Investing Campaign Resource Center at the Boston College Institute for Responsible Investment. She is also affiliated as a Research Associate at the Oxford University Centre for the Environment, School of Geography, and as a Research Fellow at the University of North Carolina at Chapel Hill, Center for Community Capital. In July 2008, she completed her appointment as a Research Fellow at the Labor & Worklife Program, Harvard Law School working on the Pension Funds & Urban Revitalization Initiative funded by the Rockefeller and Ford Foundations. Lisa Hagerman was previously a Vice President of Economic Innovation International, a Boston consulting firm that builds privately capitalized community equity funds. Prior to her consulting work Ms. Hagerman was with Wells Fargo Bank, San Francisco, as Assistant Vice President in the Government Relations group and also worked for Citibank, New York, for seven years in the Latin American Marketing Division. She completed her doctorate in economic geography at the University of Oxford on Public Pension Fund Investment in Urban Revitalization. Ms. Hagerman received her B.A. from Bucknell University and her M.A. in political science from the University of North Carolina at Chapel Hill.

**Tessa Hebb** is the Director of the Carleton Centre for Community Innovation, Carleton University, Canada. Her research focuses on the financial and extra-financial impact of pension fund investment in Canada and internationally with particular emphasis on Responsible Investment and Corporate Engagement and is funded by the Social Sciences and Humanities Research Council, Government of Canada. The Carleton Centre for Community Innovation is a leading knowledge producer on social finance tools and instruments. Dr Hebb is also a senior research associate with the Oxford University Centre for the Environment and the Initiative for a Competitive Inner City. In 2008, she completed a multi-year research project funded by Rockefeller and Ford Foundations on the role of US public sector pension funds and urban revitalization, based at the Labor and Worklife Program, Harvard Law School. Dr Hebb has published many articles on pension fund investing policies and is the coeditor of the volume *Working Capital: The Power of Labor's Pensions*. Her new book *No Small Change: Pension Fund Corporate Engagement* was published in September 2008 by Cornell University Press.

**Paul Langley** studied politics, history, and international political economy at the University of Newcastle-upon-Tyne. He is currently Senior Lecturer in Politics at Northumbria University. Paul recently completed a three-year term as Convenor of the International Political Economy Group (IPEG) of the British International Studies Association (BISA), and is presently an editor of the *Review of International Political Economy Series* (Routledge). He is the author of *The Everyday Life of Global Finance: Saving and Borrowing in Anglo-America* (OUP, 2008), and *World Financial Orders* (Routledge, 2002). His most recent research has focused on the intersections between housing, financial, and mortgage markets in the context of the sub-prime crisis, and has been published in *Economy and Society*. During 2009–10, Paul will hold a Fellowship at the Institute of Advanced Studies (IAS), Durham University, and will be exploring "The Performance of Liquidity."

**Donald MacKenzie** works in the sociology of science and technology and in the sociology of markets, especially of financial and carbon markets. He holds a personal chair in sociology at the University of Edinburgh, where he has taught since 1975. His first book was *Statistics in Britain, 1865–1930: The Social Construction of Scientific Knowledge* (Edinburgh University Press, 1981). His most recent are *An Engine, not a Camera: How Financial Models shape Markets* (MIT Press, 2006) and *Do Economists Make Markets? On the*

*Performativity of Economics* (Princeton University Press, 2007), co-edited with Fabian Muniesa and Lucia Siu.

**Yuval Millo** is a lecturer in the Department of Accounting at the London School of Economics. He applies theoretical approaches from sociology of science and economic sociology along with a combination of qualitative and quantitative methods to the study of financial risk management and corporate governance. He is one of the leading contributors to the evolving field of the social studies of finance. His latest publication is *Market Devices* (Blackwell, 2007, with Michel Callon and Fabian Muniesa).

**Ashby H. B. Monk** is a Research Fellow at the University of Oxford and a Research Fellow at Boston College's Center for Retirement Research. He received his D.Phil. in Economic Geography at Oxford and holds an M.A. in International Economics from the Université de Paris I–Panthéon Sorbonne and a B.A. in Economics from Princeton University. His current research is on the design and governance of financial institutions, with particular focus on pensions and sovereign wealth funds (supported by the Center for Retirement Research at Boston College, the Leverhulme Trust, and the Lupina Foundation). He has published numerous academic papers related to the above, and is the co-author of a forthcoming book entitled *Sovereign Wealth Funds: Power, Governance, and Legitimacy* (Princeton University Press).

**Phillip O'Neill** is Professor and Foundation Director of the Urban Research Centre at the University of Western Sydney. His research interests are in the broad field of economic geography. Phillip has made distinguished contributions to the study of the investment and employment practices of major international corporations, the conduct of government institutions, the contemporary reformation of major cities, and the application of quantitative methods and geographic information systems (GIS) technologies to analysis of the performance of cities and regions under economic and demographic stress. His current research interests focus on the role of corporate power in the contemporary city, with an emphasis on infrastructure and infrastructure financing. Phillip is also a prominent public commentator on economic and social change in cities and regions. He is a regular op-ed columnist and commentator in the Australian national media.

**Louis W. Pauly** holds the Canada Research Chair in Globalization and Governance and directs the Centre for International Studies at the University of Toronto. A graduate of Cornell University, the London

School of Economics, New York University, and Fordham University, he has been a visiting professor at Oxford University, Northwestern University, and Osaka City University, held management positions in the Royal Bank of Canada, and served on the staff of the International Monetary Fund. His publications include *Global Ordering: Institutions and Autonomy in a Changing World* (UBC Press, 2008), *Complex Sovereignty: Reconstituting Political Authority in the Twenty-First Century* (University of Toronto Press, 2007), and *The Myth of the Global Corporation* (Princeton University Press, 1998). With Emanuel Adler, he edits the journal *International Organization*. His current research focuses on the politics of technological innovation in East Asia and on crisis management in integrating financial markets.

**Samuel Randalls** is a lecturer in geography at University College London. Prior to that he held a James Martin Fellowship in the Environmental Change Institute at the University of Oxford and completed his Ph.D. at the University of Birmingham. His research interests and publications encompass areas of environmental finance, particularly weather derivatives and carbon markets. He is currently exploring cultural and historical aspects of climate change, the relations between businesses, meteorology and the weather, and other new corporate ventures in environmental sustainability.

**Susan J. Smith** is a Director of the Institute of Advanced Study, and Professor of Geography, at Durham University. She has recently completed a program of work, funded by the UK's Economic and Social Research Council, on the close encounter between housing, mortgage, and financial markets. Using qualitative methods alongside more conventional quantitative tools, this work has contributed to a growing literature on housing investment, mortgage equity withdrawal, and housing market risk. Among more than 100 scholarly works accounting for the economic and social geography of inequalities of all kinds, Susan has recently co-edited a theme issue on the microstructures of housing markets (Housing Studies, 2008) and the rematerialization of home (2008), as well as a Blackwell companion to the economics of housing (2009). She is currently Editor in Chief of the *International Encyclopedia of Housing and Home* (Elsevier, 2011).

**Kendra Strauss** is a Research Associate in the School of Geography, Oxford University Centre for the Environment. She holds a B.A. (Hons) in Cultural Studies from McGill University and an M.Sc. (Distinction) and D.Phil. from Oxford University. She is broadly interested in issues to do with gendered inequality, the social and cultural embeddedness of economic practices, and the future of the welfare state. Her doctoral research, which was supported by the UK Economic and Social Research Council, the Canadian Social Sciences and Humanities Research Council, and Mercer Human Resources Consulting, focused on choice, risk, and responsibility in defined contribution occupational pensions in the UK.

**Dariusz Wójcik** is a Lecturer at the Oxford University Centre for the Environment and a Fellow of St Peter's College Oxford. Prior to his current appointment he was a consultant for KPMG Poland (1996–8), a scholar of the Open Society Institute and the Foreign & Commonwealth Office and a D.Phil. student at Oxford (1998–2002), a Junior Research Fellow at Jesus College Oxford (2003–5), and a Lecturer at University College London (2006–7). He held visiting teaching positions at the London School of Economics and Political Science, and the Graduate Business School of the Hong Kong Polytechnic University, and gave invited lectures at the Annual Dublin Finance Conference and to the Polish Securities and Exchange Commission. His research is concerned with the intersection of geography and finance, with emphasis on the geography of financial services and centres, capital markets, and corporate governance. He is the guest editor of the special issue of *Growth and Change* on European Financial Geographies (2007), and a co-author of *The Geography of Finance: Corporate Governance in the Global Marketplace* (OUP, 2007). His research has been reported in the *Financial Times*, the *Financial News*, and by Bloomberg.

# Preface

This book is about the management of financial risk, drawing inspiration from a new generation of scholars working at the interface between financial markets and the academic fields or disciplines of economic geography, economics, sociology, and political science. The book is designed to showcase their research and, most importantly, articulate the links between financial processes operating at a variety of geographical scales – hence the subtitle "From Global to Local." Equally, the subtitle could be "From the Local to the Global." We leave it to our contributors to articulate the local–global–local connection in ways that help us understand what is in play in global markets, national institutions, and local communities.

The book was conceived in early 2007, before the tremors in global financial markets became a sub-prime crisis and then a global financial and economic crisis. At the time, we were conscious of an apparent yawning gap in the academic literature: for all the sophistication of mathematical financial models, we could see that asymmetries of information between market participants located in various jurisdictions and located at different levels in the spatial hierarchy of financial centers threatened the integrity of the whole. Our intuition was that the value of information for embedded market participants was being discounted by both the flow of transactions from the local to the global and by the perfection of mathematical models that deliberately eschewed local knowledge in favor of formula-based risk-management on a global scale.

Our insight in this matter was not entirely new; financial economics has always been interested in the nature and flow of information in markets – there is, after all, a premium on information that is not widely available, held by interested parties, and sold to the highest bidder. This is expressed in many different ways, including the relative sophistication of market players such as institutional investors located close to trading centers and day-traders remotely located (in time and space). Just as importantly, the flows and channels of market information have been heavily influenced by national traditions. We have worked here and elsewhere to articulate the logic whereby information asymmetries are not just a product of happenstance, always driven out of the market by virtue of efficient market pricing, but are systematically embedded in that which is inherited and that which is a product of the restless risk-seeking behavior of financial agents.

At another level, the tension between the local and the global has been one of those issues that has attracted close scrutiny over the past decade or so by those academics and market agents interested in conceptualizing market structure and performance. We refer here, of course, to the work of Clark and O'Connor on the consequences of systematic informational asymmetries for the form and functions of financial centers, the work of Moskowitz and colleagues on the market for information, and the work of Shiller on the incompleteness of macro-markets and the consequent behavioral patterns including herd behavior and "irrational exuberance." Similarly, sociologists like MacKenzie have sought to better understand how the adoption of certain analytical frameworks has effectively driven out of the market information that ought to have a price but which has been discarded because of its lack of "relevance."

Notwithstanding our analytical intuition, we were unprepared for the rapid transformation of the sub-prime crisis into a global financial and economic crisis. Whereas our approach to financial risk management is consistent with the production, spread, and depth of the sub-prime crisis, our contributors prompted us to make the widest possible links to global financial governance. Here, then, is one of the strengths of the book: we begin with this most contentious of issues and take the reader down through the spatial scale to the individual financial "actor." Along the way, our contributors reach out – upwards and downwards – showing how risk-management at one level is connected with related factors operating at a variety of scales. This, we believe, has been one of the lessons of the global financial crisis; it seems that no corner of the global financial system has been left unscathed although at its heart the costs of failure in financial governance have been heavily concentrated – just ask residents of North East England and Charlotte, North Carolina (and more besides) who have borne significant costs from the failure of regionally dominated financial institutions.

A central theme of the book is the significance of the global and local financial sector. This is shown for a variety of sectors and industries – from market structure to market performance, from models of management to individual decision-making, from housing to pensions, from urban infrastructure to development and so on. Whether it survives as such in the aftermath of the global financial crisis is difficult to know. Clearly, there will be concerted attempts to exact compensation and revenge for misdeeds and malfeasance through state regulation. But it seems to us that finance will remain important for nations and communities; indeed, it will remain one of the cornerstones of globalization. What shape it will take, how the importance we attribute to risk management will be integrated into financial decision-making, and how innovation will be managed such that the costs of failure remain located with those that promote new kinds of financial products spread around the globe are profound questions that may take another ten years to resolve.

Most importantly, our book is not so much about the sub-prime crisis and the global financial crisis as it is a report from the frontiers of academic research on topics we believe will be with us far into the future. Whatever happens to the form and structure of financial institutions, the nature and scope of regulation, and the degree to which financial institutions blur the boundaries between "public" and "private", we believe the functions of risk-management relevant to the issues raised in this book will be very important over the coming decades. Take just three examples. Given the entwining of national pension policy and financial markets in many countries over the past fifty years, without nationalization of private pensions how will pension institutions deal with risk management? Likewise, how are the risks associated with housing markets and mortgages to be managed without simply making housing a luxury good? And what about the design of carbon markets? Current models match and mimic the risk-management techniques of financial markets. Given the significance of this issue for global well-being, will government regulation be an adequate mechanism to realize the changes that must take place over the next twenty-five years?

We do not pretend to have a recipe for the future of each and every sector studied in the book. But we do think that each chapter provides a way of thinking about risk-management that steps outside of simple models to give the heterogeneity of information and behavior its due. We hope this book will promote a closer analysis of how the local became global and vice versa in twentieth-century financial markets. We also hope that articulating these linkages will encourage a view of finance that is cognizant of its practice.

*Gordon L. Clark, Adam D. Dixon, and Ashby H. B. Monk*

Oxford, October 2008

# Acknowledgments

The impetus for the book goes back to a train ride from Lancaster to Oxford in January of 2007. Having just participated in a two-day workshop on financial geographies hosted by James Faulconbridge and Ewald Engelen, we agreed with Louis Pauly that we should keep the discussion going. To that end we organized a series of invited seminars for the spring of 2007. Eight seminars took place in Oxford on the subject of financial risk management and the geography of finance from April through to June of 2008. The reception of this seminar series was extremely positive, so much so that we felt there was scope to further expand the project.

With Oxford University Press formally interested in publishing the book, we commissioned papers from our seminar participants and those we thought could take us into other important areas relevant to the local–global connection. As an interim point, we then sponsored a series of sessions on the drafts of papers at a major international conference in the spring of 2008, giving the authors an opportunity to see each others' work and write their own chapters with others' work in mind. Finally, after receiving completed rough drafts in the summer of 2008, the editors critiqued, commented and redistributed the drafts of chapters for revision and cross-referencing. Final chapters were submitted in the fall of 2008. The process in its entirety has taken nearly two years.

As the above suggests, an edited volume requires the input and hard work of many people. As such, we would like to acknowledge specific contributions of certain people and institutions. First, we would like to thank the contributors. Without their flexibility and hard work, this book would not have been possible. In addition, the project has been supported by the Oxford University Centre for the Environment and Oxford University Press. Indeed, David Musson of OUP has been instrumental in this book's success. The authors would especially like to thank Jan Burke for logistical support.

Gordon L. Clark would like to thank Shirley for her steadfast support over the past seven years. Ashby H. B. Monk would like to thank Courtney for continuing enthusiasm and interest. Adam D. Dixon would like to thank Olga for her patience and support, as well as his parents for their permanent enthusiasm.

# List of Figures

# List of Tables

# Abbreviations

| | |
|---|---|
| ABS | Asset Backed Securities |
| AIM | Alternative Investment Management Program |
| AMEX | American Stock Exchange |
| BIS | Bank for International Settlements |
| CBOE | Chicago Board Options Exchange |
| CDDs | Cooling Degree-Days |
| CDO | Collateralized-Debt Obligation |
| CDVCA | Community Development Venture Capital Alliance |
| CIC | China Investment Corporation |
| CME | Chicago Mercantile Exchange |
| CRT | Chicago Research and Trading |
| DC | Defined Contribution |
| ECB | European Central Bank |
| ECOFIN | Economic and Financial Affairs Council of the European Union |
| EDM | Emerging Domestic Market |
| ESCB | European System of Central Banks |
| ESG | Environmental, Social, and Governance |
| ETI | Economically Targeted Investing |
| FACT Act | Fair and Accurate Transactions Act |
| FOX | London Futures and Options Exchange |
| FSA | Financial Services Authority |
| FSAP | Financial Services Action Plan |
| GARP | Global Association of Risk Professionals |
| HDDs | Heating Degree-Days |
| IMF | International Monetary Fund |
| IRR | Internal Rates of Return |
| LCFI | Large Complex Financial Institution |

| LCTM | Long-Term Capital Management |
|------|------------------------------|
| MassPRIM | Massachusetts Pension Reserves Investment Management Board |
| MBSs | Mortgage-Backed Securities |
| MEL | Macro-Economic Linkages |
| MPT | Modern Portfolio Theory |
| NCREIF | National Council of Real Estate Investment Fiduciaries |
| NPSS | National Pension Savings Scheme |
| OCC | Options Clearing Corporation |
| ONS | Office of National Statistics |
| OTC | Over-The-Counter |
| P/E | Market Price To Earnings |
| PBW | Philadelphia-Baltimore-Washington Stock Exchange |
| PHLX | Philadelphia Stock Exchange |
| PSE | Pacific Stock Exchange |
| SEC | Securities and Exchange Commission |
| SIVs | Structured Investment Vehicles |
| SSF | Social Studies of Finance |
| TMT | Technology, Media, and Telecom |
| VA | Value-Added |
| VaR | Value At Risk |

# Introduction

*Gordon L. Clark, Adam D. Dixon, and Ashby H. B. Monk*

The annals of financial and economic history will mark 2007 and beyond as years of great uncertainty and historic firsts. What began as the bursting of the US housing bubble in the summer of 2007 cascaded into a global financial crisis when the market could no longer sustain continued price inflation and credit conditions began to tighten, which then led to significant defaults on sub-prime mortgage loans that had been packaged into complex structured products and sold off to investors across the world. Major players such as investment bank Bear Stearns, an institution founded in the 1920s, fell victim to the crisis from overexposure to sub-prime mortgages, as did Lehman Brothers, Merrill Lynch, and the world's largest insurer American International Group. Others, such as Morgan Stanley and Goldman Sachs, had to seek out major cash injections and transformed themselves into bank holding companies, effectively putting an end to the era of the large independent investment bank model.

Yet the majors were not the only victims. For instance, one of the first to fall was a relatively small German regional bank, Sachsen LB, after losing billions on US sub-prime mortgage investments via off-balance sheet investment conduits. This sent many wondering how a regional bank unbeknown to most outside Germany could have become so involved in the US housing market. In the UK, the bank run on Northern Rock and its subsequent nationalization was reminiscent of the Great Depression. More significantly, a little more than twelve months into the crisis the US government announced it was effectively nationalizing the government-sponsored mortgage lenders Fannie Mae and Freddie Mac, the bedrock institutions of the US mortgage system. This was done to inject confidence in the US mortgage market, and stave off further turmoil both at home and abroad as tight credit

1

conditions and market uncertainty continued to reign large. Shortly there-after, the US Congress passed a $700 billion mortgage and bank bailout.

Two general points can be made about the onset of the 2007–8 financial crisis. In the first instance, global finance has clearly become interwoven and central to economic activity and capitalist organization. In theoretical terms, it seems almost implausible to separate the "real" economy from the "financial" economy; finance represents a major source of growth and business opportunities in and of itself, and is increasingly entwined in the everyday life of individuals. In the second instance, the crisis demon-strates the complex social, political, and economic geography that is finance and financial markets. Finance, and the institutions that propel it forward, are not reducible to the basic act of intermediation between capital suppliers and capital users, nor are they completely grasped by abstract mathematical models. Indeed, variegated spaces of financial regu-lation and social practice, overlapped and interconnected by global flows of capital of different origin and intent, moving in and out of global and local financial centers, make for a multidimensional institutional space and circuitry not easily described by simple binaries, static concepts, and national boundaries.

What is more, the sub-prime crisis reveals the complex tension present between the global and the local in finance. In many ways, the sub-prime crisis occurred because the "global" ignored the complexities of the "local." Sub-prime mortgages of different local housing markets in the United States were packaged together with other forms of debt and then sold off to investors across the globe. To the architects and buyers of these products, it was thought that by bundling, repackaging, and selling debt to a multitude of investors, higher rates of return could be generated while minimizing risk. However, when local housing markets began to unravel, the underlying cash flows of these products ceased, sending their value tumbling. Indeed, sufficient attention had not been paid to the intricacies of the numerous local variables in these complex products, mainly the assumptions made concerning the sustainability of local house prices and borrowers' capacity to repay. For the local, the practice of repackaging mortgages and selling them on to global investors facilitated the rapid expansion of mortgage credit, which helped fuel local house price infla-tion. In effect, managing financial risk and discerning what risks are, are thus a matter of spatial enquiry.

The object in this introductory chapter is to advance the call for geog-raphy to become a major component to studies of finance and in expli-cating its social, political, and economic manifestations. At the same time our goal is to advance the call to the social sciences as a whole to take seriously, as more and more continue to do, the rise of finance and the evolving modes of managing financial risk involved therein. Indeed, we argue that understanding the evolving economic landscape of twenty-first century capitalism will rely crucially on understanding the global and local practices and variegated institutional configurations of finance. This chapter is organized as follows. In the first section we briefly describe the rise of finance and the variegated spatial and temporal logic of global finance and global capital flows. In following, we explore global and local representations of finance and capitalist organization with reference to recent literature on the geography of finance and reference to Clark's (2005) metaphorical abstraction that "money flows like mercury". Here, we expose the need to see finance as a global phenomenon beyond the confines of national boundaries, while remaining sensitive to the national and regional institutional variegation with which global finance interacts and influences, and which global finance is influenced by. We then offer a vignette of the sub-prime crisis following this approach. This chapter concludes with presentations of the various contributions to the volume, where various aspects of managing financial risk are discussed.

## The rise of finance

In the last three decades financial markets have become major sources of economic growth and global political–economic integration. Indeed, the globalization of the end of the twentieth century and the beginning of the twenty-first century is frequently described as financial globalization. Since the collapse of the Bretton Woods international financial system in the 1970s, states have progressively liberalized and facilitated the integration of financial markets, which in turn has redefined political–economic proximity and interdependence (Helleiner 1994; Abdelal 2007). At the same time, financial markets have facilitated corporate and industrial restructuring and relocation through mergers, acquisitions, spin-offs, leveraged buy-outs and initial public offerings (Jensen 1993). This has ultimately changed the geographic landscape of production from local to increasingly global scales and the nature of corporate competition. In a short time, financial markets have become 24-hour entities criss-crossing the globe via high-speed information and communication networks, with complex and exotic products and methods of pricing and valuing risk.

Perhaps most important to the rise of finance is the incredible accumulation of capital pools. Pension assets, mostly from Anglo-American countries, yet becoming increasingly important elsewhere due to reforms of public pay-as-you-go pension systems, have fueled the expansion of markets by providing increasing demand and critical need for investment products and investment opportunities (Clark 2000, 2003; Clowes 2000; Dixon 2008). Other large asset pools such as commodity-based wealth funds, foreign-exchange reserves generated from global financial imbalances, and bank deposits and insurance premiums augment the latter to create a massive pool or pools of trillions of dollars. In turn, these assets fuel the development of social practices and the institutions that are in the business of moving or holding capital, from pension funds, asset managers, investment banks, and insurance companies, to sophisticated hedge funds, private equity houses and investment consultancies (Knorr-Cetina and Preda 2005).

As ubiquitous as this picture of finance may seem, its structure and logic manifests various histories and geographies. The different sources of capital, from pension funds to petrodollars, have variegated origins and political–economic rationales for why they exist and why their social and economic reproduction persists. These unique origins explicitly or implicitly affect the manner in which the capital is treated and where and how it is invested (Clark 2008). For instance, pension savings, which originate from political decisions to rely on funding instead of current transfers between workers and retirees, are in practice supposed to provide a retirement income at a later point in time. This consideration ultimately affects, whether implicitly or explicitly, the manner in which the funds are allocated to different investment opportunities (Clark 2000). Risk and return and investment allocation have to be balanced with a view to the approaching divestment period in the future and the needs and life expectancy of the beneficiary at that point in time and thereafter (Campbell and Viceira 2002).

Likewise, the institutions that move and house capital have a unique geography of ownership. For instance, a large Dutch private pension fund managing the pension benefits of thousands of beneficiaries will have different priorities and decision-making hierarchies than a sovereign wealth fund from an emerging economy, where investment goals may not necessarily be exclusively commercial in nature, or based on some form of fiduciary duty, as is understood in the Western world. It is arguable, for example, that China's recent founding of the China Investment Corporation (CIC), a fund to invest a $200 billion portion of China's estimated $1.8 trillion in foreign exchange reserves, is a means for China to acquire increased access to financial expertise and give increased visibility and exposure for China in global financial markets. These effects come as extra-financial gains on top of conventional financial gains (or losses) (Monk forthcoming).

The CIC's risky $5 billion investment in Morgan Stanley for a nearly 10 percent equity stake at the end of 2007 during the height of the sub-prime crisis, is arguably an example of this. Although the investment soon eroded in value, investing at such an unstable time in financial markets and when Morgan Stanley was in need of a major capital injection was arguably an opportune time for the CIC to invest without receiving significant political resistance. The trustees of pension funds similar in size, such as ABP of the Netherlands or CalPERS of the United States, would likely find it nearly impossible to justify such a large and risky bet such as this, due to their fiduciary duty to beneficiaries (Maatman 2004; Clark 2007). On the other hand, some pension funds are leading the charge on socially responsible investment, where a sound financial return may be gained along with some other social or environmental objective in mind such as urban development (Hagerman and Hebb, this volume).

Similarly, the major investment banks, most of which originate from the United States and therefore its long and varied financial development over the twentieth century, manifest different corporate cultures and modes of governance and decision-making. Goldman Sachs, for instance, made a significant $4 billion profit hedging against sub-prime loans in 2007, after several of the firm's traders were able to convince colleagues that lending criteria had become so lax that defaults were inevitable (Bawden and Thompson 2007). The firm may have been the beneficiary of sheer luck in predicting the extent of the collapse before others, yet its unique culture of risk management was arguably an important factor. As such, different risk management cultures exist and are operationalized in different ways (Clark and Thrift 2005).

Likewise, location in different financial centers also poses potential sources of social differentiation and distinction. Although financial professionals frequently spend long periods living and working in the major financial centers, such as London, New York, Tokyo, and Hong Kong (and financial institutions make an effort to standardize their bureaucratic and cultural practices on a global level (Clark and Thrift 2005)), the local dynamics of the financial center impinge ultimately on the manner in which this process unfolds. Indeed, interpretation of the market is essential and is facilitated by proximity and social networks (Leyshon and Thrift 1997).

The point of these brief examples, of which many more exist, is to highlight the heterogeneous nature of financial practice and its institutional composition. In no way is finance a well-regulated whole following a functionalist logic, but rather an aggregation of different and unique parts. At a formal level, however, much credence and reference is given to theoretical principles of finance, those extended by mainstream financial economics, which advance particular expectations about how markets and finance should act and what finance and markets are. Models such as the Efficient Market Hypothesis, the Capital Asset Pricing Model, and the Black-Scholes option-pricing theorem form part of a common language in financial textbooks and often in investment professionals' legitimization of their investment decisions (MacKenzie 2006).

In practice, however, the behavior of financial markets, especially in times of distress, often fails to act according to these principles. This is not to imply that these models provide no ontological value in pricing risk. Rather, conceptualizing how financial markets actually work and how risk is assessed should not be left to them and them alone, and would benefit immensely from a plethora of "on the ground" analyses, both historical and actual, that can pick apart the various institutional and scalar variations present in the practice and operationalization of finance. Indeed, many of the textbook methods of pricing assets and valuing risks have given way or been augmented by more empirical methods, and even qualitative measures (Clark and Wójcik 2007).

## Money flows like mercury reprised

In advocating a role for economic geography in this effort of understanding global finance as lived, Clark (2005) volunteers the metaphorical abstraction that "money flows like mercury". In comparison to other metaphors such as water, the properties and behavior of mercury provide a compelling conceptualization of the spatial and temporal logic of global capital flows. Firstly, liquid mercury is synthesized in a chemist's laboratory. Like money, the synthesis of mercury implies a certain ownership and socio-anthropological process, that is, the chemist's knowledge and manipulation (see also Maurer 2006). Like mercury, money is a human invention with various representations and profound symbolism in quotidian life. Secondly, mercury is extremely rare in the earth's crust. As such, it is inherently valuable, just as money is inherently about value. Thirdly, mercury is poisonous, implying the need to handle it with care. Indeed, money can be easily lost, which in different ways can cause harm. Fourthly, based on its viscous properties, mercury is never randomly distributed. It forms together in pools and travels together at speed. Global finance (money) also runs together at speed and collects together in pools. One need not look further than the multi-trillion dollar 24-hour foreign exchange market, where massive flows of capital move in and out of financial centers at speed through established networks. Running together allows market agents to gauge the expectations and sentiments of others, which is crucial in an environment of risk and uncertainty. The collection and tagging of pension savings in large asset managers, which are then moved in different pools to users of capital, is a simple visualization of the latter. Neither of these is done haphazardly, nor usually without some sort of care given. Indeed, the structure and efficiency of managing money and moving money matters greatly to the overall cost, and thus financial returns.

The theoretical utility of the metaphor that money flows like mercury to the geographic imagination lies in its interaction with the global and the local. Where many social scientific enquiries tend to favor either one or the other, the behavioral properties of mercury in many ways grasp both at the same time. Mercury's viscosity and pooling behavior implies tightness to a locality, at least for a period of time. It does not spread ubiquitously across a surface as water would. This property of tightness to a location allows for the appearance of borders. Given political–economic borders are unstable over time and are generally porous, this avoids treating such borders as static. When characterizing something as global, one runs the risk of falling into the trap of ubiquity where the item in question is perceived as omnipresent, and at times omnipotent. On the other hand, mercury is liquid and moves across the surface. In that case, mercury's relationship with a locality is ultimately transitory. In effect, there is a constant tension between the global and the local.

This leads us into what we refer to as the "geography of finance" (Clark and Wójcik 2007). Our approach to the study of capitalist development, in its current form where finance and financial practice are a crucial part, diverges from more functionalist accounts of capitalist development. On the one hand, the geography of finance diverges from the view of capitalism espoused mainly by neoclassical economics and similar globalization theories, where price competition, utility maximization, and rational action will inexorably lead to the increasing spatial convergence of political economies and their institutional differences (see, e.g., Jensen 2000; Ohmae 1990). For instance, this mode of thought predicts a convergence of the way firms operate and organize themselves, suggesting there is one "best" way. As a corollary, financial practice and the spread and scope of financial markets would converge as well. On the other hand, the geography of finance diverges from contrary and similarly functionalist accounts, namely the "varieties of capitalism" (VoC) approach derived from heterodox political economy, which continues to examine capitalist organization mainly in terms of national borders (e.g., Hall and Soskice 2001). Unlike the neoclassical approach, the VoC School, and its focus on national institutional configurations, argues that countries will continue to diverge from each other along distinct paths. Due to path dependence and increasing returns to scale, institutional configurations such as corporate governance and local financial systems are predicted to resist convergence.

Importantly, however, the geography of finance shares various aspects of both approaches. In terms of the former, the geography of finance is keenly aware of the power of the capacity of markets, in a broad sense, to price different histories and geographies against competing opportunities. In a world of increasingly integrated financial markets, where many firms have partially shed their historical and national commitments in search of increased investment or market opportunities, this has significant empirical grounding. Nation-states no longer, if they actually ever were, are insulated from the pricing capacity of the markets and the power of investors. Nation-states themselves, as issuers of sovereign bonds, are equally priced against competing opportunities. This global pricing activity has the scope to remake geographies and change historical path dependencies, if not directly then through the power of such perceived pricing, whereby the local adapts (which is not equivalent to conforming) to changing global conditions. As such, the power of global finance has the capacity, to an important extent, to reshape and mould the modern corporation or the economic institutions of a particular political economy to the conventional expectations of the market and market actors. However, on the other side of the coin, the conventional expectations of the market, such as corporate governance or accounting standards, are themselves unstable and prone to change and revision. In effect, this relationship is by no means linear or one-dimensional.

What the geography of finance shares with the former, the various approaches fiercely protective of observed differences, is a sensitivity to the variegated institutional constitution and organizational manifestations present in local capitalist experience. To be sure, political economies and actors within them still face different regulations, business practices, and processes, not to mention different cultures, histories, and language. Actors and groups of actors cannot easily rid themselves of deeply embedded differences manifest in their local environments. Where our approach differs and what we share with new efforts to purge the inherent functionalism of comparative capitalist approaches is in reaffirming the role of agency (e.g., Campbell 2004; Crouch 2005). Unlike neoclassical or some cultural approaches that place a great deal of emphasis on agency, which seems to lose the salience of structure, the geography of finance recognizes that actors are both constrained by their environments but can equally utilize and adapt their environments to new means and challenges. Importantly, however, our view of institutional change does not perceive a dominant role in rational action. Although actors may appear to act in rational ways at times, institutional change does not occur always under rational intent. Rather, action is institutionally patterned (Engelen, Konings, and Fernandez 2008).

In order to understand finance, then, a broad-based social scientific approach is needed; however, one that is neither linear nor verging on some grand theory where the many ways finance operates and unfolds across different political economies and geographies are missed. By moving away from the linear modernist thought that typified so much of twentieth-century academic thought and political–economic theorizing, we open the stage for even more fine-grained empirical analysis of how finance is lived. As such, the geography of finance is not a theory per se, but a call to take global finance seriously as well as not forgetting to keep grounded in the various ways finance and financial practice unfold at the local level. In other words, global finance is actually an aggregation of numerous local practices, where understanding the global necessarily entails understanding the local. Though in a dialectical manner, truly understanding the local demands that the global, and every layer in between, is not forgotten. As we show in the following section, the sub-prime crisis is exactly one where this dialectical relationship was largely ignored.

## Sub-prime – a crisis foretold?

The looming sub-prime crisis garnered widespread media coverage in the lengthening shadows of the north summer of 2007. Across the world, banks and financial institutions began to fail prompting, in the UK case at least, queues of frightened customers seeking return of their deposits.

Once the crisis was exposed in the pricing of US housing mortgages, expectations about the ever-upwards trajectory of US housing prices began to waver; the housing price bubble was revealed for what it was – unsustainable in the face of retreating credit. As expectations switched from increasing to decreasing house prices it became apparent that the US housing market was facing a near-term surplus of supply: in many locales, developers and owners faced the prospect of not being able to realize expected sales prices and estimated mortgage values (see CBO 2008). Apocryphal stories of default began to circulate raising fears in banks and financial institutions that held sub-prime mortgages that they would not realize the value of those portfolios.

This was just the first phase of the crisis. The second phase became apparent when it was realized that the so-called "rated" quality of mortgage portfolios could not be relied upon in a situation of systemic market meltdown. The rating agencies were unable to convince the market that their data sources and rating methods could withstand scrutiny. As the crisis accelerated and the volume and scope of likely defaults grew far beyond expectations, banks and financial institutions could no longer use their mortgage-backed securities (MBS) as collateral in raising credit. Amplifying problems of market liquidity, banks fearing shortfalls on their own accounts began refusing extension of credit to customers and others banks and financial institutions (Crockett 2008). The contagion effect of these actions turned a "local" crisis into a "global" crisis (Dodd 2007; Adrian and Shin 2008). Only after extensive write-downs of bank portfolios and the sanitization of balance sheets did the interventions of monetary authorities around the world begin to stabilize the situation.

The sub-prime crisis has been told many times, with many different conclusions (including the threats to market stability posed by off-balance sheet special investment vehicles and the social costs of moral hazard). Here, we draw rather different connections and conclusions linking findings from the geography of finance with Adam Smith's model of governing trade and exchange. Basically, the sub-prime crisis was foretold by geographers and economists, albeit from two rather different vantage points and with implications that were not realized. We show, moreover, that what might have been a "local" crisis particular to the structure and performance of the US housing market and its mortgage providers became "global" by virtue of the unrequited demand for higher rates of return on investment without adequate mechanisms for governing the intermediation process. We begin with the supply of MBS, and then switch to the global demand of MBS.

In a series of papers, Andrew Leyshon and his colleagues sought to explain the transformation of the UK banking and financial services industry from one based upon "interpersonal relationships of trust" to one based upon the servicing of consumers on the basis of "at-a-distance" data bases and market intelligence (Leyshon, Thrift, and Pratt 1998). In their first paper, they suggested that traditional on-site client-specific risk assessment had given way to the compilation of multi-attribute data bases on current and potential consumers with related risk-assessments administered at-a-distance from bank branches through electronic and communication networks. For Leyshon et al. (1998), this development had enabled new competitors into the UK financial marketplace discounting the value of incumbents' branch networks as barriers to market entry. As a consequence, there were a significant number of branch closures by the major banks. Either directly or indirectly, providers of financial services assumed that the personal knowledge of consumers forgone by virtue of remote assessment was either unreliable or not so significant as to amplify the risks associated with remote mechanisms for evaluating the creditworthiness of clients. By their argument, the break with the "local" trust relationship and its replacement with "remote" credit-scoring threatened to isolate some types of consumers from the financial services industry by virtue of their risk "characteristics".

This argument was developed in Leyshon and Thrift (1999) and in Leyshon et al. (2004). In Leyshon and Thrift, the distinctive nature of the UK retail market for financial services was documented noting the diversity of new market entrants as against incumbents and their dependence upon customer scoring systems to establish creditworthiness. For Leyshon and Thrift, the issue was whether these systems were effective in resolving the inherent problem of information asymmetries – where intending customers know more about their risk profile than the institutions seeking to evaluate their claims for service. They also suggested that incumbent banks and new entrants did not trust "local" assessment – the combination of distrust of local assessment with the new scoring technologies resolved the issue of effectiveness without stress-testing. One consequence of the widespread adoption of scoring technologies was the segmentation of markets using customer characteristics to produce geographical and social subsets of the market ("ecologies") according to product-potential with appropriate marketing strategies (2004).

In their paper on the sub-prime market for financial services, Burton et al. (2004) suggest that those excluded by mainstream retail providers because of low scores on credit-worthiness were brought into the market (at a price) through securitization. Poor credit history and red-flagged characteristics could be discounted by lenders against the prospect of seizing consumers' assets in the case of default. As in the case of credit scoring, the assessment of consumers was done remotely; even the putative value of assets underwriting offers of credit in sub-prime market segments was taken remotely by "assessors" charged with closing deals rather than rejecting possible risky valuations. At best, assessors used risk-related "trips" built into software programs. At worst, these "trips" were routinely violated. The risks associated with information asymmetries, so important to Coval and Moskowitz (1999) and colleagues in their exposition of the logic underpinning the geography of finance, were deeply embedded in UK and US lending practices. Institutions systematically violated Adam Smith's dictum on the governance of trade and exchange.

Mortgage-backed securities have entered financial markets in two different ways. Normally, mortgage providers sell-on large chunks of their portfolios distributing to wholesale buyers risk-rated strips or segments underwritten by past performance and the prospect of claiming underlying assets should default be a problem. The expected rate of return on these assets is benchmarked against government and corporate bonds given the fact that their yield is priced against a premium on the discount rate and the long-term expected rate of economic growth. With respect to sub-prime MBS, new entrants to the market including investment banks also offered rated strips and segments but with a higher yield to reflect the underlying higher risks. With galloping US house-price inflation and high rates of current and expected rates of economic growth it seemed that the default risks of particular strips and segments could be discounted by the underlying assets and the spread of investment across a range of MBS.

Investment banks offering strips of sub-prime MBS benefited in three ways from such products. They claimed fees on the transactions, they booked the rate of return on MBS held in special-purpose investment vehicles, and they used the expected market value of sub-prime MBS portfolios to underwrite credit. In effect, these institutions had a strong interest in parceling together and providing to the global marketplace a never-ending stream of sub-prime investment options offering a high yield underwritten by the apparently increasing value of the asset (*contra* Leyshon et al. *2004*). These institutions relied upon market intermediaries to rate and value sub-prime strips, if need be utilizing ratings agencies to validate the methods of scoring risk if not the underlying prospects of default in varying market conditions. In effect, no market player had a pecuniary interest ("skin-in-the-game") in looking underneath the putative risk scores; the flow of transactions dominated institutions. Only after-the-fact, when banks were left holding "assets" they were unable to price, did the costs of these arrangements become apparent.

Why was there such demand for sub-prime MBS? Why was demand global not just local? There were three immediate reasons for the growth in demand. Firstly, the rate-of-return premium on conventional MBS was attractive to many institutions given the putative "insurance" offered by the underlying assets and the ratings provided by rating agencies. Secondly, the expected growth in US housing markets was such that sub-prime securities seemed to be highly liquid; institutions expected to trade-out at a profit. Thirdly, in some cases, access to sub-prime MBS through banks' special-purpose investment vehicles provided investors tax advantages and anonymity not always apparent in public markets. More importantly, in the aftermath of the 1999/2000 stock market bubble characterized by low interest rates and modest equity returns the US housing market seemed to offer higher rates of return underwritten by economic growth and sophisticated methods of risk management. For institutional investors, such as pension funds and insurance companies, facing higher-valued long-term obligations, sub-prime was a way out of calling on contributions from sponsors.

At a global level, though, the demand for sub-prime was an expression of three overlapping and reinforcing factors. Most obviously, the global glut in savings was such that opportunities for higher rates of return in western public markets were systematically undercut by the pricing and trading practices of large institutions. As public markets approached the standards of "efficiency" sought by academics, garnering higher rates was increasingly only possible by happenstance. For many European investors, hamstrung by low rates of economic growth and the fact that the flow of market-sensitive information seems to benefit "insiders" as opposed to "outsiders" (Clark and Wójcik 2007), US markets seemed to offer the long-term benefits of higher rates of economic growth and high levels of immigration as reflected in housing markets. These opportunities were deemed far more predictable given the risks associated with emerging markets. In any event, US securities markets were believed to be more transparent and better regulated than other markets, encouraging reliance upon investment banks with triple-A reputations.

Whereas Leyshon and his colleagues foretold a looming crisis of access to financial services because of the pervasive use of credit-scoring techniques, and suggested that sub-prime segments of the market would be at risk to unscrupulous sellers of financial services, it turned out that the demand for sub-prime strips and segments brought into the market many people and localities whose risk-profiles were not effectively evaluated. Whereas Moskowitz and his colleagues foretold a crisis of investment given the idiosyncratic risks embedded in geography, it turned out that the crisis was systemic by virtue of the fact that the widespread adoption of remote risk-scoring techniques systematically violated the best interests of investors (if not providers). Whereas the demand for sub-prime might have been isolated to specific localities and market segments because of the highly geographically stratified nature of housing markets, the crisis was global because of the never-ending search for higher levels of risk-adjusted rates of return. Global investors came to the US market on the assumption that reputation was a reflection of highly calibrated risk-management. In coming to market, global investors amplified the risks inherent in sub-prime; the local became global by virtue of the unsatisfied demand for investment returns.

## Managing financial risk: from global to local

Acknowledging the importance of space and place in the production and reproduction of finance at various geographical scales, the organization of the volume follows a structure of moving from matters of seemingly macro/global importance to matters of micro/local importance and effect. However, in many ways this structure is only for organizational purposes. Although grouped in these "artificial" categories, each chapter could easily be, both empirically and conceptually, recategorized and regrouped within a different scalar subset. Indeed, each chapter to a certain degree manifests the global to local continuum, either explicitly or implicitly.

### Governing global financial risk

We begin the core of the book at the global scale. This is important for several reasons. Firstly, markets are increasingly interconnected requiring political cooperation. Secondly, global financial institutions require sophisticated governance mechanisms to handle firms' global risk exposure and investment decision-making. Thirdly, financial services firms shift risk from place to place throughout the globe, making it a natural starting point in our analysis. At this level, poor governance and coordination by firms and regulators can have dangerous consequences, such as financial crisis, political instability, and negative long-term welfare.

Pauly's chapter rests on the assumption that despite the obvious moral hazards built into the system, the *sine qua non* of financial integration is that states persistently refuse to retreat in the face of systemic crises. Pauly begins with the recognition that in previous periods financial institutions were relatively contained within national borders and subject to clear "home-country" supervision and more importantly had the implicit guarantee of the national purse in times of systemic crisis, whereas cross-border operations in the current era abound, which muddles the clarity of both "home-country" supervision and implicit state guarantees to financial market stability. Pauly then looks at the changing nature of state sovereignty as regards the international integration of financial markets more generally, and at the evolving modes of political cooperation during systemic crises in particular, with an examination of current trends in Europe.

As Pauly argues, the challenge for deeper European financial integration is the absence of any cross-national "college of supervisors" and a single lender-of-last-resort. This is compounded by the problem that national authorities speak to the importance of state sovereignty, although they remain open to integration given the higher growth potential it brings. However, despite the apparent lack of collaboration on the surface and absence of formal institutions, European countries are devising innovative means of political cooperation beyond the familiar structures and borders of political accountability and obligation, leading to the deepening complexity of state sovereignty and thus limiting the threat of capital market disintegration. As regards financial risk management, Pauly's contribution demonstrates that the salience and persistence of international market integration is crucially dependent on the role of macro-level political cooperation, especially given how crises can engulf micro-level risk management.

Dymski's chapter examines the problem of financial governance from the view of macro-structural dynamics. Like Pauly, Dymski starts from the basic context that financial governance resides in two forms: bounded prudential supervision of a set of financial firms or markets, and lender-of-last-resort function to prevent financial meltdown. Like Pauly, Dymski argues that in the current era of market integration and uncertain authority, these governance functions have become less effective and less feasible. More specifically, Dymski's contribution argues that the shift to a floating-exchange-rate world, where the United States no longer acts as the sole financial hegemon as it did during Bretton Woods and where there is competition for reserve-currency status, allows countries with reserve-currency status to take on more and more risk. In countries without reserve-currency status, a financial crisis in these countries' financial systems is likely to engender a simultaneous crisis of confidence in the local currency. In turn, these countries cannot stem a crisis of confidence by providing liquidity with their own currency, which would deepen the crisis. On the other hand, countries with reserve-currency status are able to use their currency in lender-of-last-resort operations. As such, for countries without such status it is important that they limit the build-up of aggregate risks. Yet, for those with this status there is a larger capacity to build up larger volumes of risk, and in turn these countries may have a reduced incentive to rein in excessive risk-taking by private financial institutions.

Whereas Pauly and Dymski examine the lack of a global framework of financial regulation and supervision and the challenges this poses to financial risk management, Clark's contribution examines the governance of institutional investors, notably pension and retirement income funds. As most nation-states have abandoned quantitative and qualitative restrictions on cross-border investment for pension funds and insurance companies, these institutions have increasingly operated on a global scale. As such, these institutions are consigned to manage their financial risk while following their implicit or explicit mandates to maximize the rate of return on investments. Yet, just as the macro-level governance of financial markets is problematic, Clark notes that institutional governance is more often than not imperfect and subject to problems of coordination. As such, Clark provides an account of the nature and scope of financial decision-making under conditions of risk and uncertainty, demonstrating the importance of time, expertise, and collective commitment in the decision ecologies of these types of institutions. Understanding the dynamics and structure of decision-making in these institutions, Clark argues, is a necessary ingredient to any comprehensive understanding of the logic of global financial markets.

### Place, proximity, and risk

From the global scale we move to the meso-level/regional scale. This section highlights the tension between centralization and decentralization of finance and financial practice, focusing on the importance of place and proximity in financial risk management. At this level, the management of the kinds of financial risks cited above appears to be driving the centralization and decentralization of certain types of financial services and practices.

The following three chapters extend the issue of proximity regarding financial risk management in several different ways. Millo and MacKenzie's contribution begins the section with an examination of the emergence of financial risk management in markets for financial derivatives, specifically looking at the development and utilization of the Black-Scholes-Merton options pricing model and the introduction of options trading on organized exchanges. As the chapter argues, financial risk management is a loosely coupled array of techno-social practices – which encompasses different yet interrelated communities of practice, including traders, regulators, and "non-financial" specialists such as lawyers and accountants – rather than simply methods evidencing the accuracy and validity of modern financial economics. More importantly, the chapter demonstrates that although financial risk management is often assumed to be based on connections that are arm's-length, procedural and utilitarian, it actually unfolds in a network of connections where different organizational actors know each other and where these actors trust each other's judgments concerning the utility of the risk management systems.

The importance of trust is extended in the following chapter, where Engelen examines the spatial distribution of financial innovation and what the implications are for this distribution with the return of uncertainty resulting from the sub-prime crisis. As Engelen shows, until 2007 financial markets seemed to be highly transparent, arm's-length financial derivatives subject to weak ties proliferated, and actors felt increasingly confident in their risk calculations. In other words, functional, organizational, and territorial proximities lost much of their salience, as a sense of "certainty" spread in across market actors. However, the outbreak of the sub-prime crisis reintroduced great uncertainty. Faith in financial products, one's counterparties and means of calculating risk effectively disappeared: the financial "facts" that market participants had implicitly agreed upon for how markets worked fell apart. Engelen argues that the return of uncertainty might well mean the return of spatial proximity, where relational trust becomes more and more important for financial transactions.

Continuing with the issue of proximity, Wójcik's chapter analyses the role of proximity between investors and corporations with equity traded on public secondary equity markets in financial risk management. Combining insights from recent research on home and local bias in financial economics, with economic geographical research on proximity and financial markets, Wójcik argues that proximity, even if defined narrowly as geographical proximity, has significant implications for: investors (in terms of performance and trade-off with liquidity); the investment industry as a whole (in terms of size, structure, and strategy); issuers (in terms of access to capital and liquidity); communities (in terms of herd behavior and financial literacy); and policy makers (in terms of market structure, competition, and international harmonization). The consideration for cognitive, social, organizational, and institutional proximity enriches the understanding of secondary equity markets, by complementing the analysis of geographical proximity, but does not make the latter redundant.

### Urban risk

In this section we observe financial risk management at another "scale", the urban built environment. This environment has become an important financial product and a means of managing long-term risk for institutional investors. At the same time, financial markets have become increasingly concerned with managing environmental risks facing the urban system. Indeed, at this level, understanding financial risk is important for two main reasons: firstly, the urban environment has become a means of managing long-term financial risks associated with retirement; and secondly, the agglomeration of assets in urban environments presents concentrated financial risks unobserved in rural areas.

O'Neill's contribution deals with the emergence of infrastructure as a rapidly emerging urban economic sector. With increasing fiscal conservatism, cash-strapped governments and associated privatization of public utilities, infrastructure has become increasingly mobilized as a financial product. Attributes such as stable and often inflation-adjusted returns over long time periods, and usually oligopolistic or monopolistic positions in the market, have made infrastructure investing highly attractive to pension fund managers. Importantly, the financial mobilization of infrastructure, O'Neill argues, has altered the definition of what constitutes infrastructure from a set of hard physical structures to a field of urban flows and connections involving quotidian commercial, public, and private life.

O'Neill examines the issues involved in this evolution alongside the reformulation of infrastructure as a financial product via a case study of Australia's international infrastructure bank Macquarie, with a particular emphasis on its activities in Sydney. Specifically, the chapter concentrates on the strategies devised by the banks to control risk. According to O'Neill, these have a number of dimensions. One is a set of human resources strategies that mobilizes its young professionals to devise and negotiate new infrastructure products within a set of risk controls. Another is a set of strategies for managing aggregate balance sheet risk through a combination of portfolio manipulation, risk transfer to the balance sheets of associated financial entities and outright ownership shifts. Critical to the success of the banks' risk control strategies is achieving appropriate balance between financial product invention, IPOs, and holding products for capital gains and fees generation. As O'Neill argues, this means that the daily operations of the contemporary city are increasingly bound to the investment and risk management strategies of the major infrastructure banks. The implications of this entanglement are explored.

Hagerman and Hebb expand on the changing way financial markets interact with the built environment, by examining investment in underserved urban markets. Specifically, Hagerman and Hebb look at innovative practices in which institutional investors can enjoy competitive financial returns on their investment while stimulating economic growth in these communities. Over the last three decades the community-based investing industry has undergone a paradigm shift from the traditional subsidy-driven model to the market-driven model. In the capital-driven model institutional investors perceive investing in the underserved urban areas as an overlooked economic opportunity. Increasingly institutional investors identify urban investments as a means to diversify risk and achieve competitive market rates of return. Hagerman and Hebb examine how urban investments add value to a public pension fund by diversifying risk through a strategic asset allocation policy. Such policies fall under the rubric of investing in economic development and yield financial, social, and environmental returns. Specifically, the chapter examines how urban investments cross the traditional asset classes (fixed income) and alternative asset classes (equity real estate and venture capital). The role of the investment intermediary is examined in their ability to overcome investment barriers typical to the emerging domestic markets.

In Randalls's chapter we are reminded that financial risks relating to the environment are frequently concentrated in cities, both in the source of risks and in the management of those risks. Indeed, urban areas are prone to a number of environmental concerns including brownfield biodiversity, flooding and potential relations to climate change, and the effects of "everyday" environmental changes, for example the weather, on productivity. Furthermore, managing these risks is found in the city too through mainstream financial institutions like banks and insurers that seek both physical and financial protection for themselves and their clients from the worst environmental effects. One clear example is decision-making about the Thames Barrier in London, which aims to protect the financial heartland of the UK from severe flooding. At the same time, in nearby offices, a wide range of new products are being created to manage these urban environmental risks, including diverse catastrophe bonds, weather derivatives, and global warming indexes. Drawing on governmentality and poststructural approaches, Randalls highlights the ways in which environments are being made into financial risks, yet goes on to explore the possible repercussions of this form of financial risk management and what it might obscure or open up. Underlying his analysis is the recognition that environmental management through financial markets takes political action to make it work.

## Individuals in a risk world

The final section of this book focuses on risks borne by individuals and their interactions with financial markets, particularly in the areas of retirement income, consumer credit, and housing. Indeed, people's lives are increasingly "financialized" and they are thus required to make difficult financial decisions, from understanding their home as a financial product to planning for retirement. The evidence suggests that these risks are not well understood by these individuals and, as recent market turmoil testifies, by global markets.

Smith's chapter begins the section with a compelling look at the growing model of housing provision where home ownership has become a package of housing services linked to an investment vehicle, which is accessed through leveraged financing. In the "home ownership" societies of the English-speaking world, borrowers, lenders, developers, and politicians are vying for the positions that gain most, and lose least from price movements in the housing market. This positioning by economic actors is indeed unsurprising, as housing is the world's largest class of assets. Moreover, housing as an asset class has outperformed most other asset classes for more than a decade. Like other forms of investing, this system of housing is laden in financial risk. This is especially pertinent for ordinary households whose wealth is generally concentrated within a single owned home where it increasingly forms an asset base for welfare. Smith's chapter more specifically addresses the issue of why none of the financial derivatives and markets invented to manage this growing dependence on a narrow, sometimes volatile, and generally heavily leveraged, investment "portfolio" – and which protect large institutions against the ups and downs of virtually every other major asset class (commodities, equities, bonds, and more) – are yet available for housing. In what follows, Smith focuses on attempts underway to change this, while also weighing up their merits and limitations and considering whether they are likely to succeed.

In the following chapter Strauss explores another area important to individuals: retirement income. In particular, Strauss surveys research by geographers on decision-making in UK occupational pensions and examines the links between choice, risk, and responsibility in defined contribution (DC) plans. Strauss highlights the implications of the financialization of pensions, in light of behavioral biases and the labour market choices and constraints faced by workers, for pension inequality. Strauss's main focus is on the gender pension gap and the ways in which men and women face different risks in relation to poverty in old age. Moreover, Strauss argues that although the gender inequality in pensions remains a significant issue, the financialization of pensions highlights the salience of class as an axis of differentiation that cuts across the category of gender.

In the final chapter of the volume Langley takes us through the embodied economy of mass market consumer credit, an area of economic activity that ballooned at the same time as the housing market. Drawing on governmentality literature, Langley examines the ways in which the responsibilities of borrowers for outstanding credit obligations have been transformed in the booming mass market for credit cards, such that individual borrower subjects come to perform entrepreneurial self-disciplines that extend well beyond simply meeting repayments. Moreover, Langley emphasizes the intersection of the legal and extra-legal in the punishment of debtors, and how risk calculations in credit scoring can be understood as a technology of government. Langley then offers reflections on the tensions and contradictions that are experienced by individual credit card holders as the crisis unfolds, specifically arguing that self-disciplines of risk management fall short of completely containing the complexities and inherent uncertainty in economic life, such as precarious labor markets.

## References

Abdelal, R. (2007). *Capital Rules: The Construction of Global Finance*. Cambridge, Mass.: Harvard University Press.

Adrian, T., and Shin, H. S. (2008). Liquidity, monetary policy, and financial cycles. *Current Issues in Economics and Finance*, *14(1)*.

Bawden, T., and Thompson, S. (2007, December 15), Goldman Sachs makes $4bn profit on daring sub-prime bet. *The Times*, online edition.

Burton, D., Knights, D., Leyshon, A., Alferoff, C., and Signoretta, P. (2004). Making a market: The UK retail financial services industry and the rise of the complex sub-prime credit market. *Competition & Change, 8(1)*, 25.

Campbell, J. L. (2004). *Institutional Change and Globalization*. Princeton: Princeton University Press.

Campbell, J. Y., and Viceira, L. M. (2002). *Strategic Asset Allocation: Portfolio Choice for Long-Term Investors*. New York: Oxford University Press.

CBO (2008). *The budget and economic outlook: Fiscal years 2008 to 2018*. Washington: Congressional Budget Office.

Clark, G. L. (2000). *Pension Fund Capitalism*. Oxford: Oxford University Press.

—— (2003). *European Pensions and Global Finance*. Oxford: Oxford University Press.

Clark, G. L. (2005). Money flows like mercury: The geography of global finance. *Geografiska Annaler Series B-Human Geography, 87B(2)*, 99–112.

—— (2007). Expertise and representation in financial institutions: UK legislation on pension fund governance and US regulation of the mutual fund industry. *Twenty-First Century Society, 2(1)*, 1–24.

—— (2008). Governing finance: Global imperatives and the challenge of reconciling community representation with expertise. *Economic Geography, 84(2)*, 281–302.

—— and Thrift, N. (2005). The return of bureaucracy: Managing dispersed knowledge in global finance. In K. Knorr-Cetina and A. Preda (eds.), *The Sociology of Financial Markets* (pp. 229–50). Oxford: Oxford University Press.

—— and Wójcik, D. (2007). *The Geography of Finance: Corporate Governance in the Global Marketplace*. Oxford: Oxford University Press.

Clowes, M. J. (2000). *The Money Flood: How Pension Funds Revolutionized Investing*. New York: Wiley.

Coval, J. D., and Moskowitz, T. J. (1999). Home bias at home: Local equity preference in domestic portfolios. *The Journal of Finance, 54(6)*, 2045–73.

Crockett, A. (2008). Market liquidity and financial stability. *Financial Stability Review, 11*, 13–17.

Crouch, C. (2005). *Capitalist Diversity and Change: Recombinant Governance and Institutional Entrepreneurs*. Oxford: Oxford University Press.

Dixon, A. (2008). The rise of pension fund capitalism in Europe: An unseen revolution? *New Political Economy, 13(3)*, 249–70.

Dodd, R. (2007). Subprime: Tentacles of a crisis. *Finance and Development, 44(4)*, 15–19.

Engelen, E., Konings, M., and Fernandez, R. (2008). The rise of activist investors and patterns of political responses: Lessons on agency. *Socio-Economic Review, 6(4)*, 611–36.

Hall, P. A., and Soskice, D. W. (2001). *Varieties of Capitalism: The Institutional Foundations of Comparative Advantage*. Oxford: Oxford University Press.

Helleiner, E. (1994). *States and the Reemergence of Global Finance: From Bretton Woods to the 1990s*. Ithaca: Cornell University Press.

Jensen, M. C. (1993). The modern industrial-revolution, exit, and the failure of internal control-systems. *Journal of Finance, 48(3), 831–80.*

—— (2000). *A Theory of the Firm: Governance, Residual Claims, and Organizational Forms.* Cambridge, MA: Harvard University Press.

Knorr-Cetina, K., and Preda, A. (eds.). (2005). *The Sociology of Financial Markets.* Oxford: Oxford University Press.

Leyshon, A., Burton, D., Knights, D., Alferoff, C., and Signoretta, P. (2004). Towards an ecology of retail financial services: Understanding the persistence of door-to-door credit and insurance providers. *Environment and Planning A, 36(4), 625–45.*

—— and Thrift, N. J. (1997). *Moneyspace: Geographies of monetary transformation.* London: Routledge.

—— —— (1999). Lists come alive: Eletronic systems of knowledge and the rise of credit-scoring in retail banking. *Economy and Society, 28(3), 466.*

—— —— and Pratt, J. (1998). Reading financial services: Texts, consumers, and financial literacy. *Environment and Planning D-Society & Space, 16(1), 29–55.*

Maatman, R. H. (2004). *Dutch Pension Funds: Fiduciary Duties and Investing.* Deventer: Kluwer Legal Publishers.

MacKenzie, D. A. (2006). *An Engine, Not a Camera: How Financial Models Shape Markets.* Cambridge, Mass.: MIT Press.

Maurer, B. (2006). The anthropology of money. *Annual Review of Anthropology, 35(1), 15–36.*

Monk, A. H. B. (forthcoming). Recasting the sovereign wealth fund debate: Trust, legitimacy, and governance. *New Political Economy.*

Ohmae, K. (1990). *The Borderless World: Power and Strategy in the Interlinked Economy.* London: Collins.

Part I

# Governing Global Financial Risk

# 1

# The Changing Political Geography of Financial Crisis Management

*Louis W. Pauly*

The market turmoil of 2007–8 exposed the fault lines running through the terrain of global finance.[1] Risk management practices had evolved rapidly and became more sophisticated. But the turbulence emanating from the American housing market in the summer of 2007 rapidly spilled across national borders and called many of them into question. As in every analogous instance since a liberalization trend began in the early 1970s, however, the political authority to manage damaging systemic effects revealed its territorial character. Micro-level changes in risk management practices did not therefore obviate the need to improvise in the development of crisis management tools at the macro level. Private-sector innovation did not replace the occasionally urgent need for public-sector intervention in integrating markets. Nevertheless, hints of something new, or at least something more distinctly hopeful, also emerged during this particular systemic crisis.

As they had always done in similar situations before, finance ministers, financial supervisors, and central bankers assigned priority in their public pronouncements to national measures aimed at stopping panics, calming investors, and beginning painful cleanups. Behind the scenes, though, they gave a new political impetus to cross-national collaborative efforts to resolve and manage this crisis, as well as to try and forestall the next one. Not least, spokesmen for some of the leading states in the system endorsed what was considered a radical proposal even ten years ago, namely the fully coordinated supervision of large financial intermediaries. The very idea of a cross-national "college of supervisors" constructed for each such entity suggested not the obsolescence but the deepening complexity of state sovereignty. Competitive and cooperative impulses among states remained obvious, but under emergency conditions in integrating markets the inclination toward collaboration underpinned remarkably robust stabilization efforts. Something very different had occurred nearly eight decades earlier, when competitive and defensive impulses proved overwhelming (Salter 1932; Temin 1991; James 2002).

Not coincidentally, the frontier of regulatory innovation in this key sector just before the crisis broke was in Europe, where the struggle to reconstitute the very meaning of sovereignty within open capitalist systems began long ago. This brief chapter examines contemporary European efforts to manage systemic financial risks and provides an orientation to the historical and political context necessary to understand their larger meaning and potential global implications.

## Systemic risk and financial market integration

After the Bretton Woods pegged exchange-rate system began breaking down in the late 1960s, the scale and speed of international capital movements increased dramatically. In 1974, the first great systemic crisis of the new era occurred when a small German bank, Bankhaus I. D. Herstatt, failed to honor its foreign exchange contracts and a subsequent cascade of defaults brought down the Franklin National Bank of New York (Spero 1980). With the assistance of the staff of the Bank for International Settlements, but actually led by central bankers from the United Kingdom and the United States, bank supervisors soon initiated regular consultations on the appropriate division of responsibilities between the home and host states of internationally engaged financial institutions. Finance ministers and legislators became seriously interested in the new dialogue on banking supervision after the 1982 Latin American debt crisis threatened large banks at the core of national payments systems (Wood 2005). The International Monetary Fund (IMF) played a key coordinating role in that crisis, the worst since 1931, but it was not the lender or investor of last resort. Certainly with regard to Mexican debt, the largest and most prominent debtor country, everyone knew that the central bank and ultimately the Treasury of the United States would have to play exactly those roles for its key money-center banks if an actual run began. In the summer of 2007, an old-fashioned run on a relatively small bank occurred in the United Kingdom. Although the failure of Northern Rock was handled inelegantly, there was no ambiguity as to the identity of the responsible central bank and government. During the following troubled period of tightening credit and collapsing confidence, the evident fragility of much larger and much more globally expansive financial intermediaries exposed once again the political dilemma glimpsed during the Herstatt crisis.

When societies seek real economic growth rates in excess of those capable of being generated by domestic savings, they must confront the question of how the actual benefits and costs of financial openness are to be distributed. Once markets are open, new kinds of financial crises can be generated, and the question cannot be avoided. The immediate costs of financial crises can be huge, their social and political effects insidious and lingering. Nevertheless, by the 1980s it had become clear that states constructing the international economy had collectively moved away from one set of policy trade-offs and toward another. Immediately after World War II, they had sought to reconcile their new-found desire for exchange-rate stability with their interest in maintaining independent monetary policies; they therefore had to tolerate limits on inward and outward capital flows. Now, capital mobility and monetary autonomy were privileged, and they were willing to tolerate floating exchange rates as well as a degree of volatility in their expanding financial markets (Clark and Wójcik 2007; Obstfeld and Taylor 2004; Underhill and Zhang 2003; Cohen 2002; Tirole 2002; Lamfalussy 2000; Helleiner 1994). Despite a clear trend toward capital market liberalization, however, no binding or broadly based international rules analogous to that governing trade flows emerged to codify a multilateral understanding on the trade-offs implied by financial openness (Abdelal 2007). Although some promoters of liberalization saw the necessity of new and enforceable rules, many apparently hoped that global markets would more or less automatically remain resilient over a full economic cycle. That hope rested on the idea that the main role of governments was simply to reinforce confidence by pursuing sound macroeconomic policies, an idea that would soon be sorely tested (Bordo and Eichengreen 2002; Alexander et al. 2006).

Before the Asian financial crises of the late 1990s, prominent voices advocated an explicit amendment to the 1944 Bretton Woods Agreement that would have had the effect of extending the IMF's formal jurisdiction over restrictions on current account transactions to a full range of imaginable restrictions on capital account transactions. When calm returned after financial emergencies spread rapidly from Asia to Russia to Wall Street, the broad movement toward capital market openness continued, even as governments refused unambiguously to embrace the principle that capital had an inviolable legal right to cross borders or the idea that an ultimate global authority was required to manage shared risks. National authorities instead opted to allow the financial institutions they themselves continued to license reciprocally to expand their international operations on the understanding that emergencies could be prevented or managed by national regulators collaborating to the minimum extent necessary (Andrews 2008; Honohan and Laeven 2005; Roubini and Setser 2004; Hoelscher and Quintyn 2003; Bryant 2003).

Such an outcome would surprise no one familiar with the way most policies are actually constructed in democracies, the form of government shared in the states that first began rebuilding the world economy after 1945 (Fligstein 2001; Seabrooke 2006). The definitive articulation of policies in a broader than national context remained difficult, the coordination of those policies episodic at best (Wray 1998; Greenfield 2003; Pickel and Helleiner 2005; Friedman 2005).

The main multilateral consultations on systemic risk focused until recently on banks at the core of vital payments systems. As Kapstein (2006, 1998) clearly demonstrated in his study of the Basel Committee on Banking Supervision in the post-Herstatt era, risk mitigation was from the beginning mixed together with a mandate to level the competitive playing field in international banking. This led it first to an agreement on the division of responsibilities between home and host country supervisors, prompted it later to clarify the responsibilities of "consolidating" supervisors, and still later to accommodate legislative changes in the United States and the European Union by strengthening the role of host supervisors of banks from countries deemed weak in their capacity for consolidated supervision. The Committee also initiated protocols for minimum standards for back-up capital reserves to be held by banks.

In 2006, the "Basel II agreement" allowed internationally active banks to bring sophisticated risk-management techniques into the calculation of their capital requirements. For the largest banks, heavy reliance was now placed on internal value-at-risk models maintained by the banks themselves. Under the terms of Basel II, smaller banks and banks not based in advanced industrial states typically faced the less flexible capital requirements of Basel I. Along with the stabilizing "pillar" of minimum capital requirements, the Basel II agreement stressed the importance of two additional pillars: adequate supervisory review and "market discipline." To improve the latter and to provide signals that might prompt early intervention by official overseers, the agreement recommended various mechanisms for increasing the disclosure of information by banks, information that would allow credit rating agencies and market counterparties to render judgments on their ability to meet their obligations (Kaufman 2002).

It would be hard to sustain the argument that the main architects of today's international capital markets did not make progress in the years preceding the summer of 2007. The Herstatt crisis, the Latin American debt crises of the 1980s, the American savings and loan disaster of that same decade, the later BCCI and Barings Bank failures, the Asian and Russian crises of the next decade – none caused a systemic meltdown, even though they did spread much pain, especially in the developing world (Eichengreen 2003; Mishkin 2006; Woods 2006; Stiglitz 2006).

The crisis of 2007 followed the familiar pattern, and the damage was extensive. Nevertheless, even as that crisis was unfolding, leading states and their most powerful constituents continued pressing the cause of globalizing private finance. For their part, newly industrializing states, most obviously in East Asia, sought to limit associated risks by building up regional arrangements and costly levels of national monetary reserves, while the poorest states remained largely ignored. Within Europe, however, the quest for durable instruments for crisis prevention, management, and resolution at the regional level had already been launched. This particular crisis starkly revealed that such a quest could not stop at Europe's borders.

## Market integration and risk management in the European Union

The Commission of the European Community began working on the coordination of member-state banking regulations in the early 1960s (Pauly 1988, 170–7). But the most significant stimuli to integration in EU money and capital markets came in 1993 with ratification of the Maastricht Treaty, and in 1998 with the creation of the euro and the abolition of national currencies among a subset of EU member-states, and finally in 1999 with the launch of the Financial Services Action Plan (FSAP). While one might have expected the European Central Bank (ECB) officially to have guided the subsequent deepening of European markets, the reality was more complicated.

In practice, the ECB is a collaborative instrument and agent only for national central banks now formally linked through the European System of Central Banks (ESCB). Its formal mandate focuses on monetary policy and emergency liquidity assistance in the Eurozone. At the end of every year, profits earned by ECB operations are distributed to the members of the ESCB, each one of which maintained whatever historical role it already had in the management and supervision of local financial systems. The effect of irrevocably linking wholesale markets in the new currency, however, was profound, and pricing rapidly converged in intra-European interbank markets. The ECB has some capacity to provide immediate liquidity support for them, and it can muster more through its member banks. In the summer of 2007, it used that capacity effectively to stabilize the Eurozone payments system. Not coincidentally, the ECB has a deepening interest in extending its supervisory authority outward from that base. However, neither its member banks nor their counterpart governments clearly anxious to preserve their own flexibility, have demonstrated much enthusiasm for extending to the Bank anything beyond a watching brief on financial stability issues on behalf of the ESCB (Issing 2003). On the critical question of access beyond short-term liquidity to the fiscal resources necessary to prevent or cope with major crises within the Economic and Monetary Union, the "Eurogroup" of finance ministers remains dominant. Among the key players missing from that group is the United Kingdom, which just happens to provide the home base for London, arguably the actual financial capital of Europe.

In recent years, banks from certain member-states, notably Germany, Austria, Sweden, and Italy, have taken very prominent roles in rapidly transforming central and eastern European markets. By 2004, the top thirty European banks overall had an average of 25 per cent of their European assets outside of their home markets. Of these, nearly a dozen reported 50 per cent or more of their total banking assets outside of their home markets. Nearly fifty institutions had cross-border and cross-sectoral features capable of complicating emergency management (Goodhart and Schoenmaker 2006, 42; Rajan and Zingales 2003). On the other hand, the number of regulators with potential interests in these intermediaries changed with each new chapter in the EU enlargement saga. Moreover, in the now twenty-seven political jurisdictions within the single market project, some of which are in and some of which remain out of the monetary union, there is no common internal structure for regulating progressively integrating financial sectors.

In the late 1990s, within the policy space demarcated by the overlap between the continuing work-programs of the Basel Committee and the European Commission, European central bankers, bank supervisors, insurance supervisors, and securities commissioners began a complex process of information sharing and aimed at convergence on best practices.

A series of experiments in stress testing various markets eventually ensued. One particularly enlightening exercise took place in April 2006, when the European Commission organized a "war game" involving a large scale commercial insolvency threatening the stability of two banks with cross-border operations. Around the same time, the European Central Bank organized a similar exercise around the imagined failure of a large clearing bank, and the Financial Supervisory Authority in Britain did the same using the imagined collapse of a foreign bank subsidiary in London as the trigger (*The Economist* 2007; also see European Central Bank 2007*a*; Gieve 2006). Technical issues and not the more problematic issue of financial burden-sharing appear to have been central to the earliest simulation exercises, and the sponsors mainly publicized comforting results on the readiness and robustness of communications networks. Common sense and reflection on the international crisis episodes discussed earlier, however, would lead one quite reasonably to imagine that such exercises also hinted at deeper problems and constraints (European Central Bank 2007*b*; Bank of England 2007; IMF 2007). Indeed, stories of negotiating breakdowns, simulated head offices walking away from subsidiaries, and national treasuries shutting down in the midst of faux-crises circulated widely after the 2006 exercises.

What we do know from the kinds of low-probability/high-cost international financial crises discussed above is straightforward. A timely resolution and a workable division of the burden of adjustment can be facilitated by a legitimate and ostensibly neutral mediator and by limiting the number of parties around the negotiating table. The possibility of expansive cross-border contagion is limited when it is clear that the taxpayers of a single country will bear the costs of bailouts. Even when an institutional failure is resolved through a timely takeover by a stronger institution, authoritative political mediation behind the scenes is often crucial. Finally, the operational independence of many central banks and financial supervisory agencies today does not translate into their depoliticized access to national fiscal accounts when emergencies occur.

In the European Union today, even among members of the monetary union, there does not exist one fiscal account. Among members of the monetary union only, national fiscal policies are subject to an agreement that exerts some (weak) discipline. Again, the operational mandate of the ECB is deliberately constrained. The identities and responsibilities of the lead or coordinating supervisors of European entities incorporated as full subsidiaries outside of the home markets of their parents are not always clear. The basic approach to regulation and supervision in general still differs in subtle and not-so-subtle ways between members. And the number and diversity of players needing to be around the table in the case of a system-shaking failure by a large, complex financial institution (LCFI) is expanding.

Although the political dilemma remains evident, the likely outcome is not entirely clear. According to some scholarly experts on the subject, the very existence of lenders-of-last-resort has exacerbated systemically significant crises since 1974. According to this logic, the system now seems organized around the perverse rubric: privatize the gains of finance capitalism and, at least in emergencies, socialize the losses. Even analysts and supervisors not entirely convinced of such a view sometimes take the related position that a high degree of "constructive ambiguity" is necessary to counter the temptations confronting LCFI managers to chase ever higher returns or risk falling behind their competitors.

Despite the obvious moral hazards now built into the system, it would be facile to imagine that the prudential dilemma must lead to the construction of a clear, transparent, and robust burden-sharing mechanism in Europe, and perhaps beyond. What this would translate into in practice is an agreement on fiscal coordination, or an agreement reliably to open national treasuries under certain circumstances and up to required limits. The problem with this logic is its conflict with historical experience. Even in the post-war collaborative project now called the European Union, the big leaps forward have not typically come from functional necessity. More often they have followed crisis moments or, like monetary union, reflected acts of political imagination in unique circumstances. The key issue confronting European financial policymakers at the highest levels was therefore whether the current crisis of and the threat of a worse catastrophe in the future would motivate a creative and coherent institutional response.

## The politics of crisis management

The political authority to stabilize globalizing financial markets has an ultimate quality to it, a quality difficult to sense when those markets are functioning reasonably well. There is no reason why it cannot be delegated for a time and in a limited fashion to operationally independent central banks, financial supervisors, or even private standard-setting organizations, and there are very good reasons having to do with the chemistry of financial innovation why such delegation occurs. When such efforts accomplish their goals, markets deepen, catastrophes are avoided, few notice, and public officials stay in the background. With the aim of maintaining just such an environment, technical debate in Europe now focuses on specific modalities for constructing extensive burden-sharing mechanisms *before* a financial crisis requires them (Goodhart and Schoenmaker 2006; Schoenmaker and Oosterloo 2005; Goodhart 1998, 2000).

The idea of a reliable *ex ante* agreement on burden sharing directly confronts the questions of what Europe actual is, whether its constituent members are fundamentally obliged to assist one another in an emergency, whether they trust one another to minimize financial losses, whether they share the same risk culture, and whether they are guided by similar regulatory approaches. At the very least, it would assume continuing efforts to render national-level supervisory systems and practices more compatible, and to share both the fruits and the responsibilities of economic integration in a sustainably equitable fashion (Coleman 1996; Padoa-Schioppa 2002; Luetz 2004; Busch 2008). Even the sympathetic observer of recent developments in Europe might be tempted to call such an assumption heroic, and certainly prominent officials, including the head of the ECB, have repeatedly and publicly repudiated the idea of an *ex ante* financial burden-sharing agreement. On the other hand, an *ex post* agreement in this arena would seem beside the point; once catastrophic financial losses are realized, the damage is done. But perhaps it is not so difficult to imagine an *ex ante* understanding aimed at prevention continually being negotiated and renegotiated at the core of the European Union and left implicit. Although it could never be acknowledged by the member-states, the notion of a Europe of "variable geometry" would be relevant here. In the face of a severe and generalized financial crisis, one can imagine leading states hanging together come what may and another group being left to fend for themselves. In less than catastrophic circumstances, and given both a basic sense of trust at the core and the presence of effective instruments for market intervention and political bargaining, one can even imagine *ad hoc* agreements on burden sharing being negotiated at the moment of the crisis itself. Even if this verges on the idea of *ex post* crisis management, not entirely dissimilar processes have been evident in modern European history.

Comparative political economists working on contemporary Germany, for example, have long emphasized that country's characteristic and generalized *ex post* style of policy coordination. Given apparently strong rules and the pragmatic need for exceptions, this policy style has resembled "management by exception" (Derlien 2001; Green and Patterson 2005). It is certainly hard to argue that this approach did not work within a highly decentralized Germany after 1945. Also hard to dismiss is the argument that just such an approach opened room for maneuver (and for complex bargaining) across various issues between post-war West Germany and its partners in the European Union.

The financial vulnerabilities created by the current tensions within Europe between home and host country responsibilities and capabilities, are perhaps most visible in eastern Europe, in the Baltics, and in the Balkans. Governments now reliant on foreign-based banks to provide the lion's share of domestic financial services are not entirely confident of the durability of this situation. Widespread requirements for those banks to incorporate locally as fully capitalized subsidiaries might be taken to indicate as much, notwithstanding the original EU idea that a license in one member country should easily translate into a "passport" to do business elsewhere in the Union. For their part, contingency planning within bank headquarters to insure against losses in the portfolios of such subsidiaries would seem prudent. In an immediate sense, the regulators of those banks are surely right to focus on such things as the value of collateral held by such subsidiaries. But surely they must also consider what head offices will do if a local crisis engulfs their foreign operations. In short, they can cut and run at the risk of their global reputations, they can provide liquidity and even equity support at the risk of their consolidated balance sheets, they can work collectively with other similarly situated competitors, or they can rely on their home and host states quietly to work out mutually agreeable arrangements.

Large systemic risks point in the latter direction, and it was hard to miss indications that the leading states in Europe had inclined in this direction during the summer and autumn of 2008. Perhaps it would have been preferable to have already established a neutral intermediary combining technical capability, delegated political authority, and credibility not only with finance ministries and central banks but with private-sector institutions as well. A single point of coordination has obvious benefits when extreme crisis moments arise, and its very existence and presumed legitimacy might have a preventive effect. The idea that a credible central agency will promote collaborative solutions cannot help but reduce the temptation to panic. Any moral hazard issues thereby also raised, must be weighed against the alternative of self-help, either by private intermediaries or by their national overseers. But this did not happen, and it remains hard to imagine it happening in the absence of more fundamental political integration. To be sure, the temptation to beggar neighbors had not vanished. The regional effort to move toward coordinated responses to the crisis of 2007–8, however, provided a countervailing pressure.

In the enduring Keynesian tradition, Kindleberger (1978, 1986) and Kindleberger and Laffargue (1982) repeatedly reminded us that leadership is vital either to head off financial crises or to manage them when they nevertheless occur. In the short run, cooperating monetary authorities acting as lenders-of-last-resort can play that role. As Minsky (1986) noted, however, it is fiscal authorities who ultimately must come to the fore as investors-of-last-resort. If there existed a centralized fiscal authority in contemporary Europe, it would hold the key. Like the US Treasury during the Latin American debt crisis, however, prudence suggests that it would still need political buffers and reliable instruments for surveillance, persuasion, and coercion, such as the Federal Reserve and the IMF had provided in the early 1980s (Pauly 1998). But, again, such a fiscal authority does not exist, and the mandate of the ECB is specifically limited. If unambiguous lines of supervisory responsibility could still be negotiated for the LCFIs now evolving in Europe – and if it could be guaranteed that even ineptly managed problems in more local or more specialized financial markets would not threaten systemic resilience, questions of ultimate fiscal authority and *ex ante* burden sharing might not arise in practice. To the extent such lines ever existed, they eroded rapidly as Europe's key financial institutions expanded in scope and depth (Isard 2005; Véron 2007; Nieto and Schinasi 2007; Decressin et al. 2007).

As they did not want to confront the potential implications of this fact directly, some proponents of deeper financial integration in Europe asserted their belief in the inherent resilience of innovative markets that sliced risks finely and redistributed them widely. Somewhat less optimistic observers, especially in the midst of the turbulence beginning in the summer of 2007, still professed abiding faith in the insurance provided by voluntary memoranda of understanding among national authorities. They saw such devices ably enough supported by the technical work on regulatory issues (in the so-called "Lamfalussy process" (Quaglia 2008)) of the Committee of European Banking Supervisors, the Committee of European Securities Regulators, and the Committee of European Insurance and Occupational Pensions Supervisors, supplemented on financial stability and supervision policy issues by the Banking Supervision Committee of the ESCB and by the work of more broadly based groups like the Basel Committee and the Financial Stability Forum. In the deep background, even after they repeatedly witnessed turbulence not stability emanating from US markets, perhaps some really thought that the United States could always be counted upon to help rescue crumbling European financial markets. After all, American intermediaries remained leading participants in London's wholesale markets and prominent players in a full range of continental financial markets.

Those markets, however, are indeed now more complex, and the geopolitical foundations underneath them were shifting. The resulting dangers came home to policymakers in the wake of the massive 2007–8 liquidity operations undertaken by central banks in the United States and Europe. Inside Europe, a fresh impulse was given to the ideas of constructing a regional equivalent to the systemic crisis-management role played by the IMF in 1982 (Kraft 1984).

In today's Europe, moreover, the prospect of LCFI failures leads some observers to conclude that a European System of Financial Supervisors, analogous to the ESCB at the heart of the monetary union and possibly capped by a capstone authority analogous or linked directly to the ECB, is required (European League for Economic Cooperation 2006). The more immediate idea of constructing for each of the four dozen current European LCFIs a specific "college of supervisors" led by a consolidating or lead supervisors had already emerged in policy circles before the recent crisis, and the more holistic objective no longer seemed far-fetched. Some desirous of such an outcome but less sanguine about its practicability any time soon promoted the idea of an "Nth (or 28th) regime" just for current European LCFIs that have clearly outgrown strictly national supervisory frameworks (Eurofi 2007). But both ideas begged the same questions. Who coordinates the coordinators at the moment of crisis, and who pays for any bailouts that may be necessary? For the moment, the key link in the chain remained to be forged.

Ultimately, such a link must connect the finance ministers represented in the Economic and Financial Affairs Council of the European Union (ECOFIN), the governors of Europe's national central banks, and the diversely structured agencies charged with responsibilities for financial supervision at the national level. Adjustments in monetary policy, the reliable provision of liquidity at the core of payments systems, adequate prudential supervision, and, finally, the ability to provide fiscal resources to LCFIs whose failure could be catastrophic – the coherence and effectiveness of all of these necessary responses depend upon such a link. The effort to forge such a link is underway, and despite the separate but obviously linked national measures to inject capital into systemically significant financial institutions in the autumn of 2008, it is easy to be pessimistic about its prospects. At the same time, momentum remains behind the effort to encourage financial integration across the Union, to complete the internal market in financial services. The latter suggests that the former must continue.

ECOFIN had already taken a significant step forward in October 2007, when it agreed in principle to develop arrangements for cross-border financial stability within the EU. In this regard, it called for the negotiation of a new EU-wide memorandum of understanding on the management of systemic financial crises among supervisors, central bankers, and finance ministers, and more significantly reached a consensus on nine common principles to guide future cooperation. While seeking to achieve "level playing fields," encourage private-sector solutions, and limit any commitments of public money to resolve crises, the noteworthy fourth principle states that "where a bank group has significant cross-border activities in different Member States, authorities in these countries will carefully cooperate and prepare in normal times as much as possible for sharing a potential fiscal burden" (Council of the European Union 2007, 4). The ninth principle further specifies that "the global dimension will be taken into account in financial stability arrangements whenever necessary [and] authorities from third countries will be involved where appropriate."

What ECOFIN did not yet promise, however, was a neutral arbiter legally mandated to coordinate necessarily complicated processes of emergency response. Certainly the separate directorates of the European Commission responsible for the internal market, for competition, and for economic and financial affairs lack the cohesiveness to manage financial crises. But the alternatives to an executive-level instrument, at least within the Eurozone, would be an expanded ECB or a similarly "independent" institution given wide powers in the arena of cross-border prudential supervision. Although the latest crisis gave many pause and threatened to change the situation, neither alternative was yet palatable to ultimate national authorities.

Most surprisingly, in light of his country's traditional preference for maximum discretion in the oversight of financial markets, in March 2008 the British chancellor of the exchequer (Darling 2008) wrote to his colleagues in ECOFIN emphasizing the "need to reinforce the arrangements for supervisory cooperation within the EU and crucially with key international partners too" and proposing both a "step change in European supervisory cooperation through the establishment of Supervisory Colleges...on a firm legal basis" and the setting up by member states of broader "cross-border stability groups to manage and respond to cross-border risks to financial stability where they have links with each other through systemically important financial institutions." These phrases signified a new tone and striking new impetus behind the difficult work of building more solid political infrastructure for integrating financial markets. Since they implied fiscal burden sharing in ever more readily imaginable emergencies, they also suggested that the continuing linguistic and legal difference between "intergovernmental cooperation" and "shared sovereignty" signified less and less in the real world of practical policy.

In fact, these British proposals were embedded the next month in a new Memorandum of Understanding agreed unanimously by ECOFIN (2008). Most significantly, the MOU stipulated "that sufficient cross-border procedures in normal times between all relevant authorities are put in place to enhance the availability of tools for crisis management, to ensure that decision-making procedures are in place for coordinating action between countries; and to ensure preparedness for financial crisis situations, including in light of the potential need to share financial burdens between Member States." ECOFIN left it to the Commission to propose ways to clarify cooperation obligations, including possible amendments to EU banking legislation. (In this regard, Chapter 4 of Directive 2006/48/ EC of 14 June 2006 for the first time in Community law had already set out in considerable detail the mutual consultative obligations of key supervisory authorities. New EU-level rules, for example, might specify when exceptions could be made to competition laws to allow rapid market interventions by public authorities, how the liquidation of failing cross-border institutions could be accomplished without prompting destructive rivalries over the seizure of assets, and what standards should guide national deposit insurance and other crisis-prevention schemes (Eisenbeis and Kaufman 2007; Singer 2007)).

The extension of such ideas globally received explicit endorsement from the finance ministers of the G7 at their own April 2008 meeting. More specifically, using the vehicle of the Financial Stability Forum they had established after the Asian crisis, which like the Basel Committee of Bank Supervisors continued to be hosted by the Bank for International Settlements, they mandated the establishment of such colleges for all systemically significant financial intermediaries by December 2008. They also endorsed the idea that as small a group within those colleges as necessary to be "effective and flexible" in an emergency move forward rapidly with detailed procedures for information sharing, supervisory coordination, and crisis planning (Financial Stability Forum 2008). To the skeptic, perhaps, the voluntarism inherent in both the vehicle and the mandates suggested continuing resistance to actual and reliable burden sharing. Increasingly difficult to deny, however, was the growing consensus on the need for coordinated responses to future cross-national financial emergencies: first, among the largest members of the Eurogroup, second, between the Eurogroup and the United Kingdom, and third, among the members of the G7. In the summer and autumn of 2008, that consensus became visible in massive and nearly simultaneous actions by both central banks and fiscal authorities on both sides of the Atlantic designed to keep money markets open and fluid and to bolster the capital bases of banks.

Reasonable doubts surely remained as to the probability of solidaristic responses to future crises both within and beyond the charmed circle of advanced industrial countries. Such doubts surely helped to explain the continuing insistence of many other countries on adequate local capitalization for foreign bank branches and subsidiaries, on first recourse to local collateral, and even on maintaining massive foreign exchange reserves. The less skeptical observer of recent developments in this vital policy arena is left to ground any sense of optimism on the actual experience of institution-building in Europe and beyond since the time of the Herstatt crisis. Innovations in risk management at the micro level during that period could prove useful, but, as we witnessed dramatically in 2007–8, they could also prove dangerously perverse when authoritative oversight was inadequate. The *sine qua non* of the contemporary experiment in global financial integration remains a continuing if inelegant process of cross-national regulatory innovation, ultimately resting on the refusal of the most powerful states to retreat in the face of repeated emergencies.

## Conclusion

The fragility of integrating financial markets in a system of dispersed political power was occasionally glimpsed after 1974. Crisis moments reveal the limits of risk management techniques at the micro level. Systemic risks ultimately require systemic responses. Even when related capabilities remain in the deep background, where they should usually be if markets are to function efficiently, the idea of their emergence is critical. Officials charged with ultimate oversight of integrating and innovating markets have never forgotten the lesson learned the hard way during the Great Depression. Confidence in the high probability of macro-level political collaboration when crises overwhelm micro-level risk management remains necessary if integrating markets are to endure. If such collaboration fails, self-sustaining markets of global or even regional scale are highly unlikely. Today, European authorities in particular seem unwilling to assume either that such collaboration will automatically arise when needed or that it will develop inevitably out of the technical work of central banks. What they are actually thinking and doing in this vital policy arena hardly seems exhausted by the strict intergovernmental frameworks commonly employed by political analysts to explain instances of international cooperation. Already in train in the European Union is collaboration of a depth not plumbed before outside of declared federations.

Of course national authorities in contemporary Europe must speak the public language of state sovereignty even as they remind listeners of the dangers of nationalism, for they are speaking in practice mainly about the resources of national taxpayers who bear the costs of integration that cannot reliably be exported. Of course they look to market participants themselves to help them limit systemic risks. But under the surface of transient events and in a densely technical language, they are moving beyond familiar structures of political obligation and accountability.

Unless European governments are making serious contingency plans for capital market disintegration along traditional national lines in the wake of emergencies, which would be hard to take seriously when they simultaneously continue seeking the benefits promised by deeper integration, the optimistic observer must hope that what is really going on in Europe today is analogous to the opaque debates, the constant haggling, and the politically necessary denial that often characterizes regulatory innovation and reform within established federal states. Even in the tightening union of the United States after the start of the industrial era, the conflicts and contradictions posed by interstate commerce and gradually integrating capital markets were eventually rendered more manageable by a complicated transformation and recalibration of political authority. In Europe, something similar does now appear to be underway in the arena of financial regulation and supervision (Sapir 2007; Jabko 2006; Menon and Schain 2006; Schmidt 2006; Grande and Pauly 2005; de Larosière 2009). Although there is nothing inevitable about the outcome, after all federations and confederations have fallen apart throughout history, the unavoidable question of fiscal burden sharing is now central to the idea of completing the internal market in financial services. The question it begs is "internal to what?" In the long run, the answer must be a European polity with sovereignty, and the ultimate fiscal responsibility at its core, deeply shared.

Finally, if we follow such a logic this far, how can we conclude that such an answer must remain geographically bounded? Although much more research will be required after the financial turmoil that persists even as this book goes to press, contemporary events suggest otherwise. When risk management within large financial institutions reached obvious limits, political authorities intervened to bolster confidence in markets that now spanned national borders in increasingly complicated and intimate ways. Some movement back from global to national occurred as market players and policy makers sought to minimize future losses. But behind the scenes, collaborative crisis management became the compelling order of the day. Central banks intimately coordinated their liquidity operations to safeguard money markets now deeply linked across national borders. Moreover, fiscal burden sharing implicitly occurred not through any newly constituted regional or global funding mechanism, but through effectively coordinated national interventions targeted at the local operations of national and international intermediaries. Within Europe and more broadly, *ad hoc* collaboration occurred, not dissimilar to that anticipated by experts who might have preferred prior agreement on more elegant *ex ante* mechanisms but who also understood the nature of continuing political constraints.

The kinds of innovations in risk management explored by Clark in his chapter and in this volume continue to develop in larger macroeconomic and macropolitical contexts. When more open markets are calm, authoritative overseers, lenders-of-last-resort, and especially investors-of-last-resort fade into the background, where they quietly encourage improved risk management practices by intermediaries, investors, and savers. When they are not so calm, the inherent fragility of those markets is exposed, and so too is the collaborative politics upon which they ultimately rest.

## Note

1. Some material in this chapter appeared in "Financial Crisis Management in Europe and Beyond," *Contributions to Political Economy*, vol. 27, No. 1, July 2008, pp. 73–89. For suggestions, some taken and some not, I am grateful to Sean Berrigan, Andreas Busch, Marco Buti, Servaas Deroose, Alexandre Lamfalussy, Jacques de Larosière, Edgar Grande, Charles Goodhart, Graham Hacche, Eric Helleiner, Otmar Issing, Bruce Jentleson, George Kaufman, Walter Mattli, Patrick Pearson, Christos Pitelis, Lucia Quaglia, Klaus Regling, Vijay Singh, Geoffrey Underhill, Marc Ventresca, Nicolas Véron, Max Watson, John Weaver, David Wright, Ngaire Woods, and the editors of this volume.

# References

Abdelal, R. (2007). *Capital Rules*. Cambridge: Harvard University Press.

Alexander, K., Dhumale, R., and Eatwell, J. (2006). *Global Governance of Financial Systems*. Oxford: Oxford University Press.

Andrews, D. (ed.) (2008). *Orderly Change: International Monetary Relations since Bretton Woods*. Ithaca, NY: Cornell University Press.

Bank of England (2007). *Financial Stability Review*, No. 21, April; No. 22, October, pp. 73–84.

Bordo, M. and Eichengreen, B. (2002). Crises now and then. *NBER Working Paper* 10130. Cambridge, MA: National Bureau of Economic Research.

Bryant, R. (2003). *Turbulent Waters*. Washington, DC: Brookings.

Busch, A. (2008). *Banking Regulation and Globalization*. Oxford: Oxford University Press.

Clark, G. and Wójcik, D. (2007). *The Geography of Finance*. Oxford: Oxford University Press.

Cohen, B. (2002). International Finance, Chapter 22 in *Handbook of International Relations*, edited by W. Carlsnaes et al. New York: Sage.

Coleman, W. (1996). *Financial Services, Globalisation and Domestic Policy Change*. London: Macmillan.

Council of the European Union (2007). Council Conclusions on Enhancing the Arrangements for Financial Stability in the EU, *Press Release*, 2822nd Economic and Financial Affairs Council Meeting, Luxembourg, 9 October.

Darling, A. (2008). Letter to Dr. Andrej Bajuk, President, ECOFIN, 3 March.

Decressin, J., Faruqee, H., and Fonteyne, W. (eds.) (2007). *Integrating Europe's Financial Markets*. Washington, DC: International Monetary Fund.

de Larosière, Jacques (Chair) (2009). *Report of the High-Level Group on Financial Supervision in the EU* (February 25). Brussels: European Union.

Derlien, H.-U. (2001). Germany, in *The National Coordination of EU Policy*, edited by H. Kassim et al. Oxford: Oxford University Press.

Economic and Financial Council of the European Union (ECOFIN) (2008). *Memorandum of Understanding on Co-operation between the Financial Supervisory Authorities, Central Banks, and Finance Ministries of the European Union on Cross-Border Financial Stability* (4 April).

*The Economist* (2007). Financial Fire-drill, January 20, p. 81.

Eichengreen, B. (2003). *Capital Flows and Crises*. Cambridge, MA: MIT Press.

Eisenbeis, R. and Kaufman, G. (2007). Cross-Border Banking, revised paper presented at the DG ECFIN Annual Research Conference, Brussels, September 7–8, 2006.

Eurofi (2007). *Achieving the Integration of Europe's Financial Markets in a Global Context: Conference Report*. Paris: Eurofi.

European Central Bank (2007a). The EU Arrangements for Financial Crisis Management, *ECB Monthly Bulletin*, pp. 73–84.

—— (2007*b*). *Financial Stability Review*, June.

European League for Economic Cooperation (2006). Financial Supervision in Europe, *Cahier Comte Boël*, No. 12, February.

Financial Stability Forum (2008). *Report of the Financial Stability Forum on Enhancing Market and Institutional Resilience*, Basel (April 7).

Fligstein, N. (2001). *The Architecture of Markets*. Princeton: Princeton University Press.

Friedman, B. M. (2005). *The Moral Consequences of Economic Growth*. New York: Knopf.

Gieve, J. (2006). Practical Issues in Preparing for Cross-Border Financial Crises, Financial Stability Forum Workshop, 13 November. London: Bank of England Publications.

Goodhart, C. (1998). *The Evolution of Central Banks*. Cambridge, MA: MIT Press.

—— ed. (2000). *Which Lender of Last Resort for Europe?* London: Central Bank Publications.

—— and Schoenmaker, D. (2006). Burden sharing in a banking crisis in Europe, *Economic Review*, vol. 2, pp. 34–57.

Grande, E. and Pauly, L. (eds.) (2005/7). *Complex Sovereignty*. Toronto: University of Toronto Press.

Green, S. and Patterson, W. (eds.) (2005). *Governance in Contemporary Germany*. Cambridge: Cambridge University Press.

Greenfield, L. (2003). *The Spirit of Capitalism*. Cambridge, MA: Harvard University Press.

Helleiner, E. (1994). *States and the Reemergence of Global Finance*. Ithaca, NY: Cornell University Press.

Hoelscher, D. and Quintyn, M. (2003). *Managing Systemic Banking Crises*. Washington, DC: International Monetary Fund.

Honohan, P. and Laeven, L. (eds.) (2005). *Systemic Financial Crises*. Cambridge: Cambridge University Press.

International Monetary Fund (2007). *Global Financial Stability Report*, April and September.

Isard, P. (2005). *Globalization and the International Financial System*. Cambridge: Cambridge University Press.

Issing, O. (2003). *Monetary and Financial Stability*. Basel: Bank for International Settlements.

James, H. (2002). *The End of Globalization*. Cambridge, MA: Harvard University Press.

Jabko, N. (2006). *Playing the Market*. Ithaca, NY: Cornell University Press.

Kapstein, E. (1998). *Governing the Global Economy*. Cambridge, MA: Harvard University Press.

—— (2006). Architects of stability? *BIS Working Papers*, No. 199, Monetary and Economic Department, Bank for International Settlements, February.

Kaufman, G. G. (ed.) (2002). *Prompt Corrective Action in Banking*. Amsterdam: Elsevier.

Kindleberger, C. (1978). *Manias, Panics, and Crashes*. New York: Basic Books.

Kindleberger, C. (1986). *The World in Depression 1929–1939*. Berkeley: University of California Press.

—— and Laffargue, J.-P. (eds.) (1982). *Financial Crises*. Cambridge: Cambridge University Press.

Kraft, J. (1984). *The Mexican Rescue*. New York: Group of Thirty.

Lamfalussy, A. (2000), *Financial Crises in Emerging Markets*. New Haven: Yale University Press.

Luetz, S. (2004). Convergence within diversity, *Journal of Public Policy*, 24, 169–97.

Menon, A. and Schain, M. (eds.) (2006). *Comparative Federalism*. Oxford: Oxford University Press.

Minsky, H. (1986). *Stabilizing an Unstable Economy*. New Haven: Yale University Press.

Mishkin, F. (2006). *The Next Great Globalization*. Princeton: Princeton University Press.

Nicolaidis, K. and Howse, R. (eds.) (2001). *The Federal Vision*. Oxford: Oxford University Press.

Nieto, M. and Schinasi, G. (2007). EU Framework for Safeguarding Financial Stability, Conference on Globalization and Systemic Risk, Federal Reserve Bank of Chicago, September 27–8.

Obstfeld, M. and Taylor, A. (2004). *Global Capital Markets*. Cambridge: Cambridge University Press.

Padoa-Schioppa, T. (2002). *EU Structures for Financial Regulation, Supervision, and Stability*. Brussels: European Commission.

Pauly, L. (1988). *Opening Financial Markets*. Ithaca, NY: Cornell University Press.

—— (1998). *Who Elected the Bankers?* Ithaca, NY: Cornell University Press.

Pickel, A. and Helleiner, E. (eds.) (2005). *Economic Nationalism in a Globalizing World*. Ithaca, NY: Cornell University Press.

Quaglia, L. (2008). Financial sector committee governance in the European Union, *Journal of European Integration*, 30, 563–78.

Rajan, R. and Zingales, L. (2003). Banks and Markets, *NBER Working Paper Series*, No. 9595.

Roubini, N. and Setser, B. (2004). *Bailouts or Bail-Ins?* Washington, DC: Institute for International Economics.

Salter, J. (1932). *Recovery: The Second Effort*. London: G. Bell and Sons.

Sapir, A. (ed.) (2007). *Fragmented Power*. Brussels: Bruegel.

Schmidt, V. A. (2006). *Democracy in Europe: The EU and National Polities*. Oxford: Oxford University Press.

Schoenmaker, D. and Oosterloo, S. (2005). Financial supervision in an integrating Europe, *International Finance*, 8, 1–27.

Seabrooke, L. (2006). *The Social Sources of Financial Power*. Ithaca, NY: Cornell University Press.

Singer, D. (2007). *Regulating Capital*. Ithaca, NY: Cornell University Press.

Spero, J. (1980). *The Failure of the Franklin National Bank*. New York: Columbia University Press.

Stiglitz, G. (2006). *Making Globalization Work*. New York: W. W. Norton.

Temin, P. (1991). *Lessons of the Great Depression*. Cambridge, MA: MIT Press.

Tirole, J. (2002). *Financial Crises, Liquidity, and the International Monetary System*. Princeton: Princeton University Press.

Underhill, G. and Zhang, X. (eds.) (2003). *International Financial Governance under Stress*. Cambridge: Cambridge University Press.

Véron, N. (2007). Is Europe ready for a banking crisis? *Bruegel Policy Brief*, 2007/3, August.

Wood, D. (2005). *Governing Global Banking*. London: Ashgate.

Woods, N. (2006). *The Globalizers*. Ithaca, NY: Cornell University Press.

Wray, R. (1998). *Understanding Modern Money*. Cheltenham, UK: Edward Elgar.

# 2

# Financial Governance in the Neo-liberal Era

*Gary Dymski*

The neoliberal era has been characterized in the financial arena both by banking deregulation and financial-market integration, and also by new forms of risk and recurrent financial crises. This chapter examines the problem of financial governance from a macro-structural perspective: that is, we consider the financial risks generated by aggregate financial flows and global macroeconomic imbalances in this period, and the challenges these pose for governance.

This chapter finds that the structural financial dynamics of the neoliberal era have deepened financial risk, led to more financial crises, and made financial governance less feasible and less effective than before. The situation is seen most readily by contrasting the neoliberal situation with the simplest case.

In any era, economic units take on financial risk when they make binding financial commitments: through borrowing and making contractual promises to repay, or through obligating themselves to finance an asset position. There are two fundamental types of financial risk: default risk arises for lenders whenever borrowers may be unable to meet their contractual repayment obligations; liquidity risk, whenever an economic unit may be forced to support its asset position by borrowing at rates higher than anticipated (in the extreme, resulting in negative net cash-flow).

In this basic context, financial governance has two components: prudential supervision, bounding the financial risks of a set of financial firms or markets; and lender-of-last-resort (LLR) intervention, which involves defending the integrity of the financial system when it is subject to destabilization. This "simple" case in itself poses many challenges. The supervisory agency, in effect, operates along a risk/growth continuum: at one extreme, it attempts to minimize the financial risks emitted and borne by the financial intermediaries it regulates; at the other, it ignores risk emission and encourages intermediaries' support of growth. And when the system must be defended, the lender-of-last-resort (which may be different from supervisory agency) must respond aggressively – via liquidity creation, moral suasion, or other means, to maintain public confidence in the intermediaries and markets for which it has responsibility.

The problem of regulating risk has become even more challenging in the neoliberal era. One reason is that many more financial commitments are cross-border in this era. And when an economic unit holds financial assets in one country and liabilities in another, then exchange rate risk adds a dimension to core financial risks.

Another reason is that the neoliberal age has been accompanied by rapid advances in technological and market capacity, which have permitted financial intermediaries that originate risky assets to sell them to other entities. This separation of the locus of risk-creation from that of risk-bearing has encouraged financial intermediaries to adopt what are termed here liquidity-intensive strategies, which generate net income from fees far more than from interest margin. This separation greatly complicates prudential oversight. For one thing, the use of liquidity-intensive strategies means that regulators must monitor liquidity risk not only over the business cycle, but in the context of lender strategies. For another, purchasers of credit contracts may, if they default, have recourse to lenders – an especially troublesome contingency when asset-holders are offshore.

The neoliberal age has also complicated the lender-of-last-resort problem. In the Bretton Woods period, the United States alone functioned as financial hegemon; fixed exchange rates and limited financial-market capacity restricted the scope and scale of systemic risk. In a floating-exchange rate world, with competing financial centers, there is competition for reserve-currency status.

This leads to a crucial asymmetry. A crisis of confidence in a given nation's financial system is likely to involve a simultaneous crisis of confidence in its currency. So that nation's financial authority cannot quell a crisis of confidence by providing liquidity with the very currency whose value is suspect; this would deepen – not stem – the crisis. Thus, only countries whose currency is universally accepted as means of payment can use their own currency in lender-of-last-resort operations. Other countries must have reserves of globally-accepted currency with which to either forestall or manage crises. The less the capacity of a nation to defend itself, the more important that it avoid the buildup of aggregate risks. Conversely, nations with greater capacity to intervene effectively in crises can permit the buildup of larger volumes of aggregate financial risk.

And this asymmetry, in turn, leads to a problem. Asymmetric prudential oversight tends to follow asymmetric hegemonic power. Nations with strong lender-of-last-resort capacity have a lesser incentive to rein in risk-generating behavior, as they have more capacity to protect their own nations' financial customers and intermediaries from losses. This makes crises – which may be offshore – more likely. But recurrent financial crises reduce autonomous national controls for nations that lack lender-of-last-resort capacity, while expanding market-entry and wealth-enhancing opportunities for financial firms headquartered in nations that have it. But this makes increasingly severe financial crises more likely, even while it reduces regulatory discipline. This suggests that systemic breakdowns exceeding current global lender-of-last-resort capacity may become ever more likely. This, of course, is precisely the prospect presented by the sub-prime credit crisis that has gripped so many banking firms and markets around the world.

In sum, the neoliberal era has seen an increase in the occurrences and depth of financial risk. These shifts have not only made governance more difficult, but have led to some perverse interactions between risk and governance. This finding emerges from an overview of the evolution of financial risk and governance in recent history. The next section describes the situation of financial risk and governance in the early Bretton Woods era through the late 1970s. The sections following that examine the turbulent 1979–90 period, the 1990, and the emergence of the sub-prime credit crisis in the 2000s. The final section examines the implications of this history for the future of financial governance.

## Financial risk and governance in the early Bretton Woods era

The Bretton Woods agreement of 1944 established the global economic order for the post-War period. The US dollar was fixed in value relative to gold; and most other currencies had a fixed value relative to the dollar. This arrangement embodied Kindleberger's notion (1973, 1974) that stability in global economic arrangements requires leadership by a hegemonic nation-state. The global hegemon emits a currency that circulates globally and guarantees financial stability.

Institutionally, the Federal Reserve took on the role of lender-of-last-resort, and the International Monetary Fund (IMF) was established to help nations manage currency and trade balances. The global dominance of US industry in the immediate post-war period assured a demand for dollars. The supply of dollars was provided in this period by the Marshall Plan, the Korean War, and various aid programs.

In most nations, banking systems operated either according to policies dictated by governmental authorities, or as tightly-policed circuits of dedicated finance. Banking systems focused on meeting the payments and financing needs of consumers and of business, often with the assistance of state-administered or subsidized funds. In the United States, for example, private commercial banks collected household savings and made loans to businesses; mortgage companies, and savings and loan associations emerged to collect savings and meet mortgage demands. Conservative norms guided lending decisions, as typified by the "real bills" doctrine.[1] In essence, banks' hands were tied by extensive rules governing the markets they could serve, the products they could sell, and the prices of those products.

In the Bretton Woods period, financial risks were bounded. Exchange-rate risk was largely moot because exchange rates were fixed. Default risk rose largely during business-cycle downturns. And in the 1950s and early 1960s, liquidity risk was virtually unknown: the savings that supported asset positions were largely held on the balance sheets of depository institutions; and these latter institutions' liability rates were capped by low regulatory rate maxima. Because borrowing markets were undeveloped, banks' lending was limited to the extent of the readily available deposit funds to which they could lay claim. There were, in effect, market-scope boundaries that both restrained liquidity risk and checked the extent of default risk.

In this phase, the demands on financial governance within developed nations were minimal. Bank regulators had virtually complete control over depository institutions' conditions of reproduction. The Federal Reserve was not called upon to play its lender-of-last-resort role. The principal role of the IMF was to help global-North countries with external-payments difficulties (Carvalho 2001).

However, the fixed-rate exchange rate system came under increasing pressure. The UK tightened exchange controls in 1966, and then devalued the pound sterling by 14 per cent in November 1967. The accelerating Vietnam War and inflationary pressure worsened the US external balance and highlighted the overvaluation of the dollar. Finally, the convertibility of the dollar into gold was suspended in 1971. The dollar was permitted to float against gold in August 1973, and immediately tumbled in value. The transition from the Bretton Woods system was traumatic: a severe oil-price shock and recession in 1973–4, accompanied by continually accelerating price inflation.

Systematic price inflation in the mid-1970s put increasing pressure on banking systems. Market interest rates rose above low regulatory ceiling levels for bank deposit rates. As interest rates spiked, money-market mutual funds facilitated disintermediation from regulated financial depositories. Disintermediation, in turn, hampered banks' lending capacity. This led larger firms to obtain credit directly in the financial markets: the commercial-credit market opened up for short-term borrowing, and commercial bond markets expanded. Large banks reacted by seeking out new revenue sources: they provided lines of credit and underwriting facilities for large firms in lieu of loans, and also expanded their overseas lending. In the wake of oil-price shocks and the Club of Rome report, this lending flowed heavily to resource-rich countries in the latter 1970s – especially to Latin America.

In addition to interest-rate instability, exchange-rate fluctuations in the post-Bretton Woods era gave rise to new speculative currency markets. These markets grew rapidly, due to their peculiar two-sided character: on one side, futures, options, and derivatives contracts could provide hedges – in effect, insurance – for firms exposed to exchange-rate risk; on the other, those providing this insurance could bet on market volatility.

In sum, from the mid-1960s onward, financial markets grew more complex, and began to escape the purview of government regulators. Banks made strategic adjustments that undercut regulations designed to limit bank activities and competition. Liquidity risk increased, both because of large banks' liability management and because of disintermediation. Funds leaked out of the system of regulated intermediaries. Further, while it was not recognized at the time, cross-border default risk was rising precipitously for banks, as they competed to make Latin American loans.

## Financial crises amidst controlled disintegration, 1979–90

By the end of the 1970s, the United States and global macroeconomies were in disarray. US workers were subjected to deindustrialization and falling pay. The dollar fell throughout the decade, and inflationary pressures worsened. The United States' hegemonic leadership was challenged:

Europeans viewed the United States as exporting its 1970s inflation and its recessionary tendencies (Parboni 1981).

President Carter turned in 1979 to the post-monetarist Paul Volcker to restore order. In Volcker's view, US monetary policy should intervene strategically to advance "national policy." Volcker observed in a 1979 publication that "a controlled disintegration in the world economy is a legitimate objective for the 1980s." Specifically, he wrote, "It is tempting to look at the market as an impartial arbiter... But balancing the requirements of a stable international system against the desirability of retaining freedom of action for national policy, a number of countries, including the United States, opted for the latter" (Volcker 1979, 4).

So Volcker sought to overcome the crisis of confidence in the US economic/financial system by killing off inflation, no matter the price. The Federal Reserve choked off base-money growth and forced interest rates into the stratosphere. In a complementary policy shift, exchange-rate management shifted from an active to a passive approach. In effect, the rest of the world would have to adapt to the United States' structural position.[2] Underlying this shift was the view that the "world" would happily absorb as many dollars as the United States emitted. What had once spurred irreconcilable national conflict under Bretton Woods was now re-imagined as a market-adjustment problem.

With climbing interest rates, the "high dollar" was re-established. A double-dip recession ensued. The newly-installed Reagan Administration then implemented a fiscal policy that reasserted US military might, cut taxes for the wealthy, and generated systematic budget deficits. Managing the competition between the Japanese and US economies, in the context of this budget deficit, was a crucial new consideration. In response to Japan's manufacturing pre-eminence, and to its investors' increasing purchases of US assets, the two nations met in New York's Plaza hotel in 1985, and signed the Plaza Accord. Japan agreed to refocus its investment domestically, and to increase the value of the yen relative to the dollar.

These forceful policy shifts led to distress abroad as well as domestically. Loans to resource-rich Latin America came under increasing pressure as Volcker's tight-money policy pinched. Much of this debt was made on a short-term, variable-rate basis; so the costs of refinancing asset positions leapt upward. Finally, Mexico declared a debt moratorium in August 1982. This triggered similar actions by other Latin American borrowers, creating the first international debt crisis in fifty years. This period's unprecedented nominal interest rates, combined with global stagnation, generated debt renegotiations and adjustment programs throughout Latin America (Cline

53

1984, 1996). A period of stagnation known as Latin America's "lost decade" ensued. Meanwhile, by the end of the 1980s, the Plaza Accord, after pushing funds into Japanese urban housing markets, had led to a huge real-estate bubble, which burst in 1990.

In sum, by the end of the decade, two of the United States' major global partners were frozen into crises. Latin America entered its "lost decade" in 1982. Japan's housing- and stock-market bubbles burst, leading to a period of stagnation which it has yet to completely overcome.

These episodes demonstrate the willingness of the United States, under Volcker's leadership, to seek its own position of advantage even at the expense of allied nations' distress. US policy actions hardly seemed those of a disinterested and powerful Kindlebergerian hegemon. In bringing about the promised "controlled disintegration," the United States' policies left its economy in a good relative position, but undermined prosperity elsewhere around the globe.

Hobbled by disintermediation and high interest rates, US commercial banking was substantially deregulated in 1980 legislation. The extensive government guidelines that segmented financial product markets, limited banks' geographic expansion, and governed many financial-market prices were eliminated – the 1980 legislation proved to be the first in a sequence of banking deregulation bill passed in the 1980s and 1990s, which dismantled Depression-Era restrictions on product-line and geographic competition.

This reform effort unfolded during a triple banking crisis. The Latin American debt crisis, introduced above, generated large losses and even forced the dissolution of some large banks. Second was the systemic crisis of the US savings and loan associations (thrifts), the backbone of home mortgage lending. In the early 1980s, many thrifts were forced to replace disintermediated deposit funds with short-term borrowings whose cost exceeded the return on their long-term mortgage portfolios. Experts initially diagnosed this as a liquidity problem, not a solvency problem: thrifts, it was argued, were disadvantaged by being forced to invest primarily in mortgages. National legislation in 1982 loosened thrifts' investment rules and expanded secondary markets for mortgage debt. Since some thrifts held state charters, not federal charters, numerous state regulators also loosened the rules on thrifts' permissible activities. The sometimes extreme deregulation permitted under this "two-tier" regulatory system was accompanied by loosened oversight capacity. Many deregulated thrifts thus launched investments and speculative schemes which soon came crashing to earth. A 1989 bailout bill provided massive funds needed for a public recapitalization (and reprivatization) of the new wave of failed thrifts (Jaffee 1989). The third crisis in US banking occurred in the "oil patch" states of Texas, Oklahoma, and Louisiana. The precipitous drop of global oil prices in the mid-1980s burst a development bubble in these states and led many banks operating there into failure.

Inside the United States, these events triggered a bank merger wave: many failed thrifts and oil-patch banks were absorbed by healthy commercial banks (Dymski 1999). The segmented US banking system was gradually reconfigured as a system of hierarchically-organized regional banks.

Outside the United States, this same conjuncture led to the dissolution of older banking structures and to widespread mergers. In Europe, the adoption of common financial rules and opening of Eastern Europe led to a continent-wide scramble for market share. Pressures mounted for the elimination of the idiosyncratic national rules governing financial firms and markets. In the global South, financial crises (often fueled by the lending of global-North banks) led to the softening or elimination on restrictions of the entry and activities of overseas banking firms. The balance sheets of these nations' development banks were ravaged by financial crises and the loss of fiscal capacity. Over time, development and state-owned banks failed or were privatized, while new financial markets opened.

The Latin American debt crisis, which distressed large banks around the world, demanded a dramatic regulatory response. Already by 1981, US banking regulators were demanding stricter disclosure of capital and assets by large banks, given their deteriorating capital positions (Ferguson 2003). In 1988, the Basle Committee on Banking Supervision, representing central banks in several global North countries, agreed on the Basle Capital Accord. While this association has no formal regulatory power, its standard for credit-adjusted capital adequacy became a governing criterion for internationally-active banks. The Accord's basic requirement is that banks have 8 per cent in core ("Tier one") capital against its total risk-weighted assets. The Basle Accord was controversial in the global South because it mandates financial-governance criteria without being democratically accountable.

Meanwhile, domestic structures of financial governance also cracked under the pressure of crises. In the United States, the savings-and-loan crisis exposed a major flaw in thrift oversight – the two-tier regulatory system (Barth and Litan 1998). In the two-tier system, financial authorities compete to issue charters to intermediaries that can choose among authorities. Such a system induces authorities to lower their standards regarding excessive risk-taking; and neither authority can adequately monitor overall financial risk.

The broader problem was that defaults and default risk had built up to unprecedented levels within the regulated US depository system and in cross-border lending. Discussion of appropriate policy response to the thrift and oil-patch banking crisis was dominated by the "Shadow Financial Regulatory Committee" (Benston et al. 1986), which put the blame on moral hazard in lending (see Kane (1989)): deposit insurance removes depositors' incentives to discipline intermediaries whose managers or boards take undue risks. This committee argued for continued deregulation, plus more limited but more effective regulation. Similarly, analyses of the Latin American debt crisis attributed non-payment to moral hazard, and specifically to inadequate debtor repayment "effort."[3]

The notion that reforming micro-mechanisms in financial intermediation would obviate crises overlooked the fact that resolving both the thrift and Latin American crises had required lender-of-last-resort interventions. In the thrift crisis, federal intervention had held depositors harmless while rescuing the US housing finance system.

In the end, the thrift system's default and liquidity risk problems were solved through the combination of a massive federal bailout and an enhanced securitization mechanism for moving mortgage loans off lenders' balance sheets. That is, the financial risk of regulated banks was mitigated through creating a new class of securities, mortgage-backed securities, which transferred credit obligations into the broader financial markets. A similar solution was found for the megabanks involved in the Latin American debt crisis: many of these banks' Latin American bad debts were sold off to a newly created, independent market for "Brady bonds."

These pragmatic responses to this triple crisis collectively had the effect of spreading risk across several financial sub-sectors, only a fraction of which were under a prudential-oversight umbrella. A retrospective discussion of the 1980s banking crisis by committee members and other policy insiders acknowledged that a comprehensive effort to address moral-hazard incentives had not yet been undertaken (Kaufman and Litan 1993). However, neither this review nor other contemporary analyses considered the potential macro-level incoherence that spreading risk beyond the purview of institutionally-focused regulators might introduce into financial-system dynamics.

In effect, US financial governance assigned a zero weight to financial risks and used its considerable capacity to minimize any disruption to financial processes and economic growth.

By contrast, the IMF, acting as lender-of-last-resort for Latin American borrower nations in their 1980s debt crisis, operated as if minimization of financial risk to global lenders was all that mattered. The IMF's economists argued that economic growth could come only through adoption of appropriate (neoliberal-friendly) macroeconomic policies. These countries had little or no capacity to resolve lender-of-last-resort problems on their own; consequently, their households and firms would be exposed to every form of financial risk. This risk would discipline Latin America's financial intermediaries. This, together with appropriate macroeconomic policies, should renew growth and permit overseas debt to be paid off.[4]

As Volcker had anticipated, the United States' financial hegemony constituted a crucial comparative advantage in a world of looming crises. In any case, it is the hegemon's peculiar privilege to be partially shielded from the fallout emanating from even severe crises – so long as this hegemony itself is not surrendered.

## Asymmetric hegemonic protection and financial turbulence, 1991–2001

The fall of the Berlin Wall in 1989 suggested that the 1990s constituted the beginning of a new American Century, wherein the United States would shape the geopolitics and economic rhythms of a "one-superpower" world. The Washington Consensus governed macro policy: to ensure prosperity or to recover from crises, governments should maintain fiscal discipline and permit free inflows of overseas goods and capital. As in the later 1980s, this conjuncture worked to the advantage of US economic growth: the dollar remained high, the US current account sank ever deeper into deficit, and capital inflows to the United States correspondingly grew.

Economic growth in the global South during the Washington Consensus period was considerably worse than in the Golden Age (Chang 2007). Further, global financial crises continued. The first major outbreak was Mexico's "Tequila" crisis. The passage of NAFTA in 1992 had been accompanied by privatization of Mexican banking, largely to domestic owners. Confident of its growth path, Mexico borrowed dollars on Wall Street via Tesobono bonds, which were to be paid off in pesos. A run on the peso and a collapse of the Tesobono market ensued in 1994–5. It wrecked consumer and small business incomes and devastated the balance sheets of Mexican banks, which had been promoting consumer lending. In the wake of this crisis, the Mexican government took on much of the ensuing bad debt of Mexican banks, and then sold them off to foreign-owned banks and investors.

The Tequila crisis was troubling because it was unanticipated. Obstfeld (1994) provided a plausible explanation in delineating a "second generation model" of currency crises: nonlinearities in beliefs of market participants can cause crises, *regardless* of the fundamentals of the macroeconomy or banking system. While hardly reassuring to Mexico, it suggested that crises might no longer signal structural problems; instead, early-warning systems should be refined.

Two years later, a far larger and more ominous financial crisis ensued, again in economies with apparently sound fundamentals. East and Southeast Asian nations had experienced robust levels of foreign lending and investment throughout the 1990s. These capital-account inflows facilitated these nations' urbanization processes and accelerated their incorporation into the global production nexus. These nations' robust rates of economic growth made these inflows seem secure. However, the Asian financial crisis emerged when currency crises struck Thailand and Indonesia in May 1997, and soon led to banking crises in these nations. These surprise crises spurred speculative attacks on other Asian nations' currencies, causing more balance-sheet damage. By mid-Fall 1997, the crisis struck Korea with full force.

Korea was a remarkable victim – it had applied for OECD membership in 1995, and had become the world's eleventh-largest economy. Speculators and nervous bank loan officers did not spare this poster-child for national growth under neoliberalism. Its reserves exhausted, Korea had to sign an IMF agreement on 24 December 1997. Over the next several years (Dymski 2006), Korea's banking system was wracked by solvency crises punctuated by failed efforts at rationalization. This extended multi-country episode provided yet more evidence of the power of contagion effects. Again, the country under threat (Korea) paid large sums to make its banking system market-ready, while analyses bemoaned the need for proper prudential governance of financial risk.

The final major episode of financial crisis in this time period involved Long-Term Capital Management (LTCM). LTCM was a gigantic hedge fund, one of the many such largely unregulated funds that exploited cracks in the edifice of financial regulation. Hedge funds permitted wealthy investors to amass profits through unorthodox strategies. Specifically, positive cash-flow margins were created not by emitting information-based assets to "real" borrowers, but through highly leveraged margin plays based on offsetting futures-market and derivatives contracts. Significant profits require large-volume replication of these plays – before the markets being arbitraged can react. In this brave new terrain of financial position-taking, what matters is less what you know about industries, and more what you know about the dynamics of market trading itself. LTCM got caught with an overly aggressive position vis-à-vis Russian rubles and Russian interest rates (Lowenstein 2000). The result was a run on the ruble, which damaged the currencies and growth rates not just in Russia but also in Brazil and Turkey. This crisis was resolved when the Federal Reserve coordinated a LLR response with Wall Street money-center banks.

Throughout this period, American financial hegemony appeared robust, and the dollar in high demand. The United States' liquid markets were undergirded by minimal price inflation. The United States seemed a safe harbor in a world wracked by recurrent and increasingly belief-driven crises. The IMF had sufficient capacity to rescue global-South economies, and global-North banks had sufficient equity to acquire and recapitalize the global-South banking systems that failed in such crises. And the LTCM crisis apparently proved that the Wall Street megabank complex had sufficient capacity, when coordinated via Federal Reserve LLR actions, to ensure that the failure of a large arbitrage-focused financial fund would not lead into a liquidity crisis.

But financial governance was evolving at the national and global levels. In the "Tequila" crisis, Mexico's post-crisis national oversight proved crucial; it led to purchases of local banks by multinational banks whose capacity and strategic instincts were presumably superior. No lender-of-last-resort bailout was involved: the Mexican economy was forced to absorb the effects of an internal liquidity crunch, which led to the failure of a third of small businesses in Mexico and to significantly reduced real wages. In the East Asian financial crisis, post-crisis national oversight also featured centrally. Once again, purchases of local banks by multinational banks were a prominent feature of policy response. Further, there was again no lender-of-last-resort bailout. Adjustment came through the real sector, and was often wrenching.

The crisis of LTCM did evoke LLR action, as noted; and it did lead to enhanced national-level (United States) prudential oversight: limits were imposed on hedge-fund position-taking, and greater transparency was mandated. But the rules for non-bank, arbitrage-based lending were not fundamentally altered. In contrast to the drastic measures taken to reform Asia's "crony capitalist" banks, the New York Federal Reserve Bank orchestrated an orderly workout for Wall Street investors. The impact that the financial-market tumult induced by the LTCM crisis had on global-South debt burdens and macroeconomic growth was neither calculated nor compensated.

In sum, these responses to 1990s crises increased the reach and market share of global-North banks, while pointing up the asymmetric nature of global hegemonic protection. Not surprisingly, then, the final victim of these 1994–2001 crises was the Basle Accord itself. As Basle I had not prevented new crises, it came under increasing criticism, especially because of the inflexibility of the benchmarks it established. Basle's risk-weighted adjustments did not differentiate among the different risk contexts of sectoral assets in different nations. And crucially for the LTCM crisis, Basle I did not capture the financial-risk consequences of the leveraged and off-balance-sheet commitments that were increasingly the business of upper-tier banks around the world.

Proposed rules for Basle II partially addressed these problems. A more nuanced, three-legged approach to assessing institutions' financial risk was developed; risk-weights were made more flexible. Most controversial was the treatment of the off-balance-sheet and derivatives-based risk to which global megabanks were exposed. Regulators found themselves unable to agree on a set of criteria or procedures that could accurately pinpoint risk while not being gamed. The new instruments and arbitrage- and hedge-based strategies employed by banks were so time-sensitive that no data-capture rule would provide accurate risk assessments. Further, the leveraged position-taking possibilities were so wide-ranging that financial risk could only be assessed by working through a large number of expectations-meltdown scenarios. Consequently, the megabanks engaged in such activities were made responsible for their own stress-testing.

This was a calculated surrender, since no one set of global rules prevailed regarding financial-instrument transparency or investor leverage. The premise was that the large players involved in such practices themselves had the greatest incentive to ensure that their own activities would not ruin the parameters of the markets that facilitated their revenue-seeking activities.

What this compromise did not consider was that the collective activities of each of these various players, taken together, could endogenously undermine the parameters to which each player considered individually was reacting – thus generating a systemic crisis even if banks' own balance sheets, viewed narrowly, apparently met Basle standards.

But this is precisely the systemic problem to which hedge-fund – and later, private-equity and structured-investment fund – activity can give rise. First, these funds' equity/asset ratios are not subject to regulation, as are banks'. Second, these funds are notorious "copy cats." Once one fund perfects a given arbitrage strategy, other funds can imitate it. Imitation drives down margins; so these funds expand volume to meet profit targets. In effect, liquidity-intensive strategies become prominent when income generation depends on rate mismatches. And since rate mismatches often involve risk mismatches, liquidity-intensive strategies are used first to multiply risk differentials, and then to exploit them. Third, as more participants are drawn into such ventures, their "plays" increasingly interlock participants throughout the global financial and corporate markets. That is, what constitutes risk is ever more narrowly defined, even while global liquidity is drawn on ever more heavily. These proved to be the defining features of the credit-market crunch of 2007–8.

## Sub-prime investment strategies and liquidity-intensive intermediation, 2002–8

The 2000s have witnessed the buildup of a housing-market bubble, which collapsed in 2007 when many homeowners could not support mortgage-finance commitments made in the late stages of the boom. A majority of these defaults involved sub-prime mortgages. The "sub-prime mortgage crisis" has evolved into a generalized liquidity and insolvency crisis on a global scale.[5]

The sub-prime crisis itself resulted from the convergence of several forces within the US financial system. First was a change in banking strategy. After the United States' triple 1980s banking crises, those banks that survived emphasized consumer banking in upscale retail market areas. They refined a standardized, "conventional-belief based" approach to loan-making, in which loans were increasingly made to be sold on to secondary markets. Initially, they left lower-income and minority areas to a "fringe" banking system comprised by check-cashing stores, finance companies, and pawn-brokers (Dymski and Veitch 1996). But banks eventually began to appreciate the market potential in lower-income and minority areas, and consequently increased their activities there (often through subsidiaries). In particular, banks wanted to expand their tiny share of the explosively-growing market for cross-border remittance (Orozco 2004).[6]

Second was the US history of racial inequality in credit markets, which cast its shadow over banks' increasing activity in minority areas. Over the years, federal legislation and community activists had pushed financial intermediaries to provide credit to underserved individuals and areas. In the mid-1990s, lenders came up with new credit instruments, aimed at "high risk" – initially lower-income and minority – customers. Credit was provided at high rates of interest, with high penalty costs, and high collateral requirements. The options ranged from short-term "payday" loans to consumer-durable financing to first or second mortgages for homeowners. These "sub-prime" loans were labeled "predatory" by activists. Since first being launched in the early 1990s, these instruments grew at a frenetic pace in neighborhoods historically subject to financial exclusion.

Third was the availability of intermediaries willing to absorb securities based on these high-risk loans by buying them on the secondary market. Crucial to this demand were hedge funds and private equity funds; unburdened by reporting and oversight requirements, these entities provided a launching pad for high-risk, high-leverage investment strategies. The continued growth of unregulated, hybrid financial intermediaries, whose revenues were arbitrage-based and not "intrinsic-knowledge based," fueled the demand for sub-prime credit. Soon enough, securitization was expanded to include bank bridge loans for acquisitions, credit-card debt, and so on.

The willingness of financial markets to absorb sub-prime paper transformed the landscape of strategic possibility for banks. Previously, only "conforming" (or "plain vanilla") mortgages could be securitized – that is, mortgages whose risk parameters (20% down payment, due diligence about borrower income, etc.) met Fannie Mae guidelines. Now, nonconforming mortgages were underwritten and securitized, outside Fannie Mae's orbit. Banks could make high-risk loans and then shed the risks they had taken.

So whereas previous loan-market discrimination had led financially-excluded households and areas without access to credit, many more households were now being financially included – albeit on terms and conditions that heightened default risk. Initially, sub-prime loan practices heavily impacted the elderly, people of color, and minority neighborhoods.[7]

The gathering housing boom caused home prices in some US regional markets to rise beyond the ranges of affordability, using conventional mortgages based on actual borrower incomes. This generated a need for mortgages that relied on lower-than-standard down-payments and/or made heroic assumptions about borrower loan-servicing capacity. Sub-prime mortgages provided the solution: they broadened the pool of home-buyers in overheating markets by emphasizing the dynamic price potential of the housing asset, not the solvency of the borrower.

Excessive default risk justified the high fees, rates, and penalty clauses pioneered in financially-excluded areas. Further, rapidly climbing home prices in impacted areas suggested that today's risks were tomorrow's sure bets. As the markets heated up, and more suppliers crowded in, innovations based on home-price appreciation appeared. For example, the 2/28 mortgage provided a subsidized introductory mortgage rate for two years, after which a market-based rate would be locked in for the remaining 28 years. With receptive buyers willing to bundle diverse mortgages into securities, non-conforming mortgages became the conventional choice for first-time homebuyers in some regional markets. The remarkable leverage they offered to homebuyers (culminating in the no-downpayment loans that appeared in 2005) mimicked the leveraged earning opportunities they offered to the hedge funds and banks that held them. With US financial markets awash in liquidity, mortgage-backed securities exploded in volume.

Security-holders' willingness to hold paper with the opaque risk, return, and maturity characteristics of non-conforming mortgages led banks to sell and bundle many more types of loans. Soon Mortgage-Backed Securities (MBSs) were seen as one component of a broader class of collateralized-debt obligation (CDO). The practice of dividing expected financial payouts into tranches and recombining them in new synthetic instruments reached the point where neither a security's seller nor buyer might know its precise risk characteristics. As in every period of financial excess since the dawn of time, lenders were reassured by the fact that others were using the same conventions. Many types of intermediary – private-equity funds, investment banks, and commercial banks – set up sub-prime and CDO funds, either directly or through hedge funds.

In sum, the sub-prime/housing bubble combined LTCM's arbitrage of currency/interest-rate futures, with the sheer industrial logic of the US standardized-risk-based credit machine, and linked both to a wildly optimistic vision of housing value that was validated through self-reinforcing conventional beliefs. This bubble depended on the remarkable liquidity of US financial markets; thus, at the macro level, these assets depended on the US economy's status as a global liquidity pool. Once these preconditions fell apart, so did the sub-prime market.

Prudential oversight was clearly lacking in this asset-price buildup and crash. In the United States, bank-holding company regulations were loosened in the years that sub-prime lending grew. For example, bank holding companies were able to create and hold large volumes of CDOs only because these assets were not counted against their Basle I-based capital requirements. Large global banks were in transition to the rules proposed under Basle II. The new rules mandated that all large banks run their own stress-test scenarios to ensure that their particular mixtures of derivatives, futures-market commitments, and so on, would survive various worst-case scenarios.

The sub-prime loans were made by unregulated entities. In many cases, these entities were affiliated with or originated by regulated banking firms, especially megabanks. Regarding such banks, they participated in sub-prime-mortgage origination to boost their fee-based activity; and they established funds for holding sub-prime loans as cash-flow booster funds. That these funds could be regarded as independent of their issuing banks' balance sheets – as having been made without recourse – shows how completely the lessons of the 1980s thrift crisis had been forgotten.

The step-by-step off-loading of default risk onto entities outside of the regulatory scope of the banking authorities came back to haunt US regulators in the sub-prime crisis. Further, measures that had previously been sufficient to restore markets to order fell short in this new era. Their key move during the LTCM crisis had been recruiting Wall Street's megabanks to make loans so as to permit LTCM to unwind its oversold position. This was not possible in the sub-prime crisis: many of these same megabanks themselves became over-exposed in the sub-prime market (and consequently undercapitalized). No once-and-for-all bailout measure has yet surfaced, in part because the sub-prime crisis has triggered a broader housing-market downturn, wherein many conventional mortgage-holders have homes whose value is less than their outstanding mortgage.

Those interventions that have been undertaken by the Federal Reserve thus far have focused on stabilizing the credit and mortgage-financing markets. These interventions have been undertaken in a currency whose value is falling against other global currencies. While this may hasten the demise of the dollar as global reserve currency, in this case there is no alternative.

## Implications and conclusions

The implications of the sub-prime meltdown are still unfolding; but clearly, the idea that banks and markets are able to assess and distribute financial risk autonomously has been undermined. Federal Reserve Chair Bernanke, among others, has urged tightened oversight of the risks generated in financial markets.[8]

But such admonitions do not take into account the sheer magnitude of the financial risks that regulators must oversee. The industrial logic of competition in the financial industry – which makes this industry incapable of policing its own risk-taking – generates risk at high levels of volume that can easily swamp case-by-case supervisory control protocols. So aside from their responsibilities for case-by-case accretions of risk, regulators must pay attention to, anticipate, and block behaviors and innovations whose systemic consequences for aggregate financial risk can jeopardize financial infrastructure.

How to draw the line in real time between strategies that do and do not threaten systemic stability is not the topic of this chapter. One observation might be hazarded. It does seem clear that systemic stability requires the bounding of liquidity-intensive strategies. Liquidity in financial markets is certainly linked not just to market psychology, but to the macro-structural factors emphasized here. In effect, the efficiency gains from using these strategies to maximize returns for the wealthy and market-insiders must not be given priority over the unknowable (and possibly unbounded) risks these strategies create for the global financial system.

And whatever policy measures are taken may forestall future crises or lessen their magnitude, clearly the capacity to respond effectively to crises remains fundamentally important. We have noted the paradox wherein nations with strong lender-of-last-resort capacity have a lesser incentive to rein in micro-generated risk. This does not mean that the best outcome is the arrival of a world in which no nation or no entity, in any event, possesses lender-of-last-resort capacity. Some such capacity is clearly necessary under any global scenario.

An effective system of financial governance requires an authority capable of reconstructing financial and banking relations when they generate crises; a sustainable system must administer these interventions fairly. Financial firms whose national financial systems have more advanced markets should not, at the same time, be able to plan that mistakes they make in other people's financial systems will result in asymmetric rescue operations whose costs are borne elsewhere.

This logic leads us to a difficult conclusion. Shared global financial governance is hardly in view; but systems based on national hegemonic power are prone to asymmetries in the rules regarding prudential oversight, and to asymmetries in the post-crisis resources used to restore failed markets and institutions.

Whether the United States will lose its hegemonic position, and the dollar lose its universal acceptability, is not clear at present. Nor is there clearly a hegemonic successor on offer; nor is a new Bretton Woods agreement likely. There are clearly links between global economic and political power and the distribution of hegemonic currency and financial power. Not so long ago, the American century appeared to be unfolding anew; now, yet again, American power is in eclipse. What remains to be seen is whether a single national financial hegemon can harness, at one time: the capacity to respond to crises; the discipline to regulate the financial risks of national banking firms that enjoy the cover of hegemonic currencies; and the will to restore systemic capacity post-crisis in any other national banking system than its own.

## Notes

1. This doctrine specified that default risk would rarely occur, because loans should finance real economic activity, which would readily convert into "real bills."
2. McKinnon (1979) sets out the theoretical rationale for this approach.
3. See, for example, Eaton, Gersovitz, and Stiglitz (1986).
4. This debt was never forgiven. Brazil's 1980s sovereign debt obligations were paid off only in 2006.
5. On the causes and implications of the sub-prime crisis, see Demyanyk and Van Hemert (2007), (Dymski 2008), and Kregel (2008).
6. Katkov (2002) estimates that under- and unbanked households generate $6.2 billion in annual fees.
7. A nationwide study of 2000 HMDA data (Bradford 2002) found that African Americans were more than twice as likely as whites to receive sub-prime loans, and Latinos more than 40–220 per cent more likely.
8. At a recent Chicago banking conference, Bernanke stated: "Supervisors must redouble their efforts to help organizations improve their risk-management practices" (*Bloomberg News*, 15 May 2008).

## References

Barth, J. R. and Litan, R. (1998). Lessons from bank failures in the United States. In G. Caprio, Jr., W. Hunter, G. Kaufman and D. Leipziger (eds.), *Preventing Bank Crises: Lessons from Recent Bank Failures* (pp. 133–72). New York: Economic Development Institute of the World Bank.

Benston, G. J., Eisenbeis, R. A., Horvitz, P. M., Kane, E. J., and Kaufman, G. (1986). *Perspectives on Safe and Sound Banking: Past, Present, and Future*. Boston: MIT Press.

Bradford, C. (2002). *Risk or Race? Racial Disparities and the Subprime Refinance Market*. A report prepared for the Center for Community Change.

Carvalho, F. J.C. (2001). The IMF as crisis manager: An assessment of the strategy in Asia and its criticisms. *Journal of Post Keynesian Economics*, 23(3), 235–66.

Chang, H. (2007). *Bad Samaritans: Rich Nations, Poor Policies and the Threat to the Developing World*. New York: Random House.

Cline, W. R. (1984). *International Debt: Systemic Risk and Policy Response*. Washington, DC: Institute for International Economics.

—— (1996). *International Debt Reexamined*. Washington, DC: Institute for International Economics.

Demyanyk, Y. and Van Hemert, O. (2007). Understanding the subprime mortgage crisis. Mimeo, Federal Reserve Bank of St. Louis, December 10.

Dymski, G. A. (1999). *The Bank Merger Wave*. Armonk, NY: M. E. Sharpe, Inc.

—— (2006). La crise des banques coréennes après la crise, *Revue de Tier Monde*, Special Issue on Asia, No 186, Avril–Juin, 361–84.

—— (2008). The political economy of the subprime meltdown. Mimeo, August 2008. Forthcoming, *Historical Materialism*.

—— and Veitch, J. M. (1996). Financial transformation and the metropolis: booms, busts, and banking in Los Angeles. *Environment and Planning A*, 28(7), 1233–60.

Eaton, J., Gersovitz, M., and Stiglitz, J. (1986). The pure theory of country risk. *European Economic Review*, 30, 481–513.

Ferguson, Jr., R. W. (2003). Capital standards for banks: The evolving Basel Accord. *Federal Reserve Bulletin*, September, 295–305.

Jaffee, D. (1989). Symposium on Federal Deposit Insurance for S&L institutions. *Journal of Economic Perspectives*, 3(4), 3–10.

Kane, E. J. (1989). The high cost of incompletely funding the FSLIC shortage of explicit capital. *Journal of Economic Perspectives*, 3(4), 31–48.

Katkov, N. (2002). *ATMs: Self-service for the unbanked*. Tokyo: Celent Communications.

Kaufman, G. G. and Litan R. E. (eds.) (1993). *Assessing Bank Reform: FDICIA One Year Later*. Washington, DC: Brookings Institution.

Kindleberger, C. P. (1973). *The World in Depression, 1929–1939*. Berkeley: University of California Press.

—— (1974). *The Formation of Financial Centers: A Study in Comparative Economic History*. Princeton: International Finance Section, Princeton University.

Kregel, J. (2008). Changes in the U.S. financial system and the subprime crisis. *Levy Institute Working Papers*, No. 530, Annandale-on-Hudson, New York, April.

Lowenstein, R. (2000). *When Genius Failed: The Rise and Fall of Long-Term Capital Management*. New York: Random House.

McKinnon, R. I. (1979). *Money in International Exchange*. New York: Oxford University Press.

Obstfeld, M. (1994). The Logic of Currency Crises. *National Bureau of Economic Research Working Paper*, No. 4640, Cambridge, MA.

Orozco, M. (2004). *The Remittance Marketplace: Prices, Policy, and Financial Institutions*. Washington, DC: Pew Hispanic Center.

Parboni, R. (1981). *The Dollar and Its Rivals*. Trans. Jon Rothschild. New York: Verso Press.

Volcker, P. A. (1979). The Political Economy of the Dollar. *Federal Reserve Bank of New York Quarterly Review*, Winter, 1–12.

# 3

# Risk Management and Institutional Investors

*Gordon L. Clark*

Global financial markets are curious beasts: for much of the time, they seem to be entirely stable, functionally efficient, and wholly integrated.[1] But, of course, global financial markets are also prone to seismic tremors and systemic crises of coordination. As Dymski (in this volume) notes, one source for these crises is the asymmetry of global financial governance: the fact that the risks assumed by private financial institutions in their global financial engineering are, in effect, underwritten by national financial authorities (in the first instance) in the form of bailouts and the public in general (in the final instance) in the form of lost welfare. The difficulties of cross-border supervision and the regulation of private financial institutions have no doubt amplified the systemic risks of global financial integration (Pauly, in this volume).

It is tempting, therefore, to see the issue as a crisis of multilateral governance (giving weight to the problems of state sovereignty and coordination over unruly financial interests). This is, of course, very important. But sometimes missing in these accounts is an appreciation of the nature and scope of risk management in private financial institutions that start local in the sense that they have a "home" jurisdiction but whose investment responsibilities are thoroughly intertwined with the flux and flows of global markets. Indeed, many of these institutions have a mandate to invest well beyond the borders of their home jurisdictions – recent research by the OECD (2006) has noted that most nation-states have abandoned quantitative and qualitative restrictions on cross-border investment by pension funds and insurance companies over the past twenty years. The onus has been placed on these institutions to manage financial risks against their explicit or implicit mandates of maximizing the rate of return. Many of us have a personal stake in these mandates (Clark 2000).

At issue is the institutional governance of financial decision-making with respect to risk and uncertainty recognizing that modern portfolio theory (MPT) and the related theory of institutional investment makes a virtue out of risk-taking – that is, there are rewards for risk-taking, especially in circumstances where markets are relatively inefficient or in some sense incomplete (Shiller 1993). Given the global map of financial market regulation, reflecting as it does diverse national traditions and legal codes (La Porta et al. 1997, 1998), it is not surprising that these institutions bet on the regulation of national securities markets (Bauer et al. 2008). In this chapter, I look more closely at the issue of institutional governance with respect to financial risk and uncertainty, drawing upon our work on global best practice (Clark and Urwin 2008a, 2008b). My goal is twofold: first, to provide an account of the nature and scope of financial decision-making in these types of institutions, and; second, to identify the systematic risk management problems often associated with these institutions when financial decision-making is collective or collegial.

In the next section, I focus on the challenges that face institutional investors like pension funds when operating in global financial markets. Having done so, we move to explain how and why time, expertise, and collective commitment are so important for decision-making under risk and uncertainty. This is followed by a review of recent findings in the behavioral literature regarding recognized decision-making biases, informed by our own research on the competence and consistency of pension fund trustee decision-making (see Clark et al. 2006, 2007). From there, we consider the costs and consequences of systemic failures in governance before closing with comments about the significance of "local" governance in relation to "global" governance. Basically, I develop Shiller's (2002) insight about the institutional social "ecology" of market behavior – in his case, applied to the behavior of pension fund trustees in the context of the late 1990s bubble and bust. In our case, his argument has great significance for understanding the failure of risk management in a global context.

## The ecology of decision-making

A great deal of research on financial markets and behavior stresses the role of individuals and their decision-frameworks under risk and uncertainty.

Our research program has also focused on these issues but in the context of certain types of institutions subject to quite distinctive rules, norms, and customs. In a sense, this chapter challenges the reader to match the disembodied agent of financial markets and economic theory with a certain ecology or context in which they must act and take responsibility for their actions. As might be expected, the reference institution and norms of behavior are pension funds that operate across the globe. But, I hope the point is broader even if the details are quite specific to a certain decision ecology (see also Clark and Thrift 2005 on currency trading in international banking institutions).

March (1997, 24) defined decision ecologies in terms of "the structure of relationships among individual units" and how these relationships interact with "the behaviour of these units to produce systemic properties not easily attributable to . . . individual behaviour alone." Our interviews, surveys, and experience suggest that there are three ingredients in the decision ecologies of pension funds (see also O'Barr and Conley 1992). First, by common law and/or statute, fund boards are collegial entities – board members are separately and collectively accountable for their decisions against a general rule or standard of behavior – typically fiduciary duty. In some jurisdictions, fiduciary duty is benchmarked against common sense (as in the "prudent person" standard in the UK); elsewhere, fiduciary duty is benchmarked against professional judgment in the finance industry (as in the "prudent expert" system in the United States). Either way, the judgment and opinions of individual board members on matters of substance must be reconciled such that whatever collective decision is reached is defensible against these standards.

A second important ingredient in the ecology of investment boards is the fact that, in many jurisdictions, board members are deemed to "represent" beneficiaries, shareholders, and stakeholders (Clark 2007). At one level, this means that board members ought to act in the best interests of others. At another level, this could mean that stakeholders including plan sponsors, employee unions, retirees, and the community have a legitimate claim to be heard in board deliberations. Notice, though, the ethic of "representation" is generally consistent with the theory of representative democracy rather than direct interest-group claims. This does vary by jurisdiction, by the public and private sectors, and by national political cultures (see De Deken et al. 2006 on continental European social solidarity). Consequently, the expertise of board members is more heterogeneous than the management boards typical of the retail investment management industry. Board members can have very different views about first principles: the value of time, risk, the meaning and significance of probability, and the value of information (Clark et al. 2006).

The third ingredient is the significance attributed to collective commitment. Trustees accept appointment to protect the interests of beneficiaries. They do so on very different terms than their colleagues in firms of service providers in the finance industry. So, for example, in many jurisdictions and across industry sectors, compensation is limited to token attendance fees, lost earnings, and reimbursement for the costs of attending meetings. Whether it should or should not be like this is open to debate. But it is a shared ethic that typically governs – either explicitly or implicitly – how board members understand proper behavior (cf. the behavior of people who act according to their own needs in "normal" situations). There are two important implications that follow from this ethic. Unlike corporate entities, the link between compensation and performance in board deliberation is weak and sometimes undercut by the claims of competing responsibilities that are highly compensated (as in corporate pension funds). On the other hand, collective commitment justified as it is by the interests of others is a powerful mechanism for taming the potential costs of "representation" and for reconciling very different views about decision priorities.

The premium on collegiality indicates how and why the imposition of hard and fast rules regarding effective risk-related decision-making may be overturned – not because of objections to their functionality but because of unease about rule-bound decision-making that is not sensitive to others' views. Similarly, the equitable representation of stakeholders' interests suggests a premium on the process of consultation and deference even if tactical decision-making demands short-cutting due process so as to garner advantage in situations where there is great uncertainty as to the long-term consequences of decision-making. While collective commitment provides a means of coordination in strategic decision-making, it need not provide a recipe for best-practice investment management. Given the heterogeneity of skills and expertise on many boards, it may simply reinforce the lowest common denominator driving herd behavior in circumstances that demand reasoned judgment.

In this context, effective decision-making beyond the simplest of routine issues depends upon mobilizing collective commitment in ways that sustain attention and focus upon the most important aspects of institutional performance. Otherwise, in the absence of a clear purpose, time and expertise may be wasted in a search for the basis of collective decision-making. In this respect, leadership can be thought to play a crucial role in mobilizing the resources of decision-making. Here, though, leadership is often most effective by framing the decision-making process rather than an executive-led process that circumvents the collective deliberations of the board (Clark and Urwin 2008b). Basically, leadership involves the mobilization of collective commitment to the process of decision-making and stands in contrast to leadership through the exercise of executive power (Garud and Shapira 1997).

## Institutional structure and decision-making

There has been widespread debate about the proper structure and financial performance of pension institutions. As such, twenty years has seen moments of innovation wherein national pension systems were re-designed, transforming past commitments into new institutions with quite different goals and objectives (notably Chile, Australia, Sweden, and the foreshadowed UK National Pension Savings Scheme). Whether these moments of innovation affect the introduction of "optimal" functionally efficient institutions (along the lines suggested by Merton and Bodie 2005) is open to dispute. Roe (2006), writing about the regulation of corporate governance, argues that in "reform" political interests typically trump functional efficiency; each "new" institution carries with it the compromises, lacunae, and unresolved tensions of its origins. Any reading of recent European pension reforms would surely come to the same conclusion (Clark 2003).

Pension funds and related investment institutions are, no doubt, peculiar institutions in that trustees are separately and together subject, by common law and statute, to the doctrine of fiduciary duty. But so too are others, including corporate boards of directors, governors of public institutions, and members of chartered organizations with long-term mandates. In this respect, trustees are normally required to make decisions about beneficiaries' or shareholders' best interests and are required to act in a collegial manner with respect to long-term financial objectives in the face of short-term exigencies (Clark 2007). Governance is an essential mechanism through which these imperatives are reconciled and managed; elsewhere we have identified the principles of best-practice pension fund governance focused on investment management in financial markets (Clark and Urwin 2008a).

We acknowledge that pension funds and related institutions face many issues and must make a huge range of decisions. Here, we emphasize investment decision-making under risk and uncertainty and argue that the performance of pension funds hinges on five inter-related types of decisions faced by many institutions operating in global financial markets (see also Ambachtsheer 2007; Clark 2008). In what follows, we summarize these decisions, referred to above, with reference to the nature and scope of the decisions that must be taken on boards with reference to risk management (Clark and Urwin 2008*b*). Figure 3.1 summarizes our argument with respect to the available decision-resources of an institution.

(1) *Structural decision-making* refers to the overarching goals and object-ives of the institution, oftentimes set externally by stakeholders or shareholders but heavily influenced by the assignment of roles and responsibilities in the institution and its service providers. The influence of a well-ordered and shared belief-set governing investment is similarly important in this respect. A well-governed institution has a clearly articu-lated set of goals and objectives closely linked to the formal allocation of the organization's roles and responsibilities. It forms its views about appropriate goals by board-level debate and agreement on the key invest-ment factors governing success. By contrast, poorly governed institutions are often ones in which goals and objectives are poorly specified and at odds with assigned roles and responsibilities, sowing the seeds of doubt, confusion, and conflict over risk management and the decision-making process (March 1994).

(2) *Strategic decision-making* refers to the deliberate process of setting the parameters of investment performance, matching its goals and objectives to long-term investment strategies informed by experience and expect-ations (Campbell and Viceira 2002). While the framing of investment strategy can vary by institution, in most situations the crucial decision is strategic asset allocation. This decision comes from a combination of original analysis and prior beliefs. In well-governed organizations, the efficacy of investment decision-making is judged against these parameters. Equally, in poorly governed institutions other types of decision-making are often at odds with long-term objectives. So, for example, a board pre-occupied with operational decision-making may simply miss the strategic significance of the gathering importance of systemic risk evident in imbalances in its asset allocation.

(3) *Tactical decision-making* refers to the decisions taken in response to either anticipated or unanticipated market or investment manager events given previously agreed investment strategy. In well-governed organiza-tions, investment decision-making is sensitive to the timeliness of the

issues – lack of responsiveness because of institutional inertia may impose significant costs on funds in terms of lost opportunities and higher than expected return volatility (Litterman et al. 2003). Lack of responsiveness due to a policy of matching other funds' behavior or a poorly conceived response adopted by fiat by a number of institutions can impose significant costs on the whole financial system. So, for example, a pension fund may suddenly be made aware that one of its asset managers has suffered an unexpected and catastrophic short-fall in its market position requiring an immediate response by the fund. Whether this is an idiosyncratic issue, or is indicative of a gathering problem in the market as a whole is a judgment call that can have long-term consequences.

(4) *Operational decision-making* refers to the decisions needed in order to maintain an institution's flow of investment tasks and functions. In well-governed institutions, this type of decision is typically delegated to senior executives – being subject to *a priori* rules and procedures that have effectively pre-processed the nature and significance of required actions in relation to institutions' goals and objectives (Smith et al. 1992). So, for example, a pension fund may regularly re-balance its investment portfolio to maintain its desired long-term asset allocation. This type of decision is often the responsibility of fund executives subject to reporting to the board at its next meeting.

(5) *Monitoring and oversight decision-making* refers to the routine but nonetheless crucial mechanisms whereby the institution monitors the implementation and execution of its investment decisions. In well-governed institutions, this type of function is about ensuring compliance with stated objectives as well as compliance with respect to the contractual commitments undertaken by service providers. At its simplest level, the results of these decisions are routinely fed back through to higher tiers of decision-making. At a more important level, though, knowledge gleaned through routine monitoring may prompt reconsideration of investment strategy if not the structure of investment decision-making (Clark 2007).

## Governance and decision-resources

Each and every decision is about risk management in that each carries implied costs if poorly executed – for a well-governed institution, the key to risk management is to ensure that the separate costs of poor execution are contained to the issue at hand. It is apparent that decision-makers often blur the boundaries between decision types largely because they overlap and interact with one another in practice (this is, no doubt, an important characteristic of financial markets and different from other types of industries; see Clark 2000). At the same time, in poorly governed institutions there is an ever-present danger that the risks of poor performance on each issue accumulate and overlap with one another such that the whole enterprise is threatened. In many institutions, the blurring of decision types reflects a lack of organized deliberation, priority-setting, and the effective use of decision-resources including expertise.

At issue, therefore, is the organizational capacity of institutional investors to manage themselves against these decisions in ways that mitigate the separate and combined risks of poor performance. In "extreme" situations, not only is the integrity of each institution at issue, so too is the stability of the whole market (as Shiller 2002 noted in the case of the technology, media, and telecommunications [TMT] bubble and which has come home with a vengeance in the global credit crisis). Here, we assume that any organization has three types of resources available for managing risk-related decision-making: (a) the available time of its staff and board members; (b) the expertise of those directly involved in decision-making and those that may advise and evaluate the decision options; and (c) the collective commitment and efforts of those involved in decision-making to achieve institutional goals and objectives.

These three resources are, at one level, widely accepted as essential ingredients in organizational management (see O'Connor 1997). Each has its own nuances and qualities. For example, by time we mean the hours and days allocated to the management of tasks and functions and the attention paid to those tasks and functions by those responsible for the performance of the organization. This "resource" overlaps with expertise in that the application of task-relevant skills and aptitudes to specific types of decisions may enable an institution to effectively allocate the available time of those involved. Similarly, collective commitment may speed decision-making, sustaining previously agreed protocols and responsibilities where, otherwise, distrust of the motives of those involved may delay action by amplifying the time needed to reach agreement.

As indicated in Figure 3.1, the five types of decisions make different demands on the available resources. Operational decision-making may be time-extensive rather than time-intensive compared to tactical decision-making. Strategic decision-making may require comprehensive expertise and a level of collective commitment quite different to that needed in monitoring the execution of tasks associated with lower tiers of

| | | Type of decision-making | | | | |
|---|---|---|---|---|---|---|
| | | Structural | Strategic/ upper-tier | Tactical/ lower-tier | Operational | Monitoring |
| **Resource** | Time | - Infrequent once design is complete | - Periodic - Time-extensive | - Event-specific - Time intensive | - Regular recurrent - Time intensive | - Regular - Not necessarily time intensive |
| | Expertise | - Diverse competency | - Investment specific competency | - Deep investment specific competency | - Moderate investment/ diligent competencies | - Wide-ranging competency model |
| | Collective | - Overarching process - Stakeholder empathy | - Inclusive process | - Individual accountability model | - Delegated model | - Critical for accountability - Allows adaptation |
| | | Key: Ideal resource allocation | Limited | Material | Critical | |

Figure 3.1. A resource-based typology of pension fund decision-making

Source: Clark and Urwin (2006).

decision-making. As such, each type of decision has its own rhyme and reason with the likelihood of competition over the available resources (especially if some decision-makers have a preference or predilection for one type over another). Since resources like time and expertise are expensive, it is important to structure the decision-making process according to the resource requirements implied by all types of decision-making.

This framework and schematic provide support for our proposition, shared with Ambachtsheer et al. (2008) and others, that best-practice pension governance and investment management separates board roles and responsibilities from those charged with implementing and executing goals and objectives. Structural, strategic, and monitoring decisions rely upon collective commitment and do not normally require time or expertise in a sustained manner given the routine ways in which boards are normally managed. By contrast, tactical and operational decisions make heavy demands on time and expertise and assume those responsible, like delegated executive staff, act in ways warranted by the collective commitment and the oversight of boards. In many cases, where there is conflict over authority and power in these types of institutions, there are no clear lines of distinction and separation amplifying coordination problems in response to market volatility.

From Figure 3.1, it is apparent that each type of decision makes different demands on the available decision-resources for risk management. In particular, strategic and tactical decisions make heavy demands on the available expertise whether applied to fund performance in financial markets (contingent) or applied to long-term planning with respect to fund goals and objectives and fund liabilities (in the defined benefit environment). We have also argued that there is a close relationship between contingent market performance and long-term investment management: operating in the risk domain, exploiting opportunities while constraining impulsiveness, and being innovative in the face of the competition for returns challenge the effective governance of all kinds of financial institutions. These challenges require a level of expertise that is domain-specific; the "real-life" of investment management is often poorly defined, lacking essential information, and subject to great uncertainty about the proper course of action (see Gigerenzer 2003; Kahneman and Tversky 1979).

Reviewing the cognitive science literature, Wagner (2002, 57) concluded that "the development of expertise is a process whereby broader abilities are honed to sharper ones in which extremely high levels of performance are manifested in extremely narrow domains." So, for example, having shown that fund trustees vary in terms of their competence and consistency of decision-making, and having shown that their performance in the application of probabilistic reasoning to investment-related problems is correlated with formal education and training (Clark et al. 2006, 2007), Wagner would take these observations a step further: the repeated use of these acquired skills enable qualified decision-makers to become financial experts. In essence, expertise is non-transferable between decision-domains – being a "professional" is not necessarily a strong indicator of being able to acquire financial expertise. Since probabilistic reasoning makes heavy demands on cognitive ability, financial expertise on many institutional investment boards is rarer than often acknowledged.

## Calibrating risk management

It is widely recognized that, by themselves, individuals are prone to a range of behavioral biases or "traps": people tend to be overconfident, inconsistent, and unjustifiably risk-averse. These are just three of more than forty "errors of judgement" identified by Krueger and Funder (2004, 317). For many psychologists, these lapses in judgment are profound in that they derive from human cognition; in play is the capacity of people to act in the super-charged rational manner assumed by many social scientists, whatever their circumstances, roles, and responsibilities. By contrast, there are others including Gigerenzer (2004) who follow Simon (1956) to argue that "real" behavior as opposed to cognitive pre-disposition depends, in part, upon the environment or ecology of decision-making.

Recognizing the temptations of overconfidence and confirmation bias, for example, financial institutions implement monitoring devices to oversee the actions of traders, using limits and thresholds to signal significant departures from agreed decision protocols (see Clark and Thrift 2005 on the institutional management of currency trading). Likewise, investment boards have been made aware of the costs of risk aversion especially when their own predilections for risk run counter to an institution's capacity to manage risk against prospective returns (see Clark et al. 2006 on pension fund trustees' awareness of individual and institutional risk profiles). Even so, the heterogeneity of board membership can be a significant constraint on institutional risk management.

In the academic literature, and without regard to institutional structure or decision ecologies, three common causes of poor collective decision-making are identified as follows (Raiffa 2002): (*a*) the structure of decision-making is not adequately focused upon agreed goals and objectives; (*b*) the nature and scope of the decisions to be taken are either at odds with one another and/or lack an agreed order or assigned priority; and (*c*) those involved in decision-making have very different styles of deliberation such that there is often unacknowledged and unresolved conflict over the means of finding common agreement. As suggested below, each type of problem can spill over into market performance, local and global.

*Lack of focus* in collective decision-making is owed to the separate and incommensurate interests of those involved; that is, they come to the process of decision-making without prior agreement on the purpose of deliberation. With respect to pension fund decision-making it is presumed by many that the purpose of collective decision-making is obvious: the maximization of beneficiaries' welfare. Indeed, it is arguable that collective commitment is a robust resource for just this purpose – it cuts through separate interests to a legitimate point of common concern. But, as we have seen in case studies and academic research, this rule is often too abstract to be an effective device for governing decision-making (Clark 2004). The governance of pension funds is complicated by the interests of several stakeholders, notably the sponsor, making the investment mission more subtle than is generally credited. At best, we suggest collective commitment is an umbrella principle for negotiation over target-setting prior to decision-making; at worst a rhetorical device used to block decision-making (Clark and Urwin 2008*a*).

The *nature and scope* of decisions combined with the variable complexity of those decisions often overwhelms the process of collective deliberation (Goldstein et al. 2001). Without an explicit order of deliberation, and prior agreement on the significance of the five types of decisions to be taken, decision-makers may face cognitive and communication overload. As a consequence, there is a temptation to settle on the simplest issues, or allow those with strongly held views to take others to poorly reasoned conclusions. In the context of fund governance, there are resources at hand to manage temptation including time and expertise. But, as noted above, time is scarce and expertise is expensive. Consequently, agenda-setting and the use of sub-committees to process the most complex types of decisions are crucial elements in best-practice governance. However, when collective commitment is combined with an unqualified deference to the views of others, however informed or otherwise, there is a temptation to blur distinctions between the types of decision-making and to ignore prior agreement about the notional order and significance of types of decisions. In these circumstances, there is a temptation to use time to effectively wash away dissent from executive opinions and judgment. Risk management in these circumstances is at risk of institutional inertia.

Most problematic, however, is the prospect that there are *unacknow-ledged differences* in individual decision-making embedded in collective deliberation. Different decision-making styles can prompt disagreement among decision-makers and misunderstanding of one another's action, so much so that the process of collective deliberation breaks down under the weight of mistrust. This is believed to be particularly important as the numbers involved in deliberation grow and intimacy and collective commitment is replaced by formality and decision protocols.[2] To illustrate, I now turn to a set of figures drawn from Clark and Urwin (2008*b*) designed to illustrate the ways in which unacknowledged differences in board member preferred decision-making can undercut the coherence of collect-ive decision-making thereby amplifying poor decision-making at the level of the fund and even market volatility.

Elsewhere, we have described in some detail the nature and sources of our respondents. For the purposes of this chapter, however, it is sufficient to observe that our respondents come from a number of UK and US pension institutions, complemented by a larger group of Dutch fund ex-ecutives. Here, I am not so much concerned with whether these differ-ences are representative of the coexistence of such differences across society – the point is that these differences are apparent on the boards of large, global institutional investors. Figure 3.2 summarizes how our

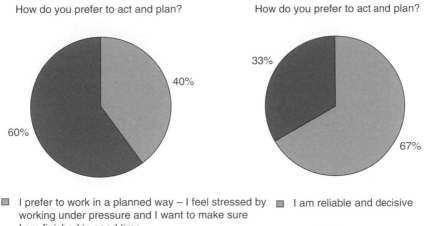

How do you prefer to act and plan?  How do you prefer to act and plan?

40%

60%

33%

67%

☐ I prefer to work in a planned way – I feel stressed by working under pressure and I want to make sure I am finished in good time

■ I often prefer to leave finishing things until the last minute, I find I do much better, more creative work when there is pressure from a deadline

☐ I am reliable and decisive

■ I am spontaneous and flexible

**Figure 3.2.** Self-assessed preferred mode of action and planning in decision-making

respondents prefer to act and plan. Not only did our respondents evince different styles of decision-making, distinguishing between being decisive and being spontaneous, they evinced two very different ways by which they prefer to plan decision-making, distinguishing between being prepared and simply responding to events. It could be that some respondents were inconsistent in their answers (switching from acting in a planned manner to being spontaneous).

Perhaps the self-assessed differences in styles of decision-making noted in Figure 3.2 can be explained with reference to the larger debate in cognitive science about the significance of intuition (Kahneman 2003). Notice, in Figure 3.3 it is apparent that these same respondents were almost evenly split in their reliance (or not) on others in working through important decisions. Respondents often rely on colleagues they trust; however, some are suspicious of others' motives and beliefs. One implication is that the degree to which a board commonly engages in decision-making is determined *ex ante* by the trust and mutual respect among colleagues.[3] For almost as many respondents, however, collegiality is not a significant factor in how they assess their own opinions and the opinions of others when considering issues to be resolved. When confronted with

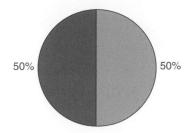

How do you prefer to focus your attention?    How do you prefer to reach a decision?

52%    48%    50%    50%

☐ If I have a problem I like to talk it through
with people I trust, talking it through helps
me to get things clear in my own mind

■ If I have a problem I need to think it
through for myself before I talk about
it with others

☐ When I am evaluating the information
someone has given me, I like to check
for any flaws or gaps in their argument

■ To really understand a situation I want
to get a feel for the motivations and
values of the people involved

**Figure 3.3.** Self-assessed confidence in personal and collective decision-making

the choice set, a significant group of respondents emphasized their own analytical skills when they come to consider shared problems.

We recognize that both approaches could produce desirable outcomes with respect to institutional risk management. Indeed, throughout, we make no normative claim about what should be seen as the "proper" response in each and every instance. Decision styles are best thought of as intuitive best-guesses about what respondents believe they would do when faced by issues that are domain-specific, are constrained by the issues at hand, and require immediate response (Hogarth 2001). Our point is that the coexistence of quite different styles of decision-making could derail the process of decision-making in circumstances that demand extraordinary attention to time-sensitive risk-management issues unless steps are taken to manage the process of decision-making in a deliberate and constructive manner that retains collegiality.[4]

On these grounds, we would contend that *both* the structure and the management of the decision-making process are essential ingredients in driving the performance of investment institutions. Whereas decision-making can be managed through the application of time and expertise, leadership through agenda-setting and recognition of the extant styles of decision-making is integral to sustaining board members' commitment to the decision-making process. In this sense, fund leadership respects styles of decision-making; leadership is an important decision-resource that can articulate underlying differences in approaches to institutional risk-management. By this logic, the patterns identified by Shiller and others, typical of the response of these types of institutions to unexpected market volatility, can be sheeted home to the governance of investment institutions as functional entities fit-for-purpose (or not as the case may be).

## Regulation and supervision

There is little doubt that pension funds and related retirement income institutions are important in the flux and flow of global financial markets. At one level, the placement of their assets in national and international securities markets has underwritten financial market liquidity as well as market integration challenging inherited nation-state financial institutions to respond to the imperatives of portfolio investors. So, for example, it has been shown that some of Europe's largest corporations have "reformed" their governance policies and practices so as to be consistent with market expectations and the interests of institutional investors (see Bauer, Braun, and Clark 2008). Perhaps just as importantly, the power of pension institutions in global markets combined with their apparent significance for financial innovation and risk management have led some governments to establish institutions that emulate their management practices and global scope (see Dixon 2008 on the development of related institutions in continental Europe).

However, in many countries pension and retirement income institutions have not carried the same kinds of regulatory obligations as banks and insurance companies. In much of the Anglo-American world, solvency requirements have been balanced against plan sponsors' long-term commitments, and asset-liability matching for defined benefit plans has only recently been made a standard practice in the light of new standards promulgated by the International Accounting Standards Board. Of course, the regulation of pension plans and the nature and scope of their risk management practices vary by country and by nation-state regulatory traditions. But typically shared across jurisdictions is a commitment to the principle of fiduciary duty – that trustees and their agents are bound by expectations of behavior consistent with professional standards and the interests of beneficiaries. As noted above, this principle is at the heart of common commitment, an important decision resource for financial decision-making and risk management.

Notice, though, for many years fiduciary duty was the single most important "regulatory" instrument for governing behavior in these institutions. But it served as a principle or rule rather than a policy and set of regulations. Where governments were uncomfortable with the scope implied by such an open-ended mandate, limits were imposed on the nature and scope of permitted investments including restrictions on the assets an institution could allocate to domestic and international equities and bonds etc. In effect, governments sought to limit the risks assumed by trustees and their agents recognizing that fiduciary duty otherwise provided for an unfettered scope of activity. As also noted above, however, these restrictions have been largely removed in most OECD countries over the past fifteen to twenty years in the interests of broadening the scope of asset classes and the geographical range of these institutions. For commentators, the growing volume of assets to be invested combined with the unfettered scope of financial risk has empowered financial innovation and the dominance of the Anglo-American economies (Clark 2000).

In this sense, the burgeoning financialization of modern economies can be traced, in part, to the reliance of many governments on a very simple but powerful decentralized risk-regulation instrument – fiduciary duty. Equally, some of the problems associated with the enormous growth in global financial flows and the ever-present search for returns at the margins of market risk-pricing identified by Dymski and Pauly can be traced to institution-specific governance practices that are justified by fiduciary duty, if not bound by a cautious reading of the scope of the doctrine. It is hardly surprising, then, that the recently established sovereign wealth funds from commodity and currency rich corners of the world have tended to emulate the investment practices of these institutions even if not being bound by the professional standards implied by fiduciary duty (Monk 2008b).

Nonetheless, it should be noted that governments have sought to regulate the risks associated with pension fund investment where those risks bear upon the expected income of beneficiaries. In some cases, this has meant requiring funds to carry "reserves" so as to ensure that funds are able to meet their obligations from notional surpluses (as in The Netherlands, where pension funds are regulated, in part, by the insurance regulator). In other countries, such as the UK and the United States, governments have sponsored agencies partially funded by pension plans to ensure that should a plan not be able to meet its obligations there is at least a minimum benefit paid to claimants. This type of "guarantee" system works as long as the risk of "default" is idiosyncratic or at least localized to a certain region or industry. The problem, of course, with "reserves" and "guarantees" as risk management devices is that they are vulnerable to systemic risk – where the gyrations of global markets lead to a long-term discounting of the market value of accumulated "surpluses" and "premiums".

Equally, governments have sought to improve institutions' decision-making skills and competencies regulating the selections and training of trustees in relation to the calibration and assessment of investment risk. In the UK, nearly a decade of policy intervention on this issue has led to the Pensions Regulator setting expected albeit basic standards of knowledge and understanding. In The Netherlands and elsewhere, government has set higher standards of expected qualifications on the assumption that domain-specific skills and substantive knowledge are crucial for the informed assessment of risk, whether related to investment or the matching of assets and liabilities. In both cases, the principle of fiduciary duty has been respected while the ecology of decision-making has become the focus of risk-regulation and supervision. In effect, the scope of fiduciary duty has been retained on the assumption that those who separately and together claim the responsibilities of fiduciaries should do so with the skills and qualifications that match the nature of market-related decisions (Figure 3.1).

At the limit, the interest of regulators in the principles of best-practice financial governance represents a twofold commitment to private investment institutions: on one hand, a commitment to the unfettered scope of investment notwithstanding the risks involved in the hope of reaping a market premium on financial innovation; and on the other hand, a commitment to private solutions to the long-term financial well-being of citizens given the contested boundary between the state and the market in neoliberalism. By this account, risk management by private financial institutions is part and parcel of a state-sanctioned search for a higher rate of return that can be found in "local" economies or indeed in "national" economic growth.

## Implications and conclusions

In this chapter, we have sought to make explicit the link between the architecture of global financial markets and institutions and the governance of institutional investors, notably pension and retirement income funds. Recognizing the critical perspectives offered by both Pauly and Dymski on the incomplete global framework of financial regulation and supervision, we sought to show that institutional risk management and financial decision-making is also quite problematic. The "ecology" of these institutions in relation to the nature and scope of financial decision-making is a necessary ingredient in any comprehensive understanding of the logic of global financial markets. That institutional governance is, more often than not, imperfect and subject to significant coordination problems is one explanation of the propensity for recurrent episodes of "irrational exuberance" (Shiller 2000).

Even so, we should be careful about the implications to be drawn from these observations. Close involvement with institutional investors indicates that many are "intendedly rational"; that is, in many of these institutions there are self-conscious attempts to perfect decision-making and risk management systems (Gabaix et al. 2006). The costs of poor decision-making and risk-taking are apparent, and the benefits of risk management systems that dampen volatility in relation to expected short to long-run rates of return are significant (Clark 2008). Likewise, there have been self-conscious attempts to develop models of management that deliberately incorporate identified principles of best-practice institutional governance (Clark and Urwin 2008a, 2008b). In any event, whatever the significance of these industry initiatives, it is also apparent that many governments have sought to encourage by regulation and supervision the adoption of governance principles and practices consistent with the public interest in ameliorating the costs of market volatility.

Nonetheless, as the sub-prime crisis has shown, global financial markets remain vulnerable to herd behavior and the accumulated costs of poor risk management practices. It would appear that even "well-governed" financial institutions have been implicated in "excess" risk-taking. In what follows in this book, various explanations are offered in the hope of accounting for this fact of life. For example, Engelen suggests that the sub-prime crisis like other crises before it was precipitated by a failure of the highly calibrated risk-management systems that otherwise dominated the market-pricing of risk and reward. He, like a number of other contributors, makes a distinction between market risk and uncertainty, arguing that the former turned out not to be an adequate proxy for the latter. Millo and MacKenzie go further, in a sense, and argue that in any event risk-management systems are techno-social systems based upon accepted protocols and metrics. When effective, these systems allow market participants to focus on the accepted terms of trade while ignoring the unresolved and tangential risks. When these systems fail, no amount of due diligence can resolve market ambiguity.

There are other issues that deserve mention. In particular, there is a paradox in risk management and financial investment that drives global markets. In periods of market harmony and stability, agents refine, calibrate and price risk in ways that tend to homogenize market expectations and therefore drive down the expected rate of return. As risk management systems become accepted and market prices come to reflect accepted methods of calibration, markets become more efficient. Inevitably, it becomes harder and harder to reap above-benchmark rates of return without the deployment of expensive talent and massive data processing systems. However, there are huge incentives on financial managers to "outperform" the market. Further, there are enormous pressures on institutional investors to match if not exceed their peers; witness the implications that follow from Lerner et al.'s (2007) study of US pension fund performance against endowments. Most troubling is the fact that global financial markets are, by any account, awash with financial assets (the accumulated pension and retirement savings of the baby boom generation and the new earnings from sovereign wealth funds). With a limited supply of "quality" traded securities, over the past fifteen years or so asset prices have been bid up but real rates of return have fallen (witness the evaporation of the equity-risk premium).

So, just as risk management systems begin to claim center stage in market pricing, institutional investors begin seeking alternative investments where there remain unpriced risk-and-return premiums. These can be found in the corners of existing capital markets, emerging markets, and new kinds of securities hitherto ignored but too expensive to evaluate. For example, urban infrastructure has been brought to center stage by market intermediaries like Macquarie Bank with cost-effective valuation techniques (see O'Neill in this volume). Equally, climate change and carbon markets promise a new frontier for investment (as suggested by Randalls). Not to be outdone of course, mortgage-backed securities offered a premium on the available market rate of return. Because of the investment of institutions in risk-management systems, there is an ever-present temptation to simply apply those techniques to new kinds of products notwithstanding very different levels of market transparency. It is little wonder that what appeared in the first instance as "risk" was in fact uncertainty.

Equally, the ever-present premium on innovation and the ever-present concern about financial risk management suggests that institution-specific governance systems have two rather different roles to play. At one level, governance systems must be able to align interests with the nature and scope of the decisions that must be taken in driving the risk-adjusted rate of return. At another level, however, governance systems must be adaptive in relation to financial innovation and effective in being able to assess unpriced market risk. It may be, in fact, that best-practice institutional governance is better at the former task than the latter imperative. It may be that best-practice institutional governance is the enemy of effective risk-focused market innovation.

## Notes

1. This chapter draws upon my collaboration with Roger Urwin from Watson Wyatt on the principles of pension fund best practice. I am very grateful to him for the opportunity to develop our common interests in institution-based investment management. It reflects the comments and opinions of a variety of colleagues including Keith Ambachtsheer from the Rotman Center for International Pension Management who gave permission for the reproduction of material from a paper (joint with Roger Urwin) published in the inaugural issue of their journal (Fall 2008). I would also like to thank my colleagues in the production of this book, Adam Dixon and Ashby Monk, for their comments on previous drafts. The assessment regime used in this chapter to characterize decision-styles is based, in part, on the protocols developed by Diane Newell of Jericho Partners and Emiko Caerlewy-Smith. None of the above should be held responsible for any comments or opinions expressed herein.
2. As is well appreciated in the academic literature, the numbers of people involved in decision-making is a crucial element in coordination (Sunstein 2005). Insights gleaned from experimental economics and psychology, and common practice, suggest that the costs of coordination (time and attention) dramatically increase beyond 3–4 participants (Camerer and Knez 1997).
3. See Kihlstrom and Cantor (2000) on the significance of what they term as "social intelligence" for effective decision-making. They note the distinction made in the literature between "understanding the behaviour of others" and being able to "cope with the behavior of other people" arguing that these cognitive traits are not necessarily widely shared in the community. As such, perhaps our results reflect the diversity of social intelligence found among respondents.
4. It is arguable, of course, that the coexistence of different modes of decision-making could dampen extremes including the overconfidence of experts (Hilton 2003). However, I am not convinced by this argument principally because of the high level of expertise involved in calibrating time and space dependent risk management. In this sense, I am very doubtful of the "wisdom-of-crowds" thesis as applied to financial markets (local or global) (compare Surowiecki 2005).

# References

Ambachtsheer, K. (2007). *Pension Revolution: A Solution to the Pensions Crisis*. New York: J. Wiley.

—— Capelle, R, and Lum, H. (2008). The pension governance deficit: still with us. Rotman International Journal of Pension Management, 1, 14–21.

Bauer, R., Braun, R., and Clark, G. L. (2008). The emerging market for European corporate governance: the relationship between governance and capital expenditures, 1997–2005, *Journal of Economic Geography*, 8, 441–69.

Camerer, C. and Knez, M. (1997). Coordination in organizations: a game-theoretic approach. In Z. Shapira (ed.), *Organizational Decision Making* (pp. 158–89). Cambridge: Cambridge University Press.

Campbell, J. Y. and Viceira, L. M. (2002). *Strategic Asset Allocation*. Oxford: Oxford University Press.

Clark, G. L. (2000). *Pension Fund Capitalism*. Oxford: Oxford University Press.

—— (2003). *European Pensions and Global Finance*. Oxford: Oxford University Press.

—— (2004). Pension fund governance: expertise and organisational form. *Journal of Pension Economics and Finance*, 3, 233–53.

—— (2007). Expertise and representation in financial institutions: UK legislation on pension fund governance and US regulation of the mutual fund industry. *21st Century Society: Journal of the Academy of Social Sciences*, 2, 1–23.

—— (2008). Governing finance: global imperatives and the challenge of reconciling community representation with expertise. *Economic Geography*, 84, 281–302.

—— Caerlewy-Smith, E., and Marshall, J. (2006). Pension fund trustee competence: decision making in problems relevant to investment practice. *Journal of Pension Economics and Finance*, 5, 91–110.

—— —— —— (2007). The consistency of UK pension fund trustee decision-making. *Journal of Pension Economics and Finance*, 6, 67–86.

—— and Monk, A. H. B. (2007). The "crisis" in defined benefit corporate pension liabilities. *Pensions: An International Journal*, 12, 43–54; 12, 68–81.

—— and Thrift, N. J. (2005). The return of bureaucracy: managing dispersed knowledge in global finance. In K. Knorr Cetina and A. Preda (eds.), *The Sociology of Financial Markets* (pp. 229–49). Oxford: Oxford University Press.

—— and Urwin, R. (2008a). Best-practice investment management. *Journal of Asset Management*, 9, 17–27.

—— (2008b). Making pension boards work: the critical role of leadership. *Rotman International Journal of Pension Management*, 1, 38–45.

De Deken, J. J., Ponds, E., and van Reil, B. (2006). Social solidarity. In G. L. Clark, A. Munnell, and M. Orszag (eds.), *The Oxford Handbook of Pensions and Retirement Income* (pp. 141–59). Oxford: Oxford University Press.

Dixon, A. (2008). The rise of pension fund capitalism in Europe: an unseen revolution? *New Political Economy*, 13, 249–70.

Gabaix, X., Laibson, D., Moloche, G., and Weinberg, S. (2006). Costly information acquisition: experimental analysis of a boundedly rational model. *American Economic Review*, 96, 1043–68.

Garud, R. and Shapira, Z. (1997). Aligning the residuals: risk, return, responsibility and authority. In Z. Shapira (ed.), *Organizational Decision Making* (pp. 238–56). Cambridge: Cambridge University Press.

Gigerenzer, G. (2003). *Reckoning with Risk: Learning to Live with Uncertainty*. London: Penguin Books.

—— (2004). The irrationality paradox. *Behavioral and Brain Sciences*, 27, 336–38.

Goldstein, W. M., Barlas, S., and Beattie, J. (2001). Talk about trade-offs: judgements of relative importance. In E. U. Weber, J. Baron and G. Loomes (eds.), *Conflict and Tradeoffs in Decision Making* (pp. 175–203). Cambridge: Cambridge University Press.

Hilton, D. J. (2003). Psychology and the financial markets: applications to understanding and remedying irrational decision-making. In J. Brocas and J. D. Carrillo (eds.), *The Psychology of Economic Decisions. Volume 1: Rationality and Wellbeing* (pp. 273–97). Cambridge: Cambridge University Press.

Hogarth, R. M. (2001). *Educating Intuition*. Chicago: University of Chicago Press.

Kahneman, D. (2003). Maps of rationality: psychology for behavioural economics. *American Economic Review*, 93, 1449–75.

—— and Tversky, A. (1979). Prospect theory: an analysis of decisions under risk. *Econometrica*, 47, 263–91.

Kihlstrom, J. F. and Cantor, N. (2000). Social intelligence. In R. J. Sternberg (ed.), *Handbook of Intelligence* (pp. 359–79). Cambridge: Cambridge University Press.

Krueger, J. I. and Funder, D. C. (2004). Towards a balanced social psychology: causes, consequences, and cures for the problem-seeking approach to social behaviour and cognition. *Behavioral and Brain Sciences*, 27, 313–27.

La Porta, R., Lopez-de-Silanes, F., Shleifer, A., and Vishny, R. (1997). Legal determinants of external finance. *Journal of Finance*, 52, 1131–50.

—— —— —— —— (1998). Law and finance. *Journal of Political Economy*, 106, 1113–55.

Lerner, J., Schoar, A., and Wongsunwai, W. (2007). Smart institutions, foolish choices: the limited partner performance puzzle. *Journal of Finance*, 62, 731–64.

Litterman, R. and others (2003). *Modern Investment Management*. New York: J. Wiley.

March, J. G. (1994). *A Primer on Decision Making*. New York: Free Press.

—— (1997). Understanding how decisions happen in organizations. In Z. Shapira (ed.), *Organizational Decision Making* (pp. 9–33). Cambridge: Cambridge University Press.

Merton, R. and Bodie, Z. (2005). The design of financial systems: towards a synthesis of function and structure. *Journal of Investment Management*, 3, 1–23.

Monk, A. H. B. (2008). Recasting the sovereign wealth fund debate: organizational legitimacy, institutional governance and geopolitics. Available at SSRN: http://ssrn.com/abstract=1134862.

O'Barr, W. and Conley, J. (1992). *Fortune and Folly*. New York: Wiley.

O'Connor, E. S. (1997). Telling decisions: the role of narrative in organizational decision making. In Z. Shapira (ed.), *Organizational Decision Making* (pp. 304–23). Cambridge: Cambridge University Press.

Raiffa, H. with Richardson, J. and Metcalfe, D. (2002). *Negotiation Analysis: The Science and Art of Collaborative Decision Making*. Cambridge MA: Harvard University Press.

Roe, M. J. (2006). Legal origins, politics, and stock markets. *Harvard Law Review*, 120, 460–527.

Shiller, R. J. (1993). *Macro-markets*. Oxford: Oxford University Press.

—— (2000). *Irrational Exuberance*. Princeton: Princeton University Press.

—— (2002). Bubbles, human judgement, and expert opinion. *Financial Analysts Journal*, 58(3), 18–26.

Simon, H. A. (1956). Rational choice and the structure of the environment. *Psychology Review*, 63, 129–38.

Smith, E. E., Langston, C. and Nisbett, R. E. (1992). The case for rules in reasoning. *Cognitive Science* 16, 1–40.

Sunstein, C. (2005). Group judgements: statistical means, deliberation, and information markets. *New York University Law Review*, 80, 962–1049.

Surowiecki, J. (2005). *The Wisdom of Crowds*. New York: Anchor Books.

Wagner, R. K. (2002). Smart people doing dumb things: the case of managerial incompetence. In. R. J. Sternberg (ed.), *Why Smart People Can be so Stupid* (pp. 42–63). New Haven: Yale University Press.

Part II

**Place, Proximity, and Risk**

# 4

# The Practicalities of Being Inaccurate: Steps Toward the Social Geography of Financial Risk Management

*Yuval Millo and Donald MacKenzie*

Financial risk management is one of the fastest growing service industries in the business world.[1] According to the Global Association of Risk Professionals (GARP), one of the leading trade associations in the field, there are currently more than 74,000 financial risk managers in financial institutions.[2] Dozens of academic and professional institutions award degrees and diplomas in financial risk management and these qualifications are gaining recognition by regulators and international certification bodies. It is estimated that the daily transaction volume of financial products traded in organized exchanges that are managed using such methods exceeds 50 million transactions,[3] with many more transactions executed in over-the-counter markets. At the heart of this body of knowledge and practices (virtually nonexistent less than thirty years ago) is a set of financial economic theories, employing a variety of statistical models to assess and calculate the risks associated with a plethora of financial assets and contracts.

Is this remarkable success evidence of the predictive powers of modern financial economics? Judging from a brief review of several leading textbooks in financial economics (Stulz 2002; Hull 2005; McDonald 2006), the answer to this question is a resounding "yes": the accuracy and validity of risk models and the applications that use them are said to be tested and re-validated literally millions of times a day in the markets. This chapter aims to show that such a representation is partial at best and that the explosive growth of financial risk management cannot be explained by the accuracy of the models and methods used. Instead, the historical case study suggests that an institutional analysis of the way model-based risk management evolved is of crucial importance. In this respect, this chapter corresponds with Ewald Engelen's chapter in this volume, as the historical processes described in this chapter analyse the embryonic structures that evolved into current model-based risk management that he describes. We return to this comparative element in the conclusion.

This chapter traces the growth of financial risk management applications that made use of the options pricing model developed by Fischer Black, Myron Scholes (1972, 1973), and Robert Merton (1973): the Black–Scholes–Merton model. Arguably, this model is the crowning achievement of modern financial economics and was included in many of the pioneering financial risk management systems.[4] The history of the Black–Scholes–Merton model and that of the first organized exchange for the trading of stock options, the American Chicago Board Options Exchange (CBOE) was studied previously (MacKenzie and Millo 2003; MacKenzie 2006). However, while previous studies focused on the effect that the Black–Scholes–Merton model had on prices in options markets, this chapter examines the development of financial risk management.[5]

The initial link between practice and model-based prediction is historical-temporal: CBOE began trading options less than two weeks before the Black–Scholes–Merton model was published. These two coincident events mark the beginning of an exponential growth curve that traces both the markets for financial derivatives and financial risk management. This growth curve, the paper argues, was not fueled simply by actors persuaded by the accuracy of the model. Instead, the ability of model-based risk management applications to help in tackling a variety of operational, organizational, and political challenges is the crucial factor behind the success of modern financial risk management. In fact, as financial risk management proved to be useful in different arenas in and around the market, the accuracy of the predictions it produced, even during critical times, was much less salient than one might expect.

## Theoretical approach

Knowledge and practice are fused together within financial risk management through the notion of "management". The etymology of the word management is traced back to the Italian *maneggiare*, which means to "to handle," and especially "to control a horse" (Barnhart 1999). Controlling a horse demands both knowledge and the ability to perform that knowledge in real life. Hence, management is dependent on a successful transformation of knowledge from one realm to another: from knowledge that contains descriptions of actions to knowledge that dictates and controls these actions.

Michael Power (2007), who traced the growth of risk management as an organizational phenomenon, claims that the growth of risk management in the last two decades is related to a gradual convergence between risk calculation and risk *management*. As Power demonstrates, the historical process of convergence led eventually to a subsuming of "calculation" into "management". That is, nowadays risk is regarded as a manageable factor rather than merely a measurable, quantifiable and calculable entity. Organizational market participants re-positioned themselves vis-à-vis risk: they moved from being spectators at an external phenomenon to managers of an increasingly internal institutional resource.

If, as Power claims, a major transformation has turned descriptive knowledge (risk calculation) into (practice-oriented) risk management then an empirical examination should be expected to reveal organizational actors that direct more resources to communicating and coordinating action using risk management and pay relatively less attention to calculating risk levels. This communicative aspect of risk management also carries with it inevitable reflexive and constitutive implications. Risk management allows market participants to produce a map of risks and opportunities from which a plan of action is then derived. However, any map, be it a geographical map or a risk map, is charted while incorporating a particular perspective. An actor's point of view is the initial coordination according to which risks are defined and risk assessments are made. Consequently, since risk management is not only a description of a given reality but includes a prediction and is operated upon as a blueprint for action, it includes a constitutive (or performative) element: the way organizations depict their risks has a significant effect on the way they will, eventually, react to events and to other actors. Over time, an influential risk management system will bring about institutionalized patterns of risk embodiment.

This conceptual approach – one that emphasizes the performativity of markets – corresponds directly with developments that have taken place in economic sociology over the last two decades and most specifically, with the emergence of the social studies of finance (SSF) research agenda.[6] That said, SSF has so far paid little attention to the vital role that financial risk management plays in shaping markets. Thus, while corresponding directly with many theoretical approaches within SSF, this chapter also

uses concepts both from more "conventional" economic sociology (drawing mostly on the role of social networks in markets) as well as concepts
from Actor-Network theory from the sociology of science and technology
(Latour 2005).

Famed American sociologist Mark Granovetter (1985, 1992), referring to
economic historian Karl Polanyi (Polanyi and MacIver 1957), made the
theoretical claim that markets should be regarded as social constructions
that evolve on the basis of pre-existing social and cultural frameworks in
which markets are "embedded". Hence, the development of economic
institutions takes place through continuous interactions among actors
who hold a variety of motivations and perspectives. Other economic sociologists such as Mitchell Abolafia (1996), Wayne Baker (1984*a*, 1984*b*) and
Brian Uzzi (Uzzi 1996; Uzzi and Gillespie 2002; Uzzi and Lancaster 2003),
who built upon Granovetter's theoretical perspective, studied the interaction of a variety of individual actors in financial markets. This stream of

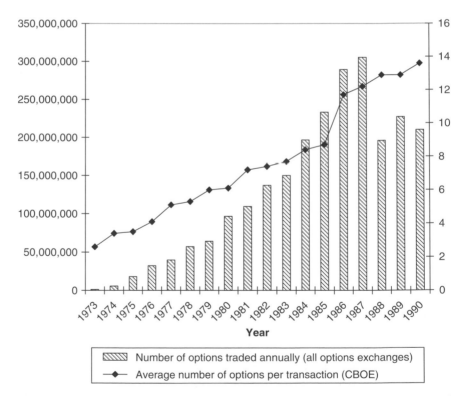

**Figure 4.1.** Number of options contracts traded in all options exchanges and
average number of contracts per transaction in CBOE, 1973–90

empirical works demonstrated persuasively that fundamental elements underpinning market behavior are regulated through dense personal networks of crisscrossing favors and animosities, which then feed into equally elaborate sets of closely guarded norms.

The "embeddedness approach" can be enriched by taking into account the role of non-human actors in the shaping of financial risk management. Financial markets are commonly described as an environment saturated in sophisticated technological artefacts. Printouts of calculations, display screens, and trading floor computer workstations, to name but a few, are indistinguishable parts of today's financial markets. As ubiquitous as these technological artefacts are the realization of the part that technology plays in shaping the structure of markets is far from common. For example, Herbert Kalthoff (2005) shows how practices that emerged around the use of computer software ("epistemic practices") crystallized institutional risk management routines. Kalthoff's findings reveal that practices did not emerge primarily from simple inter-personal interaction, but that coordinated communication was mediated by technical representations of risks and through that mediated representation risk management grew and became established. A recent paper by Miller and O'Leary (2007) draws similar conclusions regarding the role that technological materiality played in the growing efficacy of capital budgeting. Miller and O'Leary argue persuasively that the efficacy of heterogeneous networks as agents of constitutive change is dependent on their "intermediaries", the material content (e.g., written documents, technical artefacts, money) that circulates in the network and embodies, in effect, the connections among the actors.

Another important aspect that is revealed through the focus on the hybrid human-machine networks of financial risk management is the "facticity" of risk management (Latour 1988). MacKenzie (forthcoming, 2009) argues that the production of prices in financial markets is inherently intertwined with the production of validity for those prices. Hypothetically, assigning facticity to informational items can be created without the presence of machines. Nonetheless, in the context of contemporary financial markets, done manually, such a process would have practically halted activity in the markets. That is, technological actors do not merely help human market participants to perform, but by providing a stream of *methodologically* valid information (although not always realistically valid, as the chapter shows), they perform an irreplaceable and irreducible part in the constitution of markets. Indeed, inhuman speed and efficiency were the factors that kept the "facts machine" of financial risk management running smoothly.

## From risk assessment to risk management

The Black–Scholes–Merton model is a statistical model that can be used to predict options contracts' prices. The model is based on the "no arbitrage" hypothesis that assumes that prices in markets react instantly to new information that reaches them and therefore risk-free profit-making opportunities are virtually non-existent (Black and Scholes 1972; Black and Scholes 1973).[7] When the "no arbitrage" assumption is placed in a complete market setting, it dictates that a combination of options and stocks that bears no risk to its holder (risk-free) would have to generate the same cash flow as an interest bearing account (which is another risk-free instrument). Hence, the market prices of the option and stock composing such a risk-free portfolio could be discovered by comparing them with the expected yield of cash invested in a risk-free interest-bearing account. Using this initial result, the model can then be used to predict the prices of options. Similarly, because the model's calculation is based on the degree of risk related to the market positions of options, the same set of equations can be used to evaluate how much risk is embedded in holding particular market positions. The "bi-directionality" embedded in the model – the fact that it offered two equivalent procedures through which quantitative estimates of risk and prices could be calculated – was pivotal to the emergence of financial risk management.

Between 1973, when CBOE first started trading options, and 1977, volumes in options exchanges grew by more than 500 per cent, the sophistication of trading strategy increased (see endnote 6) and the number of trading firms doubled (Securities and Exchange Commission 1978). As the markets for options flourished, so did the trading firms that employed up to a dozen floor traders, along with a similar number of clerks, runners, and back-office employees (E 2000). In the larger trading firms, portfolio-wide changes could not be performed by a single trader: coordination among traders trading on the same portfolio became increasingly important so that the different trading orders would not undermine each other and Black–Scholes-based applications were incorporated into larger portfolio management systems. One of the first steps in this direction was a Black–Scholes–Merton-based trading practice known as "spreading" (Securities and Exchange Commission 1978). Spreading was a basket term for a variety of planning techniques that were all based on the same principle: finding probable discrepancies between options market prices and between their model-generated prices (this was done by computer-programmed calculations of many separate positions) and then using those results to devise a daily trading strategy.

The growth in the average number of options per transaction indicates the growing complexity in options trading strategies.[8] The decrease in trading in the last three years (1988–90) followed the market crash of October 1987, which is discussed in the final section. Number of options data is adapted from the Options Clearing Corporation's historical data archive (http://www.optionsclearing.com/market/vol_data/main/volume_archive.jsp).

Average number of options contracts per transaction is taken from CBOE's "2006 Market Statistics" report (http://www.cboe.com/data/Marketstats-2006.pdf).

These developments also had an impact on the organizational setting of the trading methods. The typical results of a spreading procedure were not predictions of specific prices, but instead produced broad guidelines that stated recommended ranges for buying and selling. Thus, at the beginning of the day, a trader would enter the trading floor, having seen the day's risk map for the portfolio he/she was trading and knowing which options were "overpriced" and which were "under priced", according to the model. The daily trading strategy was tailored with respect to these predictions. This new type of information was the basis for a development of a new practice: planning the following day's trading "game plan" on the basis of the model-generated estimates. This planning stage became an inherent part of the spreading procedure because the Black–Scholes–Merton calculations, on their own, did not produce definite sets of instructions for the following trading day. Instead, the results were discussed alongside other bits of information; risks and opportunities were evaluated and an overall picture of the trading day was generated, which led to the design of a recommended daily trading strategy. Therefore, spreading marked an important step in the unfolding of the techno-social process by which Black–Scholes–Merton-based applications gained appreciation for their communicative and managerial usefulness and by which risk assessment transformed into risk management.

As options became a more popular financial contract, option trading spread from CBOE to other exchanges. By 1977, four other exchanges were also trading options: the American Stock Exchange in New York (AMEX), the Pacific Stock Exchange in San Francisco (PSE), the Philadelphia-Baltimore-Washington Stock Exchange (PBW), and the Philadelphia Stock Exchange (PHLX) (Securities and Exchange Commission 1978). The geographical spread brought about a change in the ecology of the options traders' population. The local Chicago-based firms were gradually accompanied by large, nation-wide firms that entered options markets as an extension to their securities trading (Securities and Exchange Commission 1980).

The entrance of large investment changed portfolios management practices. The large trading firms typically had huge portfolios, containing thousands of positions, distributed among four or five different exchanges, and their trading activity was conducted by a few dozen traders. When managing a portfolio of such a size, there was little sense in asking the question: "what are the specific risks (and opportunities) involved in my current positions?" There were simply too many possible answers to this question to serve as a basis for planning a strategy.[9] Hence, the communicative and managerial challenge facing market participants in such an environment was twofold. First, to aid decision-making, it was vital that highly complex information contained in the large portfolios was simplified. Second, an agreed-upon communicative medium describing portfolio risks was called for so that the various people involved in executing trading orders and operating in different cities could coordinate their actions.

Facing these organizational challenges, trading firms started to consider a new approach to portfolio management, an approach that, for the first time, managed risk directly. This is where the bi-directionality of the Black-Scholes-Merton model had become organizationally useful. Instead of calculating theoretical prices for each of the positions and then summing up these results, the new approach took a hypothetical result as its starting point. In other words, the operational question of this new risk management method was: "what if the market drops/rises by x per cent tomorrow, how would that affect my portfolio?" To answer such a question, the methodology assumed (in fact, simulated) a market movement of a certain size, say of 10 per cent, then calculated the impact that the market movement would have on each of the positions, and finally summarized the results so as to come up with the overall implication on the portfolio. In essence, the systems simulated possible future market scenarios by using results coming from the Black–Scholes–Merton model. Although beyond the scope of this chapter, it is worth noting that this general principle was later incorporated into Value at Risk (VaR), one of today's leading financial risk management methodologies.

Scenario-simulating systems added a new dimension to the communicative function of developing financial risk management. The applications not only created a reference point for the market participants, but also represented the complex market picture in a clear and coherent way. In fact, the communicative usefulness of this new risk management methodology was such that even the information that was still originating directly from the markets was "mediated" by model-generated results. For example, in order to simplify the positions, these were presented as percentage of the previous day's gain/loss predictions and not as absolute numbers (Securities and Exchange Commission 1986). Results from the scenario-simulating systems became an indispensable mediating step between the market and its participants. When using scenario-simulating systems to design their trading strategy, market participants were no longer confined to concrete results from the market but were able to resort to predicted future situations.

The introduction of scenario-simulating systems marked a significant step away from risk assessment and toward risk management. Whereas the use of spreading merely enhanced the ability of traders to communicate their ideas about trading strategy, this new type of application became the tools with which such ideas were generated in the first place. Using spreading, a trader could only illustrate the benefits of the trading strategy he/she had already planned. In contrast, with scenario simulating risk management systems, it became possible, even likely, to receive the initial idea about possible trading opportunity by examining the application's output. For example, after the proliferation of scenario simulating applications traders started to talk about "buying volatility" or "selling volatility", when increasing the relative share of options in their portfolios. That is, model-based applications indicated that risky assets of various degrees should be bought or sold in order to balance the portfolio. Scenario-simulating did not merely supply reference points for discussions; by presenting a new discourse to the management of portfolios it made the very existence of such discussions possible.

## Financial risk management off the trading floor: Options clearing

Prices and risks related to options positions were a matter of concern not only for trading firms, but also for the options clearinghouse (Options Clearing Corporation – OCC[10]) and for the regulator of securities markets, the American Securities and Exchange Commission (SEC). In fact, this part of the historical analysis reveals the heterogeneous nature of the techno-social network from which financial risk management sprang and thus expands the notion of market participants.

Fundamentally, an options clearinghouse ensures that future obligations of buyers and sellers of options, which derive from the options contracts they buy or sell, are met. To prevent the risk of one of the parties not performing its side of the contract and to ensure that the market remains liquid and trust-worthy, the clearinghouse was assigned as the immediate buyer of options from the sellers and the immediate seller to buyers.[11] As the "other side" of the contracts (until expiry or offsetting), the options clearinghouse was exposed to considerable risks. In order to protect itself against those risks, the clearinghouse collected a portion of the contracts' value as collateral, known as "margin". Participants were required to deposit margins when they first took a position involving an options contract. Then, the margins may either decrease or increase according to daily price fluctuations.

Apart from its own margins, OCC was also responsible for the calcula-tion and collection of another set of risk-related fees – the SEC's net capital requirements. According to the SEC's net capital rule,[12] traders who regu-larly executed transactions for others, collectively known as broker-dealers (or "brokers"),[13] were required to make daily deposits of specified amounts of money, known as net capital. Unlike margins, the net capital rule's purpose was not to protect the clearinghouse, but to protect broker-dealers' customers in case their funds were inadvertently involved in risky positions held by their brokers. If such losses did occur then the pre-deposited capital would be put toward compensating the customers.

In the first three years to its operation, two different methods were used in the options clearinghouse for determining the amounts of margins and net capital requirements. For the clearinghouse's own margins, a premium based method was used. That is, a fixed premium was paid regardless of the positions' components (Seligman 1982). The net capital requirements, on the other hand, were calculated using a strategy-based method. The strategy-based method of risk-evaluation was based on a set of categories that assigned various levels of risk to the different financial assets and contracts. For example, options were considered more risky than bonds, so the required deposit for options was larger than the one for bonds.

The fact that two separate methods were used for the evaluation of the same factor – market risk – caused uneasiness among the trading firms. H, who was a senior executive at the clearinghouse from the late 1970s to the mid-1990s, described the early years of option clearing:

At about 1977–8, OCC had premium-based margin requirements [calculation methodology] and we were barraged with requests to convert the margining system to something like the way net capital rule worked at the time, which was strategy based. The requests for the changes came from the trading community, principally, and they came in with graphs and numbers and said something like: "My risk is limited to this; you should never charge me more than this in margins". (H 2000)

Brokers and other traders who had to pay both the SEC's capital requirements and the clearinghouse's margins demanded for the clearinghouse to stop charging margins according to the premium-based method and to switch to the strategy-based method. From the traders' point of view, the premium-based method was unjust because it did not reflect the growing complexity embedded in options positions and trading methods. Because options were often used to minimize risk levels, charging a flat rate for all options positions, regardless of the implied risk embedded in them, was defeating the purpose of using options altogether.

Traders were not the only ones who demanded changes in the calculation methods. Organized option trading was an emerging and highly competitive financial practice in the mid-1970s, and each of the exchanges that traded options wanted to attract customers. Since OCC was the only option clearinghouse at the time, it faced demands from all exchanges to charge less for its services. Facing those pressures, in 1977 the clearinghouse replaced its method for margin calculation from a premium-based method to a strategy-based one (Securities and Exchange Commission 1986). The new calculation method was seen as a positive move by both the brokers and the exchanges. However, from the clearinghouse's side, the move entailed some significant problems:

[The] strategy based approach, intuitively for OCC, would have complicated the nightly margin calculation process to such an extent that, because everybody was increasing volume on the CBOE, we were worried that we would not be able to get the exercising assignment notices and the reports out in time,[14] if we had to calculate margins for the entire market place. What they wanted you to do was to take large accounts with all sorts of positions and break them down into components, strategies, and minimize their margin requirements. Mathematically, it was an optimization problem that would have required iterative calculations. (H 2000)

Unlike the premium-based method, in which every transaction was charged a pre-determined rate and hence was a relatively straightforward operation, the strategy-based method required a more arduous procedure. Each portfolio (typically including between 100 and 200 different options and stocks) had to be broken down to basic positions defined in the rule; for each of those positions a risk level[15] (in the case of net capital requirements) or margin payment was determined and then the calculated amounts were summed up, producing the daily margin payment or the net capital requirement. Furthermore, because there were several possibilities for breaking down complex positions into simple ones, there also existed several alternative levels of margin payments. As a result, the clearinghouse had to perform an optimization process for each of the portfolios to determine the specific splitting of positions that would result in the minimal payment satisfying the rule. This optimization process had to be done nightly so that payments, in or out of the trader's account, could be made the following morning before the beginning of trading. Given the amount of computing power needed for completing the nightly operational task on time and considering that computers in the mid-1970s operated at a fraction of the speed of today's computers the pressure that margin calculation placed on the clearinghouse can be understood.

The SEC's division of market regulation, which was responsible for overseeing trading and clearing practices, was in charge of applying the changes made in the net capital rule and for designing, along with the self-regulatory organizations (the exchanges), new risk evaluation methods. M, who was a senior attorney at the SEC's division of market regulation from the early 1970s to the mid-1990s, explains:

> ... and then you have First Options [a large trading firm] who would have 800 large portfolios to clear and they [OCC] have to do it account by account. So it involves a lot of computing power. They would just say: "We're not going to do that one. We'll just ignore that strategy because it involves six more permutations." ... And the market maker [trader] will get angry or would question them and say: "Look. If I'm doing it then my real risk is that and you're charging me for this." [...] Our role had gotten so complicated when strategies have constantly been replaced with other strategies. It has become very hard to function in that environment. No matter what you did, there would be another one [trading strategy]. (M 2001)

As options strategies became more complex, such disputes broke out more often and this, in turn, added yet another burden on the SEC's division of market regulation. Because of the trends described above, concern was growing about the discrepancy between the sophistication of portfolio-construction methods displayed by trading firms and between the relatively crude risk-evaluation practices that were imposed by the regulator:

> I would hear [complaints about clearing], but what were we going to do? I mean, that was the rule. They [trading firms] were the ones who wanted the complicated strategies. I wasn't the one saying: "I want you to do these complicated strategies." They wanted to do them. They would, obviously, then have to do the work. (M 2001)

That discrepancy was rooted in the different viewpoints that the various market participants (i.e., trading firms, the clearinghouse, and the exchanges) held regarding the purposes of financial risk management and hence, the practice-related nature of accuracy. From the regulatory point of view, risk management was intended to protect customers by collecting "back up" funds for the case of a loss, and such money was indeed collected by the clearinghouse. Since the funds were not expected to cover fully the losses in any case, the exact amount was of little significance as long as it was above the set minimum.[16] Therefore, for the SEC, an accurate measurement of risk was less important than the fact that net capital was collected and that the rule was followed. In contrast, from the traders' point of view, sophisticated portfolio strategies were critical in reducing costs and achieving an advantage over competitors. Thus, for traders, a relatively inaccurate net capital rule would have undermined that purpose: it would not be much use to employ sophisticated strategies if those were treated as simple ones and incurred high net capital requirements. The aforementioned combination of factors – high volume of trades, sophisticated strategies, and a lagging regulator – lead the clearinghouse in the late 1970s to look for alternatives for the existing margin calculation mechanism.

In the early 1980s, two of CBOE's prominent trading firms (Chicago Research and Trading (CRT), and O'Connor & Associates) were using scenario-simulating risk management systems. When H and his team in the OCC started to examine alternatives for the strategy-based margin calculation system, they quickly encountered the new technology:

I was going to grad school and one of my grad school teachers was also a CBOE market maker [trader] and he taught me options price theory and I started to talk to him. The idea was worth a try and we convinced the board [of the clearinghouse] that they should fund some study. [An external company] began to calculate potential theoretical values for us on a daily basis for all the options series for a one year period and internally we built this program that would calculate a margin requirement equal to the worst possible loss on a line by line basis. We ran that for a year, then we wrote another report to our margin committee. (H 2000)

The system developed by the OCC applied a similar scenario-simulating principle to the one traders used to design trading strategies for the calculation of required margins. However, there was an important difference. While trading firms wanted to estimate the maximal daily loss in order to minimize it; the clearinghouse used the calculated figure as the required daily margin deposit. These two different sets of uses mark the practice-related notion of accuracy. The basic technology underlying both the OCC's and the trading firms' systems was similar, but the organizational settings and ultimate purposes were different. For the trading firms financial risk management served as a communicative and managerial tool. It provided traders with a language with which they could talk meaningfully about risk and to plan in the increasingly complex environment of the market. In contrast, one of OCC's purposes was to reduce the number of complaints regarding margins. OCC used financial risk management to establish and maintain "industrious silence" with regard to the calculations of margins: intended both internally (improving the efficiency of the calculation process) and externally (satisfying the demands of the trading firms). Again, as in the case of the trading techniques, accuracy was practice-related. As the quote above shows, OCC tested the model-based system in comparison with the existing calculation method. The results of these tests were, and are still, confidential, but interviewees' comments revealed that from an accuracy perspective the performance of the model-based system was similar to that of the rule-based one. Nevertheless, the model-based system, which, as explained earlier, was much more efficient in calculating margins than the current one, was chosen as a replacement. Hence, it was operational usefulness rather than superior accuracy that continued to pave the way for model-based financial risk management.

By 1986, when OCC fully implemented its internal financial risk management system (model-based margin calculation) model-based applications had already developed into a *de facto* standard for the communication and management of risk among trading firms and between them and the clearinghouse (Securities and Exchange Commission 1986*a*; Securities and Exchange Commission 1986*b*). Nevertheless, while the growing popularity of the financial risk management based on the Black–Scholes–Merton model brought about a standardization of risk communication, no consensus emerged regarding the accurate measures of risk. In effect, the ubiquity of model-based application facilitated the debate. For example, when traders negotiated their margin levels with the clearinghouse, which they did continually, the two parties had different opinions about the levels of risks embedded in the various options position. That is, although both sides knew that the same mathematical model was underpinning both the trading firms' and OCC's applications, the main issue they tended to debate over was not about the universally accurate measure of risk, but about the practice-related risk measure. As the interviewees from both the trading companies and the clearinghouse repeatedly stated: "each side was concerned about *their* risk" and how much they were charging or paying for it.

Consequently, both the clearinghouse and traders had stakes in the promotion of the model-based financial risk management system. Traders based their co-ordinated trading activity on it and the clearinghouse found in the model-based margining system an answer to volume and complexity challenges. In contrast, the SEC's point of view on the applications was different. While it was true that the increasingly popular options markets had brought about a significant growth in the complexity of trading strategies and that each of these strategies had to be approved by the SEC increased its work burden, the net capital rule system functioned properly – money was collected from brokers, and investors, as far as the SEC could judge, were protected. While the clearinghouse and the traders were relying on model-based applications and were eager to extend their use, the common opinion at the SEC about the application was still sceptical. This is how things stood in the summer of 1987 when staff at OCC prepared for another round of discussions with the SEC, hoping to receive a regulatory approval for their proposed model-based calculation of the net capital rule. However, before these planned discussions could take place an event occurred that dramatically questioned the accuracy and the validity of financial risk management systems based on the Black–Scholes–Merton model – the October 1987 market crash.

## Financial risk management and the 1987 market crash

By October 1987, risk management systems based on Black–Scholes–Merton were present in virtually all of the major trading firms' offices as well as in the options clearinghouse.[17] On Monday, 19 October 1987, American financial markets experienced the worst one-day price drop in asset prices since October 1929. Since stock prices dropped sharply, options (which were designed to lessen the effect of such situations) were in extremely high demand (Brady 1988). Furthermore, because many investors were selling stocks to try to cut their losses, price volatility reached record levels. Several interviewees told us that between the 19th and the 22nd of October 1987 Black–Scholes-based applications did not calculate prices and risks correctly. In fact, in a few cases it was reported that the computer systems displayed call option prices that were *higher* than the market price of the stock for which the option was written (M 2001), which, of course, makes no economic sense. This last point refers directly to the practice-oriented nature of the techno-social network that performed risk management: the theoretical Black–Scholes–Merton model could not have produced such an effect; it was the interaction between model-based computerized applications and live traders that brought it about.

Although this chapter does not discuss the possible theoretical reasons why the models were not reliable in October 1987, it is clear that some of the basic premises on which the model was established were questioned, if not shaken, because of the events. Among the questionable assumptions was the validity of the hypothesis that prices followed a lognormal distribution. Based on the lognormal distribution is the assumption that the extreme events are very rare: colloquially, the lognormal distribution is said to have a "thin tale".[18] According to this assumption (among other things), the Black–Scholes–Merton model is being used to estimate the prices of options. On 19 October 1987, it appeared that the assumption about the lognormal distribution of prices did not hold. For instance, events that had very low probabilities and, thus, were expected to occur very rarely (i.e., once in a few decades) happened a few times a day (Rubinstein 1994). For many market participants it became apparent that under such extreme conditions (for example, the NYSE dropped 21 per cent on 19 October, its biggest one-day drop since the 1920s) model-based financial risk management was not predicting risk accurately and thus could not help to manage risk appropriately.

However, despite the fact that model-based financial risk management was not proved to be accurate during the crash, the discussions between OCC and the SEC continued, leading eventually (in 1994) to the SEC granting a risk management system based on the Black–Scholes–Merton model based for the calculation of SEC's net capital requirements (Securities and Exchange Commission 1994, 1997). The system was dubbed TIMS – Theoretical Intermarket Margining System.[19] Considering the fact that for the better part of the 1980s the market regulation division of the SEC did not approve such systems, one might ask what motivated the SEC to approve TIMS when it did, at the wake of the October 1987 market crash. To understand this step, it is necessary to examine the October 1987 crash and its effect on financial risk management while taking into account the techno-social network of market participants that reacted to the events of October 1987.

M was an assistant director in the SEC's division of market regulation in the late 1980s and early 1990s; while in this position M headed the team that examined the OCC's system that was dubbed TIMS. The examination of the system took several months between 1990 and 1991, in which time the SEC and the OCC conducted comparative performance tests between TIMS and of the existing strategy-based calculation method. At the completion of the tests, it was concluded that TIMS provided more reliable and accurate results than those produced by the strategy-based system. That is,

TIMS predicted daily gain/loss amounts that were closer to the actual market results than the ones determined by the strategy-based system. That said, does this mean that this financial risk management was accurate? The period of the test was a time of relative calm in the markets and so the accuracy of TIMS was not tested during periods of extreme volatility such as those that existed in October 1987. The results meant that under ordinary market conditions TIMS would provide appropriate amounts of net capital, but what would happen in times of extreme market conditions? The SEC's answer to this question was simple:

[TIMS] is good for business purposes. Obviously, a businessman should know what his risk is from day to day. He should also have an idea of what the worst thing [is] that could happen to him, more or less. [I]n the ordinary circumstance, not much capital is needed from day to day. You only need it in stress times. Stress times don't occur that frequently. So the model is always wrong! Because it will not give that stress capital. (M 2001)

M, like many other market participants was aware of the fact that under extreme conditions Black–Scholes–Merton-based applications did not provide accurate results. Nevertheless, as the quote shows, from a regulatory point of view, it was more important to approve a financial risk management system that was acceptable by virtually all market participants, albeit being unreliable under infrequent extreme conditions, than to have a system (strategy-based rules) whose most market participants had complaints about its usefulness. This argument is rooted deeply in the practical intention behind the net capital rule. The rule was designed to protect customers from the possible adverse consequences of positions they did not explicitly intend to hold. That is, if a broker constructed risky positions using customer's money without the direct intention of the customers and the positions resulted in a loss, the customers were entitled to compensation. However, in times of extreme volatility, when prices in the markets *as a whole* fluctuate wildly, even conservative positions could be risky. In other words, the net capital rule was not designed to protect market participants from events of the type that occurred in October 1987. Therefore, from this perspective it was of little significance that the model used in the rule was inaccurate when such events happened.

When the SEC tested TIMS in the early 1990s, Black–Scholes-based applications had already served as the agreed-upon communicative and organizational basis for options trading and for the calculation of margins by the clearinghouse. The regulatory approval of TIMS, indicated not only that the preferences of the SEC regarding options markets changed, but also that a more fundamental change took place. The dominance of model-related practices in the options market environment had a significant impact on the SEC's perspective of the markets. In particular, the concept of the "common businessman" was influenced by the awareness that the model had become the common language in the market. When M, the SEC's senior employee, mentioned that "a businessman should know what his risk is from day to day", he did not merely make a normative conviction that was based on the rules and the regulations of the SEC, but one that drew its power from a more general set of values. That is, market participants should use financial risk management on a daily basis not because the system produces accurate results (at critical times it does not!) but because the different systems based on the model proved to be very useful. Financial risk management systems facilitated the growth of the market through their use by the trading firms (where they facilitated efficient organizational communication) and by the application by OCC (where it solved the bottleneck problem of calculating margins). The techno-social network of financial risk management replaced accuracy with usefulness.

## Conclusion

As implied in the title of this chapter, in many respects the story of the establishment of the Black–Scholes–Merton model simply marks the emergence of contemporary financial risk management. However, the current dominance of the risk management methods (and the failure of these methods, as Engelen shows us) resulted in the fact that financial risk management is not limited only to financial markets. Instead, contemporary capitalism is dependent on model-based risk management for a variety of managerial decisions, from the amounts paid as equity-based bonuses to corporate executives to the degree of risk associated with exploring new oil fields. Considering this perspective, can we draw a lesson from the history of financial risk management in early derivatives markets for other areas? Can a more general insight be derived from the specific historical case analysed in this chapter?

One possible direction is to examine the mechanisms through which knowledge is dispersed from one realm of practice to another. The case shows that the small trading firms of early CBOE used model-based application (Fischer Black's sheets) as a trading aid for the single traders.

Then, when larger firms entered the options exchanges, model-based applications served as tools for organizational communication. The clearinghouse, in turn, developed a solution to a technical-operational problem using the model. Finally, the SEC approved an application that performed a regulatory function. This process of gradual dissemination of knowledge includes two elements. First, the transfer of knowledge regarding the Black–Scholes–Merton model was not simple diffusion of information, but was an interpretive process. The actors analysed the practices in which the model took part, "distilled" from them the features that could be useful in their realm of practice, and employed those feature in the new set of applications, in a process that is similar to the one described schematically by Engelen (this volume). However, unlike the process that Engelen describes, the dissemination of knowledge related to the model included a second crucial element: the gradual accumulation of model-based technologies and practices. The combination of these two elements – the bare-bones "technical" usefulness of the model and the social, emerging usefulness that derived from the fact that others also use it – is responsible for the widespread development and adoption of model-based applications.

Again, in similar manner to the way Engelen analyses the contemporary reliance on financial risk management, this chapter shows that the strength of the "social usefulness" is highly related to the fact that financial risk management emerged through a network of connections. The accumulation of implicit trust in the usefulness of the model, in spite of the different practices involved, reminds us of the phenomenon the American sociologist Ronald Burt (2005) defines as "closure". Closure among two actors exists to the degree that the two have strong connections with other mutual actors and it tends to be positively correlated with the density of the network. When closure exists, the interdependency created through the structure of connections tends to bring about trust or at least trust-like effects. This description implies the existence of a social-organizational structure of a very different nature from the one commonly assumed to exist in financial markets. While financial risk management is connected frequently with procedure-based, utilitarian, arm's-length type of connections, the development of financial risk management systems analysed here reveals a different type of dynamics: not only did the different organizational actors know each other well, but they also trusted each other's judgment about the usefulness of the systems.

## Notes

1. Special thanks go to Adam Dixon, Gordon Clark, and Ashby Monk for their insightful comments. A previous version of this chapter was presented in a seminar at the school of Geography, University of Oxford where useful comments were received. A longer version of this paper was published in *Accounting, Organizations and Society* under the title "The usefulness of inaccurate models: Towards an understanding of the emergence of financial risk management".
2. http://www.garp.com/about/archive.asp (accessed on 30 March, 2008).
3. http://www.sungard.com/sungard/ (accessed on 30 March, 2008).
4. Merton and Scholes received the Nobel Prize in Economics in the 1997 for their work on the model. Black died in 1995, but was mentioned as a contributor by the prize committee.
5. The empirical material in this chapter is based on interviews and primary documents. More than thirty interviews were conducted with leading figures from the CBOE, the Options Clearing Corporation (OCC), and the Securities and Exchange Commission (SEC) who played central roles in the unfolding of the events analysed here. All interviews were recorded and transcribed in full. Since several interviewees requested anonymity, it was decided not to single out by name the ones who agreed to be recognized and thus all interviewees are identified by a single letter. In addition, extensive archival research was done. The archives used were those of the SEC and the Federal Reserve Board in Washington, DC and private collections of documents in Baltimore, New York, and Chicago.
6. Collections of articles devoted to SSF are Knorr Cetina and Preda (2005) and Kalthoff, Rottenburg, and Wagener (2000). Other noteworthy contributions include Abolafia (1996, 1998), Arnoldi (2004), Beunza and Stark (2003, 2004, 2005), Clark (2000), Fenton-O'Creevy et al. (2005); de Goede (2005), Hertz (1998), Holzer and Millo (2005), Izquierdo (2001), Knorr Cetina and Bruegger (2000, 2002a, b), Lépinay (2007), Levin (2001), Lipuma and Lee (2004), Maurer (2001), Millo (2007), Millo et al. (2005), Muniesa and Callon (2007), Podolny (1993, 2001); Preda (2001a, b, c, 2004, 2006), Riles (2004), Thrift (1994), Tickell (2000), Uzzi (1999), Zaloom (2003, 2004), Zorn (2004), and Zuckerman (1999, 2004).
7. Robert Merton's (1973) theoretical reasoning for the model is different from the one offered by Black and Scholes, but both approaches support the same mathematical model.
8. The average number of options is also related to the average size of transaction, and hence, to the number of options traded. However, since trading grew by over 300 times while the average number of options per transaction grew by less than seven times, it is clear that the number of transactions grew immensely, while the size of transaction only grew so as to accommodate the increasingly complex options trading strategies.

9. Large investment companies managed multi-exchange portfolios before exchange-traded options appeared. Yet, the level of coordination necessary in options trading was much higher than in stock trading as the vast majority of options positions were composite: composed of stock positions and one or more option positions that were bought and sold simultaneously, frequently at different exchanges. The growing complexity of options positions over the years is expressed in Figure 4.1.

10. Since OCC was the only options clearinghouse for organized exchanges at the discussed period, we refer to it as "the clearinghouse".

11. The concept of the modern options clearinghouse was developed by the CBOT team who set up the first options exchange. Indeed, the concept of a clearinghouse as an entity separate from the trading community played an important role in the approval of the options exchange itself (R 2000).

12. The rule to which this chapter refers to is the revised net capital rule from 1975. Prior to the 1975 amendments (the net capital rule was first written in 1942), brokers had to deposit a set amount of capital at the beginning of a trading day, regardless of the risk level associated with their positions (Seligman 1982).

13. The largest group of traders (although there were others) handling accounts of others were broker-dealers, who were bounded by the SEC's net capital rule.

14. Exercising assignment notices informed trading firms about the amount of daily margin they were required to pay.

15. Risk levels were expressed in the form of "haircuts" – discounts applied to the original value of the positions. The riskier the position was, the larger the haircut was.

16. The minimum value of net capital for registered broker-dealers (after their first year as broker-dealers) was set at \$250,000 or as $6\frac{2}{3}$ per cent of the total debts (SEC 1975).

17. Another pricing model, which is a variant of the Black–Scholes–Merton model, was developed by John Cox, Stephen Ross, and Mark Rubinstein (Cox, Ross and Rubinstein 1979; Ross 1977; Rubinstein 1994) and also gained significant popularity during the time period described in this chapter.

18. The lognormal distribution, being one-sided, has one "tail".

19. The SEC issued a "no-action" letter about the use of TIMS in 1994 (Securities and Exchange Commission). The meaning of the letter was that no action would be taken against bodies that used TIMS. The final, unrestricted approval of the system was granted in 1997.

# References

Abolafia, M. Y. (1996). *Making Markets: Opportunism and Restraint in Wall Street.* Cambridge, MA: Harvard University Press.

Abolafia, M. Y. (1998). Markets as Cultures: An Ethnographic Approach. In M. Callon (ed.), *The Laws of the Markets* (pp. 69–85). Oxford: Blackwell.

Arnoldi, J. (2004). Derivatives: virtual values and real risks. *Theory, Culture & Society*, 21, 23–4.

Baker, W. E. (1984*a*). The social structure of a national securities market. *American Journal of Sociology*, 89, 775–811.

—— (1984*b*). Floor Trading and Crowd Dynamics. In P. A. Adler and P. Adler (eds.), *The Social Dynamics of Financial Markets*, (pp. 107–28). Greenwich, Conn.: JAI Press.

Barnhart, R. K. (1999). *Chambers Dictionary of Etymology*. London: Chambers.

Beunza, D. and Stark, D. (2003). The organization of responsiveness: innovation and recovery in the trading rooms of lower Manhattan. *Socio-Economic Review*, 1, 135–64.

—— —— (2004). Tools of the trade: the socio-technology of arbitrage in a Wall Street trading room. *Industrial and Corporate Change*, 13, 369–400.

—— —— (2005). Resolving Identities: Successive Crises in a Trading Room after 9/11. In N. Foner (ed.) *Wounded City: The Social Impact of 9/11* (pp. 293–320). New York: Russell Sage Foundation Press.

Black, F. and Scholes, M. (1972). The valuation of option contracts and a test of market efficiency. *Journal of Finance*, 27, 399–417.

—— —— (1973). The pricing of options and corporate liabilities. *Journal of Political Economy, 18*, March–April, 637–54.

Brady, N. (1988). *Report of the Presidential Task Force on Market Mechanisms*. Washington, DC.

Burt, R. (2005). *Brokerage and Closure: An Introduction to Social Capital*. Oxford: Oxford University Press.

Clark, G. (2000). *Pension Fund Capitalism*. Oxford: Oxford University Press.

Cox, J., Ross, S., and Rubinstein M., (1979). Option pricing: a simplified approach. *Journal of Financial Economics*, 7, 229–36.

Fenton-O'Creevy, M., Nicholson, N., Soane, E., and Willman, P. (2005). *Traders: Risks, Decisions, and Management in Financial Markets*. Oxford: Oxford University Press.

de Goede, M. (2005). *Virtue, Fortune, and Faith: A Genealogy of Finance*. Minneapolis: University of Minnesota Press.

Granovetter, M. (1985). Economic action and social structure: the problem of embeddedness. *American Journal of Sociology*, 91, 481–510.

—— (1992). Economic institutions as social constructions: a framework for analysis. *Acta Sociologica*, 35, 3–11.

Hertz, E. (1998). *The Trading Crowd: An Ethnography of the Shanghai Stock Market*. Cambridge: Cambridge University Press.

Holzer, B. and Millo, Y. (2005). From risks to second-order dangers in financial markets: unintended consequences of risk management systems. *New Political Economy*, 10, 223–45.

Hull, J. C. (2005) *Options, Futures and Other Derivatives*. London: Prentice Hall.

Izquierdo, J. (2001). Reliability at risk: the supervision of financial models as a case study for reflexive economic sociology. *European Societies*, 3, 69–90.

Kalthoff, H. (2005). Practices of calculation: economic representations and risk management. *Theory, Culture and Society*, 22, 69–97.

—— Rottenburg, R., and Wagener, H.-J. (2000). *Ökonomie und Gesellschaft, Jahrbuch 16. Facts and Figures: Economic Representations and Practices*. Marburg: Metropolis.

Knorr Cetina, K. (2005). How are Global Markets Global? The Architecture of a Flow World'. in K. Knorr Cetina and A. Preda (eds.), *The Sociology of Financial Markets* (pp. 38–61). Oxford: Oxford University Press.

Knorr Cetina, K. and Bruegger, U. (2000). The market as an object of attachment: exploring postsocial relations in financial markets. *Canadian Journal of Sociology*, 25, 141–68.

—— —— (2002*a*). Global microstructures: the virtual societies of financial markets. *American Journal of Sociology*, 107, 905–51.

—— —— (2002*b*). Inhabiting technology: The global lifeform of financial markets. *Current Sociology*, 50, 389–405.

—— and Preda, A. (eds.) (2005). *The Sociology of Financial Markets*. Oxford: Oxford University Press.

Latour, B. (2007). *Reassembling the Social: An Introduction to Actor-Network-Theory*. Oxford: Oxford University Press.

—— (1988). Mixing humans and nonhumans together: the sociology of a door-closer. *Social Problems*, 35, 298–310.

—— (2007). Decoding Finance: Articulation and Liquidity around a Trading Room. In D. MacKenzie, F. Muniesa, and L. Siu (eds.), *Do Economists Make Markets? On the Performativity of Economics* (pp. 87–127). Princeton, NJ: Princeton University Press.

Levin, P. (2001). Gendering the market: temporality, work, and gender on a national futures exchange. *Work and Occupations*, 28, 112–30.

LiPuma, E. and Lee, B. (2004). *Financial Derivatives and the Globalization of Risk*. Durham, NC: Duke University Press.

Maurer, B. (2001). Engineering an Islamic future: speculations on Islamic financial alternatives. *Anthropology Today*, 17, 8–11.

McDonald, R. L. (2006) *Derivatives Markets*. London: Addison-Wesley.

MacKenzie, D. (2001). Physics and finance: s-terms and modern finance as a topic for science studies. *Science Technology and Human Values*, 26, 115–44.

—— (2006). *An Engine, Not a Camera: How Financial Models Shape Markets*. London: The MIT Press.

—— (forthcoming, 2009). *Material Markets: Facts, Technologies, Politics*. Oxford: Oxford University Press.

—— and Millo, Y. (2003). Negotiating a market, performing theory: The historical sociology of a financial derivatives exchange. *American Journal of Sociology*, 109, 107–45.

Merton, R. C. (1973). Theory of rational option pricing. *Bell Journal of Economics and Management Science*, 4, 141–83.

Merton, R. C. and O'Leary, T. (2007). Mediating instruments and making markets: capital budgeting, science and the economy. *Accounting, Organizations and Society*, 32, 701–34.

Millo, Y. (2007). Making Things Deliverable: The Origins of Index-Based Derivatives. In M. Callon, Y. Millo, and F. Muniesa (eds.), Market Devices Oxford: lackwell.

—— Muniesa, F., Panourgias, N. S., and Scott, S. V. (2005). Organized detachment: clearinghouse mechanisms in financial markets. *Information and Organization*, 15, 229–46.

Muniesa, F. and Callon, M. (2007). Economic Experiments and the Construction of Markets. In D. MacKenzie et al. (eds.), *Do Economists Make Markets? On the Performativity of Economics*. (pp. 163–89). Princeton, NJ: Princeton University Press.

Podolny, J. M. (1993). A Status-based Model of Market Competition. *American Journal of Sociology*, 98, 829–72.

—— (2001). Networks as the Pipes and Prisms of the Market. *American Journal of Sociology*, 107, 33–60.

Polanyi, K. and MacIver, R. M. (1957). *The Great Transformation*. Boston: Gower Beacon Press.

Power, M. (2007). *Organized Uncertainty: Designing a World of Risk Management*. Oxford: Oxford University Press.

Preda, A. (2001a). The rise of the popular investor: financial knowledge and investing in England and France, 1840–1880. *Sociological Quarterly*, 42, 205–32.

—— (2001b). In the enchanted grove: financial conversations and the marketplace in England and France in the 18th century. *Journal of Historical Sociology*, 14, 276–307.

—— (2001c). Sense and sensibility: or, how should social studies of finance behave, a manifesto. *Economic Sociology: European Electronic Newsletter*, 2/2, 15–18.

—— (2004). Informative prices, rational investors: the emergence of the random walk hypothesis and the nineteenth-century "Science of Financial Investments". *History of Political Economy*, 36, 351–86.

—— 2006. Socio-technical agency in financial markets: the case of the stock ticker. *Social Studies of Science*, 36, 753–82.

Riles, A. (2004). Real time: unwinding technocratic and anthropological knowledge. *American Ethnologist*, 31, 392–405.

Ross, S. (1977). The capital asset pricing model CAPM, short-sale restrictions and related issues. *Journal of Finance*, 32,177–84.

Rubinstein, M. (1994). Implied binomial trees. *Journal of Finance*, 69, 771–818.

Securities and Exchange Commission (1975). Securities Exchange Act of 1934, Rule 15c3–1. Code of Federal Regulations, 17 part 240.

—— (1978). The SEC Speaks.

—— (1978). Report of the Special Study of The Options Markets to the Securities and Exchange Commission. Securities and Exchange Commission, Washington, D.C.

—— (1980). The SEC Speaks.

—— (1986). Self-Regulatory Organizations; Options Clearing Corp.; Order Approving Proposed Rule Change. Release No. 34–23167; File No. SR-OCC-85–21. 51 FR 16127.

—— (1986). Self-Regulatory Organizations; Options Clearing Corp.; Proposed Rule Change. Release No. 34–22844; File No. SR-OCC-85–21. 51 FR 4257.

Securities and Exchange Commission (1986*a*). Self-Regulatory Organizations; Options Clearing Corp.; Order Approving Proposed Rule Change. in Release No. 34–23167; File No. SR-OCC-85–21, vol. 51 FR 16127.

—— (1986*b*). Self-Regulatory Organizations; Options Clearing Corp.; Proposed Rule Change. in Release No. 34–22844; File No. SR-OCC-85–21, *vol. 51 FR 4257*.

—— (1994) Release No. 33761 (Proposing Release). Washington, DC.

—— (1997) Release No. 34–38248; File No. S7–7–94. Washington, DC.

Seligman, J. (1982). *The Transformation of Wall Street – A History of the Securities and Exchange Commission and Modern Finance*. Boston: Houghton Mifflin.

Stulz, R. (2002). *Risk Management and Derivatives*. Boston: Thomson Learning.

Thrift, N. (1994). On the Social and Cultural Determinants of Financial Centres: The Case of the City of London. In S. Corbridge, and R. Martin (eds.), *Money, Power, and Space* (pp. 327–55). Oxford: Blackwell.

Tickell, A. (2000). Dangerous derivatives: controlling and creating risks in international money. *Geoforum*, 31, 87–99.

Uzzi, B. (1996). Embededdness and economic performance: the network effect. *American Sociological Review*, 61, 674–98.

—— (1999). Embeddedness in the making of financial capital: how social relations and networks benefit firms seeking financing. *American Sociological Review*, 64, 481–504.

—— and Gillespie, J. (2002). Knowledge spillover in corporate financing networks: embeddedness, network transitivity and trade credit performance. *Strategic Management Journal*, 23, 595–618.

—— and Lancaster, R. (2003). Relational embeddedness and learning: the case of bank loan managers and their clients. *Management Science*, 49, 383–99.

Zaloom, C. (2003). Ambiguous numbers: trading technologies and interpretation in financial markets. *American Ethnologist*, 30, 258–72.

—— (2004). The productive life of risk. *Current Anthropology*, 19, 365–91.

Zorn, D. M. (2004). Here a chief, there a chief: the rise of the CFO in the American firm. *American Sociological Review*, 69, 345–64.

Zuckerman, E. W. (1999). The categorical imperative: securities analysts and the illegitimacy discount. *American Journal of Sociology*, 104, 1398–438.

—— (2004). Structural incoherence and stock market activity. *American Sociological Review*, 69, 405–32.

# 5

# Learning to Cope with Uncertainty: On the Spatial Distributions of Financial Innovation and Its Fallout

*Ewald Engelen*

The final year of the latest boom will enter financial history books as a Janus-faced year.[1] While the problems that were ultimately to unlock the triumphant course that the financial markets from 2003 onward had taken, had been brewing in their nooks and crannies for quite some time, disaster nevertheless struck unexpectedly in August 2007. The increasing degree of self-confidence demonstrated by financial agents up to July 2007 was shattered in a mere couple of weeks. The expectation, of regulators as well as market participants, that the financial sector, because of new technologies, techniques and instruments, had finally mastered the trick of turning uncertainty into calculable risk, was proven false. Financial innovation, the rise of new financial agents and financial internationalization were seen by practitioners as having resulted in a world in which risk was spread so thin over so many different markets, localities, and institutes as to have become virtually irrelevant. Regulators, who from time to time voiced their worries over what they perceived as rising opaqueness and innovation run wild, were told by industry representatives that these worries were unfounded because we had entered a world in which opaqueness was simply the counterimage of the increasing fragmentation of risks. Moreover, new risk management techniques, the so-called "Value-at-Risk" modeling tools, based on increased computing powers as well as new "financial facts", were said to ensure that the few remaining risks would be easy to check and control (see Augar 2005, 125ff.; www.riskglossary.com).

History proved otherwise. Within a few weeks self-confidence was shattered, the beliefs in the rise of a new lightweight and risk-proof financialized economy were gone, while regulators suddenly faced a crisis of distrust among bankers, who, because of the wide dispersal of "toxic" financial products, were unwilling to grant each other liquidity. At the time of writing, this is still the case; banks are unwinding their "toxic" entanglements with other players one step at a time in order to preclude a giant meltdown, resulting in jittery markets that are easily spooked even when the main causes behind the credit crisis, that is, the problems in the US sub-prime mortgage market, have slowly receded in history.

Although the regulatory stance toward financial innovation has always been problematic and spatially diverse, the general trend was nevertheless toward more self-regulation; let financial agents control their own risk profiles for they know best, have the best tools and have the most interest in "continuing the dance". That too has radically changed since August 2007. Regulators worldwide are currently discussing new constraints to save financial markets from themselves. Measures under discussion range from higher levels of mandatory capitalization, redesigning bankers' remuneration packages, better international regulatory coordination, and shifting part of the over-the-counter (OTC) derivative trade to formal exchanges, to more transparency, more public control over rating agencies, and improved risk management techniques.

While suggesting a truly *political* analysis of financial markets, this chapter focuses not so much on the costs and benefits of these regulatory responses but uses the return of uncertainty to test the usefulness of a number of more classic sociological claims concerning the importance of social, spatial, and reputational proximity for inter-organizational trust-building. While spatial variance, despite the strong homogenizing expectations voiced by some (O'Brien 1992; Strange 1996; Castells 1996; Cairncross 1998), has remained causally relevant for the functioning of financial markets, as is demonstrated by the undiminished importance of financial centers (see Cassis 2006), the return of uncertainty implies a simultaneous replay of the importance of proximity and the "thick" knowledge it generates about the trustworthiness of counterparties to overcome the atmosphere of suspicion which has soured the financial markets in 2007.

As such, this is a study in the sociology of finance, which sees the crisis of 2007 as a unique chance to investigate the microsociological foundations of contemporary finance and their diverse spatial articulations, suggesting that the functionality of proximity for the workings of the financial "system" is a variable not a constant, which depends crucially on the extent to which markets, agents, and the techniques that are available to them are able to transform uncertainties in risks. That ability, in turn, is itself a conjunctural feat that is subject to the dynamics of financial markets (Kindleberger 2000). In other words, in periods in which markets resemble the picture painted by mainstream finance, "financial facts" are largely self-evident, allowing for more or less anonymous exchange on spot markets, while in periods of uncertainty in which markets behave more like the "price discovery machines" described by Austrian economists like Hayek, Schumpeter, and Von Mises, "facts" are contested, resulting in patterns of trade that are built around more proximate modes of trust.

The structure of this chapter is as follows. The second section gives a brief overview of the radical rupture that global financial markets experienced in 2007. On the basis of some empirical exhibits it gives readers a sense of the stark contrast in moods and sentiments experienced by traders, asset managers, and bankers. The subsequent section builds upon this and describes, first, the extent of financial innovation and its unequal spatial consequences and, second, the spatial effects of the rise of uncertainty. The fourth section uses sociological literature to understand the different empirical responses to the return of uncertainty. This chapter ends in a speculative mood by attempting to answer the question what the spatial consequences might be of the different ways of coping with uncertainty.

## A Janus-faced year

The year 2007 was a year with two faces. Until early August daily turnover at the worlds' financial exchanges was continuously breaking records, while banks, hedge funds, and other financial agents reaped bumper profits, and politicians and regulators were anxiously discussing deregulatory measures to accommodate the wishes and preferences of financial agents in order to ensure the continuing competitiveness of their jurisdictions. From August onward this turned into its opposite. Markets ran dry, prices and values collapsed, banks had to announce big write-downs and credit losses, while financial centers rapidly lost employment. Just like seven years earlier a fresh round of financial hubris came crushing to the ground.

In the middle of 2007, financial markets reached their – as of yet – historical zenith. In global currency markets the value of daily trade had approximately tripled in fifteen years, from $650 billion in 1989 to well over $3.2 trillion in 2007 (BIS 2008*a*, 4). A similar picture emerges from developments in other financial markets. The annual turnover of exchange traded bonds, for example, underwent a fourfold increase in value. Equity trade boomed tenfold over the same period, from $5 billion in 1990 to $70 billion in 2007 (WFE 2007). This had everything to do with the increasing popularity of "logarithmic trading", the rise of active traders such as "Quants" and other hedge funds, and the simultaneous demise of the patient investor.

However, these figures are dwarfed by the size of global derivate markets. Encompassing a range of financial products that share the property of being "derived" from the value of underlying assets (hence the name: "derivative" from "being derived from"), derivatives have become the bread and butter of modern financial markets, generating growing shares of the fee incomes of investment banks. This decade has seen an enormous expansion of the underlying assets that banks use to construct new "synthetic" financial products. While derivatives used to be backed by equities, bonds, and commodities, increasingly they are "derived" from consumer debts, mortgages, student loans, car loans, credit card debts, debit cards, intellectual property rights, in short anything that generates a steady income stream. Although the oldest derivate markets were set up to facilitate the trade of "futures" on agrarian commodities and can be traced back as far as several centuries ago (London, Amsterdam, Paris), most formal derivate markets are linked to the rise of finance since the mid-1970s (see Kynaston 1997).

Most derivates, however, are not traded on exchanges at all, but are traded bilaterally between two parties or, as it is called, Over-The-Counter (Morgan 2008). While hard to quantify, triannual surveys of the Bank for International Settlements (BIS) demonstrate that these markets have experienced the strongest growth of all financial markets (BIS 2008*a*). From a negligible size in the early 1970s, OTC derivative markets have reached a size of $596 trillion in notional outstanding amounts in 2007, compared to $28 trillion of outstanding futures contracts and $55 trillion of outstanding options on formal derivative exchanges (BIS 2008*b*). It is the OTC market that has spawned all these new "synthetic" products that are referred to as "alphabet soup" in the business press. Their construction was made possible by the rise of new mathematical techniques (Efficient Market Theory, Black–Scholes theorem, Option Pricing Theory; see MacKenzie 2006), the virtualization of exchange-based trade, the availability of new forms of Information and Communication Technologies (ICT) and expanded calculative powers, as well as the construction of "new financial facts" – that is, pricing hard to price securities – by risk specialists like Standard & Poor's, Moody's, and Fitch (see MacKenzie et al. 2007).

Many of these products date from the late 1990s and represent the most profitable segments of the world's financial markets (see Tett 2006, 2008). However, given the inability to attach intellectual property rights to these financial innovations, and the ensuing quick turnaround of these new instruments, resulting in rapidly declining rates of profits, there is an enormous urge to innovate (Tufano 1989; Augar 2005). While good empirical research on the institutional, organizational, social and cultural conditions of financial innovation is lacking, the spatiality of financial innovation suggests that these have to do with concentration, proximity, scale, and diversity. For anecdotal evidence clearly demonstrates that most innovations originate from trading desks in the biggest and most sophisticated investment banks that are primarily located in the biggest financial centers, that is, New York and London (Augar 2005; Knee 2006; Erturk and Solari 2007; Tett 2006, 2008).

This is demonstrated by the geographical distribution of gross values of securitized assets, presented in Figure 5.1. These figures show the disparities between different places in terms of the underlying value of the assets being securitized. As such, this suggests an unequal distribution of the conditions of innovation – i.e. concentrations of sophisticated financial agents, pools of liquidity, dense networks of traders, consultants, bankers and their clients, and, finally, diverse pools of expertise, biographies, human capital, trading techniques, heuristics, financial markets, and financial instruments – over space. Apparently, the United States is and remains the largest pool of capital and the main locus of financial sophistication, generating a level of securitized assets that is seven to tenfold that of Europe.

Within Europe too, there are telling differences between levels of securitized assets, as is demonstrated by Table 5.1. The largest issuers by far are the UK, the Netherlands, Spain, and Italy, while big European economies such as France and Germany score much lower. These differences reflect different degrees of sophistication of national banking systems as well as differences in the organization of national housing markets, given that the securitization of residential mortgages is the largest category.

What these exhibits also show is the dual-faced nature of 2007. An advertisement of Standard & Poor's that was carried by a 2006 special issue of *Institutional Investor*, a professional investor periodical, on the prospects of securitization, is telling in this regard. The cover of the issue, depicting rays of hope and glory that surround the globe, clearly

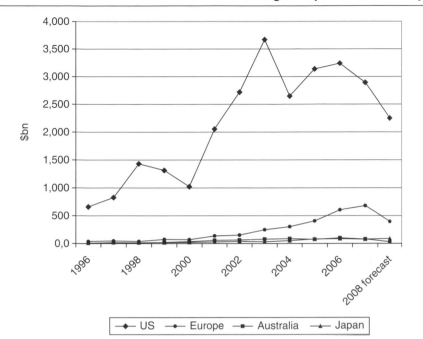

**Figure 5.1.** Trends in securitization issuance

*Source:* IFSL, Securitization Report (2008).

speaks of the bullish mood of the markets in 2006. Likewise, the Standard & Poor's advertisement offers data services to buyers and sellers of securitized products, suggesting that experience and reputation are sufficient to be able to steer a risk-free route through the increasingly opaque and continuously shifting mass of securitized assets. The main message reads:

You know the big providers of securities evaluations. But do you know what makes Standard & Poor's different? With over 35 years of experience in the prizing business, we're continuously expanding to meet your evolving needs. ABS, MBS, CMBS, CDO's and more – we've got you covered. And, we work closely with you to anticipate and address new market developments. Knowledge, independence, and direct access to the professionals behind the thinking. It's what you expect from a market leader. (Institutional Investor News 2007)

What is striking about this quotation is not so much the self-confidence of which it speaks, but rather the promise of security it performs; "we've got you covered", as if the public role of the private corporation of Standard & Poor's is comparable to that of the police in guaranteeing domestic security. It is suggested that expertise, experience, and professionalism are

125

**Table 5.1.** Securitization issuance by country of collateral

|  | 2007:Q1 | 2007:Q2 | 2007:Q3 | 2007:Q4 | 2007 Total |
|---|---|---|---|---|---|
| Belgium | – | 0.2 | 3.9 |  | 4.1 |
| Denmark | 0.1 | 0.4 | – |  | 0.5 |
| France | 1.3 | 1.8 | – | 0.8 | 3.9 |
| Germany | 3.5 | 8.2 | 1.8 | 5.1 | 18.6 |
| Greece | – | 1.5 | 1.3 | 2.5 | 5.3 |
| Ireland | 2.9 | 3.2 | 2.3 | 2.0 | 10.4 |
| Italy | 6.7 | 4.1 | 3.1 | 2.5 | 26.3 |
| Netherlands | 5.8 | 10.6 | 11.5 | 12.9 | 40.8 |
| Portugal | 2.9 | 2.4 | 2.6 | 2.9 | 10.8 |
| Spain | 16.5 | 14.4 | 14.5 | 15.7 | 61.1 |
| Switzerland | 0.4 | 0.3 | – |  | 0.7 |
| UK | 62.5 | 62.1 | 30.2 | 17.8 | 172.6 |
| Multinational | – | 3.2 | 1.9 | 2.4 | 7.5 |
| Total | 102.8 | 123.9 | 73.3 | 65.0 | 365.0 |

*Source*: ESF (2008), ESF Securitization Report 2007.

sufficient to tame chance, so buyers and sellers of securitized assets have nothing to fear as long as they use the securities evaluations of Standard & Poor's; "we've got you covered!" As has become clear since the credit crunch, rating agencies such as Standard & Poor's have systematically overrated the values and underrated the risks of securitized assets, raising worldwide concerns over conflicts of interests and the need to rate and regulate the rating agencies; "qui custodiat custodes"?

Given the unequal spatial distribution of financial innovation (and its rewards), it should come as no surprise that the fallout from innovations gone sour has also taken an unequal spatial pattern. At the moment of writing, more than $1,000 billion of financial assets have melted away. Most of these losses have been booked by financial firms that are located in the very same places and territories that were identified earlier as the main locations of financial innovation. The biggest losers have been big US and UK financial groups such as Citicorp, Wachovia, Washington Mutual, RBS, HSBC, and Barclays, while a further band of losers can be found in North-Western Europe, suggesting a strong causal linkage between the degree of involvement in financial innovation and the extent of damage inflicted. However, some observations do not fit this narrative. For instance, some regional German banks, while outside the main circuits of financial innovation, were nevertheless severely hit by the credit crunch, as were sophisticated Swiss and American investment banks such as UBS, Credit Suisse, Bear Sterns, Merrill Lynch, and Lehman Brothers, suggesting that the fallout followed a core-periphery pattern; victims were either located at the core of financial innovation and hence so much implicated in those categories of assets that they could not divest them quickly enough, or they were so much at the periphery of financial innovation that they simply did not know what they were buying and were hence caught unawares when the mood suddenly turned foul. As such, the fallout too followed a very particular spatial pattern that had everything to do with the flows of knowledge within the network-based structures of contemporary finance.

## From risk to uncertainty

There are (at least) four lessons that can be drawn from the narrative presented above. First, despite strong claims by pundits, practitioners, and academics that financial markets had finally transcended the economy of blood, sweat, and tears, the credit crunch has clearly demonstrated that to be a false presumption. Despite their increasingly ethereal and esoteric nature, the synthetic products that are being traded on the OTC derivative markets are thoroughly grounded in the economy of everyday life. The US sub-prime mortgage market where the August 2007 crisis originated, was built on a business model that was viable as long as housing prices increased. When that expectation was no longer met, households started to recognize that they had shouldered debts that transcended the value of their collateral. The ensuing "voluntary evictions" had an immediate downward impact on the value of the MBS's that were constructed on the back of these mortgages. That in turn led to a drying up of the secondary market for mortgages and a sharp increase in the price for insurance against possible defaults provided by the so-called "monolines". Suddenly, a wide variety of financial agents – sophisticated as well as mainstream – were seen to possess an uncertain amount of "toxic" products that had become unmarketable. And since agents were unable to assess the extent of the fallout on the books of their counterparties, liquidity in the interbank market dried up, worsening the prospect of attaching sound values to derivatives. In other words, it was developments in the so-called "real economy" that stood at the cradle of the credit crunch, while the credit crunch in turn will have substantial effects on the "real" economy; estimates have it that the American writedowns will add up to $400 billion, equivalent to 1 to 1.5 percent of the annual US GDP (IMF 2008).

Second, contrary to expectations of market insiders, market risks were not distributed thinly over many different financial agents and were hence negligible. Until August 2007, regulators like IMF and BIS harbored the expectation that because of financial innovation and the rise of new financial agents such as hedge funds and private equity funds and the transformation of sleepy institutional investors into active financial players that had mopped up most of the excess liquidity, risk was distributed much more widely than before, resulting in a more robust financial system. Rather, what happened after the outbreak of the sub-prime mortgage crisis suggested the reverse. Big multi-divisional banks and bulge bracket investment banks still appeared to play central roles in the global financial system, meaning that most of the toxic products ended up in their books. The web of finance may have become larger, more complex and denser, but it is still held together by only a limited number of nodes.

Third, despite new global regulation (Basel II) and increasing calculative powers, transparency has not proven to be the "best disinfectant". When many derivatives had overnight become highly toxic, it became apparent that no one had an adequate estimate of their size, type, and distribution. Any counterparty could well be the owner of large parcels of toxic products, greatly endangering its existence over time. The distrust that slowly crept into the interbank markets has caused a gradual drying up of liquidity, which is only partially and temporarily alleviated by the huge amounts of liquidity that central banks have pumped into those markets.

Finally, and this is the lesson that is at the core of this chapter, the claim that uncertainty was finally transformed into calculable risk was powerfully refuted. Despite the impressive concentration of expertise, manpower, and calculative capacity in locations like London and New York, financial markets were suddenly seen to behave in irrational ways. Apparently, real existing financial markets contained an indefinable residue that escaped the models of modern finance theory, turning what had appeared to be calculable risk into paralyzing uncertainty.

The distinction between risk and uncertainty was minted by the founder of the Chicago school of economics and erstwhile Max Weber translator, Frank Knight. As Knight famously wrote in his 1921 classic:

The fact is that while a single situation involving a known risk may be regarded as "uncertain," this uncertainty is easily converted into effective certainty; for in a considerable number of such cases the results become predictable in accordance with the laws of chance, and the error in such prediction approaches zero as the number of cases is increased. (Knight 1921, 42)

In other words, given a large enough sample, variance can be turned into probability and hence can be priced away by means of insurance techniques. However, what is crucial about Knight's insight is that it is not always possible to make enough observations or to determine to which category these observations belong, suggesting that not every uncertainty can actually be transformed into risk.

That is precisely what the credit crunch demonstrated. Suddenly financial markets started to behave in a manner that was out of sync with the expectations of traders, which were informed by the mathematical models that were supposed to describe the workings of these markets. In other words, there suddenly appeared to be a mismatch between "model" and "muddle", raising pressing questions about the ontological status of mainstream finance theorems. While those questions cannot be discussed here, there are at least two considerations that should be faced.

First, does the credit crunch disprove the performativity thesis that has been proposed by scholars like Michel Callon (1998; Callon et al. 2007) and Donald MacKenzie (2006; MacKenzie et al. 2007)? Since that thesis is embedded in a constructivist perspective on social reality and hence conflates epistemology and ontology, in fact claiming that theoretical frameworks do not represent a given social phenomenon but are performing these phenomena, it does not allow for ontological residues that turn against the "engines" that are supposed to generate them. But that seems precisely to have occurred with the credit crunch. That social reality does not follow the scripts laid out by "performativity theories" suggests that the observation of performative effects has more to do with a temporary alignment of theory and reality than with the actual conflation of epistemology and ontology that performativity theory implies. In fact, crises like the credit crunch indicate that the conflation of theory and reality that performativity theory postulates is actually a classic example of the "epistemic fallacy" for which post-modern thought is castigated by critical realists (Bashkar 1975; Sayer 2000, 27). While Millo and MacKenzie in their contribution to this volume speak of the "inaccuracy" of risk management models and explain their successes (*sic!*) by their "social usefulness" and hence seem to backtrack from MacKenzie's earlier performativity claim, the chapter is much more about the way in which these "technologies" solve social coordination problems, stressing intersubjective acceptance, than about the real effects of their empirical inaccuracy. So in my opinion the jury is still out on whether the credit crunch can be reconciled with the performativity thesis.

Second, what caused the mismatch between "muddle" and "model"? Is it something which merely requires further elaboration of the premises underlying current models of risk management and is it hence compatible with the reigning neoclassical framework or is it intrinsically incompatible with such a framework and are we hence in need of a different economic paradigm? A number of explanations floating around suggest the former. The increasing reflexivity of market participants suggests that more complex risk management models are needed. The same is true for claims that perverse incentives or faulty data are the root of the problem. In all these cases, the problem is quantitative not qualitative, so to speak. It is a matter of further refinement or adding further complexity, not one of radical overhaul.

Some, however, do claim that that is needed. Following his Austrian predilections, former Fed-chairman Greenspan maintained in an op-ed piece in the *Financial Times* that risk management models were intrinsically unable to model adequately "the human passions" and the large movements between fear and euphoria they incited. "Current systems of risk management", thus Greenspan:

[D]o not fully capture what I believe has been...only a peripheral addendum to business-cycle and financial modelling – the innate human responses that result in swings between euphoria and fear...This, to me, is the large missing "explanatory variable" in both risk-management and macroeconometric models...(Greenspan 2008)

What we have here are two diametrically opposed theoretical perspectives on economic life. The first postulates a world that is inherently knowable and quantifiable, inviting agents to rationally plan their future courses of action, as if their preferences and the future ways of satisfying them are completely transparent. The second stresses complexity and multi-causality, and contrasts these with the limited cognitive capacities of agents, implying that notions like maximization and rationality belie reality. While both deliver strong pro-market arguments, they could hardly be further apart. Whereas the neoclassical paradigm emphasizes the *allocative* efficiency of market exchange, resulting in economy-wide equilibrium, the Austrian school of economics praises markets for their *dynamic* efficiency, meaning their ability to discover new preferences and new ways to satisfy them (see Hayek 1949; Hodgson 1993).

Widely being seen as diverging paradigms within economics, it is striking that the two theoretical frameworks appear to have empirical leverage over the two parts of 2007. The first half of 2007 by and large answered the calls of the neoclassical paradigm, while the second half, with its high degree of uncertainty and its sudden opaqueness, was more in line with the tenets of Austrian economics. How can it be that two diametrically opposed theoretical frameworks are empirically adequate during different parts of a single year? This raises interesting questions on what the nature of economic reality has to be in order to make these two frameworks subsequently true.

## Social responses to uncertainty

Whereas uncertainty is the "repressed other" of neoclassical economics, in some strands of economic sociology it is the main independent variable that explains the nature of the social relations that agents construct. In a recent overview of the state of the art in economic sociology Neil Fligstein and Luke Dauter distinguished three approaches of the market within economic sociology on the basis of their respective causal mechanisms. The first is "performativity", the second is "institutions", and the third is "networks" (Fligstein and Dauter 2007). It is the latter that is relevant here. Harking back to Granovetter's seminal 1985 paper, the network approach in economic sociology takes the social embeddedness of economic ties as being functional for the construction of long-term relations, which help to decrease the uncertainty that economic agents face in view of the "big divide" that separates the supply and demand sides of markets (see Granovetter 1985; Fligstein and Dauter 2007). The key concept is "trust". Trust is the emergent property of ongoing exchanges between agents. Since each next moment of exchange allows agents to punish the other for breaching formal and informal rules, the continuation of the exchange signals both the value that the partners attach to the exchange relationship as well as the mutual trustworthiness of the exchange partners. Despite being infected by functionalism, the latest manifestations of network theory appear especially useful to analyze the fallout from the current credit crunch, since, as many commentators have emphasized, it is not so much a crisis of liquidity or solvency as of confidence and trust.

Network theorists have stressed that trust has efficiency effects that go beyond those postulated by neoclassical economics. The degree of confidence on the side of agent A that B will abstain from opportunism, which is the essence of "relational trust" in an economic context, determines the costs of actually accomplishing a transaction. As such, trust is functionally equivalent, albeit economically superior, to formal contracts that allow arm's-length economic exchange. More recent network research, however, has indicated that these efficiency effects are not universal but context dependent. Much depends on the level of uncertainty surrounding the exchange. Under conditions of high uncertainty the trust that is implicated in "strong ties" appears to be functional. Under conditions of low uncertainty, however, "strong ties" lose their functionality, while at the same time tying agents to networks that could block their move to other networks that offer more profitable exchange opportunities. The latter effect was nicely captured by Granovetter's "strength of weak ties" (Granovetter 1981) and Burt's notion of "structural holes" (Burt 1992), capturing the importance of combining two kinds of ties (strong and weak ties, bridging and bonding relationships) to give agents access to different kinds of information and hence to different market opportunities.

Until July 2007, the financial economy appeared to be highly transparent, resulting in an increasing proliferation of weak ties, simultaneously spanning and crossing functional, sectoral, and territorial boundaries. While "distance" did not disappear, the functional, organizational, and territorial proximities that are required under conditions of uncertainty arguably lost much of their salience. As the earlier discussion suggested, the production of trust ("we've got you covered") was largely outsourced to quasi-private rating agencies. As long as one could trust the empirical adequacy of the ratings of Moody's, Fitch, and Standard & Poor's, there was no reason to doubt the quality of the underlying instruments or the stability and creditworthiness of their "producers" and hence no need to check and double-check the flow of information on which these quasi-official assessments were based.

This radically changed in August 2007. Accustomed to an environment of calculable risk, financial agents suddenly found themselves unprepared for a situation of deep, ontological, uncertainty. The immediate effect was a return to well-tried strategies to diminish uncertainty and find a new equilibrium between information requirements and information processing capacities. According to Joel Podolny, we have to distinguish between two types of social responses to the onset of market uncertainty (Podolny 1994). The first one is well known from earlier network theorists and has played an important role in the attempt to carve out a distinct niche for economic sociology vis-à-vis neoclassical economics, namely trust building and reproduction through reiterated exchange. Under conditions of uncertainty, agents restrict their scope of action to transactions with well-tried, trusted partners.

The second one has received less attention in economic sociology and has to do with market reputation. Under conditions of uncertainty, reputation serves as a marker of trustworthiness that is functionally equivalent to the trust that is generated by reiterated exchange. As such, market reputation is especially important for less reputable agents who are "located" at a social, cultural, and territorial "distance" from the reputable agent in question, but who, because of increased contextual uncertainty, have a growing need for more and better guarantees of the trustworthiness of counterparties.

The credit crunch is an excellent example of a changing context, which has led to a general increase in the need for extra assurances of trustworthiness that fall outside the scope of the immediate observation capacities of agents. As a result of a sharp rise in cross-border financial transactions, many new financial players have simply found it impossible to assess the trustworthiness of counterparties using the well-tried techniques of repetition and proximity. Instead they have been forced to rely upon reputation. According to Podolny, the reputation effect is based on the particular way in which a field (or a market) is stratified, implying that agents predominantly prefer to trade with agents that are known to occupy the pinnacle of the market hierarchy.

In his 1994 study, Podolny demonstrated this effect through a case study of investment banking relationships. Podolny found that market reputation is a "positional good" (Hirsch 1976), or an intersubjective value that is attached to a relative position within a hierarchically stratified field. Market insiders determine the status of an agent on the basis of the relative status of its main exchange partners. In investment banking, the relative status of agents can be read off easily from the position of the name of the agent on so-called "tombstones": that is, public announcements of the relative contribution of investment banks to structured loans or emissions that are published in the business press. According to Podolny, this results in markets that are structured on the basis of status homophily, suggesting that markets with a high degree of uncertainty are hardly accessible to newcomers (Podolny 1994).

Newspaper reports of the credit crunch have amply demonstrated these two responses to uncertainty among financial agents. It was striking, for instance, that the immediate response of "bulge bracket" investment banks to the new condition of uncertainty was to cut off hedge funds and private equity funds from the existing circuits of capital. The "flight to security" that was caused by the credit crunch was in a very true sense also a "flight to familiarity"; traders and firms simply cut back on their interactions with "strangers" and newcomers and resorted to counter-parties with whom they had long-standing trading relations. In a mere couple of weeks, global trading networks were reduced to a core of long-established trading patterns in order to overcome information asymmet-ries and reduce paralyzing uncertainties.

Reputation too was in high demand, as is demonstrated by the growing market share of Goldman Sachs in the most important investment bank-ing markets (M&A, IPO's, and prime brokerage) as a result of the superior way in which it has weathered the credit crisis. However, as this example indicates, the status of financial agents appears to be highly dependent on their internal risk management procedures, implying that high pre-crunch reputations were no guarantee of good post-crunch performance. A case in point is the predicament of UBS. Highly esteemed for its suc-cessful integration of investment banking and private banking, it has become one of the main victims of the current credit crunch, earning it the moniker of "Used to Be Smart". In other words, under conditions of high volatility reputation is no longer an anchor of stability, allowing agents to determine each other's trustworthiness, but is subject to the same shifts and changes as wider market conditions, raising questions about its usefulness as a guide through uncertainty.

While the relative status position of agents is traceable through public manifestations in the form of credit ratings, quarterly reports, tombstones, and annual rankings and hence ought to be transparent for outsiders too, the huge investments in "bulge bracket" investment banks by Asian and Middle-Eastern sovereign wealth funds suggest that there are nevertheless different status perceptions by market insiders and market outsiders. According to Bloomberg the write downs and credit losses of banks as a result of the sub-prime mortgage crisis had added up to a sum total of $232 billion in August 2008 (FT 2008). As a result banks have been forced to find fresh sources of capital to shore up their tier 1 capital ratio. Right before the fall of Lehmann, banks had received a total of $84 billion in capital injections, most of it from capital providers from South-East Asia and the Middle East. While the recipients are highly reputable banks such as Merrill Lynch, Citigroup, Barclays, UBS, and Bank of America, the fact that Western institutional investors shun the shares of these banks raises interesting questions concerning the distribution of reputation-related information. Apparently there is a certain time-lag between different types of investors in their response to the ups and downs of reputations in volatile market conditions, suggesting the importance of direct linkages to the core of the financial market networks and indicating the relatively peripheral position within these networks of most sovereign wealth funds—although it is fair to say that next time around that will probably be different.

A response to market uncertainty not discussed by Podolny but clearly relevant for an adequate understanding of the current credit crisis, is the complete breakdown of market exchange. Striking about what happened after the sub-prime mortgage crisis in the United States broke out, is the steep fall in the sale of securitized assets in both the United States and Europe. For some securitized asset markets this means a virtual disappearance. Apparently, uncertainty can reach such levels that liquidity dries up, resulting in an inability to determine prices or in erratic price formation, which in turn enhances the solvency problems of banks and sharpens the downward pressures on activity in financial markets that in a substantive sense have nothing to do with the valuation problems in the markets where the credit crisis originated.

## What are the spatial consequences?

Throughout this chapter I have suggested that the return of uncertainty might well mean a return of spatial proximity. While transparent markets can never be a-spatial, since in a deep sense every mode of social action takes place in a spatio-temporal "fluidium", market contexts that are highly similar to spot markets and are hence built around transparent products whose trading is free from information asymmetries, generally lack the social structuring that is caused by "spatial variegation" (Brenner, Jessop, and Peck 2009). Here I play upon the distinction drawn by Andrew Sayer between space as "medium", space as "effect", and space as "cause" (Sayer 2000, 106–29). While ontologically speaking every social action has to occur within the medium of space, it is much rarer that space has an empirically identifiable causal effect on that action. That is to say, human action always has spatial articulations, but is only rarely causally determined by those articulations.

While this proposition has universal theoretical validity, geographers have so far failed to consider to what extent its validity is determined by contingent conditions. As this chapter has tried to argue, space is more causally relevant under conditions of uncertainty than under conditions of risk. In other words, it is the nature of the available information on which agents base their actions that determines to what extent space is merely a medium or has causal effects. The analysis given above indicates that conditions of risk generate different spatial patterns than do conditions of uncertainty. Under conditions of risk, information asymmetries are few and far between, and are thus only of limited value to market participants, resulting in expanding trading networks and increasing reputational egalitarianism. Since all relevant information is immediately and equally available to all, in theory there can be no cognitive differences between agents and hence there is no need for extra-market guarantees. Of course, this is a verbal description of the empirical implications of the mathematical assumptions of Efficient Market Theory and hence an idealized description of the financial markets up to July 2007. Nevertheless, by and large financial agents and markets functioned as if the description was empirically adequate, lending a large dose of empirical validity to MacKenzie's performativity thesis.

However, since August 2007, space has become causally relevant again. The drying up of markets has clear spatial consequences in the sense that it has resulted in a diminished accessibility of financial markets for marginal and peripheral agents, suggesting that trading relations are once again determined by the locality of the counterparty. Striking is the indirect spatial effect this has had on the investment strategies of the most nimble financial players around, namely investment banks, and the investment banking units of commercial banks. The drying up of markets in the core regions of the world has led to a significant shift of resources and capital to newly arising investment banking markets in South-East Asia and South America. Many investments banking units now have just as many high-ranking officers in Asia as they have in Europe and the United States, suggesting a long-term structural economic power shift to what used to be described as the "periphery" in Wallerstein's World Systems Theory (Wallerstein 1974; see Mahbubani 2008).

The increased functionality of network generated trust to overcome the insecurities of uncertainty also has spatial consequences, which feed back into the market structure and can hence be said to have spatial effects. If we limit our analysis to investment banking, the credit crunch is pushing the remaining investments banks from "transaction banking" back to the earlier business model of "relational banking" (Augar 2005; Knee 2006). This can be seen to strengthen the importance of historically vested relations between banks and bankers and hence of proximity for the enactment of financial transactions. Of course, due to modern transportation and ICT, proximity does not automatically entail co-location, but it does denote the salience of physical interactions in order to have access to extra-economic sources of information on the trustworthiness, cognitive capacities, and risk assessment qualities of counterparties.

Finally, the importance of reputation under conditions of uncertainty also appeared to be clearly spatially determined, albeit in a rather paradoxical way. That has to do, first, with the functional equivalence of reputation-effects to proximity-based trust, which is especially useful for peripheral agents who are at a distance from the core of financial market networks. So, although reputation works across space, its increasing salience under conditions of uncertainty indicates a financial field that is itself spatially structured. Second, there appears to be a delay in the speed with which new information affecting the reputation of agents gets digested by counterparties. That is to say, the field of finance is hierarchically stratified, implying that reputational damages at the top reach agents located at the base last. The massive way in which peripheral sovereign wealth funds have invested in endangered American and European banks suggests that they have based their decisions on the reputations of yesterday and have failed to factor in more recent information about the extent to which these banks have been implicated in financial innovations gone sour.

In a more theoretical vein, the analysis presented in this chapter suggests strong similarities between the research agendas of network theorists and financial geographers. Both aim to determine the importance of social and hence spatial structuring for the functioning of markets, without claiming, however, that that is all there is to know. While it is obvious that every economic action is simultaneously social, in a theoretical sense this is not a very illuminating proposition. What we need to know is under which conditions socio-spatiality is causally relevant and under which conditions it is merely a medium of articulation. Using the latest research from economic sociology and geography this chapter has tried to provide a tentative answer to this question for the highly complex, immensely fascinating, and morally extremely ambiguous field of finance.

## Note

1. An earlier version of this chapter was presented at the 2008 Annual Meeting of the Association of American Geographers in Boston, during a session organized by the editors of this book. The author wishes to thank the editors for their initiative and the valuable feedback received over the course of this project. The research on which this chapter builds forth was made possible by a VIDI-grant

from the Dutch Scientific Council, grant number 452-05-347. Of course, I take full responsibility for any sins of omission and commission.

## References

Augar, P. (2005). *The Greed Merchants. How the Investment Banks Played the Free Market Game*. London: Allen Lane.

Bashkar, R. (1975). *A Realist Theory of Science*. Leeds: Leeds Books.

BIS (2008*a*). OTC derivatives market activity in the second half of 2007. In www. bis.org, accessed 10 September 2008.

BIS (2008*b*). Statistics on exchange traded derivatives. In www.bis.org, accessed 10 September 2008.

Brenner, N., Peck, J., and Theodore, N. (2009). Variegated neoliberalization. Geographies, modalities, pathways. Unpublished manuscript. Center for Urban Economic Development (CUED), University of Illinois, Chicago.

Burt, R. (1992). *Structural Holes. The Social Structure of Competition*. Cambridge: Harvard University Press.

Cairncross, F. (1998). *The Death of Distance. How the Communications Revolution Will Change our Lives*. London: Orion Business Books.

Callon, M. (1998). *The Laws of the Markets*. Oxford: Blackwell.

—— , Méadal, C., and Rabeharisoa, V. (2005). The economy of qualities. In A. Barry and D. Slater (ed.), *The Technological Economy* (pp. 28–50). London: Routledge.

Cassis, Y. (2006). *Capitals of Capital. A History of International Financial Centres, 1780–2005*. Cambridge: Cambridge University Press.

Castells, M. (1996). *The Information Age. Economy, Society, and Culture*. Vol. 1: *The Rise of the Network Society*. Oxford: Blackwell.

Erturk, I. and Solari, S. (2007). Banks as continuous reinvention. *New Political Economy*, 12, 369–88.

ESF (2008). ESF Securitisation Data Report 2007. In www.europeansecuritisation. com, accessed 10 September 2008.

Fligstein, N. and Dauter, L. (2007). The Sociology of Markets. *Annual Review of Sociology*, 33, 105–28.

FT (2008). Writedown League Tables. In www.ft.com, accessed 10 September 2008.

Granovetter, M. (1981). The Strength of Weak Ties. A Network Theory Revisited. Paper presented at the Albany Conference on contributions of network analysis to structural sociology, April 3–4, 1981.

—— (1985). Economic action and social structure. The problem of embeddedness. *American Journal of Sociology*, 91, 481–510.

Greenspan, A. (2008). The world must repel calls to contain competitive markets. *Financial Times*, 6 August 2008.

Hayek, F. A. (1949).The use of knowledge in society. *American Economic Review*, 35, 519–30.

Hirsch, F. (1976). *Social Limits to Growth*. London: Routledge & Kegan Paul.

Hodgson, G. (1993). *Economics and Evolution. Bringing Life Back into Economics*. Cambridge: Polity.

IFSL (2008). Securitisation 2008. In www.ifsl.org.uk/research, accessed 10 September 2008.

IMF (2008). *Global Financial Stability Report*. Washington: IMF.

Institutional Investor News (2007). *The 2007 Global Securitization Guide. A Compendium of Legal and Market Developments in Securitization*. New York: Institutional Investor.

Kindleberger, C. P. (2000). *Manias, Panics, and Crashes. A History of Financial Crises*. New York: Wiley.

Knee, J. A. (2006). *The Accidental Investment Banker*. New York: Random.

Knight, F. H. (1921). *Risk, Uncertainty and Profit*. Boston: Houghton Mifflin.

Kynaston, D. (1997). *LIFFE: A Market and its Makers*. Cambridge: Granta.

MacKenzie, D. (2006). *An Engine, Not a Camera. How Financial Models Shape Markets*. Cambridge: MIT Press.

—— , Muniesa, F., and Siu, L. (eds.) (2007). *Do Economists Make Markets? On the Performativity of Economics*. Princeton: Princeton University Press.

Mahbubani, K. (2008). *The Rise of the Eastern Hemisphere. The Irresistible Shift of Global Power to the East*. New York: Public Affairs.

Morgan, G. (2008). Market formation and governance in international financial markets. The case of OTC derivatives. *Human Relations*, 61, 637–60.

O'Brien, R. (1992). *Global Financial Integration. International Capital Markets in the Age of Reason*. London: The Royal Institute of International Affairs.

Podolny, J. (1994). Market uncertainty and the social character of economic exchange. *Administrative Science Quarterly*, 39, 458–83.

Sayer, A. (2000). *Realism and Social Science*. London: Sage.

Strange, S. (1996). *The Retreat of the State. The Diffusion of Power in the World Economy*. Cambridge: Cambridge University Press.

Tett, G. (2006). The dream machine. *FT Weekend Magazine*, March 25, 20–8.

—— (2008). Derivative thinking. *FT Weekend Magazine*, May 30, 1–5.

Tufano, P. (1989). Financial innovation and first-mover advantage. *Journal of Financial Economics*, 25, 213–40.

Wallerstein, I. (1974). *The Modern World System I. Capitalist Agriculture and the Origins of the European World-Economy in the 16th Century*. New York: Academic Press.

WFE (2007). Annual Report 2007. In www.world-exchanges.org, accessed 10 September 2008.

# 6

# The Role of Proximity in Secondary Equity Markets

*Dariusz Wójcik*

Equity is considered a high-return–high-risk class of assets. Between 1900 and 2000 the US equity markets have yielded an arithmetic average of 8.7 per cent per year above inflation, with the standard deviation of 20.2 per cent, compared to US bonds with real returns of 2.1 per cent per year and standard deviation of 10 per cent (Dimson et al. 2002). While the attraction of investing in equity is obvious, the challenge of managing risks involved in such investments is steep. The most powerful invention that has responded to this challenge, the Modern Portfolio Theory (MPT), tells investors to diversify investments as widely as possible, moving toward a portfolio with equity from individual countries held in proportion to their share in the global equity market capitalization. This prescription, however, is based on the assumption that equity markets are informationally efficient, that is, all information relevant to equity prices is built into them, and consequently it is impossible to beat the market other than by chance and by incurring unnecessarily high risks. Contrary to the assumption of the MPT, information on equity markets is not ubiquitous; it is not available to everybody at negligible cost. This chapter will show that an important way in which investors on equity markets manage their risks is by taking advantage of proximity to the sources of information relevant to equity prices.

The key source of information relevant to equity prices and investigated in this chapter will be equity issuers themselves. This chapter will argue that proximity between investors and corporations (equity issuers) plays an important part in explaining the behavior and performance of investors in secondary equity markets. By extension it provides a significant insight into the performance of equity markets themselves. It should be made clear from the outset that this chapter does not focus on the role of proximity or closeness between investors themselves or issuers themselves, or between stock exchanges on one side and corporate issuers or investors on the other. Nor does it focus on the position of equity analysts or market makers in relation to other actors and institutions. It goes without saying that investors and issuers are the central actors for whom secondary equity markets actually exist. While actors such as stock exchanges, analysts, or market makers provide important infrastructure and services, the key to understanding the secondary equity markets lies in the relationships between investors and equity issuers. To be sure, other types of relationships and proximity will not be ignored. They will be considered to the extent they relate to the proximity between investors and issuers. Readers interested in these other types of proximity in their own right are referred to Wójcik (2007) and Lo and Grote (2002).

The role of proximity between investors and issuers on secondary equity markets will be explored by investigating the following issues. How important is proximity in managing risks involved in equity investments? Why is it important? What are the implications of its role for secondary equity markets and beyond these markets? What are the limits to the role of proximity and how is it likely to change in the future? To address these issues I use recent research findings from both financial economics and economic geography. Combining the two bodies of research, I hope to show in detail how and why both global and local factors matter in financial markets, and to uncover some of the intricate relationships between place, proximity, and financial risk management.

## Proximity matters – evidence on home bias and local bias

In the first step of exploring the role of proximity in managing equity investment risk, I will focus on two related facets of investors' behavior – home bias and local bias. There is mounting evidence that investors exhibit a preference for trading and holding domestic shares, issued by companies in their home country, and within the home country they prefer to trade and hold shares of companies that are headquartered close to the location of investors in question. This applies to both institutional and individual investors, who by doing so forgo the potential benefits of portfolio diversification both at the international and domestic level. The magnitude of what has been termed as "home bias" and "local bias" respectively, is significant. According to Stulz (2005) in 2003 US investors held more than 85 per cent of their equity portfolio in domestic equities, while the share of the US equity market in the world equity market capitalization was approximately 45 per cent. Coval and Moskowitz (1999) estimate that in the United States approximately one in ten companies in a fund manager's portfolio is chosen because it is located in the same city as the manager. Ivković and Weisbrenner (2005) document that on average a US individual investor holds approximately 30 per cent of his/her equity portfolio in the stocks of companies headquartered within 250 miles, while the share of such firms in the total US equity market is on average only approximately 10 per cent. Loughran and Schultz (2004) show that firms in blizzard-struck cities in the United States see a dramatic trading volume drop in their stocks compared to firms in other cities, and that the Yom Kippur holiday dampens trading volumes in companies located in cities with large Jewish populations. While the bulk of research on proximity in secondary equity markets is based on the US data, "home bias" is well documented across at least developed economies (e.g., Sorensen et al. 2004, cited in Stulz 2005), while countries for which evidence on local bias is available include also China, Germany, Sweden, and Finland.

There are different types of proximity to issuers that seem to matter for investors. Home bias goes beyond simple preference for domestic vis-à-vis foreign stocks. It has been shown that investors are more likely to hold and trade foreign stocks from countries that are closer in terms of physical distance, travel cost or adjacency. In addition, Portes and Rey (2005) show that cross-border equity flows are also related positively to the telephone call traffic between countries, a variable that can represent economic and cultural ties. Hau (2001) documents that traders trading on proprietary accounts in the German blue-chip stocks, and located in Germany, Austria, or Switzerland outperform traders located in non-German speaking countries.

Most studies on local bias have used administrative boundaries within countries, analyzing investors' preference for in-state vis-à-vis out-of-state investments (Huberman 2001) and for investments in firms headquartered within an arbitrarily determined radius from an investor's location (Coval and Moskowitz 2001; Ivković and Weisbrenner 2005). Here, the thresholds of 250 or 100 kilometers have been most commonly used for distinguishing between local and non-local investments. There are however studies that account for other types of proximity than that between investor location and issuer headquarters. Bodnaruk (2004) finds that Swedish investors are more likely to hold shares in companies that have an establishment, but not necessarily the headquarters, located nearby. Grinblatt and Keloharju (2001) demonstrate that Swedish speaking investors living in Finland are more likely to trade stocks in companies that publish their annual financial reports in Swedish in addition to the Finnish language, and in those that have Swedish speaking CEOs. Finally, Massa and Simonov (2006) show that Swedish investors are more likely to invest in companies that have the same area of activity as the investor's profession. However, they find that geographical proximity is more important to portfolio composition than professional proximity.

The significance of proximity is also shown in a dynamic context, accounting for the mobility of investors and issuers. Available studies are rare, nevertheless they provide significant results. For Sweden, Massa and Simonov (2006) show that individual investors who moved recently or changed or lost their job exhibit less local bias. Bodnaruk (2004), however, documents that when individuals move they do sell stocks of companies from their old locations and buy those from new locations. With regard to the issuers, Prinsky and Wang (2006) find that in the United States, when a company moves headquarters, the co-movement of its stock market price with companies from old location declines, and that with companies from the new location rises.

Summarizing, research on home and local bias has generated dozens of papers in the leading journals in finance, some of which have received prestigious awards (Coval and Moskowitz 1999; Hau 2001). In short, the evidence on the role of geographical proximity in secondary equity markets is well established and is here to stay. There can be no doubts that home and local bias are fundamentally related to investors' perception and approach to risk, as it is impossible to assume that investors in so many different contexts simply consider domestic and local stocks as those offering higher returns regardless of risk. However, can one really claim that the geographical biases reflect any conscious act of financial risk management that goes beyond mere ignorance and uncertainty about far-away firms? The multiple and often complex ways in which proximity matters to individual as well as institutional investors suggest the operation of real risk management, but to answer this question satisfactorily we need to delve deeper into the issue of why home and local bias exist. In what follows I focus on explanations based on information.

## Explaining investment bias with information

According to Merton, "investors buy and hold only those securities about which they have enough information" (1987 cited in Massa and Simonov 2006, 640). But what does "enough" information mean? And what kind of information? To put it crudely, in order to invest in a security an investor has to know of it and something about it. In other words, he/she has to be familiar with it. Geographical proximity is without doubt an instrumental factor of familiarity. Investors' knowledge about the world of equity is biased toward local equity, as they consume products and services of local companies, have colleagues who work for local firms, and are exposed to local media that write about local economy. Put differently, firms are more visible to local investors than to remote ones. As Barber and Odean (2008) argue, with approximately 7,000 listed companies in the United States the world of equity investments is a world of information overload, and investors are bound to use mental shortcuts to make investment decisions. As a result home and local bias could be just behavioral biases.

If home and local bias were nothing more than behavioral biases driven by pure familiarity, they would give investors no edge in relation to non-proximate (foreign or non-local) investors. This contention, however, is unsustainable in the view of evidence that investors can earn superior returns on proximate stocks. Shukla and van Inwegen (1995) find that UK mutual fund managers investing in the US underperform relative to their US colleagues. Coval and Moskowitz (2001) show that mutual funds generate large gains from local investments (defined as holdings within 100 km of the fund headquarters), outperforming distant holdings by as much as 3 per cent per year, and outpacing local stocks not held by 4–5 per cent, on a risk-adjusted basis. Hau (2001) documents that traders proximate to the headquarters of issuers generate superior returns from intraday trading in the stocks of these companies. Ivković and Weisbrenner (2005) show that the US households on average generated an additional annualized return of 3.2 per cent from their local holdings relative to non-local holdings. Superior returns from local investment have also been documented for individual investors in Sweden (Massa and Simonov 2006; Bodnaruk 2004) and China (Feng and Seasholes 2004). Research testing the performance of actors other than investors also, albeit indirectly, lends support to the role of local informational advantage. Malloy (2005) demonstrates that in the United States geographically proximate equity analysts produce more accurate forecasts and recommendations than other analysts, while Madureira and Underwood (2007) analyze market making in Nasdaq stocks, and find out that market makers located within 100 kilometers of a firm provide more liquidity and contribute more to price discovery than more distant market makers.

Growing evidence that local investors can outperform remote investors on local stocks, does not imply that familiarity effect does not exist. Rather it suggests that investors can turn familiarity to their own advantage by gaining superior information in relation to non-local investors. In other words, there is an information asymmetry between local and non-local investors. What information then could be available to local investors that is not available to the remote ones? Local investors can talk to employees, managers, and suppliers of the firm; they may obtain information from local media; they may use the company's products and services more often and be better able to judge their quality; and they may have personal ties with corporate executives (Coval and Moskowitz 1999). Geographical proximity may help better understanding of the technical aspects of a firm's operations, as well as the cost of evaluating intangible factors such as management ability and corporate culture (Gaspar and Massa 2007). It also improves information about the local business climate. Information with regard to which local investors have an advantage is usually associated with soft (in contrast to hard) and private (in contrast to publicly available) information. The term soft information is usually used interchangeably with tacit information (Gertler 2003) and means information that is hard to communicate to others, let alone capture in written documents. Private information can be defined as that obtained from corporate insiders and not available to the public. Geographical proximity can be crucial in helping investors to access and interpret soft and private information relevant to the value of corporate equity. A remote investor can access public and hard information, for example, by reading local newspapers from far-away places on the internet, but may have difficulty to interpret this information, and may be right to suspect that many local investors will have already had this information for some time.

The role of soft and private information can be corroborated with research showing how different characteristics of stocks affect the existence and degree of local bias and superior performance of local investors. There is evidence that local bias applies particularly to investment in small, highly levered firms that produce non-traded goods, for example, firms in the services sector (Coval and Moskowitz 1999). Non-local investors are less likely to be familiar with and possess high-quality information about small firms that do not sell their products or services on a country-wide basis. A similar logic applies to firms with high leverage, which means that firm profitability is particularly sensitive to small changes in revenue and/ or costs. It is with regard to such firms that the informational asymmetry between local and non-local investors seems to be the largest. In addition, there is evidence that superior returns realized by local institutional and individual investors are particularly high for investment in smaller companies located in remote areas of the United States (Coval and Moskowitz 2001; Ivković and Weisbrenner 2005). This suggests that barriers experienced by geographical outsiders are more pronounced with regard to firms from small towns and rural areas than those from large urban centers. Importantly, the results on market makers and equity analysts also show that the superior performance of local actors is particularly strong in relation to small firms and firms located outside major metropolitan areas (Malloy 2005; Madureira and Underwood 2007).

What type of local investors would we expect to possess more informational advantage? As individual investors are less sophisticated, that is, they have on average smaller resources and less expertise than institutional investors, we can expect them to exhibit more familiarity bias. Findings by Grinblatt and Keloharju (2001) for Finland, seem to support the role of investor sophistication by showing that local bias is less prominent among investment-savvy institutions (corporate, for-profit institutions) than among households and less investment-savvy institutions (government and non-profit institutions). The role of investor sophistication is further supported by Massa and Simonov (2006), showing that the degree of local bias is related negatively to individual investors' wealth. To the best of my knowledge, however, there is no research yet that relates the local information premium to investors' sophistication or wealth.

There is a potential use of information on local issuers that we have not yet mentioned. Investors can buy or sell local stocks based on positive or negative signals, but instead of selling that may also influence the management of the issuer, for example, by communicating the threat to "walk away" through informal channels like phone calls or meetings with the management. Of course, the power of investors to exercise voice in place of exit would depend on the size of their shareholdings, and as such is likely to be of particular significance for large individual or institutional investors. Consistently with this proposition, Gaspar and Massa (2007) show that firms that have a larger fraction of shares owned by local in relation to remote mutual funds exhibit better corporate governance, reflected in lower investment rates and fewer but better acquisitions. This suggests that proximity between investors and issuers could reduce agency problem, that is, the problem of aligning managerial (agents') incentives with investors' (principals') interests. The role of proximity in corporate governance should be highlighted as an important subject for further research.

The last question we need to address in our exposition of theories explaining home and local bias with information is whether the informational advantage of local investors is enhanced by social interaction among investors themselves. In other words, the question is whether social proximity among investors affects their informational advantage and how it relates to proximity between investors and issuers. After all people talk about the prospects of the local economy and local companies as a matter of everyday life. Indeed, Hong, Kubik, and Stein (2004) demonstrate that in the United States the more socially active households are more likely to invest in the equity market. Prinsky and Wang (2006) document strong co-movement in the stock returns of firms headquartered in the same area, and attribute this finding to the proposition that physical proximity enables social interaction, which in turn promotes the transmission of investment sentiment and information among members of the community.

While we need to appreciate the role of social interaction among investors, findings by Feng and Seasholes (2004) suggest that proximity among investors plays a secondary part to proximity between investors and issuers. The paper analyzes trades of investors in Guangdong in southern China, who for years queue and place their orders at one and the same of a number of brokerage houses, as well as trades of investors from Shanghai, with all trades referring to stocks of firms headquartered in Guangdong. One result is that the correlation of net trades within brokerage houses in Guangdong is not higher at all than the correlation across the brokerage houses in the province. There is, in turn, a significant negative correlation between the net trades of investors in Guangdong and Shanghai. When Guangdong investors are net buyers (sellers), the Shanghai investors tend to be net sellers (buyers), and typically investors from Guangdong time their trades more profitably than their Shanghai counterparts. The authors conclude that these results rule out group psychology as the predominant force driving investment decisions.

Summarizing the section, recent research makes a strong case for the explanation of the home and the local bias based on information. This explanation addresses the major weakness of the Modern Portfolio Theory and the Capital Asset Pricing Model, that is, the assumption of ubiquitous information, and the resulting universal recommendation of portfolio diversification. As Mark Twain put it in his definition of success in 1894: "Behold, the fool saith, 'Put not all thine eggs in the one basket' – which is but a manner of saying, 'Scatter your money and your attention'; but the wise man saith, 'Put all your eggs in one basket and watch the basket'." (cited in Ivković and Weisbrenner 2005, 267). It appears that proximity is crucial to both choosing and watching the basket.

## Alternative explanations of the investment bias

To be sure there are alternative theories that try to explain the investment bias without recourse to information. Let us start with alternative explanations for the home bias. First, international diversification could be hampered by formal restrictions on cross-border equity trading. Available research, however, suggests that capital controls have been largely removed, at least between developed economies (Kaminsky and Schmuckler 2003). In addition, if formal restrictions were to blame, why would we still find a high degree of home bias within the European Union including Euro zone (Wójcik 2002)? Another alternative is that investors face higher transaction costs, such as brokerage commissions or clearing and settlement costs, in trading equity across borders than in trading domestically. While this is a valid factor, seeing it as a major determinant of the home bias would be inconsistent with findings that cross-border equity trading actually exhibits higher frequency than domestic equity trading (Tesar and Werner 1995). Yet another explanation has been that a large fraction of the capitalization of foreign markets is simply not available on public stock markets, as it is controlled by dominant owners, including home country governments (Stulz 2005). This proposition modifies the recommendation of the Modern Portfolio Theory, whereby investors should diversify their equity portfolio according to the market value of the free-floating equity. This, however, can explain home bias only to a small degree, and in particular, is inconsistent with low shares of US equity in the portfolios of non-US investors (Dahlquist et al. 2003).

Moving to the factors underpinning local bias, there are three groups of explanations competing with the information effects. First, investors may feel more charitable about the familiar and local companies, and feel a desire to invest in them rather than in unfamiliar companies. Second, they may obtain or at least hope to obtain non-investment benefits that will compensate them for the opportunity cost of investing in local companies (Landier, Nair, and Wulf 2009). They may be employees who invest in their own companies, hoping that this increases their chances of keeping their jobs. They may be their neighbors, including shopkeepers hoping to contribute to the prevention of high unemployment and all its negative economic and non-economic implications in the community. Finally, according to the third explanation investors could face competition for local resources, such as real estate, labour, and services, within their community. If supply of these resources is relatively inelastic, their price goes up with the wealth of the community. Investors may hedge against the risk of local price increases by tilting their portfolio toward local stocks (Bodnaruk 2004; DeMarzo, Kaniel, and Kremer 2004).

It should be noted that the roles of charitable motives, non-investment benefits, and local competition in explaining home bias are all about proximity between investors and issuers, represent profoundly economic geographical issues, and as such are extremely valuable directions for future research. Nevertheless, they represent alternatives to the explanations based on information. While they all suggest plausible factors behind local bias (and by extension potentially home bias as well), they cannot explain why investors can obtain superior returns on local investments, and as such do not undermine the explanation based on information.

## Implications for investment firms and issuers

So far it has been shown that investors can obtain superior returns on local investments, and that this is most likely due to the use of soft and private information in contrast to hard and public information about issuers. This has significant implications for the size and structure of investment firms, and by extension the whole investment industry. According to a model developed by Stein (2002), "small firms are at a competitive advantage in evaluating investment projects when the information about these projects is soft and cannot be credibly communicated from one agent in the firm to another. In contrast, large firms do relatively well when information about investment projects can be easily 'hardened' and passed along within the hierarchy" (Berger et al. 2005, 239). This does not rule large firms out altogether, but it means that large firms that want to use soft information effectively need to avoid high levels of centralization and hierarchy. In Stein's words (2002, 1894): "holding the firm's size and scope fixed, the softness of information will tend to imply that a flatter organisational structure, with fewer layers of management, is more attractive". What is therefore suggested is an inverse relationship between the degree of centralization and hierarchy in investment firms and the role of soft information in investment projects they deal with. To put it simply, to take advantage of soft information in secondary equity markets you may need to be close to issuers, but you may also need to be small. And if you want to run a large investment institution that is close to many different places, and at the same time enjoys economies of scale, you need to be careful to maintain a relatively decentralized and non-hierarchical organization. In other words geographical proximity can be overcome with organizational proximity but only to a certain extent, and only under certain conditions. Empirical research in both geography and financial economics illustrates the implications of proximity and soft information for investment firms. Jones (2002) shows that branches of international investment banks enjoy a relatively high degree of autonomy in decision-making. Chen et al. (2004) demonstrate that small mutual funds are not only more likely than their larger counterparts to invest in local stocks, but they also earn superior returns on these investments.

We can also look at the relationship between investment firm size and soft information from the perspective of equity issuers or firms seeking capital in general. If financing a firm involves a relatively large amount of soft information (due to the nature of the projects to be financed and/or the nature of the firm, in particular its smallness) then the suitable sources of finance would be investment firms that are local and small rather than remote and large, or at least large investment firms whose local units have sufficient decision-making power. This resonates with Klagge and Martin (2005, 414) arguing that "[...] the presence of local critical mass of financial institutions and agents – that is, of a regionally identifiable, coherent and functioning market – enables local institutions, small and medium size enterprises, and local investors to exploit the benefits of being in close spatial proximity". In other words, the spatially limited circulation of soft and private information implies a certain degree of spatial fragmentation of secondary equity markets, limited mobility of capital, and spatially restricted access to capital. Of course, secondary equity markets are not a direct source of capital for firms. Potential for an active and highly liquid secondary market for a security, however, is crucial, as it improves the chances of the security being issued in the first place. If investors tend to trade in local stocks, then rural and provincial firms could find it more difficult to access equity markets, since these areas offer fewer potential investors than large urban centers. Consistently with this proposition, Loughran and Schultz (2006) find that rural firms wait longer to go public, are less likely to conduct seasoned equity offerings, and have more debt in their corporate structure than otherwise similar urban firms. Wójcik (2007*b*) documents that in Europe, the United States, and Japan, large firms from capital cities are more likely to be listed on stock markets than their provincial counterparts. The role of proximity in the circulation of information on secondary equity markets could influence firms' access to capital but also firms' capital structure, as firms facing barriers to access equity market turn to debt financing.

## The limits to proximity

### Trade-off between proximity and liquidity

If it is so well documented that proximity can improve investors' information about opportunities and risks of equity investment, why are not secondary equity markets exclusively local markets? One important, though not exclusive, explanation involves a trade-off between informational benefits afforded by proximity and liquidity. What is crucial is that an informational advantage to local investors is a disadvantage to non-local investors. The larger the local informational advantage, the less likely non-local investors are to trade a given stock. Local investors can enjoy informational benefits that could improve the risk-return characteristics of their equity investments, but suffer from liquidity risk, the risk of not having a liquid market where they can exit from their investments. At the extreme, with very high local informational advantages, local investors would have nobody but themselves to trade with, and firms would have nowhere but the local pool of investors to draw their equity capital from.

The proximity–liquidity trade-off creates incentives for issuers but also for investors to support the developments that lower the informational disadvantages perceived and experienced by non-local investors. Investors may for example support regulatory measures aimed at increasing corporate transparency. Issuers can actively try to overcome the informational disadvantage to non-local investors by increasing their visibility in non-local markets, providing non-local investment communities with more and higher quality information, and introducing measures, such as internal control procedures and external audits, that minimize the leakages of inside information from the company. For small firms, it may be too costly relative to the firm's resources to overcome these barriers and they are likely to settle on a combination with high level of proximity-based investment and low level of liquidity. Fortunately in a sense, small firms may also have relatively small needs for equity capital, which can be satisfied on local markets. Firms producing non-tradeable goods and services (in contrast to high-technology firms that may obtain high visibility relatively easily) and provincial and rural firms may find themselves in the worst situation. Due to their sectoral and geographical nature, non-local investors may perceive their informational disadvantage as so large, that to overcome these barriers would be too costly for firms. At the same time, there may not be sufficient capital available locally. Consistently with this proposition, Loughran and Schultz (2005) suggest that in the United States, controlling for other factors such as size and sector, rural stocks have lower liquidity than urban stocks. It is possible that this gap can be filled with other sources of finance, such as credit (Loughran and Schultz 2006), but it is also possible that some firms will end up incurring a higher overall cost of capital (see Francis, Hasan, and Waisman 2007 on higher cost of debt capital in rural United States).

There is a further complication of the proximity–liquidity trade-off that appears if we consider that local investors can use voice in addition to exit. This implies that local informed investors could improve the governance of the issuer and induce shareholder value enhancing decisions such as less over-investment, and fewer but better acquisitions. The benefits of improved governance could then be shared with all investors, including non-local and non-informed ones. To be sure, however, local investors would still have informational advantage with adverse impact on liquidity. Thus, on the one hand the stock price could go up (and the risk premium required by investors go down) due to improvements in governance; on the other it could be reduced (risk premium increased) by adverse impact on liquidity. Research on the net effect is only emerging, with Dass and Massa (2008) suggesting that more local banking relationships of issuers in the United States improve their governance and bring stock market liquidity down, but the net effect on firm value (measured as Tobin's q and stock price appreciation) is positive. Thus, the trade-off between proximity and liquidity is not just about the relationship between local and non-local investors, it is also about the balance of local ownership and monitoring versus liquidity.

### Beyond the distinction between soft and hard information

In my view the main weakness of the existing research in financial economics analyzing the role of proximity in secondary equity markets is not its reliance on proximity defined as physical distance (which is considered as an empirical necessity rather than a conceptual statement), but the simplistic and often silent assumptions about the nature of the distinction between soft and hard information. First, soft information, defined as information that cannot be transferred over distance, is by definition local, and consequently soft information *from* individual issuers is as dispersed as the location of their decision-making establishments (or simply headquarters). This, however, does not mean that all soft information *about* issuers is dispersed. Successful assessment of investment opportunities and risks in equity markets requires comparisons between companies, knowledge of whole sectors, comparisons across sectors, and the knowledge of non-local and global business climate. Information, often of qualitative nature, that allows such assessments may also be local, but is likely to be concentrated in large urban financial centers, with large institutional and individual investment communities and intensive interaction among them, both inside organizations and between them. Importantly, large urban financial centers are also concentrations of issuers' headquarters.

Second, soft information in secondary equity markets should not be associated with sophisticated information in contrast to hard information considered unsophisticated. Mathematics and economics involved in equity trading may range from simple ratios such as P/E (market price to earnings) to complex mathematical formulae used in arbitrage and derivative trading, but arguably even the understanding of a P/E ratio is not common among individual investors. Sophistication in the use of hard information, combined with the use of soft information local to large urban financial centers can compensate for the lack of proximity. Corroborating this hypothesis, Malloy (2005) reviews research showing that in Latin America foreign equity analysts outperform local analysts; in the Taiwanese market foreign equity analysts that have a local research group outperform foreigners without local presence, but also outperform local analysts; while in Europe home country analysts outperform foreign analysts. These results underscore the significance of investor sophistication and financial literacy. If proximity ruled the world of investment unchallenged, non-local investors could only pursue passive investment strategies, leaving all active investment (stock picking) to locals. In reality, foreign investors can be active and successful.

My argument is not about a world of secondary equity markets where local investors use soft information from local issuers and compete against non-local investors who leverage their chances with soft information about markets as a whole and with the sophistication in the use of hard information. This picture would miss a part of the investment industry that is trying to follow both strategies, by combining local information with global information. Combining information and people from different places can help such firms to achieve some degree of cognitive distance between professionals within a firm, which is desirable for innovative investment activity (Boschma 2005). For example, a person from a local branch may recommend buying stocks based on soft information on a specific issuer, but analysts at the headquarters may disagree based on their interpretation of hard information and their judgment of the whole sector or market. Arguably, investment success or indeed innovation in investment can be achieved through such confrontations of different types of information from different sources. As literature suggests, both too much and too little cognitive distance may be bad for innovation. Financial experts, however, use common language and English financial terms, and a common toolbox of financial theories (Clark and Wójcik 2007), which may assure that even combining people with their ideas from different places may not create a too large cognitive dissonance within organizations.

The argument in favor of the use of information sources that are both local and non-local to specific actors on secondary equity markets resonates with that of Bathelt et al. (2004), who claim that knowledge creation in firms depends on the coexistence of high levels of local buzz and pipelines – channels of communication with non-local actors. The metaphor of local buzz may in fact be very useful in the context of secondary equity market for yet another reason. Buzz contains both grains and chaff, and it may be difficult to separate one from the other. As such, local information may fuel local herd behavior. Following DeMarzo, Kaniel, and Kremer (2004), imagine an IT engineer in Silicon Valley who decides to invest a lot in IT stocks. His neighbors, who do not work in IT, have a good reason to follow, as their income is less dependent on the IT boom, but their costs of living very much so. While an IT engineer may engage in pure speculation, his neighbors hedge their consumption. Thus, consumption motives may aggravate localized herd behavior. On the other hand, Coval and Moskowitz (2001) use evidence from the United States to argue that fund managers herd most strongly in distant firms and break away from the herd in their local investments. According to the authors this reveals fund managers' tendency to free ride on the information of others by following the herd in remote stocks.

Thus, we have established that there is a price to pay for exercising proximity in secondary equity markets. One is the cost of lost liquidity. Another is the threat of investors relying on local information at the expense of external pools of knowledge that may also be valuable to investment activities, and central to innovative investment. A related threat is that of local information being too homogeneous and fueling herd behavior. In other words, secondary equity markets may be localized or embedded in a locality to the extent that threatens the competitiveness of both local investors and issuers, and consequently that of a local economy (see also Clark and Wójcik 2007).

## Changing institutional environment of information circulation

The roles of proximity and soft local information in secondary equity markets are not set in stone, as the broader institutional environment in which information on these markets circulates changes. One major trend involves increasing production of hard information but also conversion of what used to be soft information into hard information. Consider, for example, the level of detail that now has to be disclosed by firms in most developed economies on corporate directors, their credentials, remuneration, and shareholdings. What increases is not just the amount but also the frequency and timeliness of information disclosure. Think of transition from annual and half-yearly to quarterly financial reporting by listed companies in many European countries as well as shortened deadlines for preparing and making reports publicly available. Beyond regulatory changes, rating agencies, investment analysts, and the rest of the burgeoning sector of financial infomediaries, represent a virtual factory of hard information for investors, and are biting the edges of what used to be reserved as the realm of soft and/or private information.

Another major change in the institutional environment of information circulation involves the international harmonization of accounting and corporate governance standards, with the spread of the International Financial Reporting Standards and the OECD Principles of Corporate Governance in the lead. By making "the rules of the game" on equity markets (and beyond these markets) more similar across countries, international harmonization may be seen as reducing institutional distance between investors and issuers across national borders, and reducing the role of geographical proximity. In normative terms, however, whether it introduces a more level playing-field between local and remote investors is a contestable issue. As indicated earlier, non-local investors may possess an advantage over local investors due to a higher level of investor sophistication, which outweighs local investors' advantageous access to local information. As such the issues of financial literacy and sophistication should not be overlooked when considering the implications of the international harmonization of equity market regulation.

To be sure, the changing institutional environment of information circulation is not neutral in terms of power relations and involves political processes. It could be in the interest of large investment firms to "harden" the part of soft information that is local, while guarding the part of soft or sophisticated information which they are most likely to produce. Consider, for example, patents in financial products and services, becoming popular in the United States and contemplated in Europe (Lerner 2001). On the other hand, powerful incumbent local investors as beneficiaries of soft local information may oppose the conversion of soft into hard information. The political economy of information in secondary equity markets should not, however, be reduced to the level of a zero-sum game between large international companies and community-based investment. Advancement in information technology and growing mobility of investors and issuers can in their own right erode the significance and value of geographical proximity. With moving investors and issuers the circuits of soft information exchange are less likely to be geographically localized. Mobile investors and issuers may thus represent a growing constituency that requests a more level playing-field between local and remote investors.

Arguably, the redoubt of the role of proximity in secondary equity markets can be found in the nature of human cognition and behavior. Even if formal institutions surrounding secondary equity markets converge, will differences in terms of informal institutions such as customs and habits also be reduced? And will not local companies always be more visible to local than to remote investors? Perhaps the evidence on the persistence of local bias in the United States, where there is relatively little institutional diversity, is the ultimate evidence that proximity will remain important?

## Final remarks

In this chapter I have investigated the role of proximity between investors and issuers in secondary equity markets with respect to financial risk management. I have demonstrated that proximity, even if defined narrowly as geographical proximity, has significant implications for investors (in terms of performance and trade-off with liquidity), investment industry as a whole (in terms of size, structure, and strategy), issuers (in terms of access to capital and liquidity), communities (in terms of herd behavior and competition), and policy makers (in terms of market structure, competition, regulation, and financial literacy). This reminds us that the role of geographical proximity is anything but an outdated or anachronistic idea. The consideration for cognitive, social, organizational, and institutional proximity enriches the understanding of secondary equity markets, by complementing the analysis of geographical proximity, but does not make the latter redundant.

What are the implications of these findings for other financial markets? First of all it should be noted that proximity effects are also found beyond secondary equity markets. Evidence is available for primary equity markets, corporate and municipal bond markets, real estate markets, loan markets, as well as markets for corporate cash management and other financial services. In other words, financial agents take advantage of proximity whenever it promises access to valuable information. In fact, the existence of the proximity effects in these markets is mostly explained with soft information, quite along the lines discussed in this chapter. It is not unreasonable to expect that the proximity–liquidity trade-off applies across different financial markets and products. Further research on the role of proximity in markets other than those studied here would be a welcome contribution to the understanding of finance and geography.

In this chapter, I have tried to reverse the order usually found in texts on financial geography. A typical paper starts with arguments from the world of finance, which seem to doom the future of geography, and then uses geographical analysis to prove that "local" and geography still matter in finance. Here, I started with empirical research in finance arguing in favor of the local, and then used insights from geography to demonstrate the limits of the "local" and to argue how both "global" and "local" matter in finance. In this way I hope to contribute to literature that dispels the myth that financial economics is about the ignorance or an attack on the "local", and that geographical research on finance is about the defense of the "local". In the times where, struck by empirical evidence, economics is diversifying into new theories, there is hopefully more room than before for rapprochement between financial economists and economic geographers (Clark 2005). As Huberman (2001, 659) eloquently commented on the existence of home bias: "[ . . . ] investors should soon start gobbling up foreign shares in record numbers. If they do not, economists may have to diversify into other theories." Geographers could definitely contribute to this process of diversification.

## References

Barber, B. M. and Odean, T. (2008). All that glitters: The effect of attention and news on the buying behavior of individual and institutional investors. *Review of Financial Studies*, 21, 785–815.

Bathelt, H., Malmberg, A., and Maskell, P. (2004). Clusters and knowledge: local buzz, global pipelines and the process of knowledge creation. *Progress in Human Geography*, 28, 31–56.

Berger, A. N, Miller, N. H., Petersen, M. A., Rajan, R. G., and Stein, J. C. (2005). Does function follow organizational form? Evidence from the lending practices of large and small banks. *Journal of Financial Economics*, 76, 237–69.

Bodnaruk, A. (2004). Proximity Always Matters: Evidence from Swedish Data. EFA 2004 Maastricht Meetings Paper No. 3765, July 29, 2004. Retrieved 12 August 2008 from: http://ssrn.com/abstract=565345.

Boschma, R. A. (2005). Proximity and innovation: a critical assessment. *Regional Studies*, 39, 61–74.

Chen, J., Hong, H., Huang, M., and Kubik, J. D. (2004). Does fund size erode mutual fund performance? The role of liquidity and organization. *American Economic Review*, 94, 1276–302.

Clark, G. L. (2005). Money flows like mercury: the geography of global finance. *Geografiska Annaler B*, 87, 99–112.

—— and Wójcik, D. (2007). *The Geography of Finance: Corporate Governance in the Global Marketplace*. Oxford: Oxford University Press.

Coval, J. D. and Moskowitz, T. J. (1999). Home bias at home: local equity preference in domestic portfolios. *Journal of Finance*, 54, 2045–73.

—— —— (2001). The geography of investment: informed trading and asset prices. *Journal of Political Economy*, 109, 811–41.

Dahlquist, M., Pinkowitz, L., Stulz, R. M., and Wiliamson, R. (2003). Corporate Governance and the Home Bias. *Journal of Financial and Quantitative Analysis*, 38 (1), 87–110.

Dass, N. and Massa, M. (2008). The Bank–Firm Relationship: A Trade-off Between Better Governance and Greater Information Transparency. Working Paper. Retrieved 12 August 2008 from: http://siteresources.worldbank.org/INTFR/Resources/The_Bank_Firm_Relationship_A_Trade_off_between_Better_Governance.pdf.

DeMarzo, P. M., Kaniel, R., and Kremer, I. (2004). Diversification as public good: community effects in portfolio choice. *Journal of Finance*, 59, 1677–715.

Dimson, E., Marsh, P., and Staunton, M. (2002). *Triumph of the Optimists: 101 Years of Investment Returns*. Princeton: Princeton University Press.

Feng, L. and Seasholes, M. S. (2004). Correlated trading and location. *Journal of Finance*, 59, 2117–44.

Francis, B., Hasan, I., and Waisman, M. (2007). Does Geography Matter to Bond-holders? FRB of Atlanta Working Paper No. 2007-2. Retrieved 12 August 2008 from: http://ssrn.com/abstract=962888.

Gaspar, J.-M. and Massa, M. (2007). Local ownership as private information: evidence on the monitoring–liquidity trade-off. *Journal of Financial Economics*, 83, 751–92.

Gertler, M. S. (2003). Tacit knowledge and the economic geography of context, or the undefinable tacitness of being (there). *Journal of Economic Geography*, 3, 75–100.

Grinblatt, M. and Keloharju, M. (2001). How distance, language, and culture influence stockholdings and trades. *Journal of Finance*, 56, 1053–73.

Hau, H. (2001). Location matters: an examination of trading profits. *Journal of Finance*, 56, 1959–83.

Hong, H., Kubik, J. D., and Stein, J. C. (2004). Social interaction and stock-market participation. *Journal of Finance*, 59, 137–63.

Huberman, G. (2001). Familiarity breeds investment. *Review of Financial Studies*, 14, 659–80.

Ivković, Z. and Weisbrenner, S. (2005). Local does as local is: information content of the geography of individual investors common stock investments. *Journal of Finance*, 60, 267–306.

Jones, A. (2002). The "global city" misconceived: The myth of "global management" in transnational service firms. *Geoforum*, 33, 335–50.

Kaminsky, G. and Schmuckler, S. (2003). Short-run Pain, Long-run Gain: The Effects of Financial Liberalization. NBER Working Paper No. 9787, Cambridge (Mass.).

Klagge, B. and Martin, R. (2005). Decentralized versus centralized financial systems: is there a case for local capital markets? *Journal of Economic Geography*, 5, 387–422.

Landier, A., Nair, V. B., and Wulf, J. (2009). Trade-offs in staying close: corporate decision making and geographic dispersion. *Review of Financial Studies*, 22, 1119–48.

Lerner, J. (2001). Where Does *State Street* Lead? A First Look at Finance Patents, 1971–2000. Working Paper. Retrieved 12 August 2008 from: http://www.hbs.edu/research/facpubs/workingpapers/papers2/0001/01–005.pdf.

Lo, V. and Grote, M. H. (2002). Where Traders Go When Stock Markets Go Virtual – Concentration, Dissemination or Persistence? In M. Balling, F. Lierman, and A. Mullineux (eds.), *Technology and Finance: Challenges for Financial Markets Business Strategies and Policy Makers* (pp. 190–203). London: Routledge.

Loughran, T. and Schultz, P. (2004). Weather, stock returns, and the impact of localized trading behavior. *Journal of Financial and Quantitative Analysis*, 39, 343–64.

Loughran, T. and Schultz, P. (2005). Liquidity: urban versus rural firms. *Journal of Financial Economics*, 78, 341–74.

—— —— (2006). Asymmetric Information, Firm Location, and Equity Issuance. Working Paper. Retrieved 12 August 2008 from: http://leeds-faculty.colorado.edu/yungc/Seminar%20Papers/location.pdf.

Madureira, L. and Underwood, S. (2007). Geography and equity market making. Retrieved 12 August 2008 from: http://ssrn.com/abstract=1032633.

Malloy, C. J. (2005). The geography of equity analysis. *Journal of Finance*, 60, 719–55.

Massa, M. and Simonov, A. (2006). Hedging, familiarity and portfolio choice. *Review of Financial Studies*, 19, 633–85.

Portes, R. and Rey, H. (2005). The determinants of cross-border equity flows. *Journal of International Economics*, 65, 269–96.

Prinsky, C. and Wang, Q. (2006). Does corporate headquarters location matter for stock returns. *Journal of Finance*, 61, 1991–2015.

Shukla, R. K. and van Inwegen, G. B. (1995). Do locals perform better than foreigners? An analysis of U.K. and U.S. mutual fund managers. *Journal of Economics and Business*, 47, 541–54.

Stein, J. C. (2002). Information production and capital allocation: decentralized versus hierarchical forms. *Journal of Finance*, 57, 1891–921.

Stulz, R. M. (2005). Presidential address: the limits of financial globalization. *Journal of Finance*, 60, 1595–638.

Tesar, L. and Werner, I. M. (1995). Home bias and high turnover. *Journal of International Money and Finance*, 14, 467–93.

Wójcik, D. (2002). Cross-border corporate ownership and capital market integration in Europe: evidence from portfolio and industrial holdings. *Journal of Economic Geography*, 2, 455–92.

—— (2007*a*). Geography and the future of stock exchanges: between real and virtual Space. *Growth and Change*, 38, 200–23.

—— (2007*b*). Do Stock Markets Represent Economies? Working Paper. Retrieved 12 August 2008 from: http://ssrn.com/abstract=998814.

# Part III

## Urban Risk

# 7

# Infrastructure Investment and the Management of Risk

*Phillip O'Neill*

One of his greatest executive talents was his ability to foster an extraordinarily entrepreneurial culture, while implementing a high risk management regime to ensure that the bank's capital was protected.

Karen Maley, "Fair and frank, boss closes his account", *Australian Financial Review* 21 May 2008, p. 58.

Here Malcy refers to Alan Moss in her piece on his retirement in 2008 as CEO of Macquarie Bank, a position he had held for fifteen years. In this period Moss oversaw the spectacular growth of Macquarie Bank from a small Sydney offshoot of the British merchant bank, Hill Samuel & Co Ltd, into a global infrastructure financier, dealer, and manager. As we see in this chapter, the story of Macquarie Bank's success has involved the mobilization and control of risk; the formulation of the idea of urban infrastructure as a financial product; the development of a highly motivated, highly skilled team of risk-conscious finance professionals; and a keen awareness of the desires and constraints of investors, especially funds managers from the superannuation and pension savings sector.

Of course, like many of the world's financial institutions involved in recent times in the creation and aggressive marketing of financial products, Macquarie Bank has experienced a severe decline in its share price as a result of the loss of investor confidence in financial stocks during the current global financial and economic crisis. This decline, though, has tracked closely falls in the finance sector index, the MSCI World Diversified Financials Index, suggesting that Macquarie has no extraordinary exposures or vulnerabilities. Indeed, the bank's investor briefings

available from its web site (www.macquarie.com.au) at the time of sub-
mission of this chapter (November 2008) explicitly dispel charges of fragility. The bank claims that it has no problem trading or material problem
credit exposures, no exposure to structured investment vehicles (SIVs), no
sub-prime lending, no problems with debt underwritings, only modest
holdings of highly rated debt instruments partially backed by US sub-
prime mortgages, no underwriting of leveraged loans, very little underwriting of corporate loans, modest credit exposures to the hedge fund
industry, and no material exposures not already known to investors. It
also claims to be well funded, with liquid assets of over A$20 billion. Such
evidence, assuming it is robustly collected and honestly delivered, shows
that Macquarie Bank remains a solid financial entity. Importantly for the
argument here, the evidence portrays Macquarie as an institution capable
of surviving calamitous financial circumstances with its approaches to
risk and risk management intact. These approaches are the subject of
this chapter.

This chapter commences with an overview of the infrastructure sector,
explaining why infrastructure has become a prominent investment item;
indeed an economic sector in its own right. A discussion of risk follows.
This discussion points to the centrality of risk in the creation of financial
products and the parallel rise in risk management practices and their
associated technologies, metrics, and risk amelioration strategies. The
chapter then turns to Macquarie Bank as a case study of the insertion of
risk into financial circuits of capital alongside the development of risk
management strategies in the corporate world more generally. At the
heart of the story is Macquarie's embrace of risk as a device to be mobilized
in the creation of financial products out of infrastructure items. Three of
Macquarie's strategies for dealing in risk and dealing with risk are explored. One is the bank's policy of "adjacency" in the selection of both
new product markets and new geographical domains for expansionary
investments. Another is the bank's "freedom within boundaries" policy
which seeks to build a risk-taking culture within the bank parallel to a set
of complex risk assessment and containment procedures. Central to the
"freedom within boundaries" policy are the bank's recruitment, remuneration and performance management practices, all demonstrative of awareness within the bank of the embodied nature of work in the finance sector
(see McDowell 1997). The third strategy within the bank's set of risk
strategies is balance sheet monitoring, involving cutting edge measurement and assessment practices that set limits on the bank's exposures to
downside risks while supporting the venturesome nature of the bank's

development and growth activities. This chapter concludes with an evaluation of the consequences of liquefying urban infrastructure by its conversion into risk infused financial products.

## Infrastructure

Infrastructure is a relatively new, rapidly growing urban economic sector. Its emergence is due to a variety of forces including fiscal conservatism by governments and the associated privatization and corporatization of public utilities. As we see below, the trend to infrastructure privatization has created opportunities for infrastructure to be mobilized as a financial product. The distinctiveness and attraction of infrastructure as a financial product, though, requires it to be assigned specific and unique attributes. One is that urban infrastructure generates predictable, stable, and often inflation-adjusted returns over long time periods. This characteristic makes infrastructure investments attractive to funds managers who have responsibility for generating consistent returns on members' savings well into the future, especially when faced with increasingly volatile returns from equity and property markets. Another is that infrastructure assets typically have a monopoly or an oligopolistic position in a market, with demand behavior that is typically inelastic and recession-proof. For example, the usage rates of a city's water supply or of a key inter-urban motorway are predictable year in, year out, because users have little scope to vary consumption as a result of variations in income or user charges. A related quality, which also shores up future earnings prospects, is that the privileged position of the infrastructure operator in an urban market is commonly guaranteed by legislation or through the compliance of an industry regulator or even through direct earnings assurances. Such protection is often delivered by governments in order to sweeten public infrastructure asset sales and public–private partnership bids.

Importantly, the emergence of the infrastructure sector and its attractiveness to long-term investors have seen a broadening of the definition of what constitutes infrastructure. Obviously, infrastructure developers and financiers are keen to expand the notion of infrastructure beyond a limited set of hard urban physical structures such as roads, rail and bus systems, and water, electricity and gas utilities. Increasingly, the category "infrastructure" is extended to include packages of predictable, repeated urban flows and connections involving everyday commercial, public, and private life that are capable of generating predictable, repeated cash flows through user charges.

More practically, the development of infrastructure as a financial product has come from a widespread concern that infrastructure provision in our cities is in crisis and therefore in need of new forms of delivery and financing in the face of debt-averse state treasuries. The crisis has a number of dimensions. First, the large stock of infrastructure developed to accompany nation building projects and economic growth in the post-war period is now ageing and in need of renewal. For Australia, a PricewaterhouseCoopers report for the Australia Local Government Association (PWC 2006) estimates a backlog of A$15 billion in local government infrastructure maintenance. For the United States, an American Society of Civil Engineers report (2008) estimates that US$1.6 trillion is needed in the United States over five years to bring existing infrastructure to good repair.

Second, urban growth in major cities in developed nations, especially in the outer suburbs, and surging levels of urbanization alongside rapid economic growth in large population nations, especially China, India, Russia, and Brazil, are creating substantial demand for new infrastructure rollout. For Australia, ABN Amro (2005) estimates that between A$330 billion and A$400 billion will be spent on new infrastructure projects in Australia in the next decade. For the United States, ASCE (2008) estimates that by 2020 freight volumes will be 70 per cent greater than in 1998, while population will reach 420 million by 2050, with most growth in metropolitan areas requiring major increases in infrastructure capacity and operation. For China, the Population Reference Bureau (2008) estimates a net increase in its urban population of 350 million by 2030; and for India, an equivalent increase of 290 million people. The growing demand for new urban infrastructure as a consequence is astonishing.

Third, new technologies are producing shifts in the nature of infrastructure requirements with rising demand for networked infrastructure, including integrated freight handling systems and high speed broadband communications access. One manifestation is the erection of networks of mobile phone towers across the urban landscape that have become in revenue terms the telecommunications equivalent of toll plazas on motorways. Accordingly, in neighborhoods where revenue streams are weak, telecommunications coverage is thin.

Fourth, methods for financing, delivering, and managing infrastructure are no longer certain or agreed on. Uncertainty stems directly from far-reaching changes in the fiscal and regulatory behaviors of the state (Altshuler and Luberoff 2003; Brenner 2004). Here, limited capacity, or obstinate unwillingness, by governments to borrow for capital investment generates a search for alternative funding arrangements involving consistently, now, a high level of private provision. The transfer of financing responsibility from public to private balance sheets creates enormous earnings possibilities for infrastructure financiers and operators. Brookings Institution speculates, for example, that the introduction of road pricing in America's largest 98 metropolitan areas would generate annual revenues of $120 billion per annum (*The Economist*, 28 June 2008, p. 40). Yet in many circumstances private sector participation in key projects has been reluctant or insufficient.

Fifth, sustainability concerns, especially in the context of extreme weather events and the high probability of climate change, have generated questions about the long-term viability of holding large scale infrastructure items in traditional monolithic formats, especially those involving water and sewerage systems, motorways and arterial roads, and electricity grids (Bulkeley and Betsill 2003). Yet the break-up of the metropolitan authorities and utilities for commercialization or privatization typically invites the retention and protection of monopoly supply rights. The process often diminishes the prospects of private ventures as appendages to a networked or distributed system of supply, and the capacity of the state to move the system toward more sustainable outcomes.

Uncertainties aside, these largely supply-side drivers of investment interest in the infrastructure sector coincided over the last decade with a fertile financial context. The key here was the rising level of personal savings lodged in superannuation and pension funds. These required management in ways that sought assured returns over long time periods. At the same time, new financial products emerged, many of them higher risk, higher yielding products; which, in turn, generated demand for moderating, longer term, lower risk, portfolio-balancing products, like infrastructure products.

At their best, infrastructure investments provide – or least posture as providing – a coincidence of patterned, predictable, reliable financial products that seem to have a transparent connection to the materialized world of urban life at a time of growing wariness about non-transparent financial products that seem to lack an identifiable, real income source. Through its visible presence in the built environment, infrastructure was able to emerge as a stable asset class, providing the type of backing that was once present in an intermediated financial world, but was increasingly absent from a financial scene disrupted by the disintermediation of securitized and collateralized debt relationships. Infrastructure products, then, offered an alternative to the synthetic financial products seen as lacking recognizable substance; and therefore reliant on ratings agencies to signal their worth using stylized short-hand codes. Its derivatives aside (for now), infrastructure became an investment product with fairly simple metrics – traffic counts, usage rates, daily toll earnings – capable of being understood and verified through desktop checks by an average funds manager. Being seen as capable of generating stable, long-term yields, then, made infrastructure products a natural fit for financing from superannuation and pension funds rather than, say, from marketable debt instruments. At the same time, ironically, these qualities enabled infrastructure to be transformed into a field of promised financial flows capable of being fashioned into attractive financial products.

The rise of the infrastructure sector has also generated new institutional forms within a financialized capitalism. Large scale utilities providers have created new divisions tagged with the infrastructure label. US power, utility and finance giant, General Electric, for instance, reorganized its aviation, aerospace, energy, oil and gas, transport and water processing operations in 2005 under the badge "GE Infrastructure". Major financial houses have similarly moved to create distinct infrastructure operations. In May 2008, Morgan Stanley announced the formation of a US$4 billion infrastructure fund while during the same month the giant private equity firm Kohlberg Kravis Roberts spawned its own global infrastructure practice (*Economist*, 28 June 2008, p. 39). Meanwhile, in mid-2008 the financial press cited Citigroup, Merrill Lynch, and UBS as "international rivals" to Macquarie Bank in the generation of financialized infrastructure products (Johnston and Patten 2008).

## Risk

If risk were exclusively of the nature of a known chance or mathematical possibility, there could be no reward of risk taking; the fact of risk could exert no considerable influence on the distribution of income in any way. For if the actuarial chance of gain or loss in any transaction is discernible, either by calculation *a priori* or by the application of statistical methods to past experience, the burden of bearing the risk can be avoided by the payment of a small fixed cost, limited to the administrative expense of providing insurance. (Frank H. Knight 1971 [orig. 1921] I.II.41; Part 1, Chapter 2 para 41)

Risk and its management have always been intrinsic to successful business. Yet, one can easily surmise that the presence of risk in business transactions today far exceeds its presence nearly a century ago. One can now observe that as the state withdrew its largely Keynesian economic and social support mechanisms over the last three decades and as markets globalized, private sector risk was exacerbated, requiring greater management attention. In addition, as global circuits of financial capital deepened and intensified, finance became ". . . a central conduit of risk shifting and social change" (Martin et al. 2008, 122).

At one level, the nature of a risk can be described, assessed and exploited, or mitigated. Yet, as Frank H. Knight famously observed in 1921, risk is never fully discernible. With contingency always in play, risk assessment can never be an exact statistical science; and, therefore, investment decisions will always be risky, however diversified or hedged an investment portfolio might be. Certainly, general rules about risk can be ascertained but investors can never know how these rules will play out in the actual circumstances of their existence.

Given these simple yet intriguing truths, it is not surprising that as the range of investment options expanded, especially the ever expanding range of financial products, so has the study of the management of risk proliferated, both as a normative advisory literature and as critical analysis. As part of the latter, Miller et al. (2008) see risk management as a "particular type of rationality" and "a moral technology", a way of making the future manageable in a very specific way (see also Ewald 1990, 1991; Knights and Vurdubakis 1993).

Risk, then, inevitably flows from the presence of unknowable elements and unknowable outcomes. Successful business practice responds to these uncertainties in ways that diminish them; and, therefore, in ways that transcend crude arbitrage behavior – ". . . the exploitation of minor differences that engender volatility" (Martin et al. 2008, 130) – and the similarly opportunistic practice of disguising or divesting risk through product placement in satellite financial vehicles. Dealing with and in risk have become deliberate business engagements replete with sophisticated technologies and management practices.

The most orthodox and longstanding risk management practice is portfolio diversification. The logic of portfolio diversification stems simply from the application of probability theory to business management such that the chance of an aggregated balance sheet loss is eliminated by enrollment in sufficient investment events where the chances of success are independent of each other and where yield rates are at least equal to the chance of failure. Portfolio diversification is achieved by operating in diverse markets, be they different product markets or markets in different geographic regions. Risk management of a diverse portfolio of investments, then, involves the application of risk measurement and assessment practices across the range of business decisions. Sometimes, too, it can involve the establishment of separate management divisions, separate product divisions, or separate divisions based on geographic regions, designed to ensure the knowledge and the management of risk in a specific part of an investment portfolio are optimized. Risk management through diversification, then, has become a basic business practice.

The safety valve in portfolio management is liquidity. Risk is dissipated by liquidity. The attribute of liquidity enables convenient exit from a specific investment. By definition, financial products are more liquid than investments in localized productive assets. Monk (this volume) distinguishes between universal and localized investment products. The attraction of universal products is their qualification for entry to high volume trading markets. Examples of universal products include the rights to output from an oil field, the trademark rights to a reputable global clothing brand, and the interest payments on a stable government bond. Localized products, though, are able to be converted into universal products through their decomposition into derivative products. A privately operated, fees-generating inter-urban motorway, for instance, can be disaggregated into a number of derivative products such as: the rights to predictable cash flows over the next five years; the rights to more uncertain cash flows in the longer term when unknown technologies or transport options produce different competitive environments; the rights to billboard advertising; ownership of motorway maintenance contracts; even rights to earnings from traffic infringements.

Thus, drawing on Martin et al. (2008, 121), the derivatization of an investment product – including through the use of securities and hedging options – is more than "...a mathematical exercise of creating and trading financial products for hedging financial exposures." The substance of derivatization is its enactment of a transformation of a localized (in time and space) income stream where,

...the dismantling process enables the attributes of any asset to be configured as universally recognizable and generic, and therefore tradable, irrespective of the particularity of the asset itself. A unique asset, for which there may be quite a small market, can be dismantled into generic attributes, for which there is a large market. By 'dismantling' assets into tradable attributes, the focus shifts from the particularity of the asset itself to the universality of its attributes. (ibid. 127; see also Bryan and Rafferty 2006)

Two understandings are pertinent at this point, especially in respect of infrastructure as an investment product. First, the transformation of the infrastructure asset into a tradeable financial product involves the sale of the outcomes of the performance of the asset but not the asset itself. Mostly, the sale is of the rights to the income stream generated by the performance of the asset; or, at least, the sale of rights to an anticipated income stream based on projected performance. Second, and therefore, the nub of the transformation here is the transfer of a risk of failure to secure anticipated earnings away from the owner of the asset and onto the owners of a variety of dependent (or derivative) financial products. In this way, the transformation (or derivatization) is not so much the sale of an asset but the buying and selling of risk itself.

Using these two understandings, we can see that the derivatization process provides a very specific, immensely believable way of making a risky future manageable (after Miller and Rose 2008, 2). Prosaically, Martin et al. (2008, 131) describe this transformation as,

... a shift into the time of the end-brought-to-life, of the future-in-the-present, by which decisions made about promises to come pre-empt the image of a world yet to come.

In respect of the new private western Sydney orbital motorway, the M7, for example, the transformation fixes an image of the future operation of the motorway and its externalities as a set of determinable probabilities relating to traffic flows; land use configurations; government transport and climate change policies; and individual housing and consumption preferences. The financialization of the motorway brings into trade a product that contains a reconciliation of future operational possibilities – with varying upsides and downsides – via the incorporation of risk characteristics that expand the possibilities for derivatization and thereby the saleability of financialized infrastructure products to investors.

In brief, then, infrastructure has become a financial sector as much as it survives as a hard physical structure or a set of urban services. And key to this creation has been the development of an extraordinary capacity by finance professionals to not just do deals where prices and claimed-for yields are calculated using advanced risk assessment calculations but to create financial products that transfer risk itself. The important role of these finance professionals within Macquarie Bank is analyzed below.

So what opportunities have arisen for the financial institution in the infrastructure transformation? Urban infrastructure, having been made available to investors as an array of financial products, now intersects with the risk management practices of infrastructure financiers and investors in two quite opposite ways. First, as we have seen, infrastructure can act within an investment portfolio as a risk ameliorator: a mature product with a low risk profile and stable returns often guaranteed by the state for a long time period. But, second, the infrastructure asset can act via the derivatives process as a set of financial products that, instead of being stable, are more or less risky. These dueling properties play out in what might be seen as an infrastructure product life cycle (Figure 7.1). Thus infrastructure banks, especially Macquarie Bank because it has been in the forefront of financialization of the infrastructure sector, have over time become specialists in the management of financial products along the infrastructure product life cycle, even in securing the confidence of governments to advance an item of infrastructure beyond stage one of the cycle.

In other words, Macquarie Bank, and financial services institutions like it, inscribe risk onto an infrastructure item by bringing risk into previously or otherwise reasonably certain futures. They take infrastructure from a relatively stable operational world and insert it into the risk taking world of finance. They do this in four ways: first, by steering the infrastructure asset into private hands with the imposition of a fees payment for its use; second, by inserting financial instruments into its makeup; third, by breaking up the infrastructure item and the financial flows it generates into separate financial products; and, fourth, by mimicking the transformation process by converting other repeated urban life flows – for example, the use of luggage trolleys at an airport, the fees payable for tenure at a retirement village, the use of a taxi configured for wheelchair access, and secure access to a dedicated urban emergency services radio frequency (all being ventures of Macquarie Bank) – into quasi infrastructure products and financializing them in the same way as the motorway or the water supply. Critically, as far as is believable, the transformation process takes place with an encouraged understanding that being infrastructure products, these products are by definition, intrinsically, low-risk financial products. Perhaps, though, this belies their true composition.

In summary, then, the creation of an infrastructure product life cycle has transformed infrastructure from an urban fixture with characteristics of universality, with costs that are amortized through fiscal and inter-generational frameworks, and with externalities that are available free – characteristics designed historically to eliminate the risk of some

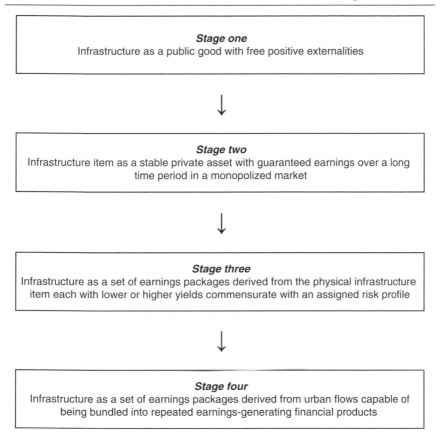

**Figure 7.1.** The life cycle of infrastructure as a financial product

parts of the population not having access to its use, on the one hand, and of reducing the risks of urban living in general, on the other – to a set of financial products devised as highly liquid conduits for the capturing of recession-proof cash flows capable of being generated over long periods of time in accordance with the necessities and predictabilities of urban life. Never has ordinary urban life been so elevated in value.

## How an infrastructure bank controls risk

Intriguingly, if infrastructure products were so plain, so lucrative, so reliable, and so capable of spawning derivative financial products, they would have been snapped up years ago all over the world and Macquarie Bank would be one of many institutions selling infrastructure products in a crowded market. Yet this is not the case. Macquarie Bank led the mobilization and securitization of earnings from the once-state-owned utilities in Australia, the United Kingdom, and in many sectors in Canada, and the United States. More recently it has sought to be the market leader in China and Russia (Korporaal 2007; Florence 2007). Macquarie Bank and few others seem to "do" infrastructure in ways that remain competitive (and government preferred) in different markets.

My argument is that Macquarie Bank has stayed ahead of the infrastructure pack because of its approach to risk. To Macquarie Bank, risk is not something to be mitigated, or eliminated. Rather, it is something to be inscribed as a quality of an infrastructure product; something to be steeped into Macquarie Bank's organizational form, its culture and performance metrics; and something to be embraced by the bank's highly skilled young international workforce. Core to all of these, as we have seen, is the transformation of infrastructure into an array of financial products that correspond to the hunger of financial circuits of capital over the last decade or more to find conduits for risk shifting and storing. Macquarie Bank is highly skilled at transforming infrastructure into a risk shifting and storing device. As a consequence it can devise infrastructure deals that produce value promises that investors will purchase, so elevating infrastructure asset valuations which justify Macquarie Bank's handsome bids and curry government favor.

The remainder of this chapter analyzes the way Macquarie Bank deals with risk; and deals in risk; how it mobilizes its staff as risk takers; and how it envelops its expansive corporate structure and reach with advanced risk management procedures – but, distinctively, by embracing risk within its operational world rather than seeking to eliminate risk from it.

Hence, the case study concentrates on the strategies devised by Macquarie Bank to confront risk. One set of strategies arises from the bank's services to an investment community created by financialization where "... finance decomposes assets into their exposures and commensurates their values" (Martin et al. 2008, 127). Another is a set of human resources strategies that mobilize the bank's young professionals to devise and negotiate new infrastructure products within a set of risk controls. And another is a set of strategies for managing aggregate balance sheet risk through a combination of portfolio manipulation, risk transfer to the balance sheets of associated financial entities, and outright ownership shifts. As we see below, pivotal to the success of the bank's risk control strategies is achieving appropriate balance between financial product invention, IPOs, and holding products for capital gains and fees generation.

Macquarie Bank has become Australia's premier international infrastructure bank and a global leader in the creation and management of financialized infrastructure products. Rather than follow the model of many international investment banks of riding the bull by trading in principals, Macquarie Bank's business model has focused on providing services, chiefly to its institutional clients and to the clients it has created, the specialist infrastructure funds. Maley (2008) writes that this strategy has so far insured Macquarie Bank against the current shake-out in global financial markets since, as primarily a fees generator, its balance sheet seems to have had minimal exposure to assets that required write downs.

In 2007, Macquarie Bank restructured in order to match better its organizational form with its aspirations. The bank separated its banking activities from its capital products creation and management activities. This also helps it meet Basle 2 regulations. A by-product of the restructuring was a name change with the bank now operating as Macquarie Group Ltd. In this chapter, as is the case in popular usage, we continue to use the term "Macquarie Bank" to refer to the entire Macquarie Group Ltd entity, unless otherwise stated.

As shown in Figure 7.2, Macquarie Bank's core business is the provision of services. Overwhelmingly it gets its income from fees for these services

| Macquarie Group Limited | | | |
|---|---|---|---|
| Group wide services<br>Finance, risk management, taxation, human resources, etc. | | | |
| Banking group | | Non-banking group | |
| Banking and securitization group | Funds management group | Macquarie capital | Certain activities from equity markets group and treasury and commodities group |
| Equity markets group | Real estate group | | |
| Financial services group | Treasury and commodities group | | |

**Figure 7.2.** The corporate structure of Macquarie Group Ltd

*Source*: Extracted from Sheppard (2008, slide 10).

**Table 7.1.** Macquarie Bank's operating income, 2007–8 fiscal year (ending March)

| Business segment | Contribution to total earnings (%) | Growth on prior fiscal year (%) |
|---|---|---|
| *Capital markets, advisory and securities* Mergers and acquisitions, advisory, underwriting and principal transactions Institutional cash equities Financial products | 42 | 75 |
| *Lending* Banking and securitized lending Equipment and other leasing Real estate lending Other lending | 10 | 23 |
| *Asset and wealth management* Infrastructure, real estate and other specialist funds Retail and wholesale funds management and private client broking | 27 | 39 |
| *Financial markets* Commodities Foreign exchange, futures, treasury and debt markets Equity derivatives | 21 | 34 |

*Source*: Extracted from Sheppard (2007).

(Table 7.1; see Jefferis and Stilwell 2006 for analysis). Macquarie Bank's lending spreads are a relatively minor income earner, which is unusual for a bank. Instead, as a specialist in the creation, sale and management of financialized infrastructure assets and securitized infrastructure earnings, Macquarie maximizes its income from fees collections: fees to financialize the infrastructure item, fees to package infrastructure earnings into securitizable instruments, fees to launch companies and trusts to control these instruments, fees to finance these vehicles, and fees to manage the intricate long-term relations it devises for its clients.

As infrastructure markets are typically local and monopolized, Macquarie Bank has had to shift continuously into new infrastructure products and new geographic markets in order to maintain growth. As a consequence, Macquarie Bank has become an extraordinarily complex entity by product and by region. In early 2008, it held over 110 major infrastructure assets and 700 large real estate assets in 21 nations across the world. Sheppard (2008) reports that 63 per cent of the bank's assets are comprised of communications infrastructure (11% of all assets under management), utilities (21%), airports (12%), and roads (21%). The remaining assets under management are various forms of real estate (13%) and investment funds (6%).

Macquarie Bank's discrete capability is in harnessing earnings from these assets and converting them into financial products that traverse time and space, while retaining characteristics that make them recognizable and comprehensible to investors and funds managers. Investors and funds managers can read a prospectus and find simple data describing daily takings from, say, a luggage trolley service at Logan Airport, or the water usage rates for residents along Kilburn High Road in London; and then assess the qualities of the security or interest rate product that Macquarie Bank derives from these revenues wherever they might be sourced across the globe. Macquarie Bank's core skill is being able to turn the risky peculiarities of how someone uses a luggage trolley or a water tap into universally comparable and tradeable products that are consistently popular with their investor clients.

Since risk is the business of Macquarie Bank, risk determination and management bind the group's banking and professional services functions. The bank claims it manages its finances on the basis of market downturns being normal despite their being unpredictable. The bank's way of embracing risk without being foolhardy is to set risk limits such that taking a risk outside these limits is unacceptable; indeed designated as a "breach" of bank policy "whether or not [the investment proves to be] profitable" (Macquarie Group Ltd 2008a). Even in a time of global financial crisis, the bank's presentations to analysts and investors have continued to boast its risk-taking culture albeit within sophisticated management frameworks. Macquarie Bank explains that it is an organization that searches for ways to find and securitize predictable long-term cash flows. Figure 7.3 shows how the Macquarie Group does its business. The figure lists the group's main operational domains: infrastructure, telecommunications-media-entertainment-technology, resources, property, financial institutions, and industrials. It shows how it launches ideas which have potential to become "principals" – the actual financial products and their long-term yields – and then the group's fees generators.

However, like all ideas, especially risky ones, most of the bank's ideas are never realized. In the first quarter of 2008, only 30 of 150 ideas that were formally mobilized by the bank graduated to become principals in the Macquarie Bank portfolio. Likewise, of 100 serious engagements with funds for the purposes of lodging principals just 27 were completed (Macquarie Group Ltd 2008a, slide 37). In other words, engineering a successful financialized product from the array of cash-generating activities in the infrastructure sector is a highly risky business. Certainly, graduating products have a history of being very lucrative. But, as Figure 7.4

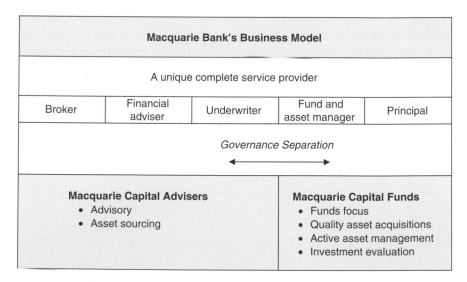

**Macquarie Group: Leveraging Opportunities**

| Idea → Brokerage → Advice → Underwriting → | Funds → | Principal → |
|---|---|---|
| Infrastructure | e.g., MIG | e.g., Aquarion |
| Telcos, media and entertainment technology | MCG/MMG | e.g., Gateway casinos |
| Resources | e.g., Opportunity | e.g., Boart longyear |
| Property | Real estate group | |
| Financial institutions | MCAG/MGOP | ATM solutions |
| Industrials | MCAG/MGOP/RVG | e.g., Icon parking |

**Figure 7.3.** How Macquarie Group does business

*Source*: Extracted from Macquarie Group Ltd (2008, slide 35).

**Macquarie Bank's Business Model**

A unique complete service provider

| Broker | Financial adviser | Underwriter | Fund and asset manager | Principal |
|---|---|---|---|---|

*Governance Separation*
← →

**Macquarie Capital Advisers**
- Advisory
- Asset sourcing

**Macquarie Capital Funds**
- Funds focus
- Quality asset acquisitions
- Active asset management
- Investment evaluation

**Figure 7.4.** The Macquarie Group business model

*Source*: Extracted from Macquarie Group Ltd (2008, slide 36).

shows, even the ideas which fail to graduate generate fees for the bank along the way. The bank consciously engages at every step along the financial product life cycle adopting every service role that is available and charging fees for their delivery.

Thus Macquarie Bank is structured in ways that maximize its chances of securing earnings – fees and profits, plus gains from asset sales – through the transformation process. This process is more complex, and more risky, than a more conventional financial services firm earning fees through advisory and management services. Moreover, the transactions which generate fees are generally non-recurring once the life cycle is completed. So very little of Macquarie's earnings comes from high volume, repeated services provision. In the main, Macquarie sells out of the product it has developed and moves on to a new venture and new risks. This capacity to reposition gives the bank its competitive market position.

Macquarie Bank has three approaches to its mobilization and management of risk. These are, first, a preference for "adjacency" in its new ventures; second, a staff management policy known as "freedom within boundaries"; and, third, an intricate modeling approach to the insertion of risk into its balance sheet. These are now dealt with in turn.

## Adjacency

Adjacency first appeared in Macquarie Bank's reports in early 2005 when the bank's chief financial officer, Mr Greg Ward, unveiled it as a financial investment strategy. Ward provided two examples of adjacency. One involved the bank's advance into forward gold trading in the commodities sector after learning the skills of gold spot trading. Adjacency led it then into the financing of gold mines and thereafter into the financing of oil and gas wells. Ward's second example showed how Macquarie Bank progressed via adjacency from delivering general financing services to arranging specific funding for Sydney's M2 Motorway and then building from this experience into the formation of specialist infrastructure funding vehicles such as the Macquarie Infrastructure Group (Ward 2005).

Subsequently, adjacency has been put forward in Macquarie Bank's presentations as a risk handling device (e.g., Sheppard 2007, 2008). Table 7.2 shows the strategy at work in Macquarie Bank's expansion into the management of infrastructure assets in China. Extracted from Sheppard (2008), the ventures shown in the table illustrate the way Macquarie Bank slides geographically and functionally between product and financial sectors to

**Table 7.2.** Adjacency at work in China

| Project | Stake | Description |
| --- | --- | --- |
| Hua Nan Expressway | Macquarie International Infrastructure Fund has 81% stake | 31-kilometres toll road across the centre of Guangzhou |
| Infra Vest | Macquarie International Infrastructure Fund invested 13.3 million euros | Operator of wind farms in Taiwan |
| Ambow Education Group | Macquarie has direct ownership | Leader in China's education services sector |
| Changshu Xinghua Port | Macquarie International Infrastructure Fund has a 38% equity interest | Multi-purpose cargo terminal near Shanghai |
| First China Property Group | Joint venture between Macquarie and Schroder Asian Properties | Residential housing in Shanghai and Beijing |
| Schroder Asian Properties | Macquarie has established investment fund | Investing in real estate in China and Asia generally |
| Macquarie Global Property Advisors | Macquarie has a 49% interest | Private equity real estate funds management business which invests in China and Asia generally |
| Macquarie Goodman Asia | Joint venture with Macquarie Goodman | Hong Kong wholesale fund with interests in 7 Hong Kong industrial properties |
| Shopping Centre Fund | Macquarie owned | Fund which owns 9 shopping malls across China |
| Taiwan Broadband Communications | Owned by the Macquarie Media Group | Cable television service provider in Taiwan |

*Source*: Extracted from Sheppard (2008).

carry expertise and experience into areas that are not too different to domains already operated within successfully.

The adjacency strategy acknowledges the capability of the Macquarie Bank organization and the skills of its staff to recognize and secure a deal so long as the environment that is being surveyed and harvested is sufficiently recognizable such that it can be navigated confidently. Risk engagement is the objective, so risk management is crucial. Risk taking is encouraged in the geographical zones or physical products which are adjacent to the zones and products where Macquarie Bank enjoys current success; but discouraged in ventures that are in relatively unknown or non-adjacent territories, because then the risk cannot be known adequately. Adjacency, then, goes hand in glove with risk encouragement and management.

## Freedom within boundaries

The second embrace of risk is via the staff management practice called "freedom within boundaries." This was first formally referred to in Macquarie Bank's 2006 annual report (Macquarie Bank Ltd 2006) and has been used commonly in investor presentations by senior staff ever since (e.g., Macquarie Bank Ltd 2007). Like adjacency, the phrase is used to refer simultaneously to the encouragement of risk taking as well as to the management of the consequences of more or less risky ventures or holdings.

Freedom within boundaries is demonstrative of Macquarie Bank's high order understanding and mobilization of risk. Because judgments are risky, the chance of securing a high yield means accepting high risk. The task of the finance professional is to produce a financial product that the investor – typically a funds manager – assesses as good value commensurate with known risks; but because the funds manager is a trustee of pooled savings requiring consistent returns over long time periods, his or her preference is for products with as low a risk profile as is possible.

Critical to Macquarie Bank being able to create financial products that can satisfy these tensely composed demands is the behavior of the Macquarie Bank finance professional. This is an acknowledgment, of course, that the process of creating and selling risk products is embodied. Labour does not operate at arm's-length from the financialization process. As noted by Martin et al. (2008, 127),

The skill of the derivative designer, as with the Fordist production engineer, is to unbundle capital into as many constituent elements as they can imagine.

So, according to Martin et al. (2008, 123),

Risk becomes not simply a form of calculation, a way of knowing, but also invites a kind of being.

where,

... labour [is] also treated as a form of capital, a risk to be decomposed, priced, hedged and managed. (Martin et al. 2008, 122)

As Macquarie Bank is in the risk business, then, it embraces risk takers as core staff, selling, in the end, not just infrastructure deals to governments and products to funds managers but also equity to shareholders, private equity to institutions and so on. The freedom-within-boundaries policy is elaborated as:

> Within Macquarie's risk framework the aim is to give business heads a high level of entrepreneurial freedom to develop and implement business unit strategy, new products and services, new market initiatives and domestic and international alliances. These areas are tightly controlled because they have implications outside the business. We call this Freedom within Boundaries. (Macquarie Group Ltd 2008*a*, slide 94).

Thus Macquarie defines the liberty component of its freedom-within-boundaries policy as an entrepreneurial license to develop and implement strategic approaches to the infrastructure field, create new products and services, structure markets in different ways, and build new domestic and international alliances. The bank's formal risk controls can circumscribe the boundaries but not the field within. Notably, in propagating its freedom-within-boundaries approach, Macquarie Bank makes no policy distinction between the act of risk containment and the entrepreneurial encouragement to take risk. Indeed, within the volatility of a financialized capitalism, Macquarie Bank's finance professionals intersect with financial products and risk calculations in ways that are impossible to fully prescribe; indeed the existence of financial products and their risk profiles are fully dependent on the ways finance professionals work, both as managers and as constrained employees. And central to this is an acceptance of freedom to create financial products.

Hence, by nurturing finance professionals as product creators, within a freedom-within-boundaries environment of work, the skills of the finance professional cannot be limited to those acquired in formal training. On one hand, the skills of the finance professional embrace creativity and adventure as new products and new urban rhythms are explored. Macquarie Bank's recruitment pages on its website emphasize the desirability of these qualities in new recruits as paralleling the bank's keenness to build an entrepreneurial spirit which matches the financial services model of the firm. Macquarie Bank is mindful of these qualities not just in personnel management but in the vital process of recruiting.

> We built this team by insisting on quality in recruiting and by helping the team to perform to the best of its ability. We have a very high retention rate. This is an environment where people can achieve. It's also an environment with strict risk-management controls. (Retiring Macquarie Bank CEO Allan Moss, quoted in Maley 2008, 58)

Macquarie Bank maintains its active recruitment process even through the current global credit crisis (AFR 20 June 2008, 1 and 12). Macquarie Bank openly publicizes its ongoing aggressive recruitment practices, its rapidly expanding staff numbers and its generous remuneration practices. By March 2008, the Macquarie Group had 12,400 staff in 25 nations, up from 3,119 in 1999 and 5,716 in 2004. About 40 per cent of current staff, or 7,493, are in Australia and New Zealand; 1,923 in Asia; 1,676 in North America; and 1,254 in Europe (Macquarie Group Ltd 2008*a*, slide 97; Macquarie Group Ltd 2008*b*). Recruitment at Macquarie Bank starts with a well-organized summer vacation program in the year before graduation as an early recruitment exercise. Training placements and part-time university arrangements are prominent especially in IT appointments. A major bonus is the bank's access to the multi-ethnic Sydney graduate market especially with its concentration of young men and women from Asian ethnic backgrounds and thereby the language proficiencies integral to the bank's Asian expansion.

On the other hand, though, the freedom-within-boundaries policy places constraints on inappropriate behaviors by encouraging a decision-making framework where personal ethics of honesty, loyalty, and hard work prevail. So there are two sides to Macquarie Bank's boundaries. There are specific rules and procedures to be abided by which define the field of endeavor for the Macquarie Bank employee. As well, though, there is a call by Macquarie Bank on those qualities of its staff that might be categorized as ethics or common sense, the natural inclination of successful, law-abiding young graduates to choose those investment pathways where there are high probabilities of good gain but where the chances of undesirable outcomes are minimal. The bank is a rule maker, to be sure, but at the same time it places considerable trust in the powers of individual staff to anticipate what the bank might see as the rules of behavior in the new and often unanticipated circumstances that the employee assays in the process of devising new financial products.

Thus, the finance professional, especially the young finance professional, the one working and living in the field, is encouraged to personalize the urban landscape to find opportunities for the financialization of infrastructure. Yet, by also using the strategy of adjacency, he or she carries best practice from one set of circumstances to the next. The risk of failure is ameliorated by the limits of the journey that best practice can take; the limits being the adjacent product category, or nearby geographic region. And so the policies of adjacency and freedom within boundaries become complementary in the management of risk and in its engagement.

## Managing aggregate balance sheet risk

As with any corporation, Macquarie Bank's businesses deal with a range of risk: credit risk, market risk, funding risk, operational risk, regulatory compliance, IT standards, and reputation risk. On top, though, the construction and disbursement of risk saturated products, being Macquarie Bank's core business, intensify all these risks. The liberal choreography encouraged by adjacency and by freedom within boundaries, while good entrepreneurial practice, is insufficient for the risk management of a formal financial institution and a large public corporation. Regulators, shareholders, and the public demand more. Not surprisingly, then, Macquarie Bank has deep, active and reportable risk assessment, management and containment practices in place.

The first of these is the bank's powerful, well staffed Risk Management Group. This group services both Macquarie Bank Ltd and Macquarie Group Ltd. It has a staff of 312 (at July 2008), 202 in Australia and 110 overseas in London, New York, Seoul, Hong Kong, Singapore, Toronto, and Auckland. The head of the group is on Macquarie Group's executive committee and extensive risk reporting is provided to every board meeting. In addition, and reflecting the integrated nature of risk involvement in Macquarie, 690 Macquarie employees are identified as having a prime risk management role while being placed within Macquarie's business groups rather than in the Risk Management Group (Macquarie Group Ltd 2008*a*, slide 97).

The second practice involves the operation of a complex model of risk assessment which the bank runs on a daily basis. The chief indices rolled into the model are the value at risk (VaR) measure and the macroeconomic-linkages (MEL) measure (Macquarie Group Ltd 2008*c*, esp. 30–51). VaR measures the group's daily exposure to potential losses in the trading value of the Macquarie Group. The model generating the VaR metric is a Monte Carlo simulation with approximately 1,000 data inputs indicative of financial behaviors, using both patterning of historical pathways and contemporary dynamic inter-relations. The model is used to assess the extent to which value in the group is threatened by exposures to market volatility in general and to specific events in different locations. Prior to the major crashes in the second half of 2008, Macquarie Bank claims that it had never experienced a one-day loss outside the possible variations predicted by its VaR modeling (Macquarie Group Ltd 2008*c*, 45). Whether possible variations have subsequently been exceeded is unknown. In any event, the risk management consequences of the VaR modeling involve constant surveillance of the group's operational activity to protect shareholder wealth from unnecessary exposures. Crucially, the firm's free-dom-within-boundaries policies are informed by the VaR modeling.

The MEL measure assesses Macquarie Bank's vulnerability to stresses across global markets especially where the negative relationships between performance variables become exaggerated in times of crisis, including credit market turbulence, market contagion, stock market crash, and downward shocks; all being terms used in the Macquarie Group's explan-ation of risk assessment in its 2008 annual report (Macquarie Group Ltd 2008c, 44–5). The MEL measure incorporates a range of scenarios to explore the impacts of crisis on the group's assets and operations. The group claims its MEL measure enables an assessment of the bank's aggregate market risks in the context of changing market dynamics, especially those which are unable to be predicted within historically based VaR modeling. Significantly, Macquarie claimed in early 2008 that its forecasting using the MEL measure revealed the group as having very limited vulnerability to major financial shocks, an outcome so far reflected in Macquarie Bank's reasonably assured share market performance during the global financial crisis so far. The bank claimed in early 2008 that its risk management approaches had proven adequate to the task of not only protecting the bank's viability during crisis but of enabling the bank's continued expan-sion with its risk culture intact (Macquarie Group Ltd 2008a, slide 102).

Thus, the bank's capacity to learn and adapt continues. This is revealed in its more recent embrace of private equity placements. Commentators note that,

About 85% of the $22.4 billion raised by Macquarie Bank last fiscal year [2007–8] was directed into unlisted funds or syndicates . . . to avoid market volatility and aggressive financial engineering. (Swift 2008, 21)

This follows a strategic growth of private equity placements in the context of global debt and equities volatility. Hence, private equity placement too has become a risk confrontation and amelioration strategy for Macquarie Bank. Unlisted specialist funds contributed $226 million in performance fees to Macquarie Bank earnings in 2007–8 fiscal year on a base of $31 billion in unlisted specialist fund equity raised between 2002 and 2006, with some pre-financial crisis estimates pointing to a potential flow of $1 billion in performance fees from these funds over the next five years (Johnston 2008; Jury 2008).

## Conclusion

The success of Macquarie Bank's penetration and appropriation of urban infrastructure and thereby the extension of the financialization process into urban life have major implications for the daily operations of the contemporary city. Of course, this means that the daily operations of the contemporary city are increasingly tied to the investment and risk management strategies of the major infrastructure banks. The implications of this entanglement are in need of exploration.

It is enticing to watch Macquarie Bank's boldness and, it seems, its continued success in new markets and new geographic regions as it rolls out its infrastructure model. We should remember, though, what the bank is doing. There have been claims that Macquarie Bank is a Ponzi scheme, or even an Enron model (see analysis in McLean 2007; Haigh 2007), involving an exaggeration of asset values and the payment of unsustainable salaries and dividends beyond earnings by borrowings or by stripping real capital from the bank's balance sheet. The evidence for improper behavior, though, is meager and the extent of the conspiracy required for its continued enactment makes belief difficult.

A different concern survives, though, perhaps one more serious than a charge of financial fraud and the potential collapse of a financial entity valued at A$27 billion at its peak in mid 2007. At risk is the way we approach the infrastructure assets of our cities. Macquarie Bank's ability to persuade state agencies to hand to it control over their utilities and urban services is arresting. At a time when the quality of an urban life depends increasingly on the nature of infrastructure and on access to it, we are not just witnessing the privatization of its procurement and provision, but transformation of infrastructure's earnings into universal financial products with performance obligations not to a city's citizenry – who may well be core funders of the infrastructure product through superannuation savings – but, instead, to global financial investors.

Once we embraced urban infrastructure, like roads, water supply, public transport, parking areas, and so on, as public goods that delivered free and universally accessible positive externalities. We could today reconfigure this idea and say that urban infrastructure, when provided as a public good, is an effective way of reducing the risks of urban living: through improved public health, safer travel, easier living, and so on. In contrast, under the Macquarie Bank model, there is an argument that infrastructure's free positive externalities disappear. In their place, the household becomes the site of risk amelioration through its capacity to pay to use infrastructure; with its own pension savings underpinning the cost and risk of its provision.


# References

ABN Amro (2005). *Australian Strategy*, September, ABN Amro, Sydney.

Altshuler, A. and Luberoff, D. (2003). *Mega-projects: The Changing Politics of Urban Public Investment*. Washington: Brookings Institution.

American Society of Civil Engineers (2008). *Raising the Grades: Small Steps for Big Improvements in America's Failing Infrastructure*. Reston, VA: ASCE.

Brenner, N. (2004). *New State Spaces: Urban Governance and the Rescaling of Statehood*. Oxford: Oxford University Press.

Bryan, D. and Rafferty, M. (2006). *Capitalism with Derivatives: A Political Economy of Financial Derivatives, Capital and Class*. Basingstoke: Palgrave.

Bulkeley, H. and Betsill, M. (2003). *Cities and Climate Change: Urban Sustainability and Global Environmental Governance*. London: Routledge.

Ewald, F. (1990). Norms, discipline and the law. *Representations*, 30, 138–61.

—— (1991). Insurance and risk, in G. Burchell, C. Gordon, and P. Miller (eds.), *The Foucault Effect: Studies in Governmentality*. London: Harvester Wheatsheaf.

Florence, C. (2007). MacBank takes its toll on China. *The Australian*, 8 November 2007, p. 23.

Haigh, G. (2007). Who's afraid of Macquarie Bank? The story of the millionaire's factory. *The Monthly Essays*, July, 25.

Jefferis, C. and Stilwell, F. (2006). Private finance for public infrastructure: the case of Macquarie Bank. *Journal of Australian Political Economy*, 58, 44–61.

Johnston, E. (2008). Macquarie cautious on outlook. *Australian Financial Review*, 21 May, pp. 1 and 59.

—— and Patten, S. (2008). Consideration to de-listing due to volatility of equity markets. *Australian Financial Review*, 24 July, pp. 1 and 20.

Jury, A. (2008). The two faces of Macquarie. *Australian Financial Review*, 21 May, p. 72.

Knight, F. H. (1971) [orig. 1921]. *Risk, Uncertainty, and Profit*. Chicago: University of Chicago Press.

Knights, D. and Vurdubakis, T. (1993). Calculations of risk: Towards an understanding of insurance as a moral and political technology. *Accounting, Organizations and Society*, 18, 729–64.

Korporaal, G. (2007). You can bank on us, Putin pledges APEC 2007. *The Australian*, 10 September 2007, p. 8.

Macquarie Group Ltd (2006). *Annual Review*. Download, www.macquarie.com, accessed August 2007.

—— (2007). *Operational Briefing: Presentation to Investors and Analysts*, 6 February. Presentation download, www.macquarie.com, accessed April 2008.

Macquarie Group Ltd (2008*a*). *Operational Briefing: Presentation to Investors and Analysts*, 6 February. Presentation download, www.macquarie.com, accessed April 2008.

—— (2008*b*). *Ten Year History.* Download, www.macquarie.com, accessed July 2008.

—— (2008*c*). *Annual Review.* Download, www.macquarie.com, accessed July 2008.

Maley, K. (2008). Fair and frank, boss closes his account. *Australian Financial Review*, 21 May, p. 58.

Martin, M., Rafferty, M., and Bryan, M. (2008). Financialization, Risk And Labour, *Competition & Change*, 12, 121–33.

McDowell, L. (1997). *Capital Culture: Gender at Work in the City.* Oxford: Blackwell.

McLean, B. (2007). The Real Macquarie: Macquarie Bank has made infrastructure funds a smoking-hot investment class. *Fortune* (European Edition), 156(6), 74–81.

Miller, P. and Rose, N. (2008). *Governing the Present: Administering Economic, Social and Personal Life.* London: Polity Press.

—— Kurunmäki, L., and O'Leary, T., (2008). Accounting, hybrids and the management of risk. *Accounting, Organizations and Society*, 33, 942–67.

Population Reference Bureau (2008). www.prb.org, accessed June 2008.

PricewaterhouseCoopers (PWC) (2006). *National Financial Sustainability Study of Local Government.* Commissioned by the Australian Local Government Association, PWC, Sydney.

Sheppard, R. (2007). *Investor Presentation: JP Morgan Conference, New York and Edinburgh.* Presentation download, www.macquarie.com, accessed February 2008.

—— (2008). *Deutsche Bank – Access China 2008 Conference.* Presentation download, www.macquarie.com, accessed April 2008.

Swift B. (2008). Macquarie's $830m retreat. *Australian Financial Review*, 17 June, pp. 1 and 21.

Ward, G. (2005). *CS First Boston 2005 Asian Investment Conference*, 17 March. Presentation download, www.macquarie.com, accessed May 2007.

# 8

# Balancing Risk and Return in Urban Investing

*Lisa A. Hagerman and Tessa Hebb*

Institutional investors are increasingly seeking innovative investment strategies in their search for fund performance.[1] Large, sophisticated pension funds are at the forefront of this trend. Faced with declining public equities markets, turbulent credit markets, and varying degrees of unfunded liabilities, pension funds are driving a search for "alpha" within the investment community.[2] Not surprisingly pension funds' investment strategies increasingly include hedge funds and alternative investments as a way to achieve out-performance. Many of these funds have indeed out-performed standard financial indexes, providing evidence that these alternative investments can pay off for savvy investors. From 2002 to 2006 US pension funds alone increased exposure to alternative investments from an average asset allocation of 7.5 to 10 per cent (Greenwich and Associates 2007). The challenge for these funds is how to achieve stellar financial returns while mitigating the additional risk inherent in these types of investments. Many are turning to targeted urban investment as part of their alternative investment program.[3]

Achieving optimal returns while reducing risk is key to pension funds' strategic asset allocation policy. Asset allocation remains the cornerstone of all investment decision making and underpins investors' ability to minimize risk while maximizing return.[4] Such investment decisions are guided by the principles of modern portfolio theory and the notion that investors can maximize return by increasing variance through the appropriate diversification of their portfolios (Markowitz 1952). However, the earliest understanding of modern portfolio theory made no temporal differentiation in optimal portfolio design. It was assumed that investors were myopic in the choice of the optimal portfolio mix (Tobin 1958; Merton 1969; Samuelson 1969; and Fama 1970). But institutional investors particularly pension funds, are characterized by their long-term investment horizons (Clark 2000; Davis and Steil 2001; Hawley and Williams 2000; Monks 2001; Clark and Hebb 2004). It is the long-term nature of pension fund investing that requires strategic asset allocation to take into consideration the temporal nature of their investments (Campbell and Viceira 2002). Such long-term strategic asset allocation includes an array of alternative investment products alongside the tradition asset mix of stocks, bonds, and cash. These alternative investment products include real estate, private equity, hedge funds, and increasingly infrastructure investments.

It is not surprising, given the size of assets held by today's institutional investors, that their direct investment in the urban and rural built environment has attracted the attention of some economic geographers. Clark (2000) was first to explore the characteristics and potential impacts of pension fund capitalism. Clark diverges from many economic geographers who leave the role of investment in firm-level productive function almost completely untheorized (Dicken and Thrift 1992; Thrift and Olds 1996; Scott 2000; Dicken 2001). Clark's work has spawned an examination of the role of investors in global finance witnessed through a geographical lens (Clark 2005; Hebb and Wójcik 2005; Clark et al. 2007; Torrance 2007).

In contrast some economic geographers see the financialization of the built environment as indicative of the dangers of neoliberalism and the distorted power relationships that overprivilege the owners of capital (Swyngedouw 1993; Tickell 2000; Peck and Tickell 2002). The work of David Harvey (1982, 1996) is reflective of many economic geographers who contend that investment with its tendency to "uneven development" is a negative force. For these scholars such private investment is the manifestation of capitalism's need to deconstruct the built environment in order to ensure the free mobility of capital, labor, and information. Contrary to these arguments, we find that investment in urban environments can be a positive force generating both urban revitalization and financial returns for pension fund beneficiaries over long-term time horizons.

Over the last three decades targeted urban investment has undergone a paradigm shift from the traditional subsidy-driven model to the market-driven model. In the capital-driven model, institutional investors perceive investing in the underserved urban areas as an overlooked economic opportunity. But such overlooked opportunities are not without attendant risk. The capital-driven model of targeted investment recognizes and seeks to control the risks inherent in this type of investment. The cautionary tale of past economically targeted investing is that these risks should not be underestimated or ignored. Our research shows that structural aspects of public sector pension funds make them systemically prone to both the financial and political risks inherent in targeted investing. Best practice in this type of investment requires pension funds to structure their targeted urban investment policies in a manner that acknowledges their own weaknesses and guards against them.

First and foremost is financial risk. While returns can be higher than public markets, the risks associated with such illiquid investments are also greater. Pension funds use a variety of techniques to mitigate the financial risks involved in these illiquid investments. The pension fund's strategic asset allocation policy is at the core of their investment philosophy and governs their ability to minimize their investment risk. Pension funds make no exceptions for targeted investments in their asset allocation no matter what ancillary benefits could be derived. For most pension funds, targeted programs make up no more than 2 per cent of their portfolio.

Direct urban investment is fraught with asymmetric information problems that raise risk in such transactions (see particularly Akerlof 1970; Spence 1973; and Stiglitz 2000 on the impact of information asymmetries on risk). Given the information asymmetries in urban investment, pension funds utilize the knowledge and expertise in this market gained through specialized investment vehicles (Bodie and Merton 1993). They seek top-quartile performers with lengthy track records in targeted investing using exactly the same standards they apply to all other investment decisions.

As urban investment usually has a geographic focus (in the United States this is often state-based), targeted investments lack geographic diversification. Again best practice recognizes the risks involved when diversification is curtailed. Pension fund investors seek investment vehicles that provide pooling thus spreading risk across multiple partners. We find fund-of-funds structures increasingly popular with today's large pension funds.[5] Another tool for achieving diversification in urban investing is through reciprocal targeting where investment vehicles provide financial returns based on broad national or regional portfolios while simultaneously placing targeted investment within the investors' own jurisdiction. Such mechanisms used to control financial risk in urban investment are explored in more detail later in this chapter.

While controlling financial risk is necessary for successful targeted urban investment programs, the political risk associated with these investments must also be acknowledged. First, the targeted nature of these investments results in increased scrutiny by plan beneficiaries, politicians (especially those who disagree with targeted investment), and the media. Should these investments fail they tend to receive greater negative publicity than other failed investments in the pension fund portfolio. Secondly, given that these programs are usually undertaken by public sector pension funds, their own structure leaves them prone to political interference in investment selection that has so often marred these programs in the past. The governance structure of most public sector pension fund boards includes trustees and ex-officio members who are regularly lobbied by a variety of local constituencies. The presence of an in-state targeted investment program is often seen as a way to achieve a variety of social objectives, particularly if the state is in an economic downturn. Best practice recognizes and addresses these tendencies by insulating the pension fund from investment decisions within their own state. Often the targeted urban policy dictates that the economic health of the state be taken into account in the investment decision-making process, explicitly allowing for the possibility of no investment taking place if conditions do not warrant it.

After setting a broad geographic target, external managers are then selected through the same process as all other investment selection by the pension fund. Top quartile past performance and lengthy track records are as essential here as in any other alternative investment. External managers, either through limited and general partnerships or through fund-of-funds structures, are mandated to follow the broad geographic target set by the fund while generating the best financial returns with risk characteristics similar to other investments in the pension portfolio without regard for any anticipated social and ancillary benefits of the investment. In this way investment vehicles can review all targeted investment opportunities presented to them, while being unencumbered in the investment selection that is based purely on expected risk-adjusted returns. By following these best practices, pension funds are able to undertake targeted urban investing without falling prone to bad investment decisions that are clouded by too many non-financial objectives.[6]

This chapter examines in detail the balance between risk and return that is inherent in alternative investment strategies. It is organized in the following manner. The second section deals with strategic asset allocation and details how the appropriate policy formation and investment selection process are key to mitigating the risks inherent in these types of illiquid investments. The third section examines the range of investment opportunities available in targeted urban markets and the variety of risk factors that should be considered in these types of investments. The fourth and fifth sections highlight the management of the information and transaction costs inherent to imperfect markets that allows knowledgeable investors to net profitable returns. Here sophisticated investment intermediaries are key to unlocking value while reducing risk. We conclude this chapter with implications for the future of urban investment with its complex balance of risk and return.

## Strategic asset allocation and investment selection

Harvard Business School Professor Michael Porter (1995) highlighted the "competitive advantages" of the inner city and untapped economic opportunity in terms of the strategic location, unmet local demand, integration with regional clusters, and available human resources. Various stakeholders (institutional investors, investment fund managers, community based organizations) have different levels of criteria for what defines an underserved market and generally the criteria includes three key elements: a region (urban and rural) with limited access to investment capital; a diversified community and management composition (woman or minority ownership); and the firm in which investment is made must employ labor from a low- to moderate-income area (Green 2006). A real estate investment opportunity in an emerging domestic market may have little significant new investments yet with characteristics of being a "transitional" neighborhood with few abandoned buildings, relatively low crime, and signs of rising property values (Rivlin 2007). In thinking about the opportunities of emerging domestic market (EDM) investments they generally reach people and places overlooked from the mainstream markets that take advantage of the economic opportunities missed by conventional investors. These investments can also fall more broadly under the rubric of responsible investment that incorporate environmental, social, and governance (ESG) analysis into the investment decision-making process (Wood and Hoff 2007).

Investments in EDMs cross the three asset classes of fixed income, equity real estate, and private equity – venture capital. The decision to invest across the asset classes forms part of an institutional investor's strategic asset allocation policy. A public sector pension fund seeks to outperform the market (alpha) through a strategic investment decision-making process. Central to a pension fund's investment philosophy is their strategic asset allocation policy. The policy governs the fund's ability to minimize its investment risk and maximize return. Public pension fund trustees are increasingly looking for ways to yield higher returns and are guided by principles of modern portfolio theory and the notion that investors can maximize return by increasing variance (Markowitz 1952).

Investors seek to optimize their portfolio by minimizing risk and aim for the highest possible return through portfolio diversification. Through a spectrum of asset classes public pension funds can spread their risk across different types of investments – including EDMs. A strategic asset allocation policy helps a pension fund strike a balance between seeking opportunities and safely meeting their liabilities given the fluctuation in the markets. Chief investment officers know the importance of optimizing risk/return characteristics by investing across the spectrum that includes traditional investments (domestic and international equities and fixed-income) and alternative investments (value-added and opportunistic real estate, venture capital, and hedge funds). EDM investments are illiquid, long-term investments. Public sector pension funds are interested in these investments as they provide an opportunity for superior returns, albeit with greater risk involved. In this process the investor seeks to construct an "efficient frontier" that offers the maximum possible return for a given level of risk. The more a pension fund understands a potential investment's risk and return characteristics the more they are able to make sound investment decisions. In choosing an EDM investment fund manager to invest in the underserved markets, pension funds consider all the risks involved. The process follows rigorous selection criteria like any other traditional investment.

Generally, if a public sector pension fund seeks to invest in the underserved markets their targeted investment policies will target a goal of 2 per cent of their total portfolio, evidenced by CalPERS, CalSTRS, NYCERS, New York State Common, and MassPRIM. While the percentage is small the impact can be significant given the size of assets, with the highest being CalPERS at $250.4 billion as of December 2007. In the CalPERS example a targeted investment policy of 2 per cent equates to a capital commitment of $5 billion. Policies can include a geographic target and a requirement to fill a capital gap in low-income and underserved areas.

In the case of the Massachusetts Pension Reserves Investment Management Board (MassPRIM) the investment selection process follows the same rigorous investment criteria as traditional investments and in the process chief investment officers and analysts seek to understand the potential fund manager's track record and ability to mitigate risks. The policy includes five economically targeted investing (ETI) criteria with parameters.

The criteria include that investments should target risk-adjusted market-rate returns and provide net returns equivalent to or higher than other traditional investments, at equal levels of risk. The policy emphasizes that ETI ancillary benefits (e.g., jobs created, affordable housing units, green buildings) will not justify higher investment risk.

The policy states that the MassPRIM staff along with its consultants will seek out guarantees, third party recourse, hedging, and other risk management vehicles to reduce or eliminate risk in ETI investments. In addition the investments must not exceed a reasonable weighting in the portfolio that includes tracking the level of exposure to the Massachusetts economy as well as maintaining an appropriate geographic diversification. The MassPRIM staff and consultants, with counsel from the investment committee, manage the distribution of assets across both traditional and alternative assets, seeking to appropriately spread their risk. The committee, will take part in a rebalancing policy that is triggered when an asset class exceeds or falls below its target allocation range (Hagerman et al. 2007a). Table 8.1 illustrates MassPRIM's long-term asset allocation targets; should the distribution of assets fall outside the long-term policy target rebalancing is required.

Targeted investments form a part of this larger strategic asset allocation policy and aim to spread risk across various asset classes. A pension fund might also engage consultants with research staff that track investment fund manager performance. They manage databases of information and analyze a fund manager's ability to react to shifts in the market and achieve

**Table 8.1.** MassPRIM asset allocation as of June 30, 2007

| Asset Class | 6/30/2007 Allocation (%) | 2007 Long-term policy target (%) |
|---|---|---|
| US equity | 25.1 | 21 |
| Portable alpha | 4.8 | 5 |
| International equity | 21.0 | 20 |
| Emerging markets equity | 5.5 | 5 |
| US bonds | 10.9 | 10 |
| TIPS | 4.5 | 5 |
| High yield and emerging mkt debt | 4.6 | 5 |
| Real estate | 8.6 | 10 |
| Alternatives – private equity | 6.7 | 10 |
| timber | 3.2 | 4 |
| Absolute return | 5.1 | 5 |

*Source*: PRIT CAFR (2007, p. 59).

their targeted investments. However, consultants tend to not engage in the assessment process of targeted investments as they are more time-consuming, and the process is left to pension fund officers and staff. Targeted investments form part of an actively managed portfolio. A public sector pension fund's prudent investment philosophy is made up of a combination of an actively managed and passively managed portfolio. Combining a core passive portfolio with active peripheral holdings, such as development oriented or targeted investments, forms part of a pension fund portfolio (Litvak 1981). Targeted investments are actively managed, time intensive, riskier investments but they also form part of a strategic asset allocation policy combining active and passive investments and spreading risk along the continuum of investment portfolio management.

## Investment opportunities and risks in the underserved markets

Institutional investors invest in the emerging domestic markets across three asset classes: fixed income, equity real estate, and private equity–venture capital. Fixed income is a debt-based real estate and small business development finance product, equity real estate is a real estate finance product investing in the potential growth in market value of the investment property, and private equity (early and later stage venture capital) is the business finance product investing in mission-oriented venture capital companies (Hagerman et al. 2007b). This discussion on the investment opportunities and risks in the EDM will focus primarily on equity real estate and to a lesser extent private equity (venture capital) investments – both providing a higher risk and higher return potential to the equity investor. The equity investor in EDM equity real estate and venture capital investments provides risk capital in exchange for an equity ownership in the real estate development or mission-oriented company. The discussion briefly covers fixed-income investments, given it is a debt based product with limited downside risk.

Investment intermediaries, both investment vehicles and community partners, working with significant patient capital from institutional investors (banks, foundations, insurance companies, and public sector pension funds) can unlock the investment potential in these underserved markets (Hagerman et al. 2007b). Real estate investment vehicles investing in value added and opportunistic real estate[7] may identify areas of potential growth such as transitional neighborhoods with relatively low crime and demographic changes showing increased demand for housing, jobs, and signs of rising property values. Such opportunistic real estate might include links to transportation hubs and take advantage of historic buildings, parks, and universities with a strong fabric of social community, yet has been overlooked by conventional investors. Urban markets can offer strategically located land, existing zoning and entitlements, infrastructure, consumer demand for national retailers, and government support. Within venture capital investments it is the proximity to transportation nodes and the size and availability of the workforce that inner city companies find as their competitive advantage. The niche of many inner city companies is to provide back-office support services to the major industry clusters in the area such as hospitals, education, and financial services. Other product focused venture capital investments may specialize in emerging markets such as clean-technology and the "green" evolution.

There are various risks associated with these types of opportunistic investments in emerging domestic markets. Investments are long-term and illiquid with returns not realized until generally five to ten years out. In opportunistic real estate, Turner (2004) identifies "opportunity fund risks" typical to opportunistic equity real estate investments. In doing so Turner outlines conditions in place in the urban context that can mitigate those risks. Factors such as transportation linkages and infrastructure already in place, subsidized land costs, and an increasing population and income can offset the perceived risks of these investments. Table 8.2 highlights some of the opportunity fund risks and the expected risk mitigation in an urban investment.

An obvious advantage to investing in US emerging domestic markets is no repatriation, nationalization, or currency risk. That said, there are opportunity fund risks, as the table highlights, that come with investing in opportunistic real estate.

Venture capital investments in the underserved markets also carry with them risks to the equity investor that debt-based products do not bring with them. Some of these investments are intended to support the initial phase of business conception that can carry with it its associated risks. The trade association for community development venture capital funds, Community Development Venture Capital Alliance (CDVCA), sets forth some of the business risks of these types of investments, that can include management risk, technology/production risk, financial risk, market risk, exit risk, and policy risk. Factors such as a company's barrier to entry in an industry, the company's ability to sustain an economic downturn, and its management of human capital and financial capital all come into play.

**Table 8.2.** Opportunity fund risks and risk mitigation

| Typical opportunity fund risks | Risk mitigation expected in urban investment |
| --- | --- |
| ■ Transportation linkages | ■ In place |
| ■ Utilities/Infrastructure | ■ In place |
| ■ Land costs | ■ Subsidized or lower cost |
| ■ Construction costs | ■ Process may be aided |
| ■ Zoning risks | ■ Entitlements as a right |
| ■ Permitting risks | ■ Some costs waived, process aided |
| ■ Interest rate risk during construction | ■ Subsidized interest rates |
| ■ Interest rate risk, permanent | ■ Subsidized interest rates |
| ■ Parking | ■ Public assistance, bonding |
| ■ Real estate taxes | ■ PILOT, abatements |
| ■ Labor costs, tenants | ■ Job tax credits attract employers |
| ■ Recession | ■ Higher sales per square foot+income density |
| ■ Demographics | ■ Increasing population and income |
| ■ Repatriation risk | ■ Not applicable |
| ■ Nationalization risk | ■ Not applicable |
| ■ Currency risk | ■ Not applicable |

*Source*: Turner (2004, p. 44).

## Managing risk in urban investments

Urban investments in equity real estate and venture capital (early and later stage) are inherently riskier than traditional investments. Traditional investors often overlook investments in the underserved markets due to their perceived market imperfections. Conventional fund managers are not able to appropriately manage risk and choose to overlook these markets. Managers do not adequately pool nor spread risk among institutional investors nor price the transaction up to the associated risk. Due to insufficient information and high transaction costs traditional investors may only see lack of growth and not the inherent opportunity in the inner city (Daniels 2005). Former California State Treasurer Phil Angelides (2000) comments on the reality of imperfect markets, noting how easily capital flows to the emerging countries with high political and currency risk, yet is not invested in their own backyard. In imperfect markets the ability of clever private equity investment fund managers to reduce the high information and transaction costs (that deter traditional investors) translates into profitable returns on specialized investments.

Investment intermediaries, both investment vehicles[8] and community partners, can provide knowledgeable expertise on how to mitigate the associated risks of urban investments. An investment vehicle has in-depth expertise investing in large-scale property development and mission-oriented companies. Pension funds provide the long-term patient capital (considering the illiquidity and higher risk nature of urban investments) and the investment vehicle is able to pool assets and reduce transaction costs to achieve scale and its return objectives.

An investment vehicle's competitive advantage is in overcoming investment barriers typical of the underserved markets. They are able to manage the inherent risk in these transactions by pooling assets and spreading risk across investors. For equity real estate investments an investment vehicle may establish itself as a commingled limited partnership. In such a commingled fund the investment vehicle reaches scale by pooling assets from several institutional investors in one fund, thus enabling the fund to take a larger position in the investment venture. The commingled fund takes part in reciprocal investing by targeting geographic areas based on the public sector pension fund's (as limited partner) investment percentage in the fund.[9]

The investment fund manager's ability to manage risk requires complex financial engineering in how they source and execute deals. The use of leverage plays an important role and in the case of the USA Fund they seek out third-party debt financing of up to 75 per cent of the project cost. Managers might also take advantage of government subsidies to buoy the investment venture such as low-income housing tax credits, new markets tax credits, and real estate tax abatements. The investment fund manager's expertise is in sourcing deals in which the fund staff perform their due diligence and assess factors such as market conditions, demographic trends, and locational advantages of the investment project site (Hagerman et al. 2007c).

Community partners also play an important role in mitigating the risks of urban investments. Community partners can offer significant resources to the investment vehicle and provide the link to the community development area. Steiger et al. (2008) highlights the resources they bring that lessen the risks involved in the transaction. The resources or "toolkit" they bring includes financial tools, social and political tools, and material tools. In particular in equity real estate investments, community partners provide financial tools in the form of land zoning and easements (land preservation/conservation agreements between a landowner and a municipality), low-income housing tax credits, new markets tax credits, and other subsidies in the form of grants or loan guarantees. Community organizations are entrenched in the community and bring the relationships with key stakeholders often needed to get a development project approved. Further, community partners can bring material tools such as a land or a community facility that supports the investment.

Within the fixed income asset class in which the products are debt-based, the risks are greatly reduced with government guarantees. Investors exchange higher returns for the security and predictability of these products. The New York City Employees' Retirement System makes forward rate commitments through its Public-Private Apartment Rehabilitation Program, that includes a 100 percent guarantee from the State of New York Mortgage Agency.

## The rewards of higher risk investments

Investing in the underserved markets brings greater risk and thus higher returns. The financial returns are being measured and adjusted for illiquidity and risk of the investment. The returns are generally reported as internal rates of return (IRR). Calculating the IRR is a complex process and is the annualized rate of return of a certain set of cash flows from an investment. The IRR is the return on the investment less the cost of capital and calculates what the investor would have earned over the time horizon of the investment. The IRR formula calculates the pre-money company valuation, cash outflow (the investment), and cash inflow (cash the fund receives when it exits). The calculations can also take into account follow-on financing, exit options, and interim interest or dividend payments. The IRR is generally reported net of the investment fund manager management fees. The returns can also be calculated in terms of investment multiples calculated by adding the remaining value reported and distributions received (cash out) and dividing it by the total capital contributed (cash in).

The financial returns are reported against established benchmarks or industry standards. In fixed income the benchmark is the Lehman Aggregate Bond Index. In private equity it is the Thomson Financial Venture Economics venture capital index, which includes a Custom Venture Economics Young Fund Universe that compares a public pension fund's young funds (still in the early stage of its investment life in the first five years) to a similar universe. In equity real estate the index is the National Council of Real Estate Investment Fiduciaries (NCREIF) Property Index.

However, NCREIF is meant for more stable leased assets and has its limitations as a benchmark for comparing value-added opportunistic real estate with inherent higher risk.

In venture capital investments the early returns are often very low or negative due to the "J-Curve effect" when funds have not yet exited on the investment yet are absorbing high management fees (Hebb, 2005). That said, CalPERS, one of the more transparent pension funds in their reporting, posts returns on their Alternative Investment Management Program (AIM). The AIM program includes the California Initiative whose objective is to invest in California's underserved markets and address a capital gap in those areas. The California Initiative is CalPERS' private equity investments targeted to underserved capital markets with an emphasis on California. CalPERS allocated $480 million to the California Initiative beginning in 2001. In 2006, CalPERS further allocated another $500 million in California Initiative II. Despite the young age of the program (with average age of 2.5 years as of October 2007) the since-inception return on California Initiative Fund I is 20 per cent, with a one-year return of 70 per cent (as of October 2007) (Mark 2007).

In real estate investments the CalPERS Cure (California Urban Real Estate Initiative) has also reported strong results. A CalPERS investment committee report (September 2007) indicates that the Cure Program has generated total nominal annual returns before fees of 20.0 per cent since inception in 1997. Its five- and three-year total nominal annual returns before fees are an impressive 32.3 and 36.8 per cent, respectively (Sept. 2007). These returns significantly outperform the benchmark NCREIF Property Index of 14.8 per cent five-year and 18.0 per cent three-year returns.

The economic returns on the affordable housing investments, debt-based fixed income product, consistently outperformed the established benchmark or industry standard – the Lehman Aggregate Bond Index. The NYCERS ten-year net return (as of 12/31/06) forward-rate commitment program yielded 8.19 per cent, outperforming the Lehman Aggregate Bond Index of 6.24 per cent. NYCERS affordable housing investments are often supported by government guarantees such as the State of New York Mortgage Agency and generally yield lower returns.

In addition to the financial returns, urban investments produce positive social benefits for the employee, the community, and the environment. The "extra financial" returns move beyond the financial and have a broader socio-economic and environmental impact on the investment area. Social returns can include increased jobs, benefits such as healthcare, wealth creation, affordable housing, and green certified buildings. While social returns never compensate for a lower financial return on an investment, after a risk-adjusted competitive rate of return is delivered the social returns are important to understanding the larger impact on the investment area.

## Conclusion

Targeted urban investment requires a careful calculus to balance the risks inherent in these long-term, illiquid investments in opaque markets. Savvy investors who utilize sophisticated investment intermediaries in these markets reap financial benefits. But in order to be successful a number of key ingredients are required. First and foremost is the strategic asset allocation policy of the institutional investor. Asset allocation is fundamental to institutional investors' risk reduction and financial performance.

However, not all risk in urban investment can be mitigated through strategic asset allocation. Other risks to be factored include diversification risk, as often these investments target specific geographies and therefore place constraints on the portfolio. Additionally urban markets are often information asymmetric and opaque and therefore involve financial risk. Such investments are long-term and illiquid, increasing the exit risk of the transaction. Given their inner city location such investments also face policy risks and demographic risks. Finally we find urban investment, with its high profile targeted nature, involves significant political risk for the institutional investor.

Yet the risks in urban investment can be mitigated through a number of effective strategies and when successful, the rewards can be substantial. Such risk management is predicated on the deployment of knowledgeable investment intermediaries who specialize in urban investment. Intermediaries can overcome diversification risk through fund-of-fund structures and through reciprocal targeting that offers local investment opportunities while providing financial returns based on the total assets under management. Investment intermediaries also bring expertise that lowers the cost of both information and transactions in urban markets, thereby reducing several of the risks identified above. However, while investment intermediaries are essential for risk management in urban markets, it falls to institutional investors to understand and insulate themselves from the political risks inherent in these markets.

Over the last three decades, targeted investment has undergone a paradigm shift from a traditional subsidy-driven model to a market-driven model. This shift has been fundamental to the success of such investments. In the 1970s and early 1980s the first generation of urban investment was a purely subsidy-driven approach. Investors sought and received government monies to entice them into development of America's urban cores.

Second-generation projects came on stream in the late 1980s and early 1990s. There was a move away from purely subsidized projects toward market-based approaches with these types of investments. The term most often used was "economically targeted investments" or "ETIs". These investments were said to provide both market-rates of return and collateral benefits for the community. But too often collateral benefits trumped the market-based returns in investment decision-making. Political interference was often a factor. Many in-state pension fund investments failed to deliver financial returns. As a result ETIs lost their appeal.

Beginning in the late 1990s a new, third generation in urban investment has developed. Increasingly pension fund investment in underserved capital markets is judged primarily by the financial returns they generate. It is recognized that when investment is successful it has both positive risk-adjusted rates of return and a significant impact on its location. Ancillary benefits include affordable housing, improved infrastructure, increased employment opportunities, and expanded tax bases. In short, such investment leads to significant urban revitalization. But savvy investors no longer factor in the ancillary benefits when making investment decisions in underserved capital markets. In the capital-driven model institutional investors perceive investing in the underserved urban areas as an overlooked economic opportunity.[10]

Some final thoughts on the implications of the capital-driven model of urban investment for the future are as follows. First and foremost, success in urban investment must be measured by risk-adjusted rates of return. This discipline ensures that institutional investors put in place all necessary policies and programs to reduce risks and achieve financial returns in urban markets. In most cases this means in the face of investment programs that can be construed as political in nature, institutional investors must ensure the same standards in investment selection are followed as in their mainstream investment program. Such standards include asset allocation, diversification, and investment vehicle selection. Policies must give the investor the option not to invest in the targeted region when economic conditions would hinder financial returns. In other words, market-driven urban investment must insulate itself from political interference that perceives these investments as opportunities to gain ancillary benefits for a region without the necessary financial objectives that should govern investment selection. The success of market-driven urban investment lies in understanding that when risk and return are carefully balanced in these markets, they pay off for everyone.

## Notes

1. We would like to thank the foundations for their generous financial support of the Pension Funds & Urban Revitalization Initiative that made this research possible: The Rockefeller Foundation and Darren Walker, and the Ford Foundation and Katherine McFate and Rick McGahey. We would like to thank Dr Elaine Bernard and the Labor and Worklife Program of the Harvard Law School for their support. We also wish to thank the pension funds: CalSTRS, CalPERS, NYCERS, New York Common, and MassPRIM for their contributions to this research. We also would like to acknowledge the valuable support and guidance from the editors: Gordon L. Clark, Ashby H. B. Monk, and Adam Dixon.
2. Alpha is defined as the financial return of an asset that is greater than that of the market as a whole. The return of the market as a whole is termed beta. The search for alpha requires active investment management.
3. Targeted urban investments by large US public-sector pension funds have doubled from $6 billion in 2004 to $12 billion in just four years.
4. Some say asset allocation accounts for all portfolio performance over time. See Ibbotson and Kaplan 2000, and Drobetz and Kohler 2002 on this point.
5. The largest American public sector pension funds are increasingly utilizing fund-of-funds investment vehicles for targeted and specialized programs in an effort to streamline the number of external fund managers within their investment portfolios.
6. Here we take issue with Lerner et al. 2007, as our research indicated that when public sector pension funds follow best practice as indicated they can indeed achieve out-performance in their targeted private equity portfolios.
7. Kaiser (2005) distinguishes between the terms core (investments in fully leased multi-tenant properties), value-added (redevelopment or leasing of a property to increase its potential value at rate above general market trends), and opportunistic (purchase of distressed properties at low prices and their redevelopment, as well as new property development and heavily leveraged property ownership).

8. See Hagerman et al. 2007*b* for a detailed description of some of the investment vehicles across the asset classes of fixed income, equity real estate, and venture capital.
9. For example the USA Fund (a New Boston Real Estate Fund) has capital committed from MassPRIM and the Connecticut State Retirement System and through their commingled fund invests proportionally in projects in each of these states.
10. For an in-depth analysis of the three generations of targeted investment see Daniels and Nixon 2000.

# References

Agtmael, A. W. V. (1984). *Emerging Securities Markets: Investment Banking Opportunities in the Developing World*. London Euromoney Publications.

Akerlof, G. (1970). The Market for Lemons: Quality Uncertainty and the Market Mechanism. *Quarterly Journal of Economics*, 84(*3*), 488–500.

Angelides, P. (2000). The double bottom line: investing in California's emerging markets. California State Treasurer's Office. Sacramento, CA.

Bodie, Z. and Merton, R. (1993). Pension Fund Benefit Guarantees in the United States: A Functional Analysis. In R. Schmitt (ed.), *The Future of Pensions in the United States* (pp. 194–234). Philadelphia: University of Pennsylvania Press.

CalPERS (2007). Investment Committee: Real Estate Portfolio Performance Report, Sacramento, CA, 30 September 2007.

Campbell, J. Y. and Viceira, L. M. (2002). *Strategic Asset Allocation: Portfolio Choice for Long-Term Investers*. Oxford: Oxford University Press.

Clark, G. L. (2000). *Pension Fund Capitalism*. Oxford: Oxford University Press.

—— (2005). Setting the agenda: the geography of global finance. *Oxford University Centre for the Environment, Working Paper Series*, WP 05–03, Oxford. Retrieved February, 2008, from http://www.geog.ox.ac.uk/research/transformations/wpapers/

—— and Hebb T. (2004). Corporate Engagement: The fifth stage of capitalism. *Relations industrielles/Industrial Relations*, 59, 142–70.

—— —— and Wójcik, D. (2007). Institutional investors and the language of finance: the global metrics of market performance. In J. Godfrey and K. Chalmers (eds.), *Globalisation of Accounting Standards* (pp. 15–33). Cheltenham: Edward Elgar.

Daniels, B. (2005). Maryland family of funds market assessment & investment strategy. Economic Innovation International, Inc. Report and presentation to the Maryland Community Equity Fund Working Group. Baltimore, MD.

—— and Nixon, J. (2003). Making markets work for inner city revitalization. Paper presented at the Inner City Economic Forum Conference, New York, 16 Oct. 2003.

Davis, E. P. and Steil, B. (2001). *Institutional Investors*. Cambridge, MA: MIT Press.

Dicken, P. (2001). *Global Shift*. New York: Guilford Press.

Dicken, P. and Thrift, N. (1992). The Organization of Production and the Production of Organization. *Transactions of the Institute of British Geographers*, 17, 279–91.

Drobetz, W. and Kohler, F. (2002). The contribution of asset allocation policy to portfolio performance. *Journal of Financial Markets and Portfolio Management*, 16(2), 219–33.

Fama, E. F. (1970). Efficient capital markets: a review of theory and empirical work. *Journal of Finance*, 25, 383–417.

Greene, D. (2006, Spring). The California Initiative Revisited. *Journal of EDM Finance*, 12–18.

Greenwich and Associates (2007). Report on Pension Fund and Endowment Asset Allocation Trends. Retrieved February, 2008 In http://www.greenwich.com/WMA/greenwich_reports/

Harvey, D. (1982). *Limits to Capital*. New-Verso edn. London: Verso.

—— (1996). *Justice, Nature and the Geography of Difference*. Oxford: Blackwell.

Hagerman, L. A., Clark, G. L. and Hebb, T. (2007*a*). Massachusetts Pension Reserves Investment Management Board: Urban Investing Through a Transparent Selection Process. *Oxford University Centre for the Environment Working Paper Series*, WP 06–16. Retrieved February 2008, from http://www.geog.ox.ac.uk/research/transformations/wpapers/

—— —— —— (2007*b*). Investment Intermediaries in Economic Development: Linking Public Pension Funds to Urban Revitalization. *Community Development Investment Review of the Federal Reserve Bank of San Francisco*, 3(1), 45–65.

—— —— —— (2007*c*). Investment intermediaries in economic development. *Oxford University Centre for the Environment Working Paper Series*, WP 07–09. Retrieved February 2008, from http://www.geog.ox.ac.uk/research/transformations/wpapers/

Hawley, J. P. and Williams, A. T. (2000). *The Rise of Fiduciary Capitalism*. Philadelphia: University of Pennsylvania Press.

Hebb, T. (2005). California Case Study A: Private Equity CalPERS' California Initiative. *Oxford University Centre for the Environment Working Paper Series*, WP 05–15. 1–28. Retrieved February, 2008, from http://www.geog.ox.ac.uk/research/transformations/wpapers/

—— and Wójcik, D. (2005). Global standards and emerging markets: the institutional investment value chain and CalPERS' investment strategy. *Environment and Planning A*, 37, 1955–74.

Ibbotson, R. and Kaplan, P. (2000). Does asset allocation policy explain 40, 90 or 100 per cent of performance? *Financial Analyst Journal*, 56(1), 26–33.

Kaiser, R. W. (2005). Investment styles and style boxes in equity real estate: can the emerging model succeed in classifying real estate alternatives? *Journal of Real Estate Portfolio Management*, 11(1), 5–18.

Lerner, J. et al. (2007). Smart Institutions, Foolish Choices: The Limited Partner Performance Puzzle. *Journal of Finance*, 62(2), 731–64.

Litvak, L. (1981). Pension funds and economic renewal. In M. Barker (ed.), *Studies in Development Policy*, Vol. 12. Washington, DC: The Council of State Planning Agencies.

Mark, J. (2007). CalPERS Alternative Investment Management Program, Investing in California's Underserved Markets, Power Point Presentation to Inner City Economic Forum Summit, Philadelphia, PA, 18 October 2007.

Markowitz, H. (1952). Portfolio selection. *The Journal of Finance* 7 (1), 77–91.

Merton, R. C. (1969). Lifetime portfolio selection under uncertainty. *Review of Economics and Statistics*, 51, 247–57.

Monks, R. A. G. (2001). *The New Global Investors*. Oxford: Capstone Publishing Ltd.

Peck, J. and Tickell A. (2002). Neoliberalizing Space. In N. Brenner and N Theodore. (eds.), *Spaces of Neoliberalism: Urban Restructuring in North America and Westeren Europe* (pp. 33–57). Oxford: Blackwell.

Porter, M. E. (1995, May/June). The competitive advantage of the inner city. *Harvard Business Review*, 73, 55–71.

Rivlin, A. M. (2007). Targeting urban revitalization. *Federal Reserve Bank of Boston Communities & Banking*, 18(1), 12–15.

Samuelson, P. (1969). Lifetime Portfolio Selection by Dynamic Stochastic Programming, *Review of Economics and Statistics*, 51, 239–46.

Scott, A. J. (2000). Economic Geography: The Great Half-Century. In G. Clark, M. Feldman and M. Gertler (eds.), *The Oxford Handbook of Economic Geography* (pp. 18–44). Oxford: Oxford University Press.

Spence, A. M. (1973). Job market signaling. *Quarterly Journal of Economics*, 83, 355–77.

Steiger, A., Hebb T., and Hagerman, L. A. (2008). The Case for the Community Partner in Economic Development. In D. Fabiani and T. F. Buss (eds.), *Reengineering Community Development for the 21st Century* (pp. 60–75). Armonk, New York: M. E. Sharpe.

Stiglitz, J. E. (2000). The Contributions of the Economics of Information to Twentieth Century Economics. *Quarterly Journal of Economics*, 115(4), 1441–78.

Swyngedouw, E. (1993). Communication, mobility and the struggle for power over space. In G. Giannopoulos and A. Gillespie (eds.), *Transport and Communications in the New Europe* (pp. 305–25). London: Belhaven.

Thrift, N. and Olds, K. (1996). Reconfiguring the Economic in Economic Geography. *Progress in Human Geography*, 20(3), 311–37.

Tickell, A. (2000). Finance and Localities. In G. L. Clark, M. P. Feldman, and M. S. Gertler (eds.), *The Oxford Handbook of Economic Geography* (pp. 230–47). Oxford: Oxford University Press.

Tobin, J. (1958). Liquidity preference as behavior towards risk. *The Review of Economic Studies*, 25, 65–86.

Torrance, M. (2007). Forging glocal governance? Urban infrastructures as networked financial products. *Oxford University Centre for the Environment Working Paper Series*, WP 07–05. Retrieved February 2008, from http://www.geog.ox.ac.uk/research/transformations/wpapers/

Turner, R. (2004, Spring). Investing in Urban Real Estate for Profit or Not For Profit. *PREA Quarterly*, 38–49.

Wood, D. and Hoff, B. (2007). Handbook on Responsible Investment Across Asset Classes. *Boston College Institute for Responsible Investment*, Retrieved February 2008, from http://bcccc.net/index.cfm?fuseaction=page.viewPage&PageID=1869

Yago, G, Zeidman, B., and Schmidt, B. (2003). Creating capital jobs and wealth in communities. *Milken Institute*, Retrieved February 2008 In http://www.milkeninstitute.org/publications/publications

# 9

# Managing Financial Risks in Urban Environments

*Samuel Randalls*

Urban areas inspire a diversity of environmental discourses, with cities being seen equally as a significant source of environmental pollution such as $CO_2$ (carbon dioxide) emissions, but also as sites for reinvigorating societies on more environmentally friendly pathways (Bulkeley and Betsill 2005). While mass transportation and dense housing both lead to lower $CO_2$ emissions per person, urbanites also require more imported food and consume large quantities of energy and water. This rational calculation of the environmental impacts of cities is supplemented by a vivid imaginary where cities become examples of what might happen if urgent action is not taken against environmental threats. Sea-level rise and flooding have probably been the most dramatic of these scenarios partly due to the relatively low-lying nature of cities such as the city of London or Manhattan, and partly through the contemporary focus on climate change as the predominant environmental issue.

Films, novels, and other popular media generate images of aliens, terrorists, or tornadoes destroying cities, whereby the city becomes a site of vulnerability that exposes the fragility of modern life (Davis 1999). The concentration of significant numbers of people provides fertile territory for the "what if" imagination (Furedi 2007): what if X event happened in downtown New York? Emerging in response to these threats are various forms of risk modeling and mapping, preparedness exercises and scenario planning. Each of these are committed to "...conjuring up, and then institutionally preparing for, the very worst" (Masco 2006, 16) as well as the more extensive number of smaller events. These scenarios are bolstered by a number of recent events including Hurricane Katrina, which uprooted the already strained social fabric of New Orleans, or the 1995 Chicago heat wave that exposed the extant inequities that frame heat-wave exposure (Klinenberg 2002). What these examples demonstrate is that mapping urban environmental risks is equally mapping social and economic inequalities, cultural assumptions, and governance mechanisms that play such a significant role in the geographies of casualties (Klinenberg 2002).

What has this to do with financial risk? Ironically, while the catastrophe seems to loom larger, these events are increasingly perceived as manageable risks (Furedi 2007). The urban environment becomes subject to numerous engineering projects, disaster preparedness exercises, and financial or insurance products that will either directly or indirectly protect against the worst effects of a catastrophic occurrence. Increasingly the management of urban environments has been transformed into a neo-liberal approach that prioritizes market strategies and individual responsibility for protection as opposed to direct government intervention. What this means is that governments have legitimated and regulated industries, such as insurance companies, to perform both a recovery function in providing disaster relief and a prevention function through the pricing of contracts in ways that discourage risk-taking behavior. This leads to insurance companies taking on centralized expertise to calculate risks and at the same time maximizing the individual's responsibility in ensuring adequate protection (Bennett 1999). As governance strategies expand the role of risk management and insurance in providing protection, there has been an impressive development of new products in alternative risk markets. These are more frequently financial products rather than strictly insurance products, as regulatory boundaries of insurance restrict the innovation that is possible compared to capital markets. Weather derivatives, catastrophe bonds, and hurricane contracts are all examples of new financial products that have emerged within this space.

This management of urban environmental risks as environmental finance is the subject of this chapter, which explores the diverse and innovative new products that are emerging as risk management mechanisms. It is not straightforward, however, to map environmental dangers into financial risks; this is a process that requires work involving datasets, models, pricing equations, maps, and many other tools of actuarial or financial practice. Only once these tools are constructed, legitimated, and fungible is it possible to financially manage the financial risks arising from environmental events. In addition, emerging markets in $CO_2$

emissions, for example, highlight that preventing the environmental events has also become a site for financial innovation and development.

The topic of quantification has proved particularly important in recent times. The sub-prime crisis has brought into focus the role of numbers and ratings in aiding the circulation of finance, but it has also highlighted the difficulty of actually tracking down what these numbers mean or represent. Environmental finance offers new topics for these questions given the necessity of homogenizing and standardizing carbon for the emissions markets or calculating risk and return rates for hurricane markets. Understanding the normative assumptions that guide these industry or regulatory mathematical accounts of risk can make explicit the political commitments embedded within today's financial markets (de Goede 2004).

This chapter is therefore not focused on the technicalities of financial risk management, but rather follows that of scholars interested in the politics and governance of finance through theoretical approaches that draw inspiration from Foucaultian governmentality and poststructural International Relations (e.g., Ewald 1991; Ericson, Barry, and Doyle 2000; O'Malley 2003; de Goede 2004). These approaches engage with fundamental questions about the management of financial risks through examining the ways in which risks are understood and perceived to be manageable, the tools and techniques enrolled in this management, and the political repercussions of imagining risks this way. Critically examining the role of various examples of what might be termed a neo-liberal approach in which the state becomes a facilitator of financial mechanisms, rather than acting as a guardian (O'Malley 2003), becomes a crucial part of understanding the centrality of finance in society today. Thus, these literatures provide a valuable approach to explore a topic like environmental finance, because there is so much politically at stake here.

In this chapter some of the key instruments for managing environmental financial risks will be outlined highlighting the ways in which environments have to be made into financial risks. Then it will go on to examine the repercussions of this management and what it might obscure or open up. Finally it will conclude by suggesting that this neo-liberalizing of environmental management through financial markets also requires political work to support it. The focus in this chapter will be on climate-related risks, partly because climate change debates render urban environments as "at risk" sites and partly because climate finance may currently be considered an evolving and innovative sector within finance.

## Making environmental finance

Before it is possible to imagine managing urban environmental financial risks, environments must first be seen in terms of risks that need managing and secondly as quantified financial risks able to be traded within financial markets. The latter decades of the twentieth century saw the rise of risk-based governance within social and environmental regulation, whether this is attributed to the emergence of new types of risks as in Beck's (1992) argument about a "risk society" or to the growing centrality of risk as a device to manage uncertainty in approaches to regulation (a good discussion is in Rothstein, Huber, and Gaskell 2006). Risk, however, could not simply be a measure of harm or a technical topic. As Jasanoff (1999) points out, risk must be understood as a social, political artefact. Environments in this sense are not inherently risky, but rather the urban environmental risks arise through cultural-political practices that designate certain types of threats as controllable or in need of reduction. As Meyer (2000) highlights, throughout history snow has variously been deemed a hazard or resource in relation to different organization of transport systems, water systems, cultural activities, etc. and their changing exposure to snowfall. There is nothing inherently risky about snowfall.

The construction of environmental risks, allied to increasing corporate and governmental attention, has promoted a range of new modeling and mapping exercises. Environments are recorded, monitored, mapped, and experimented upon in the production of new series of datasets, statistics, and models that can provide quantitative evidence (and quantitative bounds on uncertainty) and a fungible measure of environmental value that allow environments to become part of economic calculations. Snow, for example, is measured, forecasted, mapped, and modeled as an environmental phenomenon to be most effectively managed to reduce the costly risks and maximize the benefits, through, for example, snow warnings or reservoir water planning.

Through the 1980s and 1990s the environment has been increasingly managed in quasi- or explicitly economic terms. This can be seen in concepts such as critical load in acid rain policies (Asdal 2008) and climate stabilization to prevent "dangerous anthropogenic interference" in climate change policies, whereby the atmosphere becomes a quantified resource through which companies can efficiently (through markets) determine the most cost-effective use of that air pollution capacity. These, however, are not explicitly financial risks and it is only in the markets that result from these policies (e.g., markets for Sulphur Dioxide or $CO_2$) that environmental risks become translated into financial risks. Nevertheless imagining environments economically becomes an important first step toward opening up the space for a financial rendering of environmental issues.

If it was simply pollution markets then the question of financialization of environmental issues would rapidly become one of effectiveness of those policies, but nascent environmental finance has been far more innovative and wide-ranging than that. Activities range from markets in wetland banking, weather derivatives, catastrophe bonds, biodiversity offsets, water futures, and carbon finance, through to the rise of sustainability indices, clean technology hedge funds, carbon accountancy schemes, and a multitude of other organizations or indices that are underpinning the environmental finance industries. This is a creative arena where the number of different products has been growing rapidly as investors explore alternative, uncorrelated investment opportunities,[1] and companies make greater environmental commitments. Take the example of wetland mitigation banking where wetlands can be traded in one area to be "re-built" elsewhere allowing development projects to proceed (Robertson 2007). Or consider the financing deals concerning biodiversity (swapping genes for debt relief) whereby genetic material becomes quantified in relation to extant monetary loans and commitments (Castree 2003). Environmental finance is a creative and vibrant sector bolstered by companies and governments progressively translating environmental issues into manageable risks, indeed ones that must be managed. Industry journals such as *Environmental Finance* and its sister publication *Carbon Finance* demonstrate the growing interest and diversity of products within this sector. The environmental finance industries are innovating new financial mechanisms through which previously difficult decisions can be made more palatable, for example, the exchange of ecologies from one area to another or the reduction of $CO_2$ emissions or managing the growing costs of flood insurance coverage.

One difficulty that arises in creating financial products on these environmental issues is the complexity of quantitatively mapping and estimating damage curves under various scenarios. As Ramamurtie (1999, 174) puts it, "...insurability is a function of the measurability of the phenomenon against which protection is being sought." If the environment cannot be measured, indexed, and modeled then it is hard to justifiably write insurance or capital market products. Modeling environmental risk is frequently a very sophisticated process, practiced by government agencies, university professors, private consultancies, and specialist risk companies

213

such as Risk Management Solutions. These models draw upon a wide range of data sources and theoretical equations to produce sets of maps or figures that highlight areas of concern under various risk scenarios. Risk modeling, however, involves intellectual commitments too including a belief in the calculability of risks and knowability of future scenarios. This is represented for example in the famous statement that there are no bad risks, only mis-priced risks (cited for example in Bennett 1999, 199). As Bougen (2003) highlights one of the problems for initially attracting capital market interest for catastrophe insurance is a degree of incredulity at the possibility of being able to quantify such an unknowable risk. The difficulties in modeling these risks become further compounded within corporate financial risk management where portfolio management of environmental risks can become quite tricky given the risks embedded within the initial set of outputs, whether these are in the form of modeled future events or prices. Risk can be generated as much as reduced by innovative financial products where the indices appear to drift away from the initial object the product is purported to manage and where regulation struggles to grapple with the rate of innovation (Tickell 2000; Arnoldi 2004).

In the following section a number of these financial products will be examined in relation to urban areas and climatic risks, after which some initial conclusions will be drawn about the implications of managing urban environmental risks through financial markets.

## Examples of environmental finance

Insurance products are traditionally considered when managing the costs of environmental risks. Their function is relatively straightforward as householders or companies buy protection coverage for their property or activities. The insurance company collects a premium, where the price is modeled on past event frequencies and damage costs, and then will normally package up a number of these risks and transfer them to the reinsurance markets. The re-insurers circulate these risks, spreading them across a wide range of companies such that in the event of a payout it is unlikely that any individual company will be left holding a bill that is larger than the capital they can raise. This basic protection mechanism has provided stability to insurance products thus forging belief and trust in the system, even if there is an insurance capacity cycle resulting from the consolidations and mergers that regularly follow a catastrophic event. It must also be noted that governments regulate insurance coverage and prices to prevent widespread reduction of coverage in the aftermath of a severe event and, as McLeman and Smit (2006) note, insurance is also frequently subsidized. For example, in the United States, flood insurance policy premiums may be 40 per cent lower than the modeled cost of coverage (McLeman and Smit 2006).

Increasingly, however, insurers have come under pressure from the rising payouts that each event generates and from fears that the industry could fail in the event of a severe scenario or systemic risk (e.g., a direct hurricane hit on New York). Can the insurance industry cope given this scenario? While some insurers lay the blame at the feet of anthropogenic climate change, there is significant evidence that the rising costs in weather and climate insurance are primarily related to societal changes including house building in "at risk" locations, greater coverage of products, and larger insured losses per storm (Changnon 2003; Pielke et al. 2008). There is nothing particularly uninsurable about climate change risks though increased premium costs or reduction in coverage are sometimes justified on this basis. Nevertheless fears of adverse effects of climate change on insurance affordability and availability have encouraged the creation of innovative products and public–private partnerships to engage with this risk (Mills 2005; Walker, Eyre, and Punter 2005). One example is the US government's search for new products for flood-prone areas to replace traditional insurance coverage (Bougen 2003).

Insurance products are relatively tightly regulated, so new capital market products can be more innovative and less demanding in terms of government intervention or capital protection against a payout. It is important to stress with Ewald (1999, 21) that "... there is no such thing as insurance in general," and the following should be seen as examples of new capital and insurance products to manage these risks each of which have their own histories and networks. They have emerged, however, from the failure of insurance to deal with certain types of risks, for example, the non-extreme weather risks that form the heart of the weather derivatives market, and the fears of exposure in the insurance industry that have led to the creation of new methods of making insurance risks into capital market products to thereby spread the risk further. While there has been a limited market in pluvius insurance, which can mitigate the costs for local fetes of rainy days, many non-extreme weather risks are difficult to write into insurance contracts due to certain legal clauses. In an insurance contract there must be both an insurable interest (something that stands to be lost if a particular event occurs) and proof of loss (that the loss was directly sustained because of that event). It is frequently difficult for businesses to prove losses from non-extreme, or everyday, weather events and thus new markets have grown up within the capital markets to service these "uninsurable" risks.

Increasingly re-insurers have been turning to new products that straddle the divide between insurance and capital markets in attempts to ensure that catastrophic events will still be insurable in the future (i.e., that allow payments to be made on the occurrence of catastrophic events without collapsing the insurance sector). This has been accompanied by calls from both private companies as well as government for decreasing regulation and state intervention in these markets to allow private market initiatives like catastrophe bonds to develop. Catastrophe bonds allow the reinsurance risk to be securitized through capital markets, quantifying the risks to meet demand (and money) from the capital markets for new tradeable exotic products that allow the diversification of investment strategies (Bougen 2003). Both insurance and capital markets gain from this.

In Guy Carpenter and Company's (part of Marsh and McLellan) annual review of the catastrophe bond market they estimated that by the end of 2007 there was an outstanding risk capital of $13.8 billion, up from $8.5 billion in 2006, and $7 billion in publicly disclosed bond issuances (again up from $4.7 billion in 2006 and $2 billion in 2005) (Guy Carpenter 2008). US earthquakes, US hurricanes, European windstorms, and Japanese earthquakes are the most popular products in terms of total risk capital (Guy Carpenter 2008), and urban areas are clearly the most feared strike locations. A critical component of the rise of catastrophe bonds has been the growing belief in the calculability and modeling capacity for catastrophic risks that provide semblance of justifiable price and damage estimates for the capital market traders to work with. The ability to trade catastrophe risk in the capital markets allowed new forms of coping mechanism within the insurance industry that could at least partly bypass the re-insurance companies. An early example of this was Tokyo Disney's 1999 securitization of $200 million of earthquake property damage in the capital markets (cited in Bougen 2003, 265). Catastrophe contract payouts can be triggered in two primary ways, though hybrids of the two approaches are also possible. These are an indemnity approach that functions as an insurance-style contract and is based on the actual payout of losses, or index-based approaches that pay out on a particular event occurring regardless of actual recorded losses making it a derivatives-style contract. Apart from the different regulatory regimes implied by these differences, the first is substantially more costly, more difficult to trade and slower in providing payout than the second approach, though it suffers less from basis risk (the difference between the payout from the contract and the actual cost sustained) and does not incorporate derivatives accountancy rules (e.g., mark-to-market accounting) (Guy Carpenter 2008).

These products cannot only be seen as a risk-spreading mechanism, they are far more innovative in that they encourage taking on catastrophe risks as a profit-making strategy (Bougen 2003). Risk here is very productive (Zaloom 2004) in that these products actively require (acceptable levels of) risk to be seen as potential profit. Indeed as re-insurers claim that certain risks are no longer calculable and therefore insurable, capital markets can provide new opportunities that will limit the risk of high prices or limited capacity from the traditional re-insurance market by opening up spaces for index-based contracts for which direct proof or calculation of losses is not important. While these inevitably lend an element of risk in terms of payout, they are easier to calculate and price and due to the index becoming the risk traded rather than the payout total, they are usually cheaper too. Catastrophe bonds provide insurance in terms of trading around an index, an approach also characteristic of the weather derivatives market.

If catastrophe bonds transgress the insurance and capital markets divide, then weather derivatives present a further example of this intertwining though they are focused more on everyday weather than extreme weather. Weather derivatives are financial contracts where payment is related to a meteorological index usually derived from a particular meteorological station's instruments. This index can be based on temperature, snowfall, precipitation, or alternatively on a related measure such as heating or cooling degree-days (HDDs and CDDs), which were originally energy sector indices scaled according to the temperature at which no heating or cooling is usually required (18 °C; 65 °F). Weather derivatives are cash-settled, index-based products that can be used to mitigate short term or seasonal weather. Emerging in the US energy sector in 1997, weather derivatives have subsequently spread to most continents and into many different economic sectors from agriculture to golf courses (Clemmons 2002). One potential advantage of this more pro-active financial management of environmental costs should be cost savings that can be passed on to consumers. The recorded statistics for the weather derivatives market, collated by PriceWaterhouseCoopers for the Weather Risk Management Association, show the 2006–7 market had a total notional value of $19.2 billion, vastly reduced from 2005–6's $45.2 billion, but still sizeably larger than 2004–5's $8.4 billion (PriceWaterhouseCoopers 2007). Much of the growth is related to the rise of the Chicago Mercantile

Exchange's weather market, which has become a critical actor in enabling investors and hedge funds to engage in alternative investment opportunities, thus providing increased liquidity for companies looking to hedge their risks.

It is not coincidental that most weather derivatives are traded on city airport meteorological data records; these being both secure and located near the main areas of demand for energy companies, the key protagonists in establishing weather derivatives. Weather risk for the UK, for example, will frequently be traded through London Heathrow temperatures based on the excellent correlation between that dataset and UK energy demand. This is because even if temperatures vary across the UK they do so in reasonable correlation to London (at least as implied by energy demand). The important point to note here is that it is not necessarily that the urban center is most "at risk" from environmental changes, but rather that these sites become the nodes through which the trading is channeled. This pattern is further re-enforced by the Chicago Mercantile Exchange's choice of listing weather contracts on cities such that the exchange market becomes heavily focused on urban weather risks too. Managing the urban environment stands in for managing environmental risks more generally.

While contracts have been taken out in Japan to protect construction companies when there are a below average number of typhoons in a year and they have less rebuilding and demolition work, the listing of a hurricane index for trading on the Chicago Mercantile Exchange since 2007 has extended the possibilities of trading contracts based upon the number of severe weather events or the highest magnitude event in any given year. Carvill, a reinsurance intermediary focusing on hurricane risks, designed this index that incorporates an anticipation of the potential damage from a storm through a constant re-assessment of the meteorological nature of the hurricane as it approaches land. The land is split into six regions from the US Gulf and Atlantic coasts, covering in totality from Brownsville in southern Texas (on the Mexico border) to Eastport in the Northeastern corner of Maine. The more financially damaging a hurricane is likely to be (depending on whether cities or oilfields are in its path) the higher the index will rise. This allows for companies to financially protect themselves against potentially high payout events. This index-based trading does not depend upon proof of loss in which the payout is linked to the damage actually caused so these contracts are more flexible, but potentially harder to accurately match potential cost and contract payout amounts (i.e., an event can occur and the payout be too small if the index undervalues the risks, or alternatively too large if the event causes less damage than was suggested by the index value). These products not only provide coverage, they also generate speculative possibilities that, given the more visible post-Katrina focus on hurricane prediction, allows companies to trade on the basis of increasingly sophisticated hurricane models. There is a certain irony that depending upon the positions taken a trader could end up requiring a devastating hurricane to ensure a payout.[2] Equally, without the liquidity these speculators and investors bring to these markets there would be little additional risk protection available for companies that would be severely exposed in the event of a damaging hurricane. Even more innovatively there may be different responses to hurricanes in weather and energy markets that could also be exploited to provide innovative risk management or profitable cross-correlations. One example would be to manage hurricane exposure through energy markets knowing that a direct hit on the Gulf Coast would likely increase the price of gas and oil futures contracts.

Weather products, however, do not just exist as a function of the desire to mitigate the costs of weather or as creative finance that opens up investment opportunities. As Pollard et al. (2008, 619) put it, "[f]irms now find themselves in a cultural and financial environment that is becoming less tolerant of weather-related losses." Weather and climate risk management through financial products is (slowly) becoming a normalized business practice. This implies a rather important point about environmental finance. The existence of environmental risks does not necessarily lead to a prescription of a financial response or the necessity of any response; rather, environmental finance becomes necessary as a result of social, political, and economic developments that create a regulatory or economic need for environmental markets to manage urban environmental risks as a result of a cultural change in envisioning those risks. Weather risks may have been accepted as part of business fluctuations in the past, but weather exposure has come to be seen as increasingly risky, hence in need of management.

If urban centers are perceived as at greatest risk from various climatic changes (whether justified or not), then managing the financial costs of climate change is also likely to be city-focused. Connected to this, cities are increasingly playing a visible role in carbon reduction measures to prevent "dangerous" climate change, through various forms of taxes, governance of the populace and, within the European Union, an international carbon market (Slocum 2004; Bulkeley and Betsill 2005). Creating a market for carbon trading is not straightforward given the many difficulties in calculating emissions and reductions (Lohmann

2005; MacKenzie 2007). Nevertheless this government-led approach to managing emissions has grown in importance to companies with large emission profiles even if the political caveats and allowances thus far have somewhat weakened actual emission reductions. Emissions markets are cap-and-trade markets that involve a total number of carbon credits in the market, but the allocation of them after the initial distribution to companies, is related to the amount of $CO_2$ produced. Should a company emit more $CO_2$ than they have credits they have to purchase more in the marketplace and should many companies require these at the same time, the price of a credit will rise.

A market for carbon futures has subsequently developed on the European Climate Exchange, enabling the carbon market to function similarly to other financial markets (MacKenzie 2007). $CO_2$ prices in the EU market have been somewhat volatile thus far, but one factor that will be important is the weather. Cold winter weather frequently leads to energy companies requiring more $CO_2$ credits as they have to switch on or increase production at coal-fired power stations to meet rising demand. Hot summers when nuclear power productivity is down or dry periods in Scandinavia reducing hydropower production are also important weather events reducing the availability of credits in the marketplace. These linkages between emissions and weather lead to some interesting hedging opportunities to manage both these risks as well as energy prices through the energy markets (Jewson and Jones 2005). Again urban areas will play a significant role in the development of this market being the sites of much of this energy demand and the site of the relevant thermometers.

Cities, then, will be at the center of both mitigation and adaptation agendas around climate change. In 2008, UBS explicitly linked these agendas through the launch of their Global Warming Index, which integrates a 50 per cent component from the EU emission credit prices and a 50 per cent component from temperature degree-days. This "global" index of climate change allows the management of short and medium distance futures and directly ties together a temperature change and emission price changes. While context might seem to be erased within the UBS Global Warming Index, it is importantly reinscribed in that it reproduces the energy and urban focus of the weather derivatives market more generally as well as the industrial-sectoral biases of the emissions markets. These innovative financial responses to climate change, therefore, reproduce a climate policy focused on energy and cities that create cities as sites of risk and exemplars of change.[3] If cities are threatened by long-term climate change, can these products also be adopted to manage the long distance future?

Speculatively, an international climate change market could develop that would allow companies to trade global mean temperature (as a proxy for various climate risks) further into the future than a couple of years ahead. The UBS index may be the initiator of this, and it must be recognized that the EU emissions market, with a possible international version in the future, already provides a proxy of global climate damage that is to be avoided by placing an upper limit on $CO_2$ emissions. A climate change index would become the global expression of "geomoney" (Pryke 2007), literally remaking the world's climate through a market and then compensating the losers from the new climate regime. This financial management of weather and climate risks provokes a number of issues relating to the implications of this management on people around the world and these are the subjects of the following section.

## Managing environments as financial risks

What does the management of environmental risks in urban areas as environmental finance imply about the ways in which governments and businesses are responding to perceived or actual environmental threats to the city? Clearly managing financial risk becomes as important as managing environmental risks, indeed they directly relate to each other. This raises two particular sets of issues. Firstly, and most importantly, how managing the risk becomes about managing inputs ($CO_2$ emissions), outputs (e.g., storms), and risk potential (e.g., houses on floodplains) as directly connected parts, and then secondly about the personalization often implied in these policies.

Firstly, the management of environmental risks financially suggests a neo-liberal policy that re-orients the role of government to one of "... empowerment rather than material aid" (O'Malley 2003, 278) in the event of a disaster. This argument draws upon the international nature of environmental issues to argue that state-based regulation or management no longer makes sense. Given vulnerable individuals and new international financial networks, these two groups should be directly connected through various forms of weather protection policies such as those offered by the World Bank and backed up in the weather derivatives market (Syroka and Wilcox 2006). This approach is supported by the fact that these financial products can ensure compensation in the event of a disaster relatively quickly (certainly quicker than disaster aid) as they pay out on the event occurring not on actual proved losses. This therefore reduces immediate vulnerabilities after the event, though, unless the networks are well managed, might replace them with vulnerabilities to financial capital circuits that model, price, and delimit the coverage of these policies. Here neo-liberalized environmental finance is used for socially supportive policies, even if there is some responsibility on the individual to ensure protection. Alternatively this could be managed by a state system in which governments use hedging instruments to put money aside into a fund in case of a catastrophic event occurring or directly use catastrophe bonds as a way of immediately sourcing finance in the aftermath of an event (Kunreuther and Linnerooth-Bayer 2003).

Insurance and environmental finance can and is also being used more proactively. A common problem with insurance is the lack of incentive for individuals or companies to reduce exposure to risk by, for example, investing in floodplain protection (Kunreuther 2006). As these insurance and capital products are being developed, however, increasingly the role of insurance protection is being re-evaluated too. These financial mechanisms can be integrated into projects of urban infrastructure or made a regulatory requirement, thereby using the weather-related risk factor as a key pricing component in the decision over where and what to build. Calculating the potential financial risks of building in that area and the associated coverage costs can be used to restrict building in "risky" areas thus reducing future economic damages from hurricanes. Alternatively hurricane contracts (whether via insurance or capital markets initially) could be tied into house building projects to protect the construction company and/or their eventual owners against hurricane events, to ensure that building can proceed in "risky" areas even if traditional insurance mechanisms are no longer available. Insurance and markets thus become societal regulating devices, modes of governing (Ewald 1991), in which urban development becomes related to calculated weather and climate risks in a multitude of ways.

Thus as Block (2006) argues should happen, a fully privatized weather system can be envisaged whereby urban protection is dependent upon the ability or willingness to pay for coverage and where insurers attempt to attract sufficient business to justify investment in better modeling, prediction, and geo-engineering approaches as strategies for urban weather management. These financial contracts by themselves, however, may not prevent the building of mansions in risk-prone areas where insurance coverage may be an acceptable price for the value of the view thereby creating an insurance zoning which places the highest insurance risks into the most risky places. This is particularly the case given there is some evidence that as wealth increases, people purchase more insurance (McLeman and Smit 2006). Insurance thus could create a new socio-economic geography of cities where environmental insurance determinants (re-)enforce wealth distinctions. Equally, however, the argument can be made that providing flood insurance or government assistance in these regions simply means extracting more money from less flood prone regions to cover these losses and that a more efficient market system of insurance would provide better protection to rich and poor alike (Block 2006; McLeman and Smit 2006).

Indirectly carbon markets also control future climate risks by limiting emissions to prevent the worst environmental calamities from occurring. Joining climate and emissions, as the UBS index does, could eventually lead to a market in which the cost of emissions permits relates directly to the cost of climate damages (avoided). Insurance too could draw on its social function of providing protection against the reckless actions of other individuals or companies (Glenn 2003), by opening up the possibility of litigation if severe weather events can be attributed to large companies emissions (Allen 2005a; 2005b). The fear of litigation costs could be sufficient to drive emissions reductions. Taking the logic one stage further liability insurance against future climate change cases becomes a necessary component for $CO_2$-emitting companies, even while they engage in markets that are explicitly designed to manage their emissions and potentially while they participate in weather and catastrophe markets to protect against the effects of any climate event on their business. From mitigation to adaptation to protection, the climate becomes managed with market-based products that compensate or charge depending on the overall efforts of companies internationally. While this market-based approach has become the primary strategy for managing climate change and is undoubtedly a cost-effective method of reducing $CO_2$ emissions, the ethical question of what climate damage is considered acceptable is left untended. The point is not that managing environments through financial markets is bad or wrong as such, but rather that this approach demands a political legitimation that has already defined climatic responses in ways amenable to financial modeling and calculation. This is the central issue at the heart of managing urban environmental financial risks.

Secondly, and somewhat conversely, these managerial practices also personalize the risks in that it becomes an individual's prerogative to ensure (financial) protection (O'Malley 2003). The state as guardian is replaced by the state as enabler of insurance or capital market products that allow people the choice to purchase suitable levels of coverage. This implies a shift in accountability and approach from a public to a private environmental management scheme. This personalization is not novel to environmental risks and can be demonstrated in relation to managing personal finance too. This is explored, for example, by Clark, Thrift, and Tickell (2004) who trace the increased media focus on finance with the enlarged involvement of individuals in investment and a regulatory approach that places greater burden or incentives on individual personal financial risk management. Individuals become financial consumers, particularly with the growing personalization of long-term financial planning such as pensions (Clark, Thrift, and Tickell 2004). In a broader vein, Isin (2004) maps the rise of what he calls the neurotic citizen, one constantly worrying about personal finance, calories or environmental footprints in an attempt to ensure absolute security from threats. What is important about this is that it should not necessarily be seen as the rise of individual consumer power, but rather as an explicit governmental mechanism through which the individual becomes responsible for their own and others actions. This personalization of financial management in relation to environmental threats leaves a number of questions unanswered related to the ability of people to make these conscious decisions given the past histories and cultures in which they are embedded by virtue of, for example, where they live. In other words, are householders responsible for the desire and ability to live in houses that are built with governmental permission by house building companies on coastlines prone to flooding? Even if pricing the risks are taken into account in house building projects there still remains the question of how individuals will be implicitly affected by this market pricing of housing's risks.

This approach also places significant attention on the question of choice and with research that suggests poor people inequitably suffer most from environmental risks (e.g., Klinenberg 2002), it is clear that personalizing environmental risk management could further exacerbate these inequities. As Ericson, Barry, and Doyle (2000) note, the risk approach generates a perceived neutrality of decision making that permit neo-liberal solutions and further exacerbate societal inequalities, because they remain uncontested through that perceived neutrality. Governmentality-inflected literatures highlight that when thinking through the politics of this financial approach, the analysis should not only be focused on the technical ability to engage in risk management (de Goede 2004), but rather examination of the governance structures facilitating the centrality of finance in people's lives and the political-cultural imagination that maps environments as financial risks.

## Conclusions

The emergence of environmental finance as an innovative set of products can be related to the declining ability of insurance to keep up with the rise in payouts, the rise of investors looking for alternative mechanisms by which they can profit from non-correlated risks and governments reducing their roles as protectors in favor of individual and corporate responsibility. Within this there are also individuals and companies examining how to create new products that will be innovative and profitable as ways of managing the environmental financial risks that are becoming increasingly visible through the media and regulated by (inter-)governmental authorities. Weather derivatives, catastrophe bonds, climate change indices, and emissions trading all find their place in this contemporary approach to environmental management.

While these products are applicable more generally, there has been significant focus on urban areas. This is because cities have been both enrolled into a vivid imaginary of catastrophe as sites of most risk if an event strikes and because environmental management for issues like climate change becomes concretized within urban sustainability agendas. Urban areas also become the sites of environmental finance through the innovations of frequently city-based financial entrepreneurs and traders, as well as through the construction of markets such as weather derivatives that lend them a strong urban focus even if that is through the correlation of risks to city airport thermometer readings.

A key question about environmental finance is whether governance through markets is a sensible way of managing environmental risks, but this is not straightforward to answer. It is inconceivable to imagine that the companies involved in insurance or capital markets are not also examining the profitability of these endeavors and thus at some point environmental protection will likely translate into protecting the most valuable customers (Block 2006). Yet identifying who will gain or lose from these processes is not that easy as financial mechanisms can be set up to protect the poor as well as the rich, as is evident in some of the World Bank's climate insurance strategies that enable finance to immediately reach those that need it (Syroka and Wilcox 2006). Imagining environments in terms of financial risks has consequences, but any review must address the diversity of practices, tools and techniques that make it very hard to clearly identify a singular process of financialization of the environment as such.

The integration of environmental finance and insurance products into infrastructure projects may not have equitable results though they might be expected to reduce total costs. A property regime that explicitly incorporates environmental risk into its prices leaves open questions about what happens to people already situated in high-risk areas and the extent of the choice people have about where they live. The new risk maps will have important financial implications, for example in house or insurance prices, that will re-draw environmental risk maps as financial risk maps; geographies that, as highlighted by Klinenberg (2002), are already imbued with economic, social, and political inequities.

Finally the relationship between environmental finance and finance more generally is also worthy of note. Given the potential for abrupt shocks from environmental events, the damage to financial capital circuits more broadly could be severe, albeit undoubtedly spread over many actors. Related to this through the reverse connection is the importance of the rich availability of credit that enabled environmental financial products to rapidly proliferate as investors sought new liquid markets that would balance their portfolios of standard economic investments. It is uncertain whether, given a financial crisis, all these exotic products would survive, particularly given the relatively small numbers of traders primarily involved in them. This would focus attention on the relative strengths and weaknesses of a neo-liberal approach to environmental management and the extent of government commitment to these mechanisms. At stake should these markets fail are both unprotected people and heightened environmental consequences, a situation that may provoke some interest in "end-of-the-world" products (MacKenzie 2008).

## Notes

1. In many cases environmental products are not directly correlated with economic products and thus they provide an alternative investment opportunity that can be used to balance a portfolio.
2. If this sounds morally objectionable, consider that Enron traders' direct interventions in the Californian energy markets through strategic blackouts was far more calculating, not to mention having a direct effect, than anything involving

hurricane speculation barring the possibilities of technologically-difficult geo-engineering.

3. While, for example, the World Bank has weather derivatives projects with small farmers in India and Malawi, the industry statistics suggest there is still a strong energy focus – 70 per cent of the market (PriceWaterhouseCoopers 2007).

# References

Allen, M. (2005*a*). The Spectre of Liability: Part 1 – Attribution. In K. Tang (ed.), *The Finance of Climate Change: A Guide for Governments, Corporations and Investors* (pp. 367–79). London: Risk Books.

—— (2005*b*). The Spectre of Liability: Part 2 – Implications. In K. Tang (ed.), *The Finance of Climate Change: A Guide for Governments, Corporations and Investors* (pp. 381–394). London: Risk Books.

Arnoldi, K. (2004). Derivatives: virtual values and real risks. *Theory, Culture and Society*, 21, 23–42.

Asdal, K. (2008). Enacting things through numbers: taking nature into account/ing. *Geoforum*, 39, 123–32.

Beck, U. (1992). *Risk Society: Towards a New Modernity*. London: Sage Publications.

Bennett, P. (1999). Governing environmental risk: regulation, insurance and moral economy. *Progress in Human Geography*, 23, 189–208.

Block, W. (2006). Katrina: private enterprise, the dead hand of the past, and weather socialism: an analysis in economic geography. *Ethics, Place and Environment*, 9, 231–41.

Bougen, P. D. (2003). Catastrophe risk. *Economy and Society*, 32, 253–74.

Bulkeley, H. and Betsill, M. (2005). Rethinking sustainable cities: multilevel governance and the 'urban' politics of climate change. *Environmental Politics*, 14, 42–63.

Castree, N. (2003). Bioprospecting: from theory to practice (and back again). Transactions of the Institute of British Geographers, 28, 35–55.

Changnon, S. A. (2003). Shifting economic impacts from weather extremes in the United States: a result of societal changes, not global warming. *Natural Hazards*, 29, 273–90.

Clark, G. L., Thrift, N., and Tickell, A. (2004). Performing finance: the industry, the media and its image. *Review of International Political Economy*, 11, 289–310.

Clemmons, L. (2002). Introduction to weather risk management. In E. Banks (ed.), *Weather Risk Management: Markets, Products, and Applications* (pp. 3–13). New York: Element Re Capital Products.

Davis, M. (1999). *Ecology of Fear: Los Angeles and the Imagination of Disaster*. New York: Vintage Books.

de Goede, M. (2004). Repoliticizing financial risk. *Economy and Society*, 33, 197–217.

Ericson, R., Barry, D., and Doyle, A. (2000). The moral hazards of neo-liberalism: lessons from the private insurance industry. *Economy and Society*, 29, 532–58.

Ewald, F. (1991). Insurance and Risk. In G. Burchell, C. Gordon, and P. Miller (eds.), *The Foucault Effect: Studies in Governmentality* (pp. 197–210). Chicago: University of Chicago Press.

—— (1999). Genetics, Insurance and Risk. In T. McGleenan, U. Weising, and F. Ewald (eds.), *Genetics and Insurance* (pp. 17–34). Oxford: BIOS.

Furedi, F. (2007). *Invitation to Terror.* London: Continuum.

Glenn, B. J. (2003). Postmodernism: the basis of insurance. *Risk Management and Insurance Review*, 6, 131–43.

Guy Carpenter and Company, LLC. 2008. Guy Carpenter Publishes Sixth Annual Review of Catastrophe Bond Market, Retrieved 1 July 2008, from www.guycarp.com

Isin, E. (2004). The neurotic citizen, *Citizenship Studies*, 8, 217–35.

Jasanoff, S. (1999). The songlines of risk. *Environmental Values*, 8, 135–52.

Jewson, S. and Jones, S. (2005). Weather Derivatives and Carbon Emissions Trading. In K. Tang (ed.), *The Finance of Climate Change* (pp. 165–76). London: Risk Books.

Klinenberg, E. (2002). *Heat Wave: A Social Autopsy of Disaster in Chicago.* Chicago: University of Chicago Press.

Kunreuther, H. (2006). Disaster mitigation and insurance: learning from Katrina. *The Annals of the Academy of Political and Social Science*, 604, 208–27.

—— and Linnerooth-Bayer, J. (2003). The financial management of catastrophic flood risks in emerging-economy countries. *Risk Analysis*, 23, 627–39.

Lohmann, L. (2005). Marketing and making carbon dumps: commodification, calculation and counterfactuals in climate change mitigation. *Science as Culture*, 14, 203–35.

MacKenzie, D. (2007). The political economy of carbon trading. *London Review of Books*, 29, 7. Retrieved 8 May 2007, from www.lrb.co.uk/v29/n07

—— (2008). End-of-the-World Trade. *London Review of Books*, 30, 9. Retrieved 12 May 2008, from www.lrb.co.uk/v30/n09

McLeman, R. and Smit, B. (2006). Vulnerability to climate change hazards and risks: crop and flood insurance. *The Canadian Geographer*, 50, 217–26.

Masco, J. (2006). *The Nuclear Borderlands: The Manhattan Project in Post-Cold War New Mexico.* Princeton: Princeton University Press.

Meyer, W. B. (2000). *Americans and Their Weather.* New York: Oxford University Press.

Mills, E. (2005). Insurance in a climate of change. *Science*, 309 (5737), 1040–4.

O'Malley, P. (2003). Governable catastrophes: a comment on Bougen. *Economy and Society*, 32, 275–9.

Pielke Jr., R. A., Gratz, J., Landsea, C. W., Collins, D., Saunders, M. A., and Musulin, R. (2008). Normalized hurricaned damage in the United States: 1900–2005. *Natural Hazards Review*, 9, 29–42.

Pollard, J. S., Oldfield, J., Randalls, S., and Thornes, J. E. (2008). Firm finances, weather derivatives and geography. *Geoforum*, 39, 616–24.

PriceWaterhouseCoopers. (2007). Results of 2007 PwC survey, Retrieved 29 October 2007, from www.wrma.org

Pryke, M. (2007). Geomoney: An option on frost, going long on clouds. *Geoforum*, 38, 576–88.

Ramamurtie, S. (1999). Weather Derivatives and Hedging Weather Risks. In H. Geman (ed.), *Insurance and Weather Derivatives: From Exotic Options to Exotic Underlyings* (pp. 173–8). London: Risk Books.

Robertson, M. (2007). Discovering price in all the wrong places: the work of commodity definition and price under neoliberal environmental policy. *Antipode*, 39, 500–26.

Rothstein, H., Huber, M. and Gaskell, G. (2006). A theory of risk colonization: the spiralling regulatory logics of societal and institutional risk. *Economy and Society*, 35, 91–112.

Slocum, R. (2004). Consumer citizens and the cities for climate protection campaign. *Environment and Planning: A*, 36, 763–82.

Syroka, J. and Wilcox, R. (2006). Rethinking international development and finance. *Journal of International Affairs*, 59, 197–214.

Tickell, A. (2000). Dangerous derivatives: controlling and creating risks in international money. *Geoforum*, 31, 87–99.

Walker, G., Eyre, C. C., and Punter, A. (2005). Insuring Climate Change: Implications for the Insurance Industry. In K. Tang (ed.), *The Finance of Climate Change: A Guide for Governments, Corporations and Investors* (pp. 281–92). London: Risk Books.

Zaloom, C. (2004). The productive life of risk. *Cultural Anthropology*, 19, 365–91.

Part IV

**Individuals in a Risk World**

# 10

# Managing Financial Risks: the Strange Case of Housing

*Susan J. Smith*

## Introduction

Across the last half-century, the world's housing systems have – albeit uncomfortably and unevenly – been converging toward a single main-stream model of housing provision. This tenure *de rigueur* is a particular style of home ownership: a package of housing services tied to an invest-ment vehicle that is generally accessed through the leverage of mortgage finance. This is the model of owner-occupation that accommodates around two-thirds of households in the more developed world and which reflects the dominance of a particular mix of politics and economy (Smith 2008). On the one hand, it expresses a process of incremental expansion enabled by financial de-regulation (as, for example, in the USA, the UK, and Australia).[1] On the other hand, it is the result of a systematic transfer of stock from state or social to privatized ownership, such as occurred in the transition economies of Eastern Europe.[2] Whatever the trajectory, the spread of mortgaged owner-occupation embraces a model of housing finance that has been favored by the World Bank, and celebrated (albeit controversially) as the tenure of choice among some development theorists (DeSoto 2000).

The expansion of this style of owner-occupation has been uneven, and as a housing experience it is diverse (Scanlon and Whitehead 2004). In Iceland, for example, more than three-quarters of households are home owners, over 95 per cent of whom are mortgagors; but in Greece where home ownership is even more widespread (accommodating around 80% of households) only one-in-four has yet had to borrow to sustain this. Overall, however, throughout the OECD, home ownership has become the dominant tenure sector.[3] Across the life-course of a typical household, particularly in the English-speaking world, it is unusual not to pass through owner-occupation, and it is entirely usual to do so by taking out a loan. Whatever the impulse, and however uneven its effects, this trend has created whole societies in which the majority of households' assets and a growing proportion of personal debts are anchored in owned homes (Smith 2006; Muellbauer 2008).

The merits and limitations of this style of accommodation are highly contested and cannot be debated here. As a financial strategy, however, owner-occupation has, in the long run, tended to pay off. It has widened access to the largest class of assets in the world – to a resource which is unevenly distributed, yet far less concentrated than any other kind of wealth-holding (Smith 2005). Furthermore, house price appreciation outstripped returns on most other investments in the decade to 2007.[4] Even households with limited wealth are, on the whole, better off by owning than by renting and investing the difference elsewhere (Iacoviello and Ortalo-Magné 2002). And although views are mixed on whether a balanced portfolio can perform better for individuals than one biased toward housing, three facts are clear. Housing is the only investment for which ordinary people can secure so much leverage (in the form of mortgages which, until recently, could provide the entire capital sum); it is the only potential capital gain whose returns are usually tax-advantaged (through some degree of tax relief); and it is one of few leveraged investments which attract no "margin call" in the event of capital loss. Furthermore, by the turn of the millennium it had become easy and routine for home-buyers to use increasingly flexible mortgages to draw from (as well as inject funds into) their home (Smith et al. 2002). This allowed households to roll their home equity into day-to-day decisions around savings, spending and debt, forming both a financial buffer (Benito 2007) and a *de facto* asset-base for welfare (Parkinson et al. 2008; Smith et al. 2007, 2009).

At the same time, as noted elsewhere (Smith 2006), and as events of 2007–8 so thoroughly underline, this style of housing system is mired in financial risk. This was, for a time, masked by an era of cheap credit and rising prices. Then the "credit crunch" of 2007 brought the world's banking system to its knees and sparked a wave of bankruptcy and repossession among homebuyers. As the introduction to this volume shows, all eyes are now on the debt side of the housing equation and few would disagree that it provides a vivid example of the damage wrought by the too-close encounter of households' budgets with global flows of finance. Whether the fallout reflects a failure of economics, a tolerance for sharp practice in an unstable market place, or the fact that ordinary debtors are too easily duped, it is generally agreed that threading households' economies through the needle of mortgage debt into the fabric of financial markets is risky, and that the safe solution is to draw back.

According to this model, managing housing risk is about disentangling housing services from the excesses of mortgage and financial markets, and protecting home-buyers en route. There is, as we shall see, considerable merit in this suggestion, especially around the theme of housing debt. However, in this chapter, I want to raise the possibility that the precarious financial position of home occupiers today is only partly about the problem of mortgage debt and its links to capital markets. It also stems from the surprising fact that, hitherto, there has been practically no encounter at all between market-dominated housing systems and the wide range of financial instruments invented specifically to manage *investment* risks. Home occupiers may be at risk because mortgage markets are too closely integrated with the workings of financial markets. But equally, they may be vulnerable because that engagement has been so uneven, characterized as it is by an emphasis on credit and debt, and with limited attention paid to the role and relevance of home assets.

The next short section sets the scene, hinting that the ill-fated attempt to trade (mortgage) debts as if they are assets might have been less prevalent, and its effects less pernicious, had there been a "synthetic" (financial) market for housing equity. Then I introduce the few attempts that have so far been made to address this "gap". These are initiatives which, potentially, extend to housing markets the wide range of instruments invented to help spread the gains and share the risks of investing into almost every other asset, equity or commodity. The third and fourth sections of the discussion ask why these initiatives – attempts to create a market for housing derivatives – have failed in the past, and whether they might gain traction in the future. The essay concludes by asking whether and how current moves to integrate housing and financial markets might be geared toward protecting the material and financial well-being of home occupiers.

## Housing, mortgage and financial markets

From a household's point of view, there are two kinds of financial risk associated with housing in societies where home purchase, funded by mortgage borrowing, is the dominant and normalized tenure. *Credit risks* (the risks of mortgage default, possession, and eviction) are most often in the spotlight: their growing extent and changing character have become only too apparent in the last two years. *Investment risks* (the possibility that house prices will fall, or fail to keep pace with other investments, or that markets will be illiquid when the time comes to sell) are perhaps less talked about. This is not because house prices are stable or predictable (they are in fact notoriously volatile), but because it is only recently that the full extent of housing investment risks has come to light. The more households are forced to rely on their own housing wealth to fund (outright or as security for mortgage borrowing) a range of quite basic welfare needs, the more they depend not only on homes holding their value, but on prices appreciating fast enough to replenish any wealth eroded through mounting debt, and fast enough to keep pace with, or outstrip non-housing investments (such as pensions).

Credit and investment risks in housing markets are, of course, linked (Case and Shiller 2003; Case and Quigley 2008). When mortgage default is widespread it is a precursor to sticky or falling prices as owners race to sell; and any slowdown in housing markets tends to prompt a wave of mortgage default, as those who wish to trade down or refinance find that they cannot. It is startling, given these links – which have been documented empirically – that for homebuyers, risk-mitigation commonly concentrates entirely on the management of debt, usually in the interests of lenders. In such circumstances, borrowers are, as Paul Langley's chapter shows, drawn increasingly into a web of financial responsibility and self-discipline that is tenuously underpinned by a patchwork of (limited) state safety nets and private insurances. These latter are quite traditional debt management instruments (geared to mortgage payment protection) whose coverage is partial and whose success is variable (Ford et al. 2004; Belsky et al. 2008).

When large institutions are exposed to a mix of credit and investment risks, on the other hand, they use financial instruments that have been designed precisely to manage both sides of the risk equation. These instruments are collectively known as derivatives; they are contracts (forwards, futures, options, and swaps) which effectively separate the investment returns on an asset or security from its ownership and use. While the value of derivatives depends on the performance of underlying assets (or indices), such contracts can be traded independently, providing both an investment opportunity and a means of transferring risk. The resulting markets are large. From a tiny base in the early 1980s, the value of outstanding contracts grew to over $750 trillion (more than ten times the world's entire GNI) by the middle of 2008.[5] What is curious where housing is concerned is that whereas, theoretically, derivatives should be built around both housing equity and mortgage debt – they should be able to help manage both investment and credit risks – in practice it is only the debt side that has featured. In short, mortgage and financial markets have become very closely linked, while housing markets have remained highly tangled with the former and curiously detached from the latter.

Given the recent catastrophe in the housing economy, it is easy to argue that the distance between housing and financial markets is a good thing, which should be preserved. It is certainly true to say that the attempt to use financial markets as a means of managing mortgage debt has gone badly wrong. Although there is no space to elaborate on this, a few points are worth making. In particular, it is clear that the current credit crisis stems, in part at least, not just from the fact of securitization, but also – perhaps mainly – from the way the market for mortgage-backed securities (MBS) has been created and managed. MBS are bond-type instruments (not to be confused with derivatives as defined above) which effectively turn debts into assets by bundling them together and selling them (or more properly the returns on these debts) to investors. This in itself does not have to be problematic: it can be an effective way of raising money to improve the flow of credit to borrowers, perhaps enhancing financial inclusion (though as Van Order (2003) shows, there are other ways of achieving this).

However, turning debts into tradeable assets creates a dangerous paradox. While the most expensive loans (i.e., those which attract the highest interest payments) look on paper like the best investments (they have higher yields than cheap loans), they are also risky, because they service the "sub-prime" sector whose borrowers are most likely to go into arrears. MBS appear to solve this paradox by bundling a mix of low-return prime loans and high-return sub-prime loans together into a single investment vehicle. However, this in turn creates an illusion of diversification, so that the market for MBS-*derivatives* (a way of hedging investment portfolios too steeped in mortgage debt) was a late and limited innovation (based on the ABS-HE index which dates from 2006). Meanwhile, the complex credit derivatives into which MBS *have* been imported have proved too obscure for even the experts to unravel; this was as true for the massive losses made in the last credit cycle (Gibson 2007) as it has been more recently. Certainly, these instruments have not protected hedge funds or banks from their exposures to the mortgage market. The full story has still to be told: it is the latest chapter of a crisis-riddled financial history – perhaps the most significant since Washington shut down Wall Street in 1914 (Silber 2007).

It could, nevertheless, be argued that the mortgage fiasco of the new millennium stems not just from the principle of using financial markets to manage credit risks, but also from the many – political, professional, pecuniary – failures of putting this principle into practice, not least of which is using mortgage debt as a proxy for housing assets. It may, of course, be impossible for the instruments discussed this chapter to be used to better ends (in markets that are better regulated, ethically transformed, and so on); in which case the rest of the text is redundant. But the current crisis demands a rethink of the way the markets for these instruments work: of how they operate and who they are for. There may, then, be an opportunity and indeed a mandate to remake financial markets in radically new ways. So for the moment, I would like to press my earlier point, namely that there is an asset side to the housing equation which is central to the wealth-holding, welfare, and well-being of a majority of households in the Anglo-American world, and which is almost entirely – and strangely – neglected in debates around the creation, management, and mitigation of the financial risks associated with owner-occupation.

This is worth considering for at least two reasons. First had there been an option to invest in secondary and synthetic (derivatives) markets for housing wealth, rather than only in mortgage debt, the scale of the MBS/credit-derivatives crisis (and in particular its consequences for home occupiers) might have been less far-reaching. Second, and more critically, without a synthetic housing market of some kind, the most widely distributed class of assets in the world remains a peculiarly risky investment. Owned housing is the only significant wealth-holding for the majority of ordinary households; the only source of financial security, and the sole means of shelter, for at least half the poor (and the majority of the middle classes) in the Anglo-American world. There is no other asset so fundamental to human welfare whose risks are so squarely borne by those least-well placed, and with so few options, to manage them.

## Housing: towards a new financial order?

The formal case for creating a market in housing derivatives was set out over fifteen years ago (Case et al. 1993; Dwonczyk 1992; Gemmil 1990; Miller et al. 1989; see also Shiller 2008a). The innovation this represents for home-owners – as well as for social and other landlords, and other residential property holders – is to offer a comprehensive and cost-effective route to mitigating housing investment risks.[6] The risk-management, or hedging, function of housing derivatives is achieved by enabling property owners not only to hold their physical investment (to go long on their owned home) but also to sell (or go short on) house prices (by buying a contract which pays out if the market – measured by an index of house prices, of which more later – falls in a given time period). If the physical housing market appreciates, the cost of the contract is deducted from the gain; if the market falls, the contract pays out and some of the loss is recovered.

Some key empirical analyses find that this insurance function of housing derivatives is effective for low, as well as higher, income home occupiers (Englund et al. 2002; Iacoviello and Ortalo-Magné 2002; Quigley 2006), and this is why Caplin et al. (2003*a*) position housing derivatives as part of "the human face of capitalism," while Quigley (2005) uses them to confront the challenge of "how to improve the welfare of European housing consumers at practically no cost" (see also Quigley 2006). It is not necessary to embrace every dimension of Robert Shiller's (2003) "new financial order" to see why he is inclined to locate housing derivatives at the heart of "a radically new risk-management infrastructure to preserve the billions of minor – and not so minor – economic gains that sustain people around the world" (p. ix).

The idea is not that individual households should engage directly in trading derivatives (though there are spread-betting companies that allow this). Rather, this hedging mechanism could be packaged in a variety of ways: into a style of household (home equity) insurance that is more cost-effective and relevant than those currently on offer (Caplin et al. 2003*b*); or into a new, and safer, generation of mortgages – bringing real innovation to products that have been substantially unchanged since their invention (Liu 2006; Syz 2009). The same instruments could be used by providers to manage the capital risks of more cost-effective equity release schemes; they could be geared in a variety of other ways to the aims of social, housing, and urban policy (Smith 2009); they could even be part of the sub-prime "solution" (Belsky et al. 2008; Shiller 2008*b*).

Risk management is, of course, only half the story of derivatives. These markets need buyers as well as sellers; investors who would like to gain from house-price appreciation as well as hedgers who wish to sell their housing risk. The economic argument driving this (investment) side of the market – the logic of buying into a "synthetic" (derivatives) market for housing – is compelling. In addition to its peculiarly unprotected risk structure, residential property is a very large class of assets; it exceeds the value of equities and bonds combined and is worth much more than commercial property. Yet housing is expensive to hold, slow to trade, and is accompanied by high transactions costs. Furthermore, because housing assets are, on the one hand, so "lumpy" (they have to be bought – or not – as a whole), and on the other hand, so widely distributed among so many small investors (who both own and occupy them), there is a limit on how much of the physical stock can be traded by mainstream investors and large organizations. Without housing derivatives, the only other options are to: invest by proxy (e.g., into the construction industry, or, it seems, into mortgage-backed securities); buy up fractional or shared ownerships (a tactic which has proved hard to operationalize without the help of derivatives); invest in residential real estate investment trusts (which have not proved popular); look to residential property exchanges (which are virtually non-existent).[7] As a result, not only are all renters excluded from the financial returns of residential property, but most major investment portfolios are underexposed to housing, even though it is, in the long run, a good "alternative" investment – that is, it has historically been poorly correlated with many other assets and is therefore an aid to diversification (Labuszewski 2006).

There is, then, both an economic logic and a social case for working with housing derivatives. Yet housing remains anomalous – a stark contrast to equities, bonds, pork bellies, sulfur dioxide emissions, coal, oil, and even the weather – in not inspiring a liquid derivatives market, at a time when all the evidence suggests it should. As a consequence, it continues to be difficult for the majority of large investors, and for many ordinary households, either to share in, or maximize their returns on, home assets; and it is still impossible to insure, or "hedge", investment portfolios that are – like the wealth-holdings of so many ordinary households – disproportionately exposed to the mixed fortunes of the housing market. Irrespective of the pros and cons of this state of affairs, it is impossible not to ask how it has arisen and why it persists.

Part of the answer is historical. The history of derivatives trading long predates the advent of financial capitalism,[8] but trading instruments based on house-price dynamics was not possible until the 1980s, when it became legal to settle derivatives contracts in cash rather than by physical delivery. A requirement for physical delivery (i.e., that physical delivery had to be possible, even if it was not effected) dates from the late nineteenth century; its tenacity may have been part of the struggle to distinguish investment from gambling. Millo (2007) recounts the complex story of why and how this requirement was later relaxed, paving the way for a new generation of index-based derivatives. These in turn, with the odd exception of housing, became a centerpiece of the international economy – a "new gold", anchoring, binding, and blending the global financial system (Bryan and Rafferty 2006).

Cash-settlement was introduced in 1982; in principle, it enabled financial engineers to gather up the performance of a "basket" of properties, in the form of a price index, and use this to effectively detach housing dynamics from the locationally unique, highly heterogeneous bundles of housing services that are built into the physical form of property.[9] Once detached, these price dynamics could form the basis of a variety of derivative contracts, and these could be traded independently, as an alternative to buying physical assets, or as a way of hedging housing risk. It is perhaps not surprising (in light of the case set out above) that, toward the end of the 1980s, financial exchanges began to consider listing housing options and futures. In the end, the only initiative to get off the ground was launched by the (then) London Futures and Options Exchange (FOX) which, in May 1991, offered a variety of property futures, including housing futures benchmarked against the Nationwide-Anglia house-price index. By October this market had failed, ostensibly from a combination of bad timing and sharp practice, though as we shall see there is more to it than this. Exactly fifteen years later, in May 2006, the Chicago Mercantile Exchange (CME)[10] tried again, offering options and futures on S&P Case-Shiller house-price indices for ten US cities and – as a composite of those – for the country as a whole. This market had a slow start, but is still open. Both the United States and (to a much greater extent) the UK also have embryonic "over-the-counter" (OTC) markets for housing derivatives.[11] At the time of writing, these were the only jurisdictions whose housing dynamics were traded in this way. There are, however, signs that Canada and Australia may soon join in, and the market for commercial property derivatives is also growing.

The failure of the FOX innovation, the slow start to trading at CME, and the mixed fortunes of the OTC sector, are stark reminders that there are still a lot of unknowns around the performance of financial markets. One project of economics is to reduce this uncertainty, using a modeling exercise to identify features like cash price volatility, cash market size, and so on as key ingredients of success (Black 1996). However, as Leo Melamed, Chairman Emiritus of CME and a key player in the development of global derivatives markets observes:

Let's say there are 13 elements that are necessary for a successful market in futures. We can point to 12 of those with, probably, a great degree of certainty. Then there's the thirteenth element. We don't know what that is. (Interview, July 2006)

Just what "factor 13" – the factor that most inhibits or catalyzes new financial markets – might be where housing is concerned is open to question. The next two sections draw on observations from the FOX experiment,[12] as well as from a range of evidence (original interviews, industry documentation, and literature reviews) assembled for the period 2006–8, to consider why the early efforts did not succeed and whether the new market is likely to gain traction. This account is in part a response to Faulconbridge et al.'s (2007) call to pay more attention to specific products in the effort to understand how financial markets work; it also takes up Millo's (2007) challenge to recognize the importance of index-based financial instruments as a topic for social research. Under the broad themes of cultural economy and material sociology the following paragraphs identify some of the factors accounting for the late start and slow momentum of a financial innovation which, on the face of it, could radically transform the housing economy.

## Cultural economy

An obvious place to begin the search for "factor 13" is in the archive of what has become known as cultural economy. This multi-disciplinary effort to loosen the grip of mainstream economics on understandings of economy is now well established (see Amin and Thrift 2004; DuGay and Pryke 2002). But an early and still appealing starting point is Erica Schoenberger's (1997) study of the "cultural crisis" of the firm. Reflecting on the investment decisions of large corporations, she argues that it is not shortage of information, limitations of technology, or inflexible bureaucracies that determine whether opportunities are seized or overlooked: rather it is the influence of "corporate culture" – the way that senior managers see the world – that most affects the decisions they make. Schoenberger arrives at this conclusion having documented the way engineering giant Lockheed nearly missed the boat in shifting from aeroplanes into missiles because, as the senior vice-president of the company put it, "'We couldn't give a damn about missiles, we didn't like missiles ... the top guys at Lockheed were all airplane guys ...'"

Ideas about cultural economy have come a long way since Schoenberger spoke to the "airplane guys," and there is a now a growing literature specifically on the importance, when interrogating the dynamics of financial markets, of engaging with a wide array of shared experiences, expectations, and ways of working. As Pryke and DuGay (2007) put it: "while financial markets may seem abstract, they are all assembled through systems of meaning that are consequential" (p. 349). It is in this vein that Donald Mackenzie (2007) credits the difference between Chicago's "rough and tumble" and London's "gentlemanly capitalism" for some key differences between financial exchanges in what is sold and how. It is this ostensibly simple idea that areas of economy that should "logically" be integrated sit, in practice, either side of a professional cultural divide, which resonates most closely with the checkered history of property derivatives. Here, though, the divide marks a different kind of geography: one that distances professionals attached to the peculiar materiality of property from those who are more familiar, and comfortable, with the virtual world of finance.

A common theme in the literature, and in the interviews informing this chapter, is the extent to which, historically, there has been an enduring division of expertise, opinion, and tradition between property and financial markets. This point has been underlined at trade events, and in interview, by Paul McNamara, property investment expert and Director of Research at PRUPIM (specialists in real estate investment management). Noting that "it's hard to convey how distinct property was in the mid 1980s...very different culture, very different investment language...", he implies that early attempts to bring these worlds together may have been foiled, to an extent, because "property people didn't really understand derivatives and probably didn't trust them, and likewise, derivatives people didn't know anything about property" (interview, August 2006). On the one hand, therefore, in terms of financial instruments, property generally, and the housing sector in particular, has been relatively unsophisticated (Dwonczyk 1992). This means that even though housing derivatives tend be a relatively simple exercise in financial engineering (compared to the more exotic products underpinned by many other assets), they may not have appealed to housing professionals. Some have indeed suggested that failure of the FOX initiative may, in part, have been due to a limited understanding of the products on offer (Case et al. 1993). On the other hand, financial markets have also found property generally and housing in particular hard to accommodate. For mainstream investors, housing remains a minority asset not least because, as Peter Sceats at Tradition Property put it, experts in property derivatives were (and to an extent still are) "as rare as hen's teeth" [interview, July 2006].

Ironically, this implies that a key barrier to creating a market for housing derivatives is rooted in the very qualities of property that make it attractive to financial markets: its exceptionalism; its lack of correspondence with – its distinction from – other assets; and its complexity and inefficiency as a physical market. One major exchange does not, according to a spokesperson for product development, list housing derivatives precisely because of the danger that they would be undermined by the strength of investors' emotional attachments to property. Paul McNamara's comments again shed some light on this. He notes, in particular, the appeal to direct investors of the possibility to conjure up a little "property magic" from an inefficient physical market. This refers to the skill of identifying and buying properties that might – with or without significant upgrading and remodeling – outperform the market and give "that bit of extra return". He further points out that property "is a distinct, complex asset class, in which, to manage it fully, you need to be pretty much immersed" [interview, August 2006]. In short, derivatives were – in the early days at least – a step too far for a (property) sector so emotionally attached to the feel of bricks and mortar, and for an investment community so confident in its ability to beat the market.

Although "culture" has until recently seemed too vague an explanation to apply to the hard edge of economy, the interviews informing this study confirm that, far from being a handy catch-all when other accounts fail, culture can be a powerful market force. It can moreover be an anchor for inertia as well as a catalyst for change. Indeed, in so far as there has been a shift of orientation in recent years, it has been achieved less by the gradual, collective negotiation and integration of shared meanings around housing derivatives (though this *is* part of the picture), and more by the force of what Max Weber referred to as "charisma." Weber developed this notion alongside his interest in institution-building as a way of understanding how established ways of working – ingrained in the mix of rules, regulations, norms and practices that accumulate as bureaucracies materialize – sometimes, quite suddenly, change (see Eisenstadt 1968). Although there is a huge literature on this theme which cannot be debated here, the idea of charisma – which brings to mind qualities like vision, innovation, leadership, and energy – may be helpful in identifying some seeds of change in the world of property derivatives.

Most of the people I spoke to in the course of this study made some reference to the role of a few energetic individuals in bringing the embryonic markets for both commercial and residential property derivatives to fruition. The UK OTC market, for example, has been championed by three, perhaps four, individuals who speak at all the key trade events, who have played a major role in education as well as financial innovation, and who have not only laid the foundations for trading but have been equally influential in "talking the market" to life. There is also a sense that, in the world of financial markets, charisma refers not just to the qualities of an individual but also to the character of whole institutions. Exchanges like the CME once revolved round the energies of an individual (Leo Melamed), and the institutional culture that remains is one that valorizes innovation and positions itself at the cutting edge of product innovation. Similarly, banks like Abbey in the UK (previously a building society, now part of the Santander Group) have taken positions that enable smaller providers to market derivatives-backed products, generally in the form of house-price-linked savings accounts (Ratcliffe 2006). In the early years of the millennium, new alliances also sprang into life between derivatives specialists and property service providers, sometimes with just a single desk straddling the two (functioning as the "property" desk for the derivatives specialist, and as the "derivatives desk" for the property company). So it is that the cultural economy of the market for housing derivatives is changing, as the "magic" of property is eclipsed by the "charisma" driving institutional innovation. At least one observer – market-maker Jonathan Reiss (2009) – has argued that precisely these qualities could be critical in giving embryonic housing derivatives markets the "jump start" they need to shift from a viable but illiquid state to a usable and attractive trade.

An appeal to cultural economy may be necessary to help account for the false starts and slow momentum of the market for housing derivatives; it may also contain one or two candidates for the "factor 13" required to catalyze trading around what is perhaps the most "logical" of all derivatives. However, it is not the whole story. This much is clear as we turn to consider the exceptional qualities of housing that have distanced it for so long from so much of the financial system: its physicality, its heterogeneity, its use value, and its locational fixity; its rootedness in the material world.

## Material sociology

The advent in recent years of an interest in material sociology – in the practical, technical, technological, and bodily elements of the assemblage of economy – has drawn attention to the importance of understanding the concrete arrangements that are needed for markets to function (Mackenzie

2009). The infrastructural requirements of a market for housing derivatives are varied and far too numerous to list in detail. However, successful derivatives markets depend above all on forging a workable relationship between the underlying asset (which in the case of housing is highly heterogeneous) and any measure (such as an index) that is used to "make things the same" and therefore fungible or inter-tradeable. In this vein, Mackenzie (2007) has argued for the importance, when dealing with cash-settled derivatives, of the "facticity" of such measures: "the measure used to determine cash settlement sums – whether it be a price, an index level, an interest rate or a measurement of weather, longevity or other entity – must be *fact*" (p. 368). A house – price index, for example, must capture, to the satisfaction of market actors, the performance of the asset it represents; it must have a trace of materiality within it. It must be sufficiently like the physical housing market to remain attractive to investors (as an uncorrelated asset), and to work as a hedge. But it must be sufficiently detached from that market – sufficiently able to avoid the idiosyncratic ups and downs of individual home values – to be tradeable. Sitting between the ideal of fungibility and the practicalities of the property market is the distinctive and rather awkward materiality of housing.

Almost two decades ago, Dwonczyk (1990) identified housing as the actuary's "last big frontier," not least because house prices are a (perhaps uniquely) difficult index. Many countries simply lack the price information required to achieve this. Although this is changing rapidly (by 2006, for example, the Bank of International Settlements recognized forty countries that were regularly measuring, and publishing, house-price series), there are still few standard measurement criteria, few agreed index methodologies, few consistent reporting intervals and few coordinated collecting/reporting agencies. In most jurisdictions properties are rarely revalued, except when sold, and data tend to resolve at large spatial scales. Good benchmarking is thus in its infancy, and housing lags behind many other assets in this respect, not least because most house-price indices were not (until recently) developed with derivatives trading in mind. This in itself may be a reason why housing derivatives failed in their early incarnation.

This, indeed, appears to be Mackenzie's (2007) view, as he reflects on the limited market for property derivatives generally, and for housing in particular. Noting that the (repeat sales) index used by CME from 2006 is rather different than the (hedonic index) used by FOX in the early 1990s, Mackenzie hints that index construction might be decisive. A properly constructed index is certainly necessary, and the S&PCase–Shiller index currently used by CME may well be more accurate than the Nationwide-Anglia measure adopted by FOX in 1991.[13] The case made by CME to the Commodity Futures Trading Commission indeed begins with an eighteen-page account of the construction, quality and merits, relative to other benchmarks, of the tradeable home-price indices that are written into every option or future contract that is on offer. And at the launch of the new market, in New York, in March 2006, 17 of the 23 questions from the floor focused on the quality and computation of the index.

Nevertheless, the requirements for tradeable house-price indices are widely debated and few score well on all the key criteria (Clapman et al. 2005; Deng and Quigley 2008). In fact, it is by no means clear that repeat sales measures are "better" than hedonic indices on every count; what one achieves in accuracy the other may exceed in stability; what one secures in terms of coverage, another may counter with specificity. The "ideal" index combining all these elements may never be created. As a recent survey of UK house price indices concluded: "all indices are a blend of fact and fiction and thus lack precision" (Acadametrics 2008, p. 6).

Recognizing this, a first priority for those who trade house-price indices is to be able to "see through" them. As far as the technical specification of indices is concerned, transparency is key, far more so than correspondence, per se. The consensus seems to be that as long as traders know what goes into an index, and are sure that it is not open to corruption or manipulation, they can work with it. As market-maker Simon Smith put it: "I make my judgement based on movements I expect in the physical market, as translated through the index ... I look at the way the index is put together in order to understand how those movements in the physical markets will make the index move" (interview, December 2006). Beyond that, the importance of indices for the success of housing derivatives markets may turn less on their status as "facts," and more on the way they are used – in conjunction with other materials and devices – to address an unfortunate paradox of property which LeComte (2007) phrases thus: "property derivatives need to reflect as much as possible real estate's space-time components but the more they do so, the less likely they are to make it in the world of finance" (LeComte 2007, p. 351).

The paradox is that financial markets generally, and futures markets in particular, revolve around volatile prices that update in seconds, minutes or hours with positions changing many times a day; whereas house prices and their associated indices do not behave like this. House prices do not fluctuate from minute to minute and most indices are updated monthly or quarterly. Reviewing a range of efforts to bridge this gulf sufficiently to create a market for housing derivatives, we can identify perhaps three tactics.[14] Indices feature in all of them, but their "facticity" is the beginning rather than the end of the story.

First, technological innovation has made it possible – to an extent – to bring the rhythm of exchange trading more into line with housing market dynamics. It is hard to imagine housing derivatives trading in a pit; they do not change hands that often, and it would be surprising if market makers or locals took them on in preference to adjacent faster trades. However, with an electronic platform – such as Globex, introduced at CME in 2002 – the stakes can be changed. For example, it is much easier to keep trading open through a slow start (since traders can monitor more than one market at once); it is easier to accommodate (even encourage) "buy and hold" trading strategies; and, of course, it is easier for market-makers to "tap in" from remote locations, boosting the size of the trading pool. This technological fix for the mismatch between conventional exchange trading and the distinctive patterning of housing market dynamics turns less on the question of correspondence between the index and its underlying asset (the essence of which is taken as given) and more on the pacing of the two markets. Housing may not meet the traditional criteria for a successful futures market; but those criteria may have been rendered less important thanks to the advent of electronic trading. At the same time, the material facts of housing have impinged on the conduct of financial markets to the extent that they may challenge what a futures contract looks like. As John Labuszewski, a Director of Research and Product Development at CME, observed: "Futures have traditionally been used as high-velocity, high-volume trading vehicles and are unlike traditional buy-and-hold investments. But assets like housing may prompt exchanges that have been discouraged from creating products suited to 'buy-and-hold', by traditional futures exchange fee structures, to focus as much on open interest as on volume or turnover." In practice, this process of anchoring housing derivatives in the dynamics of their underlying market may have been hampered, at least in the early days, because only short-dated options and futures (expiring in less than a year) were available.[15] This was the case for FOX in 1991 and for CME in 2006. Now, however, the maximum period is five years, and this combination of technological fix and product adjustment could make all the difference.

A second tactic has been to develop a house-price index that brings housing dynamics more into line with other index-based derivatives. Home prices that update as frequently as every month are generally cyclical and are not very "peaky". They can also be awkward to compare, even using repeat sales methodologies, because the standard measure is in units of price-change per dwelling (a measure familiar to housing professionals but less so to financial markets). This can be a problem because as property derivatives broker Peter Sceats observes: "It costs quite a lot of money to get a futures market on the road. And, you know, futures is the derivative form that most needs the oxygen of high frequency turnover" (interview, June 2007). In 2007 Radar Logic began licensing a measure that represents US residential property prices (and in particular price volatility) rather differently than its predecessors; it records daily (as well as weekly and monthly) fluctuations of the price per square foot of dwellings. The result is both a volatile index (whose visual signature is immediately more in line with that of other tradeable financial indices), and something of an "index war" played out as the new measure vies for business with more traditional formulae. The debate this has generated suggests to me that the facticity of key benchmarks is not so much a quality that is given (in the technical properties of index construction), as a status assigned to indices as part of the struggle to create and control the market. Debates around facticity may therefore be less important for the "truths" they identify, than as an indicator that the market is alive. Certainly there is a hint that this jostling has breathed a spark of life into the US OTC market (Reiss 2009).

A third approach turns less on questions of trading technologies or index construction, and more on the design of derivatives. There are, in the UK, at least six (maybe eight) tradeable house-price indices,[16] the newer of which claim greater coverage and accuracy than the Halifax that is in common use. However, such derivatives trading as there is remains firmly anchored on this latter, more established, measure: a hedonic index with no repeat sales element based on the mortgage lending data of a single banking group. This index has a long run, is trusted, and works well enough that few debates hinge on its technical qualities. As Peter Sceats pointed out: "the best indices with the best methods often come along after a derivatives market has been started on a less-than-perfect benchmark" (interview, June 2007). By that time, however, the less-than-perfect benchmark is in place and all else being equal, it generally continues to trade: "all indices have issues, some more than others and because the market is trading one, it will tend to continue to trade that one, because that's what everyone's got positions in" (Investment banking professional, interview, July 2006).

So UK markets appear, for now, to be locked into the Halifax house-price index which, intriguingly, is not so different from the Nationwide-Anglia measure used by FOX (although it has achieved wider coverage and a much longer run). Furthermore, it offers no firm guarantee of success: the spread-betting market which used it around the turn of the millennium did not succeed, for example, whereas the OTC market that traded it in the early 2000s grew rapidly, albeit from a small base. One reason, aired by some market actors, for the success of the OTC trades hinges not on index qualities but on the fact that exchange-traded futures – a key ingredient of liquidity in derivatives trading – may be "the wrong kind of derivative" with which to kick-start a synthetic housing market. Even long-dated futures are time-limited and standardized. OTC contracts, in contrast, can be tailored to housing dynamics, with swaps extending over periods of five, ten, and even thirty years, spanning periods and containing a degree of customization that is far more in tune with what one broker calls "the heartbeat" of the housing market. So it may be significant that while the UK currently has no exchange-traded housing derivatives, there has been a lively OTC market whose comparative success may reflect the sensitivity of its carefully tailored contracts to the material world they represent.

In the end, it may be that a combination of exchange trading for liquidity, and OTC tailoring, is the recipe for success. As yet no jurisdiction has managed to get this combination into place. What seems clear, never-theless, is that the correspondence between synthetic and physical housing markets is important and that this depends on assembling a wide a range materials and devices. This assemblage depends partly on establish-ing and improving the facticity of tradeable indices, but it embraces too the design of contracts, the character of the trading platform, the outcome of licensing struggles, and the imprint of regulatory negotiations. All these affect how closely derivative contracts can follow the "heartbeat" of the housing market; and it is the plausibility and viability of the whole pack-age that seems decisive.

## Performing markets

There is a well-established tradition in economics which aims to specify the conditions that promote or inhibit the success of new derivatives markets (Black 1986). But most experts agree that there is always a "factor 13" – an element that defies generalization, yet which *can* be accounted for. I have argued in this chapter that some clues concerning the uneven fortunes of markets for housing derivatives can be wrested from the inter-disciplinary worlds of cultural economy and material sociology. Not-withstanding the vexed question of recovery following recent economic shocks, there is no sticking point that seems likely to endure, apart from the challenge of meeting a liquidity threshold. This may be overcome by an institutional "jump start" as outlined by Reiss (2009). It might emerge from the mix of OTC and exchange trading that is now networked into the two main market places (the United States and the UK). It certainly depends on rethinking the legal infrastructure for owner-occupation (Fennell 2008). However, my own view is that the bottom line rests squarely on a change in what might be termed the politics of markets.

Elsewhere, I have argued that there is an appetite among providers and consumers for innovations that separate the investment risks (and returns) associated with housing from the ownership, occupation, and use of residential property. Such instruments could – though they need not, and probably will not without deliberate effort – be used to protect home occupiers from the main financial risks embedded in the housing economy (Smith 2009; Smith et al. 2009). More radically still, they could lay the foundations for more inclusive, affordable, and effectively "tenure neutral" style of housing provision. They offer a different way of thinking about the ownership of housing wealth and the stewardship of the housing stock.

To the extent that this is a desirable end, it is a future that remains to be made; or not. And here housing is on the horns of a dilemma. On the one hand the disarray of financial capitalism has fueled arguments for a "post-capitalist" future based on cooperative, collaborative economic practices that are rooted in the material world, leaving little space for the "virtual" financial markets that have expanded so rapidly in barely two decades. The "new gold" of financial derivatives, so eloquently defined by Bryan and Rafferty (2006), would on this model very rapidly be displaced by its real predecessor. In the same vein, the marginality of housing markets to the virtual economy could be seen as a position of strength – a model for sectors retreating from the risky world of engineered finance, and a way of extracting home occupiers from the damaging strictures of financial self-discipline that are described by Langley in Chapter 12.

On the other hand, a derivatives market for housing could lead to the reform of financial markets, or at least help steer the remains of financial capitalism toward more socially valorized ends. Housing derivatives of the type discussed in this chapter are a comparatively recent innovation, depending as they do on the abolition of cash-settlement and the advent of index-based instruments. However, they have as much affinity with the commodity derivatives whose history predates financial capitalism, as they do with the complex credit derivatives that are currently in the news. No derivative has to be as complicated, opaque, or detached from the "real" economy as were those inspiring the "collapse of fact" that marked the end of a financial era (Mackenzie 2008). Housing derivatives can be quite simple instruments, which are as responsive to the needs of everyday life as they are to the wider financial system. The function of derivatives trading may, ultimately, be to make everything "the same" – so that any one element is always tradable with another. But in practice derivatives are highly diverse: they not only differ generically (an option is not the same as a swap) but they take something of their character from the qualities of the underlying entity. Since derivatives trading will be more closely regulated in future, and now that governments have rediscovered their role in shaping markets, there is a real possibility that the distinctive qualities of housing may be one opportunity to make those markets differently.

To that end, there is a growing interest in the extent to which economics and economies are "performative". This is the idea that economic mechanisms and devices are not given, but have to be actively made; that economic theories and models, far from describing the way the world works, effectively bring the economy to life. Mackenzie's (2006) research on the creation of financial markets has played a large part in developing this thesis. But by showing that economies are shaped, in part, by the practice of economics, Mackenzie and others have opened up a much bigger Pandora's box. As Pryke (2007) puts it: "Cultural economy is well-suited to the task of dismantling the making of financial markets, and thus to allow access, as it were, to their politics" (p. 586). And it follows from this not only that "free" markets acquire their "freedom" through sustained political effort (Gray 1992) but also that all markets – including financial markets – are open to revision: their "script" can be changed, their ethics revisited, their bottom lines realigned (Smith 2005). At a time when financial markets are so squarely in the political eye, the possibility of harnessing them to the aims of housing and social policy – as well as to more carefully managing the economy – may be as radical a solution as any to the problems of late modernity.

My conclusion, therefore, is that whether or not the potential of prizing apart the investment and use dimensions of housing is recognized, whether its policy dimensions are realized, may ultimately be a question of political imagination. Certainly, it is not economically inevitable. If the business community wants to invest in property without the costs of acquiring and holding a cumbersome physical asset, it can do so by using a fledgling, but flourishing, market for commercial property derivatives. The asset base is smaller than that of its residential counterpart, but the actors are more skilled financially than are home occupiers, and providers can conduct their business with minimal "reputational risk". This market can prosper without having to engage the policy community or service home occupiers; and it may well do that, irrespective of what happens to housing derivatives. If this latter market is to thrive – particularly in ways that benefit home occupiers – the catalyst may have to be political rather than economic.

Currently, a very high premium is attached to evidence-based policy in the world of housing. Rather less is heard about the importance of new ideas. Housing derivatives, however, have the potential to change the way credit as well as investment risks are experienced, and to transform the meaning and use of physical housing markets. This is a radical idea whose success, awkwardly, relies on instruments that are closely associated with a financial system whose failings are all too apparent. But there is no reason in theory why housing derivatives could not be harnessed by governments to achieve rather different, more public-spirited ends. Indeed the success or otherwise of attempts to manage the increasingly risky financial position of home occupiers may, in the end, depend on policy makers being sufficiently imaginative to engage with a new approach to housing finance, and sufficiently nimble to regulate and manage it effectively.

## Acknowledgements

This research was funded by the UK's Economic and Social Research Council (RES-051-27-0126). I am grateful to the many busy professionals and individual householders who took the time to share their experiences and ideas with me in the course of this study. Thanks, too, to Donald Mackenzie for his helpful comments.

## Notes

1. Together with some Southern European jurisdictions whose high rates of ownership were previously funded by family wealth.
2. This also occurred in in some post-welfare states like the UK (through "right-to-buy") and New Zealand.
3. With the exception of Germany and the Czech Republic where there is – just – a majority who rent.
4. There is, though, a debate on whether house-price appreciation represents a net gain in real wealth for whole jurisdictions (Buiter 2008).

5. This is the value of outstanding contracts (on-exchange plus over-the-counter) given by the Bank of International Settlements.
6. That it is the only such route is demonstrated empirically by Hinkelman and Swidler (2006), who show that no other derivative provides a suitable hedge for housing.
7. The UK's first on-line residential property stock exchange (trading shares in residential property) opened in 2005 listing 18 properties; the market closed in 2008 "due to the credit crunch and other market uncertainty."
8. In the form of "grain loans" in ancient Mesopotamia, "rice tickets" in seventeenth century Japan, grain futures in mid-nineteenth century United States, and cotton futures a few years later in India (to list but a few). The forerunners (perhaps) of housing derivatives – contracts on bricks and stones – were also traded by the Chicago Board of Trade in the nineteenth century (LeComte 2007).
9. In theory there are other ways of benchmarking housing derivatives (see LeComte 2007), but at the moment, indexing is the only one in play.
10. This was symbolically a very important initiative, as the CME was (at the time) the world's largest and most diverse financial exchange and the site around which global derivatives markets had historically formed.
11. Over-the-counter deals are privately negotiated (by an intermediary) between two parties, rather than openly traded on a financial exchange.
12. Including a file of news clippings on the FOX experiment which was kindly passed on by Donald Mackenzie.
13. Even this, while it may be highly accurate, is not always the index of choice: the US spread-betting market (Hedge Street) does not use this index; and when the Chicago Board Options Exchange published a note of intent (which was never followed up) to list home price futures in 2006, it also chose a different type of index.
14. LeComte (2007) has a different and fascinating solution whose practical implications have not yet been explored.
15. Intriguingly this *was* an index issue, turning not on the quality or construction of the measure, but rather to licensing restrictions.
16. Including "Halifax-style" hedonic indices, the mix-adjusted model developed by Acadametrics as the FT index and the repeat sales index developed Calnea Analytics for the Land Registry.

# References

Acadametrics (2008). *House Price Indices – Fact or Fiction*. London: Acadametrics Ltd.
Amin, A. and Thrift. N. (eds) (2004). *Cultural Economy Reader*. Oxford: Blackwell.
Belsky, E., Case, K., and Smith, S. J. (2008). Identifying, managing and mitigating risks to borrowers in changing mortgage and consumer credit markets. *UCC08–14*. Harvard: Joint Center for Housing Studies.

Benito, A. (2007). Housing equity as a buffer: evidence from UK households. *Bank of England Working Paper* 324.

Black, D. G. (1986). Success and failure of futures contracts: theory and empirical evidence. *Monograph Series in Finance and Economics* 1986-1. New York: Salomon Brothers Center for the Study of Financial Institutions.

Bryan, D. and Rafferty, M. (2006). Financial derivatives: the new gold? *Competition and Change* 10: 265–82.

Buiter, W. H. (2008). Housing wealth isn't wealth. *NBER Working Paper* 14204.

Caplin, A., Joye, C., Butt, P., Glaeser, E., and Kuczynski, M. (2003*a*). *Innovative approaches to reducing the costs of home ownership*. A report commissioned for the Prime Minister's Home Ownership Task Force. Canberra: The Menzies Research Centre.

—— Goetzmann, W., Hangen, E., Nalebuff, B., Prentice, E., Rodkin, J., Spiegel, M., and Skinner, T. (2003*b*). Home equity insurance: a pilot project. *Yale International Center for Finance Working Paper* 03-12.

Case, K. E. and Quigley, J. (2008). How housing booms unwind: income effects, wealth effects and feedback through financial markets. *European Journal of Housing Policy* 8: 161–80.

—— and Shiller, R. J. (2003). Is there a bubble in the housing market? An analysis. *Brookings Panel on Economic Activity* 2: 299–362.

—— —— and Weiss, A. N. (1993). Index-based futures and options in real estate. *Journal of Portfolio Management* (Winter): 83–92.

Clapman, E., Englund, P., Quigley, J., and Redfern, C. L. (2005). Revisiting the past and settling scores. *Institute of Business and Economic Research Working Paper* W04-005.

Deng, Y. and Quigley, J. M. (2008). Index revision, house price risk and the market for house price derivatives. *Institute of Business and Economic Research Working Paper* W07-003.

DeSoto, H. (2000). *The Mystery of Capital*. London: Bantam Press.

Dwonczyk, M. D. (1992). Housing: the actuary's last big frontier. *Transactions, Institute of Actuaries*: 53–74.

DuGay, P. and Pryke, M. (eds) (2002). *Cultural Economy*. London: Sage.

Eisenstadt, S. N. (ed.) (1968). *Max Weber on Charisma and Institution Building*. Chicago: University of Chicago Press.

Englund, P., Hwang, M., and Quigley, J. M. (2002). Hedging housing risk. *Journal of Real Estate Finance and Economics* 24: 167–200.

Faulconbridge, J., Engelin, E., Hoyler, M., and Beaverstock, J. (2007). Analysing the changing landscape of European financial centres: the role of financial products and the case of Amsterdam. *Growth and Change* 38(2): 279–303.

Fennell, L. A. (2008). Homeownership 2.0. *Northwestern University Law Review* 102: 1048–118.

Ford, J., Quilgars, D., Burrows, R., and Rhodes, D. (2004). *Homeowners' Risk and Safety-Nets: Mortgage Payment Protection Insurance (MPPI) And Beyond*. London: ODPM.

Gemmil, G. (1990). Futures trading and finance in the housing market. *Journal of Property Finance* 1: 196–207.

Gibson, M. S. (2007). Credit derivatives and risk management. *Finance and Economics Discussion Series* 2007-47 (Federal Reserve Board, Washington DC).

Gray, J. (2002). *False Dawn: The Delusions of Global Capitalism*. London: Granta.

Hinkelmann, C. and Swidler, S. (2006). Trading house price risk with existing futures contracts. Manuscript, Auburn University.

Iacoviello, M. and Magné, F. (2002). Hedging housing risk in London. *Journal of Real Estate Finance and Economics* 27(2): 191–209.

Labuszewski, J. (2006). *Introduction to CME CSI Housing futures and options*. Chicago: CME.

LeComte, P. (2007). Beyond index-based hedging: can real estate trigger a new breed of derivatives market? *Journal of Real Estate Portfolio Management* 13: 342–78.

Liu, R. (2006). SwapRent (SM). A new alternative for property owners. California: Advanced e-Financial Technologies.

MacKenzie, D. (2007). The material production of virtuality: innovation, cultural geography and facticity in derivatives markets. *Economy and Society* 36: 355–76.

—— (2008). End-of-the-world trade. *London Review of Books* (8 May).

—— (2009). *Material Markets: How Economic Agents are Constructed*. Oxford: Oxford University Press.

Miller, N. G., Sklarz, M., and Stedman, B. (1989). It's time for some options in real estate. *Real Estate Securities Journal* 9: 42–53.

Millo, Y. (2007). Making things deliverable: the origins of index-based derivatives. *The Sociological Review*, 55(2): 196–214.

Muellbauer, J. (2008). Housing and personal wealth in a global context. In J. B. Davies (ed.), *Personal Wealth from a Global Perspective*. Oxford: Oxford University Press.

Parkinson, S., Searle, B. A., Smith, S. J., Stoakes, A., and Wood, G. (submitted) Mortgage equity withdrawal in Australia and Britain: towards a wealth-fare state? Unpublished Manuscript (in review). RMIT University, Melbourne.

Pryke, M. (2007). Geomoney: an option on frost; going long on clouds. *Geoforum*, 38: 576–88.

—— and DuGay, P. (2007). Take an issue: cultural economy and finance. *Economy and Society* 36: 339–54.

Quigley, J. (2005). How to improve the welfare of European housing consumers at practically no cost. Plenary presentation to the European Network for Housing Research Conference, Reykjavik (July).

—— (2006). Real estate portfolio allocation: the European consumers' perspective. *Journal of Housing Economics* 15: 169–88.

Ratcliffe, G. (2006). *Residential property derivatives*. Property Derivatives Essential Guide 22-4.

Reiss, J. (2009). Creating housing futures: a view from the market. In S. J. Smith and B. A. Searle (eds.), *The Housing Wealth of Nations. Companion to the Economics of Housing*. New York and Oxford: Blackwell-Wiley.

Scanlon, K. and Whitehead, C. (2004). *International Trends in Housing Tenure and Mortgage Finance*. London: CML.

Schoenberger, E. (1997). *The Cultural Crisis of the Firm*. Oxford: Blackwell.

Shiller, R. (2003). *The New Financial Order. Risk in the 21st Century*. Princeton: Princeton University Press.

—— (2008*a*). Derivatives markets for home prices. *Cowles Foundation Discussion Paper* 1648.

—— (2008*b*). *The Subprime Solution*. Princeton: Princeton University Press.

Silber, W. L. (2007). *When Washington Shut Down Wall Street*. Princeton: Princeton University Press.

Smith, S. J. (2005). States, markets and an ethic of care, *Political Geography* 24: 1–20.

—— (2006). Home Ownership: Managing a Risky Business? In J. Doling and M. Elsinga (eds), *Home Ownership: Getting In, Getting Out, Getting From*. Delft: IOS Press.

—— (2008). Owner-occupation: living with a hybrid of money and materials, *Environment and Planning A* 40: 520–35.

—— (2009). Housing Futures: A Role for Derivatives? In S. J. Smith and B. A. Searle (eds.), *The Housing Wealth of Nations. Companion to the Economics of Housing*. New York and Oxford: Blackwell- Wiley.

—— Ford, J., and Munro, M., with Davis, R. (2002). *A Review of Flexible Mortgages*. London: Council of Mortgage Lenders.

—— Searle, B. A., and Cook, N. (2007). Banking on housing: spending the home. *ESRC End of Award Report* (RES 154-25-0012).

—— Searle, B. A., and Cook, N. (2009). Rethinking the risks of owner occupation. *Journal of Social Policy*, 38: 83–102.

Syz, J. (2009). Housing risk and property derivatives. In S. J. Smith and B. A. Searle (eds), *Companion to the Economics of Housing*. Oxford: Blackwell-Wiley.

Van Order, R. (2003). Public policy and secondary mortgage markets. Washington DC: Freddie Mac.

# 11

# Gender, Risk, and Occupational Pensions

*Kendra Strauss*

One of the key features of contemporary capitalist economies is that they are, according to many commentators, increasingly "financialized."[1] What constitutes financialization has been widely debated (see, for example, Arrighi 1994; Aglietta 2000; Boyer 2000*b*; Martin 2002; Tickell 2003; Langley 2004; Stockhammer 2004; Blackburn 2006; Erturk et al. 2007; Foster 2007), but by most accounts its key features include the growing influence of capital markets and finance capital on all spheres of life (Harmes 2001; Erturk et al. 2004), the primacy of shareholder value (Aglietta 2000; Froud et al. 2000; Williams 2000; Boyer 2000*a*; Greenfield and Williams 2007), the rise and increasing ubiquity of financial engineering (Blackburn 2006), a reduction in the levels of social protection provided by the state (Langley 2006), and the situation in which the majority of corporate profits are generated through engineering and arbitrage rather than "materially productive" activities (Boyer 2000*a*; Boyer 2000*b*). Apart from reductions in state-funded public service provision, these sound like abstract processes detached from the daily reality of most individuals. In fact, they mean that increasing numbers of people rely directly upon returns generated by financial markets, even if they are unaware of this fact.

This reliance on financial markets is strongly evident in the sphere of occupational pension provision, most notably in the private sector. The Anglo-American economies in particular have seen a shift away from traditional defined benefit (DB) or final salary pensions in favor of defined benefit (DC) 401*k* style plans.[2] The significant difference between DB and DC plans is that the former guarantee, upon retirement, a pension for life. The value of that pension is usually based on a formula involving age, salary, and years of service. In DC pensions, on the other hand, the level of the pension at retirement is based on the value of the accrued contributions, plus any gains (or minus any losses) made as a result of how the contributions were invested. In DB plans, in other words, the risk lies with the employer who has to guarantee the pension; in DC plans, on the other hand, risk is transferred to the individual, who is responsible for building up their pension over time. In the former contributions are pooled and invested collectively while in the latter, each pension plan participant acts as his/her own fund trustee.

What this means is that DC occupational pension plan participants are significantly more likely to face a choice about whether to opt in to their employer's plan, how much to contribute, and how those contributions should be invested over the entire life of the plan. This "self responsibilisation" (Greenfield and Williams 2001, 417) can be seen as a way of freeing individuals to make the choices best suited to their individual circumstances, rather than binding them to an inflexible style of pension that penalizes early leavers, lacks portability, and is thus poorly suited to the post-Fordist "individualized society of employees" (Beck and Beck-Gernsheim 2001). What this view does not acknowledge, however, is that the risks may fall on people poorly placed to cope with complexities inherent in this type of financial decision-making. Studies of the welfare effects of financialization have highlighted the ways in which it can exacerbate inequality despite claims of the "democratisation of finance" (Erturk et al. 2007).

Where occupational pensions are concerned, inequality has a particular gendered dimension (Peggs 2000; Ginn 2001; Ginn, Daly, and Street 2001; Ginn 2003; Condon 2006). Women on average earn less, are more likely to work part-time, and engage in more unpaid caring work than men do, factors that are all associated with the gender gap in pensions. Yet there is relatively little research that attempts to link up work on financialization with the body of research on gendered pension inequality. This despite the fact that research on financial literacy and planning, risk tolerance and decision-making confidence has highlighted distinct differences between men and women in all these domains.

This chapter addresses that lacuna, focusing on the UK. The first section examines the gender gap in DC occupational pensions, looking specifically at the examples of the UK and the United States. The second part of this chapter sketches the broad contours of the financialization of UK occupational pensions in order to define the processes being addressed. The third section looks first at some of the macro-level changes associated with the financialization of occupational pensions before turning to the issues of financial literacy (financial capability) and planning, risk tolerance, and confidence in order to advance two main arguments. The first is that, in addition to highlighting compelling empirical evidence of persistent inequalities in coverage, savings rates, and employer contributions, evidence from economic geography and behavioral economics suggests a counter-narrative to the discourse of the "investor subject" (Harmes 1998; Preda 2004; Langley 2006; Langley 2007) which recognizes the gendered nature of the assumptions that underpin both macro trends in pension policy, and the design of defined contribution (DC) occupational schemes. The second argument, the policy implications of which are discussed in the concluding section, is that when future trajectories for the evolution of occupational pensions under conditions of deepening financialization are considered, better and more widespread financial education to increase levels of capability *without redistribution* will fail to redress gendered pension inequality.

## The gender gap in DC occupational pensions

As the 2004 report of the UK Pensions Commission stated, current female pensioners receive much lower levels of occupational pension because of lower levels of employment, higher levels of part-time work, lower average earnings, and a greater tendency to work in service sectors with lower rates of provision (Pensions Commission 2004). These women were of working age during the "golden age" of occupational welfare; as with current levels of gendered pension inequality, their lower pension entitlements reflect not only the patterns of labor market attachment, caring, and unpaid labor over the life course but also the male breadwinner model in state and occupational pension regimes.[3] Thus inequalities in pension coverage reflect what has been called the "gender order" or "gender contract": gendered relationships of power, emotional and sexual norms, and the gender division of paid and unpaid labor and social reproduction (Ginn, Daly, and Street 1991).

In the UK, as in the other Anglo-American regimes, the trends are toward increasing occupational pension coverage for women and decreasing coverage for men against a backdrop of general decline. The number of active members of occupational pension plans peaked in the UK in 1967 at just over 12 million, falling to less than 10 million by 2004 (OECD 2005, 44). In 1987 almost two-thirds (63 per cent) of male employees working full- time were members of their current employer's pension scheme; this fell to 55 per cent in 2003/04 (ONS 2005, 45). The corresponding proportions for female employees working full-time showed a different pattern; 52 per cent were members in 1987, rising to 60 per cent in 2002/03 before falling back to 56 per cent in 2003/04 (ibid.). Among women working part-time, there was a sharp increase over the same period, from 11 per cent in 1987 to 33 per cent in 2003/04.[4] However, in 2003/2004 the proportion of all working age men and women in the UK with membership of an occupational scheme was below 40 per cent (about 32% for women and 33% for men), indicating low average rates of coverage. Average coverage rates also mask big variations in coverage among different age groups. Women aged 20 to 24 were more likely to belong to an employer-sponsored or personal pension plan than men of the same age, but this age group also had the lowest rates of coverage in 2003/04 (less than 20% and less than 15%, respectively (ibid., 47). The highest levels of membership were found among those in the 45–49 age group (just over 60% for men, and just over 45% for women); this group also had one of the widest gender gaps.

Large disparities also exist in the size and adequacy of pension entitlements. Although the Office of National Statistics (ONS) in the UK does not publish data on occupational entitlements, they do provide a snapshot of gendered inequality in private pension wealth. In 2005, 9.8 million individuals had personal and stakeholder pensions, of whom 60 per cent were men[5] (ONS 2008). Just over half of all male scheme members, and two-thirds of all females, had funds valued at less than £10,000; for men aged 50 to 54 in 2002 the median value of private pension wealth was estimated at £75,000; for women, it was £6,000. In the United States in 1998 the gender pension gap on the average accumulated in DC plans was 44 per cent (ranging from 62% among 18–26-year-olds to 21% among 54–62-year-olds), meaning that the average plan balance for men was $57,239 as opposed to $25,020 for women (Bajtelsmit 2006; Kuper 1999). These disparities are the result of the gender pay gap, significantly higher levels of part-time work among women, shorter average lengths of job tenure, and concentrations in sectors where occupational pension provision is low (Bajtelsmit 2006).

## The financialization of UK occupational pensions

While the previous section illustrated the gendered inequalities inherent in "second pillar" (World Bank 1994) pensions in the UK, it did not address financialization of the occupational pension regime. Financialization, in the context of occupational pensions, refers in a general sense to the increasing extent to which pensions are invested in, sold through, and managed by capital markets and their agents. In the 1940s and 1950s, virtually all pension fund assets were invested in government bonds but by the 1970s these were seen as a poor hedge against inflation; by the 1980s even cautious fund managers were allocating up to 80 per cent of their portfolios to equities (Blackburn 2006). Pension funds are not simply institutions affected by financialization, however: they are also seen as drivers of a number of related processes. Langley (2004) argues that the financialized and contradictory investment practices of occupational pension funds increase the concern for shareholder value; Blackburn (2006) highlights Theresa Ghilarducci's research on the effects of the obsession with shareholder value on corporate downsizing, which in turn has implications for occupational pension plans and their members. Cutler and Waine (2001) have argued that the trend to increasing DC coverage is driven by the primacy of shareholder value over acquisition of value-added (VA) by labor. And financial engineering itself has been driven in part by the investment imperatives of institutional investors such as large pension funds: "As soon as pension funds mature, their need to push the envelope of existing investment norms and practices grows, resulting in increasingly speculative behaviour and the frantic search for financial innovations" (Engelen 2003, 1366).

However, there is also a more specific set of processes at play in the financialization of pensions. The first is retrenchment, which is often used to describe the reduction in social welfare under neoliberalism (see Starke 2006 for an overview of the literature). In the context of pension systems, retrenchment describes two phenomena. One is the decrease in the proportion of retirement income provided by the state. The other is the reduction in occupational provision in the private sector (both in terms of the overall number of plans, and the number of workers covered). Both trends have been observable in the UK in the last two decades (Pensions Commission 2004; Clark 2006; Ginn 2006; Clark and Monk 2007a). The Labour government's stated aim has been to shift the balance of pension income: whereas 60 per cent of current pensioners' income, on average, comes from state sources and 40 per cent from private and occupational sources, the government's goal is to reverse this ratio such that 60 per cent of future pensioners' income will be generated from private and occupational pensions (DWP 1998). At the same time, however, the number of active members of occupational pension schemes has fallen from a high of around 13 million in 1967 to just over 10 million in 2000, and the percentage of private sector employees participating in occupational DB plans has declined from about 35 per cent to just under 20 per cent (while membership of DC schemes rose by about 3% to 5%) (Pensions Commission 2004, 80–1).

The second process of relevance is privatization. The privatization of pensions reflects the transition from PAYG pension systems to funded ones, and from public provision to private provision (Condon 2001; Street and Ginn 2001; Condon 2006). In the first instance it means that pensions are paid from accumulated funds, usually invested in financial markets, rather than the contributions of current workers directly funding the retirement of current retirees. In the second instance it means that income from private and occupational pensions becomes the primary source of income in retirement, rather than state funded public pensions. While significant shifts have occurred in the pre-funding of even state-funded public pension schemes, the primacy of occupational and private pensions remains a political aspiration rather than a reality in countries such as the UK, where current and future pensioners remain dependent on state sources for the majority of their income (Pensions Commission 2004, 146). This despite the fact that governments in the United States, the UK, and Canada have promoted individual retirement plans and offered substantial tax incentives to encourage the move to private pensions, while the notion of a crisis in especially unfunded state pensions has been energetically promoted (Harmes 2001, 107).

Third is the marketization of occupational schemes. In the literature on pensions, "marketize" is used in two ways. It refers to both the political choices that serve to link pension policy to the operation of financial markets (Condon 2001), and to the drive to privatize retirement income (Peggs 2000). To these processes I would add the creation of markets for pension-related products and services. These include the market for personal and occupational pension products, the market for asset management and administration services, and more recently the market for the management of occupational pension obligations and liabilities (*The Economist* 2008).

The fourth process involves the expansion of individual choice. Both the retrenchment of public pensions and the shift from DB to DC occupational pensions have been framed in terms of expanded possibilities for individual choice (Munnell 2006). The ideology of choice is premised on a strong model of economic rationality, which portrays individuals and natural utility maximizers (Strauss 2008*b*). DC-type plans typically allow plan participants to make choices about how they invest their contributions and allow a certain amount of switching, although the degree of choice varies widely. Concomitant with the expansion of individual choice, however, has been the individualization of risk and the reduction of both employee and employer contributions. In the UK in 2000, in occupational DC schemes with between 1,000 and 4,999 members, employer contributions averaged 4.8 per cent, compared with 15.5 per cent for DB schemes of the same size (Langley 2004, 551).

The final process of relevance, the individualization of risk, clearly illustrates the extent to which the social and economic are mutually constitutive, rather than autonomous, spheres (Crang 1997; Thrift 2000; Castree 2004; Amin and Thrift 2007). In occupational DC-type pensions, plan members bear all of the risks associated with planning for retirement. They must decide whether to join the plan, what level of contributions to make, and in many cases how to invest their contributions. The management of their pension necessitates an asset management strategy, in the same way that pension fund trustees and managers must decide how the assets of DB funds are invested. This entails deciding on the ideal level of risk and selecting investment vehicles that match the risk profile. In reality plan participants may display inertia, procrastination, risk aversion, and inconsistent preferences, while many make the "choice not to choose" and end up in the scheme's default fund (Kahneman and Tversky 1979; Tversky and Kahneman 1981; Tversky and Kahneman 1986; Madrian and Shea 2000; Choi et al. 2003; Duflo and Saez 2003; Choi, Laibson, and Madrian 2005; Clark, Caerlewy-Smith, and Marshall 2007). Thus for many DC occupational pension plan members in the UK there is a real likelihood that their pension will fail to provide an adequate level of income in retirement (Pensions Commission 2004).[6]

What these constitutive processes of financialization add up to is a transformation of the landscape of occupational pensions since the "long boom." This transformation has, at a macro level, affected the institutions of Anglo-American pension regimes and the tenor of the debate about the appropriate social allocation of economic risk; at the micro-level, it has had implications for how individual subjectivities are shaped by the exercise of power and the new discourse of opportunities and constraints. These macro- and micro-level processes and effects, which are deeply entwined, have clear implications for equality and social solidarity, and are deeply gendered.

# Financialization, risk, and gender

Despite gaps in the statistics, what emerges from the empirical evidence on the distribution of pensions entitlements and assets is a mixed picture for women. Yet the fact that there have been improvements in rates of occupational coverage for women, if not unambiguously for their accrual of pension assets, must be set against the backdrop of macro processes of economic and social change in financialized economies. Changes in the organization and distribution of paid labor have been identified as part of the "feminization of work," which refers to new jobs and occupations in the service sector, more flexible and less hierarchical forms of organization and the new management structures, but also increasingly precarious forms of employment and less linear career paths (Goldsmith and Goldsmith 1997; McDowell 1997; Beck 1999; Smart 2003). Thus both men and women in the UK private sector have experienced declining job security, the increasing prevalence of contract and temporary forms of employment, and declining levels of coverage and generosity of benefits in occupational pensions. The stubborn persistence of the gender pay gap means that women continue to build up less occupational pension wealth than men.[7]

Castells (1997) suggests that there is a structural congruence between the needs of women workers for flexible employment and the requirements of the new economy for a "flexibilisation of work" (Smart 2003, 59). But, as Pratt and Hanson (1993; see also Feng et al. 2001) argue, women's domestic responsibilities figure prominently in the explanation of their subordinate position in the labor market, despite the fact that they result from the over-generalization of one life path and one period within that life course. Moreover, as women's lives are lived through time, they are also lived in place and through space. This has been recognized by those who study women's lives through the life course when they notice, for example, that the local labor markets exert a tremendous influence on opportunities for paid employment (ibid., 30). Nevertheless, there is a systematic linkage between the global expansion of production, trade, and finance, and the increase of women in gendered forms of production, especially those that involve the informal sector, lower pay and higher levels of female migration (Pyle and Ward 2003). Waylen (2006) argues in the context of the literature on globalization that few if any studies take on the difficult task of examining how the process and structures associated with globalization are gendered: the same is true for financialization. "Also ignored are the ways in which changes in the organization of global finance structures, and the impact of financial instability that has resulted from the deregulation of capital movements, impact differently on men and women" (ibid.).

The shift from DB- to DC-type occupational pensions entails individualization of risk (see, for example, Bajtelsmit, Bernasek, and Jianakoplos 1999; Condon 2001; Blackburn 2002; Langley 2004; Langley 2006; Munnell 2006; Monk 2007b), in which the financial risk relating to providing a promised level of pension to all eligible employees borne by the employer (in DB plans) is shifted to the individual plan participant. In other words, the expectation is that the job performed by trustees and investment professionals in traditional DB plans – of determining and implementing an investment strategy tailored to the level of risk a plan can bear, determined by the workforce composition (demographics), contribution levels, past returns, etc. – is fulfilled by each individual plan participant (Strauss 2008b). The UK government's stated goal of transitioning to a system in which the majority of income in retirement comes from private and occupational sources, coupled with grim statistics about declining occupational coverage, low levels of pension saving, and small accumulated balances in the majority of DC plans, has led to an understandable preoccupation with financial literacy or, as it is also called, financial capability.[8]

The UK government's interest in financial capability has been stimulated by several additional factors: the rapid increase in levels of borrowing (including for house purchase, to finance higher education, and among "sub-prime" borrowers), the "financial literacy divide" in the UK which leads often less well-off consumers to pay more or purchase inappropriate financial products (National Association of Citizens Advice Bureaux 2001), and instances of mis-selling (such as the scandal concerning private pensions in the early 1990s). This has led to several attempts to measure levels of financial capability in the UK (Kempson, Collard, and Moore 2005).

In the most recent study the authors identified four key areas or domains to represent financial capability: managing money, planning ahead, choosing products, and staying informed (Atkinson et al. 2006). The results of their analysis indicated that most people surveyed were relatively good at making ends meet and keeping track of money but nearly half reported failing to plan ahead, many said they do not have the skills to select financial products, and there was a huge degree of variability in how informed people said they are. That planning ahead is one of the weakest domains is clearly significant in the context of pensions. Research by

Kempson and Collard (2005) indicated that most individuals seen by financial intermediaries, for example, do not seek out advice on pensions but are often spurred to consider it in the course of a general financial review.

In the study by Atkinson et al. (op. cit.) age and area effects were the most significant, with the under-30s and over-70s scoring lowest and individuals' levels of capability regarding the choice of financial products influenced by those of the people living near them. But the survey's findings also had a gendered element. The researchers did not feel that it was appropriate to condense the findings of their data analysis into a single measure, but they instead identified groups with similar factor scores and categorized these groups according to the levels of weakness they displayed in each of the domains. Those in Group D, in which people had three or more weak areas, did not do well at choosing financial products or staying informed and were far below average at keeping track of their finances, although they were good at making ends meet. Women, in particular those in middle age, were overly represented in this group.

This finding would seem to accord with generally low levels of pension saving among older women in the UK (Pensions Commission 2004). It also supports research undertaken in the United States on the importance of planning for financial security in retirement (Kemp, Rosenthal, and Denton 2005; Lusardi and Mitchell 2005; Loibl and Hira 2006; Lusardi and Mitchell 2006; Lusardi and Mitchell 2008). Lusardi and Mitchell (2008), for example, found in their study of older American savers that women display much lower levels of financial literacy than the older population as a whole and that women who are less financially literate are also less likely to plan for retirement and be successful planners. In a more general study of workers over the age of 50, Lusardi and Mitchell (2008) found that lack of planning is concentrated among groups that are at higher risk for financial insecurity in retirement, including those with low education, African-Americans and Hispanics, and women. The same groups are less likely to have an adequate level of information about financial concepts and products, indicating that financial literacy and planning are linked.

Lusardi and Mitchell's proposed solution to the problems posed by a lack of financial capability and planning, especially among older women, is better planning tools to help raise levels of financial literacy and to spur planning. This does not address a fundamental issue about the ontology of economic rationality that underpins the individualized model of saving. As I have argued elsewhere, this model of strong economic rationality posits individuals as natural utility maximizers (Strauss 2008b). By this logic people, if

267

given sufficient scope for choice, are best placed to make decisions about how much to save for retirement and how the maximize those savings. Thus equality of opportunity, rather than of outcome, is essential (Erturk et al. 2007). The design and promotion of DC pensions reflect this ideology, while at the same time allowing employers to cut costs and pass the management of, for example, longevity risk on to the individual. "Whilst firms can no longer be expected to tolerate the risk that anomalous storm conditions may undercut returns on investment, individuals are best placed to shelter from the same storms by ensuring that their savings are 'adequate' to 'live on . . . in retirement'" (Langley 2004: 554).

DC plans embody more than the ideology of *homo economicus*, however: in many cases their design reflects a particular set of assumptions about the desirability of choice and the propensity for risk. Many plans offer their members a choice of funds and asset types in which to invest their contributions. The ability to accrue sufficient assets to fund retirement is premised upon rates of return that reflect a willingness to invest in riskier assets, such as equities, particularly when plan members are young. Yet while the model is universal, the "investor subject" on which it rests is deeply gendered. As Langley (2006: 929) points out: "The investor subject remains a masculine figure who is deemed best equipped to embrace financial market risk, whereas the capacity of women investors to provide for their own retirement is constrained by caring and nurturing instincts and by an associated lack of aggression." This is the expression of what Robert O'Connell calls hegemonic masculinity (Waylen 2006: 158).

While generalizations about women's innate (in)ability to perform the investor subject identity are certainly contestable,[9] there is considerable evidence that women do have a lower tolerance for financial risk than men. This evidence has been mustered in both experimental settings using accepted test protocols (Hallahan, Faff, and McKenzie 2004; Endres 2006; Fehr-Duda, De Gennaro, and Schubert 2006; Fellner and Maciejovsky 2007) and in analyses of data on pension decision-making (Goldsmith and Goldsmith 1997; Sunden and Surette 1998; Bajtelsmit et al. 1999; Bernasek and Shwiff 2001). A recent study of risk propensity among occupational pension plan participants in the UK confirmed that women express a preference for lower levels of financial risk in their retirement savings strategies, and that women on average choose lower risk allocation strategies when faced with a hypothetical portfolio allocation task (Clark and Strauss 2008). What is important to note, however, is that socio-demographic characteristics other than gender also significantly affected risk tolerance, and that there were clear interaction effects. In the study the highest level of income, as a proxy for wealth, was shown to be correlated with lower levels of risk aversion, while age was significant in that middle-aged respondents were more likely to be risk averse than those in both young or old age groups.

Women not only have, on average, lower levels of financial capability and tolerance for risk; they also express lower levels of confidence in their ability to make financial decisions (Dietz, Carrozza, and Ritchey 2003; Lusardi and Mitchell 2006; Lusardi and Mitchell 2008). These factors highlight the complex interplay of social, economic, and cultural factors in the gendered construction of particular subject positions in financialized economies. Perceived and culturally constructed norms of risk-taking behavior intersect with differences in cognitive abilities, levels of educational attainment, and labor market opportunities as well as modes of socialization, the gendered division of labor in social reproduction, and spatial forms of embeddedness (that is, the particularity of place).

As Callon (1998) suggested, calculation has powerful constitutive and constructive effects but with any calculative frame there is also a technical issue about ability (Eturk et al. 2007, 562); that ability is itself likely to be the result of the interplay of cognition and context (Simon 1956). It is therefore possible to acknowledge that women are generally more risk averse, less confident about financial decision-making, and claim to be less financially-savvy without taking a position that women are a priori less able. Recent research has shown that widespread differences in mathematical achievement between school-aged boys and girls disappear in the test scores of children in countries with the highest levels of gender equality (namely Norway, Sweden, and Iceland); numeracy is to an extent correlated with financial knowledge (Clark, Caerlewy-Smith, and Marshall 2006; Clark et al. 2007). But the argument that financial literacy can therefore be taught and so the gender gap can be closed is circular at heart, since the countries with the highest levels of gender equality also have highly redistributive social welfare systems that collectivize, rather and individualize, risk in order to ensure broad equality among all citizens. Moreover, measures to address numeracy and deficits in financial knowledge cannot insure against "irrational" economic decision-making or inertia ("choosing not to choose") in DC pensions if the rational investor subject position encompasses gendered norms of the passivity and timidity of women and their lack of numerical ability (Mendick 2005).

Finally, it is worth noting that the behavioral economics literature has confirmed a truism of economic theory: that risk taking increases with wealth (Carroll 2000; see also Clark and Strauss 2008). Thus, it may be rational for individuals with low incomes and few assets to take less financial risk (Calvet, Campbell, and Sodini 2007; Campbell 2006). There is thus a contradiction at the heart of DC pension design. For many women, who are likely to earn less over their lifetimes, spend more time out of work, change jobs more frequently, and work in sectors with lower rates of pension coverage than their male counterparts, low levels of risk tolerance are in fact rational. At the same time, assumptions about the ability of DC plan participants to build a sufficient pension fund are often premised upon high levels of investment in riskier assets such as equities, especially when young. There is some evidence that women with occupational pensions who have partners with pensions are more risk tolerant, indicating that when risks and assets are pooled within the household women are willing and able to embrace riskier strategies (Clark and Strauss 2008). Yet the effect did not hold for low-income women, highlighting the strength of the wealth effect and the dangers of DC pensions for those unable and unwilling to take risks with their (scarce) assets.

As Froud et al. (2000) have written, the empirics of household savings through financial markets suggest two conclusions: that this form of saving directly exacerbates inequalities, and that a majority of households in the UK and United States are not saving enough through the stock market for retirement. As this chapter has sought to illustrate financializa-tion, and the processes particular to the recent changes in occupational pension provision, not only exacerbate inequalities in general but are also gendered in particular ways. Structural changes in pension institutions have been influenced by changing patterns of employment (the "feminiz-ation" of work), driven in part by the imperative of generating shareholder value, which has been concomitant with women's increased labor force participation in the Anglo-American world and higher levels of occupa-tional pension plan membership. Nevertheless, these improvements must be set against declining rates for men and an overall pattern of retrench-ment in state and occupational pensions. The shift from DB to DC pension in the private sector also has implications for gendered pension inequality. While DC pensions are more portable and flexible (and thus seen as more appropriate for new forms of work), they also transfer risk to the individual and assume a certain underlying gendered economic rationality and abil-ity to bear financial risk.

The financialization of pensions is also creating new risks not previously envisaged. What Blackburn (2006) describes as "pension deficit-disorder" has produced a new breed of financier, the "vulture capitalist," who specializes in extracting value from firms burdened with large pension liabilities (often by stripping employees of their pension entitlements). Financial liberalization has fostered growth in consumption by the most favored groups rather than productive investment, the creation of unprecedented systematic risks through hedge funds, and powerful speculative forces (Boyer 2000b, 308). And companies are increasingly selling their DB pension liabilities to insurance and specialty firms to manage, usually without consulting plan members and without a clear sense of what future risks this entails for benefits (*The Economist* 2008). These risks further exacerbate inequality, which often has a gendered dimension. The nature of that gendered inequality cannot be assumed, however: highly paid female professionals are more likely to work full-time and accrue significant retirement savings than both women and men in lower paid occupations, if not as much as comparable men. The class dimensions of pension inequality are thus equally deserving of attention, and the intersection of gender, class, and ethnicity can signal multiple sites of disadvantage for particular women and men as the disparities among different groups of women and men grow.

The question this poses is whether the likelihood of inadequate pensions for many will bring about any kind of change in the direction of current pension policy. According to Froud et al. (2000, 95): "Things have to get economically worse before they get politically better. Disappointment with, and discrediting of, the stock market is the key political precondition for serious reform." The current financial turmoil in the UK and United States (the "credit crunch" and "subprime crisis," falling house prices, rising inflation, and stagnant wages) may seem likely to generate just such a sense of disillusionment. Yet there is no likelihood of a return to the DB model of old in the private sector, which was anyway premised upon a male breadwinner model. The fact is that only a universal pension with entitlements based on citizenship rather than labor market attachment, or the adoption of policies designed to ensure that women can work full-time when their children are young, can address the structural issues relating to gendered patterns of work and norms of social reproduction. In Britain, plans for a National Pension Savings Scheme (NPSS), first mooted by the Pensions Commission in the context of a politically feasible solution to the chronic problem of under-saving for retirement, propose a model which is both contributory and incorporates DC-type features of investment choice and individualized risk. The proposals thus suggest that neither a "citizen's pension" nor the adoption of Scandinavian-type policies on childcare and parental leave are likely. With financial education unlikely to be the panacea that both government and the financial services industry would wish, gendered pension inequality is likely to persist, even if its form and extent are open to change.

## Notes

1. Thanks to for Gordon L. Clark, Linda McDowell and the editors for their comments and suggestions on earlier drafts of this chapter. Any errors or omissions are, of course, my own.
2. The Anglo-American economies comprise the US, the UK, Canada, Australia and sometimes New Zealand. In this paper the focus is primarily on the UK pension system, in particular private sector occupational pensions.
3. The fact that gendered pension inequality among current retirees reflects patterns of occupational coverage during the heyday of defined benefit schemes begs the question of how widely the benefits of the "golden age" were in fact spread. As the Pensions Commission (2004) has pointed out, moreover, the narrowing of the gender gap in occupational pensions is in part the result of declining levels of coverage and benefits for men rather an unmitigated gains for women. The exception is in the public sector, which employs a high proportion of women and where defined benefit schemes are still the norm.
4. This change can largely be explained by changes following a European Court of Justice ruling in May 1995 that made it illegal for pension schemes to exclude part-time workers.
5. Stakeholder pensions were introduced by the UK government in 2001 as low-cost products for employees without occupational pension coverage. The charges on these DC-type products are capped (1.5% of the value of the fund each year for 10 years, which reduces thereafter to 1%) and they must provide a lifestyle default option. It is mandatory for employers with more than five staff to provide access to a stakeholder pension if no other provision is made, but employer contributions are voluntary. However, stakeholder pensions have had only a limited effect in increasing pension coverage. According to the Pensions Commission (2004, 120) 65 per cent of companies with between five and 12 employees have a nominated stakeholder supplier, but regular contributions are being made in only 4 per cent of plans.
6. There is considerable debate in the UK about the role of other assets, especially housing, in providing a source of income in old age (Banks and Tanner 2007; Bardasi, Jenkins, and Rigg 2002; Disney, Henley, and Stears 2002; Hancock 1998; Hancock 2000; Smith 2005; Smith 2007; K. Strauss 2008a). While popular

discourses have reflected an apparent preference for investing in housing over pensions (Modlock 2007), evidence from countries such as the US and UK suggests that individuals are in fact more reluctant to treat their home as a fungible asset that economic theory or media accounts would suggest (Venti and Wise 1989; Venti and Wise 1990). Moreover, even if the faith in housing as a source of retirement income survives the current downturn in the US and UK property markets, there are other problems with the assumption that housing equity will solve the pensions problem. These include the claims that other expenses, such as residential and nursing care, are likely to make upon assets in old age, as well as the uneven distribution of housing wealth (both in geographical and socio-demographic terms) (Pensions Commission 2004).

7. According to the Office of National Statistics, the mean gender pay gap for full-time workers in the UK in 2007 was 17.2 per cent (the median pay gap was 12.6%) while the mean part-time pay gap was 35.6 per cent (with a median of 39.1%) (ONS 2007). This figure varies significantly by region, with the largest gap in the South East and the lowest in Northern Ireland, reflecting the fact that the gap is widest in the highest earnings quintile and lowest among the lowest paid workers (due to the existence of the minimum wage) (Pensions Commission 2004).

8. Financial literacy is perhaps the more commonly understood concept: Atkinson et al. (Atkinson et al. 2007; Atkinson, McKay, Kempson, and Collard 2006) explain that in the UK, however, the National Foundation for Educational Research's definition – the ability to make informed judgements and take effective decisions regarding the use and management of money – was deemed not to take account of the fact that the term seeks to describe a process leading to desired outcomes rather than a static set of basic skills. Financial capability is now the preferred term in the UK, but the US literature still refers predominantly to financial literacy.

9. In fact, the preponderance of women's investment clubs and their success – one famous group, the Beardstown Ladies Investment Club, has published a best-selling book – suggests that women may be enthusiastic and skilful investors (Harmes 2001). Nevertheless, the qualities to which their success is attributed are often gendered: patience, loyalty, brand awareness (in the context of consumer goods), etc.

# References

Aglietta, M. (2000). Shareholder value and corporate governance: some tricky questions. *Economy and Society*, 29, 146–59.

Amin, A. and Thrift, N. (2007). Cultural-economy and cities. *Progress in Human Geography*, 31, 143–61.

Arrighi, G. (1994). *The Long Twentieth Century: Money, Power and the Origins of Our Times*. London: Verso.

Atkinson, A., McKay, S., Collard, S., and Kempson, E. (2007). Levels of financial capability in the UK. *Public Money & Management*, 27, 29–36.

—— —— Kempson, E., and Collard, S. (2006). *Levels of financial capability in the UK: Results of a baseline survey* (Report No. 47). London: Financial Services Authority.

Bajtelsmit, V. L. (2006). Gender, the family, and economy. In G. L. Clark, A. H. Munnell, and J. M. Orszag (eds.), *Oxford Handbook of Pensions and Retirement Income* (pp. 121–40). Oxford: Oxford University Press.

—— Bernasek, A., and Jianakoplos, N. A. (1999). Gender differences in defined contribution pension decisions. *Financial Services Review*, 8, 1–10.

Banks, J. and Tanner, S. (2007). Home-ownership and saving in the UK. *Housing Finance*, 45 (February 2000), 25–9.

Bardasi, E., Jenkins, S. P., and Rigg, J. A. (2002). Retirement and the income of older people: a British perspective. *Ageing and Society*, 22, 131–59.

Beck, U. and Beck-Gernsheim, E. (2001). *Individualization*. London: Sage.

—— (1999). *The Brave New World of Work* (trans. P. Camiller). Cambridge: Polity Press.

Bernasek, A. and Shwiff, S. (2001). Gender, risk and retirement. *Journal of Economic Issues*, XXXV(2), 345–56.

Blackburn, R. (2002). *Banking on Death*. London: Verso.

—— (2006). Finance and the fourth dimension. *New Left Review*, 39, 39–70.

Boyer, R. (2000*a*). Is a finance-led growth regime a viable alternative to Fordism? A preliminary analysis. *Economy and Society*, 29, 111–45.

—— (2000*b*). The political in the era of globalization and finance: Focus on some regulation school research. *International Journal of Urban and Regional Research*, 24, 274–322.

National Association of Citizens Advice Bureaux (2001). *Summing up: Bridging the Financial Literacy Divide*. London.

Callon, M. (1998). *The Laws of the Markets*. Oxford: Blackwell.

Calvet, L. E., Campbell, J. Y., and Sodini, P. (2007). Down or out: assessing the welfare costs of household investment mistakes. *Journal of Political Economy*, 115, 707–47.

Campbell, J. Y. (2006). Household finance. *Journal of Finance*, 61, 1553–604.

Carroll, C. D. (2000). *Portfolios of the Rich*. Cambridge, Mass.: National Bureau of Economic Research.

Castells, M. (1997). *The Power of Identity*. Oxford: Blackwell.

Castree, N. (2004). Economy and culture are dead! Long live economy and culture. *Progress in Human Geography*, 28, 204–26.

Choi, J. J., Laibson, D., and Madrian, B. C. (2005). *$100 bills on the Sidewalk: Suboptimal Saving in 401(k) Plans*. Cambridge, Mass.: National Bureau of Economic Research.

—— Laibson, D., Madrian, B. C., and Metrick, A. (2003). *Passive Decisions and Potent Defaults*. Cambridge, Mass.: National Bureau of Economic Research.

Clark, G. L. (2006). The UK occupational pension system in crisis. In H. Pemberton, P. Thane, and N. Whiteside (eds.), *Britain's Pensions Crisis* (pp. 145–68). London: The British Academy.

—— Caerlewy-Smith, E., and Marshall, J. C. (2007). The consistency of UK pension fund trustees' decision-making. *Journal of Pension Economics and Finance*, 6, 67–86.

—— —— —— (2006). Consistency of decision-making: The effect of education, professional qualifications, and task-specific training on pension fund trustee decision-making. *Working Papers in Employment, Work and Finance*. Oxford: University of Oxford.

—— and Monk, A. H. B. (2007*a*). The "crisis" in defined benefit corporate pension liabilities: Current solutions and future prospects. *Working Papers in Employment, Work and Finance*. Oxford: University of Oxford.

—— —— (2007*b*). The "crisis" in defined benefit corporate pension liabilities, part II: current solutions and future prospects. *Pensions: An International Journal*, 12, 68–81.

—— and Strauss, K. (2008). Individual pension-related risk propensities: the effects of socio-demographic characteristics and a spousal pension entitlement on risk attitudes. *Ageing and Society*, 28, 847–74.

Condon, M. (2001). Gendering the pension promise in Canada: risk, financial markets and neoliberalism. *Social and Legal Studies*, 10, 83–103.

—— (2006). The feminization of pensions? Gender, political economy and defined contribution pensions. In L. Assassi, D. Wigan, and A. Nesvetailova (eds.), *After Deregulation: Global Finance in the New Century* (pp. 89–191). London: Palgrave MacMillan.

Crang, M. (1997). Introduction: Cultural turns and the re(constitution) of economic geography. In R. Lee and J. Wills (eds.), *Geographies of Economies* (pp. 3–15). London: Arnold.

Cutler, T. and Waine, B. (2001). Social insecurity and the long retreat from social democracy: occupational welfare in the long boom and financialization. *Review of International Political Economy*, 8, 96–118.

Dietz, B. E., Carrozza, M., and Ritchey, P. N. (2003). Does financial self-efficacy explain gender differences in retirement saving strategies? *Journal of Women & Aging*, 15, 83–96.

Disney, R., Henley, A., and Stears, G. (2002). Housing costs, house price shocks and savings behaviour among older households in Britain. *Regional Science and Urban Economics*, 32, 607–25.

Duflo, E. and Saez, E. (2003). The role of information and social interactions in retirement plan decisions: Evidence from a randomized experiment. *Quarterly Journal of Economics*, 118, 815–42.

DWP (1998). *A New Contract for Welfare: Partnership in Pensions*. London: Department for Work and Pensions.

*The Economist* (2008). Pension buy-outs: outliving the kitty. *The Economist*, 31 May–6 June, 42.

Endres, M. L. (2006). The effectiveness of assigned goals in complex financial decision making and the importance of gender. *Theory and Decision*, 61, 129–57.

Engelen, E. (2003). The logic of funding European pension restructuring and the dangers of financialisation. *Environment and Planning A*, 35, 1357–72.

Erturk, I., Froud, J., Johal, S., Leaver, A., and Williams, K. (2007). The democratization of finance? Promises, outcomes and conditions. *Review of International Political Economy*, 14, 553–75.

—— —— —— and Williams, K. (2004). Corporate governance and disappointment. *Review of International Political Economy*, 11, 677–713.

Fehr-Duda, H., De Gennaro, M., and Schubert, R. (2006). Gender, financial risk, and probability weights. *Theory and Decision*, 60, 283–313.

Fellner, G. and Maciejovsky, B. (2007). Risk attitude and market behavior: Evidence from experimental asset markets. *Journal of Economic Psychology*, 28, 338–50.

Feng, H. Y., Froud, J., Johal, S., Haslam, C., and Williams, K. (2001). A new business model? The capital market and the new economy. *Economy and Society*, 30, 467–503.

Foster, J. B. (2007). The financialization of capitalism. *Monthly Review – an Independent Socialist Magazine*, 58, 1–12.

Froud, J., Haslam, C., Johal, S., and Williams, K. (2000). Shareholder value and financialization: Consultancy promises, management moves. *Economy and Society*, 29(1), 80–110.

Ginn, J. (2001). *From Security to Risk: Pension Privatisation and Gender Inequality*. London: Catalyst.

—— (2003). *Gender, Pensions and the Lifecourse: How Pensions Need to Adapt to Changing Family Forms*. Bristol: The Polity Press.

—— (2006). *Pensions Policy*. Radical Statistics Briefing Paper. http://www.radstats.org.uk/PensionsBriefingsept06.pdf

—— Arber, S. (2001). A colder pension climate for British women. In J. Ginn, D. Street, and S. Arber (eds.), *Women, Work and Pensions: International Issues and Prospects* (pp. 44–66). Buckingham: Open University Press.

—— Daly, M., and Street, D. (1991). Engendering pensions: a comparative framework. In J. Ginn, D. Street, and S. Arber (eds.), *Women, Work and Pensions: International issues and prospects* (pp. 1–10). Buckingham: Open University Press.

—— —— —— (2001). Engendering pensions: a comparative framework. In J. Ginn, D. Street, and S. Arber (eds.), *Women, Work and Pensions: International issues and prospects* (pp. 1–10). Buckingham: Open University Press.

Goldsmith, E. and Goldsmith, R. E. (1997). Gender differences in perceived and real knowledge of financial investments. *Psychological Reports*, 80, 236–8.

Greenfield, C. and Williams, P. (2007). Financialization, finance rationality and the role of media in Australia. *Media Culture & Society*, 29, 415–33.

Hallahan, T. A., Faff, R. W., and McKenzie, M. D. (2004). An empirical investigation of personal financial risk tolerance. *Financial Services Review*, 13, 57–78.

Hancock, R. (1998). Housing wealth, income and financial wealth of older people in Britain. *Ageing and Society*, 18, 5–33.

—— (2000). Estimating the housing wealth of older home owners in Britain. *Housing Studies*, 15, 561–79.

Harmes, A. (1998). Institutional investors and the reproduction of neoliberalism. *Review of International Political Economy*, 5, 92–121.

—— (2001). Mass investment culture. *New Left Review*, 9, 103–24.

Kahneman, D. and Tversky, A. (1979). Prospect theory: An analysis of decisions under risk. *Econometrica*, 47, 263–91.

Kemp, C. L., Rosenthal, C. J., and Denton, M. (2005). Financial planning for later life: Subjective understandings of catalysts and constraints. *Journal of Aging Studies*, 19, 273–90.

Kempson, E. and Collard, S. (2005). *Advice on pensions and saving for retirement: Qualitative research with financial intermediaries*. Leeds: Department for Work and Pensions.

—— —— and Moore, N. (2005). *Measuring Financial Capability: An Exploratory Study*. London: Financial Services Authority.

Kuper, A. (1999). *Culture: The Anthropologists' Account*. Cambridge, Mass. and London: Harvard University Press.

Langley, P. (2004). In the eye of the 'perfect storm': The final salary pensions crisis and financialisation of Anglo-American capitalism. *New Political Economy*, 9(4), 539–58.

—— (2006). The making of investor subjects in Anglo-American pensions. *Environment and Planning D-Society & Space*, 24(6), 919–34.

—— (2007). Uncertain subjects of Anglo-American financialization. *Cultural Critique*, 65, 67–91.

Loibl, C. and Hira, T. K. (2006). A workplace and gender-related perspective on financial planning information sources and knowledge outcomes. *Financial Services Review*, 15, 21–42.

Lusardi, A. and Mitchell, O. S. (2008). *Planning and Financial Literacy: How Do Women Fare?* Cambridge, Mass.: National Bureau of Economic Research.

—— —— (2005). *Financial literacy and planning: Implications for retirement wellbeing*. Working paper 46/05. Center for Research on Pensions and Welfare Policies. http://cerp.unito.it.

—— —— (2006). *Baby Boomer Retirement Security: The Roles of Planning, Financial Literacy, and Housing Wealth*. Cambridge, Mass.: National Bureau of Economic Research.

Madrian, B. C. and Shea, D. F. (2000). *The Power of Suggestion: Inertia in 401(k) Participation and Savings Behavior*. Cambridge, Mass.: National Bureau of Economic Research.

Martin, R. (2002). *The Financialization of Daily Life*. Philadelphia: Temple University Press.

McDowell, L. (1997). *Capital Culture: Gender at Work in the City*. Oxford: Blackwell.

Mendick, H. (2005). A beautiful myth? The gendering of being/doing 'good at maths'. *Gender and Education*, 17, 203–19.

Modlock, S. (2007). *Is property the new pension?* MSN Money. http://money.uk.msn.com/pensions/articles/article.aspx?cp-documentid=4780171.

Munnell, A. H. (2006). Employer-sponsored plans: The shift from defined benefit to defined contribution. In G. L. Clark, A. Munnell, and J. M. Orszag (eds.), *Oxford Handbook of Pensions and Retirement Income* (pp. 359–80). Oxford: Oxford University Press.

Office of National Statistics (2005). *Pension Trends*, No. 1, 2005 edition. P. Pennick and D. Lewis (eds.). Basingstoke: Palgrave Macmillan.

—— (2007). *Gender pay gap*. Retrieved 6 June 2008, from http://www.statistics.gov.uk/cci/nugget.asp?id=1279.

—— (7 March 2008). *Pension trends: Individual pension wealth*. Retrieved 6 June 2008, from http://www.statistics.gov.uk/cci/nugget.asp?id=1279.

Peggs, K. (2000). Which pension? Women, risk and pension choice. *The Sociological Review*, 48, 349–364.

Pensions Commission (2004). *Pensions: Challenges and Choices. The First Report of the Pensions Commission*. London: The Stationery Office.

Pratt, G. and Hanson, S. (1993). Women and work across the life course: Moving beyond essentialism. In C. Katz and J. Monk (eds.), *Full Circles: Geographies of Women over the Life Course* (pp. 27–54). New York: Routledge.

Preda, A. (2004). The investor as a figure of global capitalism. In K. Knorr Cetina and A. Preda (eds.), *The Sociology of Financial Markets* (pp. 141–62). Oxford: Oxford University Press.

Pyle, J. L. and Ward, K. B. (2003). Recasting our understanding of gender and work during global restructuring. *International Sociology*, 18(3), 461–89.

Simon, H. A. (1956). Rational choice and the structure of the environment. *Psychological Review*, 63, 129–38.

Smart, B. (2003). *Economy, Culture and Society*. Buckingham and Philidelphia: Open University Press.

Smith, S. J. (2005). Banking on housing? Speculating on the role and relevance of housing wealth in Britain. Paper prepared for the Joseph Rowntree Foundation.

—— (2007). Owner-occupation: At home with a hybrid of money and materials. *Environment and Planning A*, advance online publication.

Starke, P. (2006). The politics of welfare state retrenchment: A literature review. *Social Policy & Administration*, 40(1), 104–20.

Stockhammer, E. (2004). Financialisation and the slowdown of accumulation. *Cambridge Journal of Economics*, 28, 719–41.

Strauss, K. (2008a). *Banking on property for retirement? Attitudes to housing wealth and pensions*. Working Papers in Employment, Work and Finance. Oxford: University of Oxford.

—— (2008b). Re-Engaging with Rationality in Economic Geography: Behavioural Approaches and the Importance of Context in Decision-Making. *Journal of Economic Geography*, 8, 137–56.

Street, D. and Ginn, J. (2001). The demographic debate: The gendered political economy of pensions. In J. Ginn, D. Sadler, and S. Arber (eds.), *Women, Work and Pensions* (pp. 31–43). Buckingham and Philidelphia: Open University Press.

Sunden, A. and Surette, B. (1998). Gender differences in the allocation of assets in retirement savings plans. *The American Economic Review*, 8(2), Papers and Proceedings of the Hundred and Tenth Meeting of the American Economic Association (May 1998), 207–11.

Thrift, N. (2000). Performing cultures in the new economy. *Annals of the Association of American Geographers*, 90, 647–92.

Tickell, A. (2003). Pensions and politics. *Environment and Planning A*, 35, 1381–4.

Tversky, A. and Kahneman, D. (1981). The framing of decisions and the psychology of choice. *Science*, 211, 453–58.

—— —— (1986). Rational choice and the framing of decisions. *The Journal of Business*, 59(4, Part 2), S251–S278.

Venti, S. F. and Wise, D. A. (1989). *Aging, Moving, and Housing Wealth*. Cambridge, Mass.: National Bureau of Economic Research.

—— —— (1990). *But They Don't Want to Reduce Housing Equity*. Cambridge, Mass.: National Bureau of Economic Research.

Waylen, G. (2006). You still don't understand: Why troubled engagements continue between feminists and (critical) IPE. *Review of International Studies*, 32, 145–64.

Williams, K. (2000). From shareholder value to present-day capitalism. *Economy and Society*, 29, 1–12.

World Bank (1994). *Averting the Old Age Crisis*. Washington, DC: The World Bank.

# 12

# Consumer Credit, Self-Discipline, and Risk Management

*Paul Langley*

The notion that a borrower is responsible for making repayments to a lender is deeply ingrained in economy and society. If an individual cannot be thrifty and frugal, then it appears that they must meet the future obligations arising from their present credit relations. Credit is thus a highly unequal relation, and the norm of borrower responsibility has been central to the power, privilege, and profits of lenders throughout the history of consumer credit (see Gelpi and Julien-Labruyère 2000). Irresponsible borrowers, those who fail to meet their obligations and become debtors, can thus reasonably expect to be morally condemned and punished. Today's debtors in the United States of America (US) and United Kingdom (UK) are not punished through incarceration in debtors' prisons, as was the case in the early-modern period. Nonetheless, the debtor continues to be represented as a guilty party who can and should expect to suffer a curtailment of freedom as their future access to consumer credit is curtailed or becomes too costly to contemplate.

The norm of borrower responsibility is, then, an important continuity that marks the history of consumer credit in Anglo-American society. In this chapter, however, I want to argue that the norm of borrower responsibility, part of what I will call "financial self-discipline", has been remade as the mass market for consumer credit has further consolidated across the last quarter of a century or so. For David Knights (1997, 224; Knights and Vurdubakis 1993, 734), the "financial self discipline" that he finds to be at work in both the nineteenth century and at the end of the twentieth century is described in precisely the same terms: "a form of discipline grounded on a social ethic which has economic rationality, planning and foresight, prudence, and social and moral responsibility among its cardinal virtues." Now, it is indeed the case that the rational and prudent meeting of credit obligations by responsibilized borrowers continues to be pivotal in the contemporary mass market that features all manner of loan products, instalment plans, and credit cards across both the "prime" and "sub-prime" sectors. But, just as the mass credit market developed and boomed through unique forms of wholesale capital market funding and the re-articulation of lenders' default risk calculations, so it became embodied in everyday life through the forging of new borrower subjectivities and self-disciplines (Langley 2008a).

This chapter will argue that the embodied economy of mass market consumer credit turns on the responsibilization of the entrepreneurial administration of outstanding obligations and uncertainty over future access to credit: that is, on self-disciplinary risk management by borrowers themselves. The argument follows from and contributes to a broader set of claims that relate embodied everyday financial transformations, on the one hand, to the reconfiguration of individual responsibilities under contemporary liberal government, on the other. The responsible individual of modern liberal society has made provision for their own freedom, security, and welfare through self-disciplinary saving and borrowing performances across several centuries. But, I claim that under contemporary liberal government, where individual responsibility for freedom, security, and welfare is reinforced and intensified, the predominant forms taken by financial self-discipline are transformed. It follows that the rise of mass stock market investment through contributions to mutual funds and pensions plans, and the associated displacement of thrift and insurance as the predominant forms taken by saving in the nineteenth century and during much of the twentieth century, is imbricated in the contemporary period of liberal government. And, as financially self-disciplined savers have become investors, the meaning and calculations of "risk" have been reworked. Thus, for the everyday investor subject, risk is no longer a possible future hindrance or danger to be managed through thrifty contributions to a deposit account or the purchase of collective insurance in the present. Instead, risk is an incentive or future opportunity to be embraced through entrepreneurial self-disciplinary performances today that include, for example, making the right mutual fund choice or, for that matter, regarding a home as an asset to be traded-up in a rising property market (Smith, in this volume). This chapter, in effect, extends this analysis of transformations in saving and so-called "asset-based welfare" to consider the ways in which an embodied transformation of rational norms and associated reworking of risk has also, and simultaneously, taken place on the borrowing side of everyday financial life.

The argument I make here moves through three main parts. To begin, I draw on the later writings of Michel Foucault (1979, 2003, 2004, 2007) to trace the complex disciplinary and self-disciplinary power relations through which borrower responsibilities are constituted in the mass credit market. Emphasis is placed on the intersection of the legal and extra-legal in the punishment of debtors, the risk calculations of credit scoring understood as a technology of contemporary liberal government, and upon the calling up of entrepreneurial borrower subjects. The second part of this chapter explores the contention that successfully meeting obligations is no longer the only self-disciplinary performance that a responsible borrower subject must undertake in a mass credit market. Specific empirical reference is made to the January 2008 decision of UK telephone and internet bank Egg to cancel the credit cards of 161,000 of its customers. This supports the teasing-out of self-disciplinary performances that, especially prevalent during the height of the consumer credit boom, sought the calculative and creative manipulation of outstanding obligations. The third and final part of this chapter concentrates on risk management by borrowers that attempts to address the uncertainties of future access to credit at affordable rates of interest. This entrepreneurial financial self-discipline appears to be coming to the fore, at the time of writing, as the "credit crunch" begins to bite. The empirical focus is upon the calculative tools provided by the credit history and scoring agencies that are designed to enable borrowers to improve their own credit histories and scores, and thereby to minimize the interest rates payable on their consumer credit obligations.

## Discipline and self-discipline

Law has certainly occupied a pivotal role in the power relations of credit and debt across the centuries. Legal provisions have ensured, for instance, the delivery of a "pound of flesh" to creditors in the Roman Empire, or the brutal imprisonment of debtors in the Anglo-American world of the early-modern period. But, in recent decades, as a mass market in consumer credit has consolidated, law has become increasingly intermeshed with the extra-legal. Legal and extra-legal mechanisms now come together in the power relations that constitute borrower responsibilities, rewarding those who continue to meet their repayments and punishing those who do not. As Rose and Valverde (1998) argue more broadly by drawing on Michel Foucault's (1979) notion of "governmentality," the privileged place of law in the past can be thought of as a reflection of a particular sovereign and centralized form of power which has subsequently been displaced but not evaporated. Law no longer occupies a privileged position in modern liberal societies where the predominant forms taken by decentralized power relations are disciplinary and governmental. In their terms, "the legal complex" has "become welded to substantive, normalizing, disciplinary and bio-political objectives having to do with the reshaping of individual and collective conduct in relation to particular substantive conceptions of desirable ends" (p. 543).

It follows, as the back-cover summary of Dawn Burton's (2008) *Credit and Consumer Society* has it, that mass market credit is "an era in which credit and debt are sanctioned, delivered and collected through new cultural and economic mechanisms." The responsibility of meeting outstanding credit obligations continues to lie firmly at the door of the borrower, not the lender, but the power relations that make this possible are transformed. Burton traces this transformation to a "shift from personal trust to institutional trust," the latter referring to the adoption of marketing, credit scoring, and risk-based pricing technologies which enable "the construction of the trustworthy consumer" (p. 47). Responding to the inherent problems of forging trust in a dispersed and decentered mass market, lenders rely, at once, on the apparently scientific and objective calculations of extra-legal credit scoring to enable the management of so-called "credit risk" or "default risk" (Leyshon and Thrift 1999; Guseva and Rona-Tas 2001; Marron 2007; Poon 2007), and on the summoning up of responsible and moral borrower subjects through their juxtaposition against an irresponsible and deviant other. Ultimately, for Burton (2008), following Luhmann (1979) and Foucault (1977), the significance of trust has been largely displaced in mass market credit by the disciplinary control exercised by market institutions through what she characterizes as the "credit panopticon" (p. 53; see also Gill 1997).

The extra-legal "marketized ordering mechanisms" (Fraser 2003, 168) of credit scoring are indeed, in one sense, disciplinary tools of synchronization, standardization, and responsibilization that penetrate deep into the conduct of everyday life. In today's "prime" credit markets, as Burton (2008) suggests, "sanctions such as blacklisting through credit reference agencies" and "the threat of being blacklisted and relegated to the subprime market is an effective control mechanism" (p. 115). As studies of the legal processes of bankruptcy in the United States show, the vast majority of debtors who default on obligations do so not because of irresponsibility, but because ill-health, unemployment, and/or relationship breakdown reduce their income levels and ability to make repayments (Sullivan, Warren, and Westbrook 1989, 2000). That said, to analyze these ubiquitous calculative technologies of risk solely in terms of the disciplinary operation of power and the codification of "docile bodies" remains problematic. As Deleuze (1992) highlights, Foucault was consistently concerned with the historical peculiarities, limitations, and transience of disciplinary societies which began to reach their height at the outset of the twentieth century. While for Deleuze there is thus a need to talk of "societies of control" which are in the process of replacing disciplinary societies, Foucault's (1979, 2003, 2004, 2007) later work, especially on "biopower," "normalization," "security," and "governmentality," also sought to capture the diffuse re-encoding of power as disciplinary societies wane. By the late 1970s in modern liberal society, discipline appeared, for Foucault (in Lemke 2003, 176), to no longer be the dominant technique of power but as an "uneconomic" and "archaic" form of power.

In the wake of Foucault's foresight in this respect, four crucial features of the constitution of the embodied economy of mass market credit are brought into sharp relief. First, "risk" in mass market credit, and in financial networks more broadly (de Goede 2004, 2005), is a category of understanding and not an intuition or sensibility. It is not, furthermore, a condition of our times in a realist sense, what Beck (1992) famously characterized as the uninsurable "risk society." Rather, as Mitchell Dean (1999, 177) has it, "Risk is a way – or rather, a set of different ways – of ordering reality, of rendering it into a calculable form." Informing this view of risk is a critical reading of Frank Knight's (1921) classic investigation of indeterminacy. Thus, the category of "risk" can be seen as distinct from uncertainty, the former as the statistical and predictive calculation of the future, and the latter as non-calculable future volatilities that are beyond prediction (Reddy 1996).

Second, the risk calculations of credit scoring that provide mass market lenders with a means of feigning control over an uncertain future are also imbricated and deployed in the apparatus of contemporary liberal government. For Foucault (1979), governmentality is "the ensemble formed by the institutions, procedures, analyses and reflections, the calculations and tactics, that allow the exercise of this very specific albeit complex form of power, which has as its target population" (p. 20). What he also calls "the art of government" and "the conduct of conduct" does not simply refer to the institutions, individuals, and groups that hold authority, but also includes those calculative technologies and expertise that are authorized within and through the population and which rationalize the exercise of power. Although the place of technologies of collective insurance and accounting in the liberal government of the population has thus been an important concern of governmentality writers (e.g., Ewald 1991; Knights and Verdubakis 1993), this certainly does not exhaust inquiry into calculation and liberal government.

Third, credit scoring calculations do not simply serve the disciplinary standardization and exclusion of deviants from the credit market, but can provide the basis for inclusion and differentiation. This is broadly consistent with the general tendencies of governmental modes of power which are distinguishable from modes of power that operate primarily through exclusion, like territorial sovereignty, and also those associated with discipline, surveillance, and division. Thus, the agglomeration of borrowers and would-be borrowers as a governable population of dispersed financial consumers can be seen as extended through credit scoring technologies during the mass market boom (Marron 2007). Indeed, when combined with marketing strategies, credit scoring makes possible the sorting, targeting, pricing, and governing of customers through the prism of so-called "risk-based pricing." In risk-based pricing, both the future and the past meet in the stratified risk calculations and pricing decisions that are made in the present by lenders. Probabilities for default for different categories of borrower are determined on the basis of inference from statistics on past credit records and behavior. Graduated rates of interest become payable by borrowers according to how they are categorized by lenders in terms of default risk. As I have shown elsewhere, for example, risk-based pricing was crucial to the legitimacy of charging graduated and much higher than normal rates of interest within the "sub-prime" sector of the mortgage market (Langley 2008b).

Fourth, the government of mass market credit can be seen to feature the moral, political, and technological assembly of self-disciplined and entrepreneurial subjects. Financial subjects are called up who not only responsibly meet their outstanding obligations, but who also manipulate and manage those obligations and their future access to credit in order to maximize their freedom and security. As Foucauldian-inspired analyses of the move to the "neoliberal" or "'advanced' liberal" government of the population note, this hinges in large part on the responsibilization of an entrepreneurial self (Rose 1996; Dean 1999; O'Malley 2004). In contemporary society, individuals are obliged to provide for their own freedom and security through the opportunities and choices apparently offered by the market economy in general, and the financial markets in particular. Thus, in the mass market for consumer credit, the important other that figures in processes of identification is not simply the irresponsible debtor who finds their material well-being, freedom, and security undermined by their imprudence, but also the individual who fails to "play the market" and maintain and expand their access to credit.

## Egg and self-discipline

The contention that successfully meeting credit obligations is not the only self-disciplinary performance that a responsible borrower subject is expected to undertake in the mass credit market is starkly illustrated by the decision of UK telephone and internet bank Egg, in January 2008, to cancel the credit cards of 161,000 customers. According to Egg, the decision to withdraw further credit from these particular customers, out of a total of 2.2 million, was a result of their "risky profiles" and "blemished credit records" (Croft 2008a). But the decision was particularly bewildering for many Egg cardholders, as included within the 161,000 were those who had responsibly met the obligations they built up as they spent on the line of credit provided by their card. Customer complaints generated a high-profile story in the financial and popular media, and senior Members of Parliament called for action. For example, for John McFall, chairman of the Treasury Select Committee, "The motives of Egg need clear explanation if this is a case of them ditching long-standing creditworthy customers because they make no money out of them. Perhaps this is an issue that requires an Office of Fair Trading Investigation" (in Mathiason and Insley 2008; cf. Farrer 2008).

As the words of McFall suggest, the common suspicion among politicians and throughout the media was that Egg had canceled the cards of responsible borrowers because, in the credit card industry, cardholders who tend to meet their obligations in full at the end of each month and minimize interest charges are the least profitable segment of the market. Such suspicions are largely affirmed by social scientific analyses. In the terms of Guseva and Rona-Tas (2001, 635), for example, "the goal of the credit card business is to extend for as long as possible the period during which interest is charged on a purchase, as interest is the richest source of profit." Furthermore, in the parlance of the industry, prudent "deadbeats" stand in contrast with "revolvers" who do not meet their obligations in full and roll their outstanding obligations into the next month. While the merchant fees paid by retailers when a sale is made do create a steady income stream for credit card providers, the interest charged on revolving balances is the key to their profitability. Indeed, and more broadly, under the calculations of credit scoring which were initially designed to enable lenders to manage repayment uncertainties in a decentered market, a "low-risk" rating for a responsible and trustworthy customer with a thrifty and/or prudent credit history does not necessarily translate into a "good" credit score.

When responding in early February to media criticism of its decision to withdraw the cards of certain customers, however, Egg stressed another threat to their profitability. For Egg, the decision was "was not . . . an excuse to exclude some 'unprofitable' customers." Rather, "In this one-off review we assessed that the credit profiles of these customers had deteriorated from the time they joined Egg . . . and that they presented a higher than acceptable credit risk to the bank" (in Elliott and Atkinson 2008, 27). This "deterioration" was reflected in a growing number of revolvers who were close to their credit limits, and who were only making minimum monthly repayments. There were also earlier indications that Egg cardholders, in profile, appeared to be more likely to struggle to keep up their repayments than the customers of many of the UK's credit card providers (Croft 2008b). In 2006, Egg was criticized by the bond rating agencies when it put in place a reduced minimum repayment plan for struggling cardholders. The plan, which featured a reduction of minimum monthly repayments from 2 to 0.86 per cent of an outstanding balance without increased interest, was said to artificially reduce the level of bad debt write-downs on Egg's loan book. Furthermore, in November 2007, Egg also sought permission from the Financial Services Authority (FSA) to remove 46,000 cardholders in arrears from the pool of assets that backed bonds issued by Pillar Trust, the securitization vehicle through which it raised capital to fund a major share of its lending.

So, depending on interpretation, the Egg decision appears at first blush to be the result of either the responsible repayment performance of self-disciplined deadbeats undermining profitability, or the future threat to profitability of an irresponsible pattern of non-payment by revolvers who had allowed their spending and borrowing to get out of control. Neither of these contending interpretations are, however, quite on the mark when it comes to understanding the Egg decision and what it reveals about the remaking of borrower responsibility in the contemporary mass credit market. Egg had started out in 1998 as the internet banking arm of the UK insurance group Prudential, and was purchased by US financial conglomerate Citigroup for £546 million in 2007 (Elliott and Atkinson 2008, 24). Upon entering the credit card market in 1999, Egg provided the first online credit card in the UK. The Egg brand was promoted extensively, and advertising campaigns featured celebrity endorsement by a hip television presenter and an Olympic champion.[1] As its playful name suggested, the Egg card cut against the grain of the stuffy and serious image of UK high street banking, and appealed to an upwardly-mobile and savvy consumer. Key in this respect were the customers that Egg reached out to through the introductory offers on its cards: a zero percent interest rate ("teaser rate") on both balances transferred from existing credit cards and new purchases for a specified period.

Such was the success of its promotional work and teaser rate that, only a few years after the launch of the Egg card, Egg was one of the three biggest credit card issuers in the UK (Elliott and Atkinson 2008, 25). Egg continued to lead the market during this period in providing canny consumers with interest rate offers. From 2003, for example, new Egg cardholders could also transfer balances from personal loans and overdrafts as well as other cards, and in 2004 an "anniversary" zero per cent interest rate window was created for existing Egg cardholders who wanted to transfer further balances built-up on other credit cards.[2] Egg was in the vanguard, then, of the calling up of a revolver subject who, responsibly and entrepreneurially, manipulated their outstanding credit obligations.

The transfer of an outstanding balance from one credit card to another, thereby taking advantage of teaser rates in order to, in effect, reduce outstanding obligations, was perhaps the signature performance of the self-disciplined revolver during the consumer credit boom. Indeed, the personal finance sections of major newspapers, as well as countless money advice Web sites, continue to provide tables listing the best available current offers that, for example, provide zero per cent interest payable on balance transfers for twelve months. A newspaper report from January 2005 suggested that nearly 4.5 million cardholders in the UK had taken advantage of teaser rates, and transferred their revolving balances to another card (Meyer 2005). The frustrations of the credit card industry with those who regularly and routinely transfer their outstanding balances from one card to another and so on, leading them to label such individuals "rate tarts," furthermore only served to reinforce such entrepreneurialism. The "rate tart" who searches online for the best deal on a balance transfer is, as in the traditional colloquial and sexist sense of the term "tart," a promiscuous woman of unsound virtue who is to be condemned. However, given the more ambiguous meaning of "tart" in contemporary parlance, especially its general association by the young with a hedonistic and free life-style, the implication is also that those represented as a "rate tart" may be gaining some considerable pleasure and enjoyment at the expense of a less promiscuous other. Some leading credit card issuers in the UK, such as Egg, Barclays, and MBNA, moved in mid-2005 to curtail these pleasures by imposing charges of around 2 per cent on balance transfers. In a period of historically low interest rates, however, large numbers of issuers continued to make it possible for canny revolvers to regularly move their balance from one card to another at no cost.

The Egg business model rested, then, on the remaking of borrower responsibility and the performance of new forms of financial self-discipline by credit card holders. Indeed, low interest rates and rapidly rising house prices, during the last years of the old millennium and the first years of the new millennium in particular, ensured that responsible and entrepreneurial cardholders did not only transfer their balances from one card to another. Simultaneous performances of borrowing across overlapping credit card, loan, and mortgage networks called up revolvers who entrepreneurially substituted credit card obligations for alternative repayments at lower rates of interest. This so-called "debt consolidation" came to concentrate on mortgage refinancing and equity withdrawal. The rates of interest payable on mortgages as secured debt are, of course, lower than those that prevail for unsecured credit card debt. Mortgage equity withdrawal in the UK increased from £1.4 billion in the fourth quarter of 1995 to £13.5 billion by the first quarter of 2003 (Anderson 2004, 49). In the United States, meanwhile, the rate of increase for total unsecured consumer borrowing slowed somewhat after 2001. But the period from 2002 through to 2007 was also marked by a sharp increase in outstanding mortgage obligations. While partly related to roaring house prices and the changing subjectivities of residential property ownership that I have discussed elsewhere (Langley 2006, 2008a, 2008b), there are also strong indications that, in the words of the Joint Economic Committee (2004, 2) of the US Senate, "many households have re-financed their homes in part to pay off higher interest debt." According to a Freddie Mac (2005) brochure, a staggering $500 billion's worth of home equity was released through re-mortgaging in the United States from 2002 to 2005. And it appears that roughly one-quarter of those who refinanced their mortgages during this time increased their mortgage obligations in order to pay off consumer debts (Aizcorbe et al. 2003, 25–6; Moss 2004).

Egg's 2008 decision to cancel the credit cards of a large number of its customers was, ultimately, a recognition of the previous failings in its own profitability calculations. It was not a consequence of the inherent threats to profitability of either deadbeats or busted revolvers. For the first five years of the Egg card, Egg paid little attention to default risk management and did not implement risk-based pricing techniques. It was only in the run-up to its acquisition by Citigroup that Egg introduced risk-based pricing which, by that time, was firmly established as the norm amongst UK credit card providers (Croft 2008a, 2008b). The differentiation and categorization of cardholders through risk-based pricing would have maximized Egg's profitability during the boom years. It would have made it possible, on the one hand, not to offer cards in the first place to "low-risk" customers who had established payment patterns as "deadbeats" with other card providers. And, on the other hand, risk-based pricing would have led Egg to charge progressively higher rates of interest to revolvers who pushed to the extreme the self-disciplinary performances of manipulating rather than simply repaying outstanding obligations. From the outset, Egg proved particularly successful at attracting and creating customers who performed the new entrepreneurial financial self-disciplines of manipulating outstanding obligations. But, those in charge at Egg did not recognize that questions of profitability no longer turned on simply charging a flat rate of interest to all cardholders once their teaser rates had expired.

## Responsible risk managers

As the "credit crunch" has gathered pace over the previous year or so, there is a widespread awareness among the specialist and popular financial media that lenders are increasingly wary of "high-risk" customers in particular, and that the withdrawal of lending to these sectors of the market is also affecting the mainstream or prime sectors. The curtailment of lending was, of course, most keenly and immediately felt in the "sub-prime" mortgage market which, in many ways, had led the way in the use of default risk management and risk-based pricing techniques in order to extend the agglomeration of a population of credit consumers (Langley 2008b). The massive investment losses on asset backed securities (ABS) issued against the future repayments of US sub-prime mortgages ensured that the wider ABS market, so significant to the funding of booming mortgage and consumer borrowing, also ground to a halt.

Thus, while prime mortgage lenders sharply tightened their criteria, withdrew certain loan products, and increased the rates of interest payable by mortgagors from the autumn of 2007, by autumn 2008 it became apparent that credit card providers were also taking action to limit future possible defaults and maximize profitability. So, for example, a report from *The New York Times* from October 2008 warns borrowers that credit card providers are in the process of limiting both further card offers and the lines of credit available on existing cards (Dash 2008). It suggests that this "pullback is affecting even creditworthy consumers" at a time when "bad credit card loans" are rising sharply. Lenders' profitability is currently undercut by bad debts, on the one hand, and the increased costs of funding their operations through the mechanisms and instruments of the wholesale capital markets, on the other. The option of increasing the interest rates paid by borrowers, a tactic that credit card providers have previously used when confronted by profitability problems, is also rendered problematic by the heightened regulatory and supervisory scrutiny that is emerging in the wake of the sub-prime crisis. What is more, and as the report puts it, lenders' actions to "staunch the bleeding" come at the very moment when "options once easily tapped by borrowers to pay off credit card obligations, like home equity lines or the ability to transfer balances to a new card, dry up."

So, where does the credit crunch leave the embodied economy of mass market consumer credit? It is tempting to conclude, perhaps, that borrowers who once successfully met and manipulated their outstanding obligations are now helpless in the face of the "risk aversion" of lenders. This representation of borrowers would suggest that the self-disciplined entrepreneurial borrower was just a figure of the boom in mass market credit, a process of identification that necessarily comes to an end as the credit crunch takes hold. It is certainly the case that, as lenders "pullback," many maxed-out borrowers are likely to scale-back. They may even come to question the positive relationship between credit and freedom and security, the moral basis of the liberal government of the mass market for credit. Yet, there are also indications that, in an amplification of previously nascent practices, self-disciplined borrowers are likely to increasingly look to entrepreneurial performances that confront uncertainties over future access to credit at affordable rates of interest. Perhaps the exemplar performance of the calculation by borrowers of these uncertainties as manageable risks is the use of tools provided by the credit history and scoring agencies. These are designed to enable borrowers to improve their own credit histories and scores, and thereby to minimize the interest rates payable on their consumer credit obligations.

In the late summer and early autumn of 2008, as the "credit crunch" that had been gathering pace over the previous year began to reverberate through to prime borrowers in the UK, Experian launched a television advertising campaign announcing a "30 day free trial" of CreditExpert. The advertisements seek to establish the timeliness of CreditExpert. They also briefly remind potential customers that the interest rates that they pay on credit are closely related to their individual credit histories and scores, and cast CreditExpert as an online tool that enables its users to take entrepreneurial action. The advertisements do not, of course, inform viewers that online products such as CreditExpert are also available from the other credit history and scoring agencies. In the UK, for example, the Equifax Credit Rating tool "makes it easy to understand your credit score, see how lenders view your credit history and get tips and advice on how to improve it."[3] It is supported by the Equifax Learning Centre. Meanwhile, in the United States, TransUnion operates TrueCredit, a website that combines the generic "information and resources you need to manage your financial profile" with "premium" and "personalized" content for "members."[4] Similarly, credit scorer Fair Isaac Corporation operates the myFICO website that, on its opening page, includes a calculator that can be used to illustrate the differential rates of interest that are payable on mortgage and car loans. The calculator works on the basis of a sliding scale of FICO scores of between 850 (the maximum) and 500.[5] myFICO also offers a mix of general and specific advice facilities that are similar to those available on TrueCredit, and a range of more or less comprehensive packages that individuals can purchase. Taken together, the tools provided by the various agencies are something of an online and interactive version of the tips, guidelines, and advice that have been available for some time in the "popular finance" sections of bookstores (e.g., Rose 1997).

A noticeable and significant feature of the representation of these various tools across the websites of the credit rating and scoring agencies is the way in which would-be users are summoned up as self-disciplined and entrepreneurial financial subjects. Experian, for example, "helps consumers to monitor their credit reports and delivers critical information that enables them to make financial and purchasing decisions with greater control and confidence."[6] Equifax's company motto, which is trademarked, features the three words "inform," "enrich," and "empower," with an arrow head pointing from inform to enrich, and from enrich to empower. To this end, a common feature of the tools is the way in which they provide access to individual credit reports in the first instance. With CreditExpert, for example, a click on the "Get your free credit report now" tile is the first step in a signing-up process that includes the entry of personal and payment details. Similarly, for TransUnion, access to the tools that it markets as TrueCredit begins by clicking the "See your credit report now" tile on its home page. Accessing a credit report is seen, then, as an initial step whereby a responsible borrower assembles the necessary personal information that they will need to take rational and entrepreneurial action. For TransUnion, for instance, getting "a snapshot of your credit history" enables you to: "find out what personal information the credit bureaus have in your file"; "understand your credit file with an easy-to-read summary of your report"; "get detailed information about all your loans and credit card accounts"; "discover who has been looking at your credit report"; and "get contact information for all your creditors."[7]

The provision of an individual credit report as the starting point for the personal risk management tools provided by the credit agencies is, in one sense, somewhat disingenuous. In the UK, the Data Protection Act gives individuals the right to request their Statutory Credit Report from agencies for a £2 fee. In the United States, and effective since September 2005, the Fair and Accurate Transactions Act (FACT Act) amendments to the Fair Credit Reporting Act entitle individuals to one-off access to their credit report during a twelve-month period. The extent to which credit agencies lure borrowers with free access to their credit reports and then automatically enroll them as users of calculative tools has, then, been something of a controversial issue. For example, in August 2005 in the United States, the Federal Trade Commission oversaw a process whereby Experian settled charges, refunded customers, and made additional disclosures on its website and in its promotional materials.

When compared with exercising the right to access a credit report, the apparent "value added" of signing-up for a tool provided by the credit agencies is succinctly summarized in a table that highlights the differences between a Statutory Credit Report and Equifax Credit Rating.[8] This reinforces that credit reports and scores are not simply something to be discovered by the individual borrower. They are also the focus for self-disciplinary and entrepreneurial performances of risk management. From the outset, the Equifax Credit Rating tool is, for example, represented as a premier package that includes information and guidance on both an individual credit report and score. In terms of an individual's credit report, then, the Equifax Credit Rating tool includes guidance on how to check that all the information that it contains is correct. Such guidance is not forthcoming with a Statutory Credit Report. Similarly, TransUnion's True-Credit tools tell borrowers, for example, to "Watch out for incorrect addresses" in the personal information section of their report because "this may be a sign that an identity thief has redirected your mail to a false address."[9] They are also warned that the credit file section of their report could contain "inaccuracies that could impact negatively on your credit standing." The detailed information that the report contains about all outstanding credit agreements may contain "accounts that are not familiar – these could be accounts that were opened fraudulently in your name."

By its very nature, a Statutory Credit Report does not include information on an individual's credit score. For Equifax, for instance, this is highly significant. In their terms, "The key factor that most lenders use to rate a potential borrower is your credit score. So it makes sense to know your personal credit score and to understand how lenders see you based on this score before you apply for credit. Equifax Credit Rating gives you just this."[10] The Equifax Credit Rating tool also claims to provide a personalized program for improving an individual's credit score: "Specific ways to improve your score and therefore your ability to obtain the credit you want at a favourable lending rate." So what, precisely, is on offer here to the self-disciplined and entrepreneurial borrower? Equifax Credit Rating includes "Score performance indicators . . . to show how you rate in each category of information used to create your overall credit score."[11] The categories of risk that are most significant in undermining an individual borrower's access to affordable credit are thus easily identified, and the availability of "additional information," a "Customer Care team," and "clear, easy-to-understand advice" provides the basis for risk management.

## Conclusion: Uncertain subjects

In this chapter, I have explored the embodied economy of mass market consumer credit that has consolidated across recent decades. I have developed the argument that this market features the entrepreneurial administration of outstanding obligations and uncertainty over future access to credit, that is, risk management by responsibilized and entrepreneurial borrowers themselves. I began by emphasizing that this remaking of responsible borrower subjects has been produced through a combination of disciplinary and self-disciplinary power relations. The rise of calculative technologies of risk in the mass market, most notably credit reporting and scoring and risk-based pricing, was understood as related to the wider forces of power in the contemporary liberal government of the population. The second part of this chapter focused on Egg's recent decision to cancel the credit cards of over 160,000 of its customers in order to draw out and illustrate the self-disciplinary performances that, especially prevalent during the height of the consumer credit boom, sought the calculative and creative manipulation of outstanding obligations. The final part of this chapter concentrated on the performances of self-disciplined and entrepreneurial borrowers as the credit crunch has taken hold, exemplified by the use of calculative tools that are designed to enable borrowers to improve their own credit histories and scores and thereby to minimize the interest rates that they pay.

To close, I want to stress that the processes of identification at work in the embodied economy of mass market consumer credit are, and have always been, incomplete, precarious, and contradictory. As I have argued previously, the responsibilized borrower subjects of the mass credit market are necessarily uncertain subjects (Langley 2008a). The point here is not simply that risk management calculations fail because otherwise rational individuals are prevented from making successful calculations by the "ecology" of the credit crunch within which they find now themselves (see Clark, this volume). Such a view follows from the postulates of "behavioural finance" that, since the collapse of the "new economy" at the outset of the new millennium in particular, have typically become the starting point for critical social scientific analysis of risk in contemporary finance. As exemplified by the work of Robert J. Shiller (2001, 2005, 2008) in particular, the behavioral finance approach begins with the assumption that recent financial excesses – the new economy stock market, the housing market bubble, and the consumer credit and sub-prime mortgage market booms – are a consequence of "irrational exuberance," of collective sentiment and herding tendencies that distort otherwise rational individual decision-making and the operation of market fundamentals. Following from this assumption, the present task becomes designing and developing structures, institutions and tools for individual decision-making that can facilitate more effective personal risk management (Shiller 2003, 2008). This is highly problematic, however, as it continues to represent the remade responsibilities and self-disciplinary risk management strategies of the mass consumer credit market as ultimately rational performances that can and should be perfected. The operation of sharply unequal power relations that sustain the privileges and profits of lenders, something that surely must be questioned if we are to genuinely move towards what Shiller (2008) calls "financial democracy," is left largely unchallenged.

As Timothy Mitchell (2002) has argued more broadly, calculative devices of risk that seek to count and account for the uncertain future always fall short of fully containing the complexities of economic life. In the mass market for credit, these contradictions are not abstract forces, but are experienced, lived, and negotiated by borrowers. The self-disciplined borrowers who are summoned up through the moral discourse and political programs of contemporary liberal government, and through calculative technologies of risk, are clearly demarcated as a monolithic subject position. But representations of borrowers as disconnected figures that are disembedded from all other social relations cannot be maintained. As Burton et al. (2004) note of credit reporting and scoring, these technologies are "constructed on the basis of a linear conception of the subject who is expected to have a stable or continuously improving employment and credit career" (p. 5). Responsible borrowing can thus be performed by self-disciplined and entrepreneurial individuals to further their own security and autonomy both in the present and into the future. But, to return to Burton et al., subjects "may not necessarily have continuous life-chance careers, and/or the stable life experiences that are the life-blood of credit scoring techniques" (p. 5). In our terms, caught amid these contradictions, individuals cannot identify with the subject position of the responsible borrower in a certain and unambiguous manner.

For some, contradictions become manifest in over-indebtedness, and insolvency and rates of bankruptcy are currently on the rise on both sides of the Atlantic. Workers on flexible and temporary contracts and low incomes are, for example, especially poorly placed to perform the financial self-disciplines of the responsible borrower. The meeting and management of repayments is reliant upon relatively predictable wages that, for those on low incomes who are most "flexible" in their work, cannot be guaranteed. Low-income individuals and households are also unlikely to be savers or owner-occupiers, such that entrepreneurial borrowing practices (e.g., debt consolidation) are not possible. Already confronted by rising living costs and knife-edge labor market flexibility, exclusion from the growth of the asset-based wealth in recent decades has left many low-income households with little choice but to extend their borrowing once again. With the credit crunch, however, opportunities for additional borrowing are closed down. Furthermore, for "asset rich" prime borrowers who are also in regular and well-paid employment, contradictions are also now beginning to surface as house prices and stock market indices fall sharply. The manipulation of outstanding obligations through credit card balance transfers and especially debt consolidation becomes problematic for prime revolvers. The individual risk management of credit reports and scores may also amount to little if the cost of credit remains high across the board, with lenders continuing to struggle to fund their operations through the capital markets. Shifting labor market fortunes, sharp falls in asset prices, and stubbornly high rates of interest all, then, significantly undermine the prospects of freedom and security that are apparently on offer from responsible and entrepreneurial risk management in consumer credit markets. Individuals may actually have little choice at present but to live with uncertainties that cannot be calculated for, and hope for the best.

## Notes

1. http://www.brandrepublic.com/Industry/FinancialServices/News/228406/ Superbrands-case-studies-Egg/
2. http://www.brandrepublic.com/Industry/FinancialServices/News/228406/ Superbrands-case-studies-Egg/
3. http://www.equifax.co.uk/
4. http://content.truecredit.com/LearningCenter/welcome.page?
5. http://www.myfico.com/
6. http://www.experian.co.uk/www/pages/about_us/index.html
7. http://www.truecredit.com/popup/singleExample.jsp?popup=true&cb=Trans Union&loc=1490&bn=null
8. https://www.econsumer.equifax.co.uk/consumer/uk/sitepage.ehtml?forward =gb_elearning_credit14
9. http://www.truecredit.com/popup/singleExample.jsp?popup=true&cb=Trans Union&loc=1490&bn=null
10. https://www.econsumer.equifax.co.uk/consumer/uk/sitepage.ehtml?forward =gb_elearning_credit14
11. https://www.econsumer.equifax.co.uk/consumer/uk/sitepage.ehtml?forward =gb_elearning_credit14

## References

Aizcorbe, A. M., Kennickell, A. B., and Moore, K. B. (2003). Recent changes in U.S. family finances: Evidence from the 1998 and 2001 Survey of Consumer Finances. *Federal Reserve Bulletin*, 89, 1–32.

Anderson, S. (2004). *The CML mortgage market manifesto: Taking the past into the future*. London: Council of Mortgage Lenders.

Beck, U. (1992). *Risk Society: Towards a New Modernity.* London: Sage.

Burton, D. (2008). *Credit and Consumer Society.* London: Routledge.

—— Knights, D., Leyshon, A., Alferoff, C., and Signoretta, P. (2004). Making a market: The UK retail financial services industry and the rise of the complex sub-prime credit market. *Competition and Change,* 8, 3–25.

Croft, J. (2008*a*, February 1). Egg cracks down on "riskier" clients. *Financial Times,* online edition.

—— (2008*b*, February 14). Customers' anger could damage Egg. *Financial Times,* online edition.

Dash, E. (2008, October 29). Consumers feel the next crisis: It's credit cards, *New York Times,* online edition.

Dean, M. (1999). *Governmentality: Power and Rule in Modern Society.* London: Sage.

de Goede, M. (2004). Repoliticizing financial risk. *Economy and Society,* 33, 197–217.

—— (2005). *Virtue, Fortune, and Faith: A Genealogy of Finance.* Minneapolis: University of Minnesota.

Deleuze, G. (1992). Postscript on the societies of control. *October,* 59, 3–7.

Elliott, L. and Atkinson, D. (2008). *The Gods that Failed: How Blind Faith in Markets Has Cost Us Our Future.* London: The Bodley Head.

Ewald, F. (1991). Insurance and Risk. In G. Burchell, C. Gordon, and P. Miller (eds.), *The Foucault Effect: Studies in Governmentality* (pp. 197–210). Hemel Hempstead: Harvester Press.

Farrer, M. (2008, February 11). OFT takes up Egg complaints, *The Guardian,* online edition.

Foucault, M. (1977). *Discipline and Punish: The Birth of the Prison.* London: Allen Lane.

—— (1979). On governmentality. *Ideology and Consciousness,* 6, 5–22.

—— (2003). *Abnormal, Lectures at the Collège de France, 1974–5.* Trans. Graham Burchell. New York: Picador.

—— (2004). *Society Must Be Defended, Lectures at the Collège de France, 1975–6.* Trans. David Macey. London: Penguin.

—— (2007). *Security, Territory, Population, Lectures at the Collège de France, 1977–8.* Trans. Graham Burchell. Basingstoke: Palgrave MacMillan.

Fraser, N. (2003). From discipline to flexibilization? Rereading Foucault in the shadow of globalization. *Constellations,* 10, 160–71.

Freddie Mac (2005). *Just the facts: How we make home possible.* Available at: http://www.freddiemac.com/news/pdf/Just_the_Facts3.pdf

Gelphi, R.-M. and Julien-Labruyère, F. (2000). *The History of Consumer Credit: Doctrines and Practices.* Basingstoke: MacMillan.

Gill, S. (1997). Finance, production and panopticism: Inequality, risk and resistance in an era of disciplinary neo-liberalism. In S. Gill (ed.), *Globalization, Democratization and Multilateralism* (pp. 51–75). Basingstoke: MacMillan.

Guseva, A. and Rona-Tas, A. (2001). Uncertainty, risk, and trust: Russian and American credit card markets compared. *American Sociological Review,* 66, 623–46.

Joint Economic Committee (2004). Household debt and the economy. Washington, DC: Joint Economic Committee. Available at: http://jec.senate.gov/_files/HouseholdDebt.pdf

Knight, F. (1921). *Risk, Uncertainty and Profit*. New York: A. M. Kelley.

Knights, D. (1997). Governmentality and financial services: welfare crises and the financially self-disciplined subject. In G. Morgan and D. Knights (eds.), *Regulation and Deregulation in European Financial Services* (pp. 216–36). Basingstoke: MacMillan.

—— Vurdubakis, T. (1993). Calculations of risk: Towards an understanding of insurance as a moral and political technology. *Accounting, Organizations and Society*, 18, 729–64.

Langley, P. (2006). Securitising suburbia: the transformation of Anglo-American mortgage finance. *Competition & Change*, 10, 283–99.

—— (2008a). *The Everyday Life of Global Finance: Saving and Borrowing in Anglo-America*. Oxford: Oxford University Press.

—— (2008b). Sub-prime lending: a cultural economy. *Economy and Society*, 37, 469–94.

Lemke, T. (2003). Comment on Nancy Fraser: Rereading Foucault in the shadow of globalization. *Constellations*, 10, 172–79.

Leyshon, A. and Thrift, N. (1999). Lists come alive: electronic systems of knowledge and the rise of credit scoring in retail banking. *Economy and Society*, 28, 434–66.

Luhmann, N. (1979). *Trust and Power*. Chichester: Wiley.

Marron, D. (2007). Lending by numbers: Credit scoring and the constitution of risk within American consumer credit. *Economy and Society*, 36, 103–33.

Mathiason, N. and Insley, J. (2008, February 3). Anger at Egg ban on prudent customers. *The Observer*, online edition.

Meyer, H. (2005, January 5). "Rate tarts" fall into card trap. *The Telegraph*, online edition.

Mitchell, T. (2002). *Rule of Experts: Egypt, Techno-politics, Modernity*. Berkeley: University of California Press.

Moss, M. (2004, October 10). Erase debt now (lose your house later), *New York Times*, online edition.

O'Malley, P. (2004). *Risk, Uncertainty and Government*. London: Glass House.

Poon, M. (2007). Scorecards as devices for consumer credit: the case of Fair, Isaac & Company Incorporated. In M. Callon, Y. Millo, and F. Muniesa (eds.), *Market Devices* (pp. 284–306). Oxford: Blackwell.

Reddy, S. (1996). Claims to expert knowledge and the subversion of democracy: The triumph of risk over uncertainty. *Economy and Society*, 25, 222–54.

Rose, I. (1997). *The DIY Credit Repair Manual*. Totton: Rosy Publications.

Rose, N. (1996). Governing "advanced" liberal democracies. In A. Barry, T. Osbourne, and N. Rose (eds.), *Foucault and Political Reason: Liberalism, Neoliberalism, and the Rationalities of Government* (pp. 37–64). Chicago: University of Chicago Press.

—— Valverde, M. (1998). Governed by law? *Social & Legal Studies*, 7, 541–51.

Shiller, R. J. (2001). *Irrational Exuberance*. Princeton, NJ: Princeton University Press.

—— (2003). *The New Financial Order: Risk in the 21st Century.* Princeton, NJ: Princeton University Press.

—— (2005). *Irrational Exuberance*. 2nd Edition, Princeton, NJ: Princeton University Press.

—— (2008). *The Subprime Solution: How Today's Global Financial Crisis Happened, and What to Do About It.* Princeton, NJ: Princeton University Press.

Sullivan, T. A., Warren, E., and Westbrook, J. L. (1989). *As We Forgive Our Debtors: Bankruptcy and Consumer Credit in America.* Oxford: Oxford University Press.

—— —— —— (2000). *The Fragile Middle Class: Americans in Debt.* New Haven, CT: Yale University Press.

# Index

# Index

# Index